WOMEN'S RIGHTS TO SOCIAL SECURITY AND SOCIAL PROTECTION

This collection examines the human rights to social security and social protection from a women's rights perspective. The contributors stress the need to address women's poverty and exclusion within a human rights framework that takes account of gender. The chapters unpack the rights to social security and protection and their relationship to human rights principles such as gender equality, participation and dignity. Alongside conceptual insights across the field of women's social security rights, the collection analyses recent developments in international law and in a range of national settings. It considers the ILO's Social Protection Floors Recommendation and the work of UN treaty bodies. It explores the different approaches to expansion of social protection in developing countries (China, Bolivia and Chile). It also discusses conditionality in cash transfer programmes, a central debate in social policy and development, through a gender lens. Contributors consider the position of poor women, particularly single mothers, in developed countries (Australia, Canada, the United States, Ireland and Spain) facing the damaging consequences of welfare cuts. The collection engages with shifts in global discourse on the role of social policy and the way in which ideas of crisis and austerity have been used to undermine rights with harsh impacts on women.

Oñati International Series in Law and Society

A SERIES PUBLISHED FOR THE OÑATI INSTITUTE
FOR THE SOCIOLOGY OF LAW

Recent titles in this series

Emotions, Crime and Justice
edited by Susanne Karstedt, Ian Loader and Heather Strang

Mediation in Political Conflicts
Soft Power or Counter Culture?
edited by Jacques Faget

Criminological and Legal Consequences of Climate Change
edited by Stephen Farrall, Tawhida Ahmed and Duncan French

Shooting to Kill: Socio-Legal Perspectives on the Use of Lethal Force
Edited by Simon Bronitt, Miriam Gani and Saskia Hufnagel

Managing Family Justice in Diverse Societies
edited by Mavis Maclean and John Eekelaar

Making Human Rights Intelligible
Towards a Sociology of Human Rights
edited by Mikael Rask Madsen and Gert Verschraegen

European Penology?
edited by Tom Daems, Dirk van Zyl Smit and Sonja Snacken

Rights and Courts in Pursuit of Social Change
Legal Mobilisation in the Multi-Level European System
edited by Dia Anagnostou

For the complete list of titles in this series, see
'Oñati International Series in Law and Society' link at
www.hartpub.co.uk/books/series.asp

Women's Rights to Social Security and Social Protection

Edited by

Beth Goldblatt
and
Lucie Lamarche

Oñati International Series in Law and Society

A SERIES PUBLISHED FOR THE OÑATI INSTITUTE
FOR THE SOCIOLOGY OF LAW

•HART•
PUBLISHING

OXFORD AND PORTLAND, OREGON
2017

Hart Publishing
An imprint of Bloomsbury Publishing Plc

Hart Publishing Ltd
Kemp House
Chawley Park
Cumnor Hill
Oxford OX2 9PH
UK

Bloomsbury Publishing Plc
50 Bedford Square
London
WC1B 3DP
UK

www.hartpub.co.uk
www.bloomsbury.com

Published in North America (US and Canada) by
Hart Publishing
c/o International Specialized Book Services
920 NE 58th Avenue, Suite 300
Portland, OR 97213-3786
USA

www.isbs.com

First published in hardback, 2014
Paperback edition, 2017

British Library Cataloguing-in-Publication Data
A catalogue record for this book is available from the British Library.

ISBN: PB: 978-1-50991-295-7
HB: 978-1-84946-692-9

Typeset by Compuscript Ltd, Shannon
Printed and bound in Great Britain by
Lightning Source UK Ltd

Acknowledgements

We wish to thank the International Institute for the Sociology of Law (IISL) for hosting our workshop entitled 'Interpreting and Advancing Women's Rights to Social Security and Social Protection' on 6–7 June 2013 in beautiful Oñati. We particularly wish to thank the incredibly efficient and generous Malen Gordoa Mendizabal and the other IISL staff for all their gracious assistance. Thanks also to Christina Ruiz López who assisted us so ably regarding the publication of our proceedings.

We would also like to thank Richard Hart, Rachel Turner and the other staff of Hart Publishing for their wonderful work on this collection.

The stellar editing assistance from Sarah Dobinson is gratefully acknowledged as is the funding of her work by the Human Rights Research and Education Centre of the University of Ottawa. This Centre also provided funding, administrative and technical support for the webinar that preceded the IISL workshop for which we are extremely appreciative.

We value the detailed and very helpful responses of the two anonymous referees who commented on our proposal for this collection as well as the efforts of the editors of the Oñati International Series in Law and Society in supporting the publication of this book.

Lastly, we would like to extend our gratitude to the contributors to this collection who came from the far corners of the world to participate in a highly fruitful and collegial workshop that has led to this collection of fascinating chapters.

Beth Goldblatt and Lucie Lamarche
April 2014

Table of Contents

List of Contributors

Pablo Arellano Ortiz is Professor of Labour and Social Security Law, Universidad Austral de Chile. PhD in Law, Université Paris Ouest Nanterre La Defense, France; Master 2 Recherche Droit Social et Droit de la Santé, Université de Paris X Nanterre, France; Master 2 Recherche Droit Social de la Université de Paris II Panthéon Assas, France. Lawyer, Universidad de Concepción, Chile. He has worked as an international consultant on social security issues and as Legal Officer in the Standard's Department at the International Labour Organization. He has published several papers in Spanish, French and English relating to the right to social security and on international labour standards, especially on the welfare state, migrants, unemployment, pensions and health, concerning Chilean and international legislation.

Sandra Fredman is the Rhodes Professor of the Laws of the British Commonwealth and the USA at the University of Oxford, a Fellow of the British Academy and an Honorary Professor at the University of Cape Town. She is South African, a graduate of the University of the Witwatersrand and Oxford University. She was made a QC (honoris causa) in 2012. She has published widely in the fields of equality, labour law and human rights. Her books include *Human Rights Transformed* (Oxford University Press, 2008); *Discrimination Law*, 2nd edn (Oxford University Press, 2011); *Women and the Law* (Oxford University Press, 1997); *The State as Employer* (with Gillian Morris) (Mansell, 1988) and *Labour Law and Industrial Relations in Great Britain* (with Bob Hepple), 2nd edn (Kluwer, 1992). She edited *Age as an Equality Issue* (with Sarah Spencer) (Hart Publishing, 2003) and *Discrimination and Human Rights: The Case of Racism* (Oxford University Press, 2001). In 2012, she founded the Oxford Human Rights Hub, of which she is the director.

Beth Goldblatt is an Associate Professor in the Faculty of Law at the University of Technology, Sydney in Australia. She is also a Visiting Fellow of the Australian Human Rights Centre in the Faculty of Law at the University of New South Wales and an Honorary Senior Fellow of the Faculty of Law at the University of the Witwatersrand, South Africa. She has been involved in research, advocacy and litigation on gender and human rights in South Africa and Australia. Her recent research concerns the right to social security from a gender perspective. She has edited a book on *Women's Social and Economic Rights* (with Kirsty McLean) (Juta, 2011) and has published on issues of gender, human rights, family law, equality, transitional justice and disability.

Lucie Lamarche is a Professor in the Faculty of Political Science and Law at the University of Québec in Montréal, Canada. She is also a professor on leave from the Faculty of Law of the University of Ottawa, Canada. This book project was co-initiated in her capacity as Research Director of the Human Rights Research and Education Centre of the University of Ottawa, where she also held the Gordon F Henderson Chair in Human Rights (2007–13). Professor Lamarche recently co-edited *14 Good Reasons for Human Rights Institutions in Canada* (Irwin Law, 2013). Recent publications include 'Human Rights, Social Security and Migrant Workers' in *Social Security and Migrant Workers* (Wolters Kluwer, 2014) and 'The Canadian Experience with the CEDAW: All women's rights are human rights—a case of treaties synergy' in *Women's Human Rights—CEDAW in International, Regional and National Law* (Cambridge University Press, 2013).

Hester Lessard is a Professor of Law at the University of Victoria in British Columbia. Her main areas of teaching and research are constitutional law, human rights and feminist legal studies. Among her publications are two co-edited volumes of essays: *Storied Communities: Narratives of Contact and Arrival in Constituting Political Community* (co-edited with Johnson and Webber) (UBC Press, 2010) and *Reaction and Resistance: Feminism, Law and Social Change* (co-edited with Chunn and Boyd) (UBC Press, 2007).

Mankui Li is a Lecturer at the School of Economic Law, and a research fellow with the Centre for Labor and Work-life Law (CLWL) at the Southwest University of Political Science and Law, Chongqing, China (since 2008). His research focus includes occupational health and safety, workers' compensation, social security systems and labour law issues.

Camille Loftus is a doctoral candidate in the Department of Social Policy at University College Dublin, researching flexicurity and its application in Ireland. Her academic research interests are in the areas of social security, gender equality and the labour market. She is currently on sabbatical from her doctoral research to undertake the role of Special Adviser to the Minister for Health.

Janet E Mosher is an Associate Professor at Osgoode Hall Law School, Toronto, Canada and has served two terms as the Academic Director of Osgoode's Intensive Program in Poverty Law. Her research explores issues of gender, poverty and violence, as well as access to justice in areas ranging from school discipline for marginalised youth, to pandemic planning and the exclusion of the homeless. Much of her work is done in collaboration with community based organisations. Current research collaborations include the Canadian Homelessness Research Network and the Assets

Coming Together from Youth community research alliance. She is editor-in-chief of Osgoode's *Journal of Law and Social Policy*—a journal that publishes works on issues at the intersections of law and society, particularly as they impact low-income individuals and marginalised communities. She is co-editor of *Constructing Crime: Contemporary Processes of Criminalization* (UBC Press, 2010) and *Disorderly People: Law and the Politics of Exclusion in Ontario* (Fernwood, 2002).

Mary P Murphy is a Lecturer in Irish Politics and Society in the Department of Sociology, National University of Ireland Maynooth. Her research interests include gender and social security, globalisation and welfare states, the politics of redistribution, power and civil society. She has published widely, most recently *Careless to Careful Activation: Making Activation Work for Women* (Dublin, NWCI, 2012) and *Towards the Second Republic: Irish Politics after the Celtic Tiger* (with Peadar Kirby) (Pluto, 2011). In 2013 she was appointed as a part-time Commissioner to the Irish Human Rights and Equality Commission.

Lorena Ossio Bustillos is Senior Researcher at the Max-Planck-Institute for Social Law and Social Policy, Department of International and Foreign Social Law in Munich. Since September 2008 her field of responsibility has been Social Protection in Latin America. She is a Visiting Research Fellow at Freie Universität Berlin, Professor of Legistics, Indigenous Law, Human Rights and Public Law at the Universities of Nuestra Señora de La Paz, Catholic University und Andina Simón and Lecturer at the German University of Administrative Sciences, Speyer. She has three books on indigenous law in Latin America, one in Legistics and several academic articles/chapters on constitutional law and social rights and social protection systems in Latin America.

Dianne Otto holds the Francine V McNiff Chair in Human Rights Law at Melbourne Law School and is Director of the Institute for International Law and the Humanities (IILAH). Dianne's research interests include: addressing gender, sexuality and race inequalities in the context of international human rights law, the UN Security Council's peacekeeping work, the technologies of global 'crisis governance' and other threats to economic, social and cultural rights, as well as the transformative potential of people's tribunals and other NGO initiatives. Her recent publications include three edited volumes, *Gender Issues and Human Rights* (Edward Elgar Publishing, 2013), a chapter in Margaret Davies and Vanessa Munro (eds), *A Research Companion to Feminist Legal Theory* (Ashgate Companion Series, 2013) and an article in *Jindal Global Law Review* (2013). She also authored a bibliographic chapter, 'Feminist Approaches' in Tony Carty (ed), *Oxford Bibliographies Online: International Law* (Oxford University Press, 2012).

Núria Pumar Beltrán is an Associate Professor of Labour Law at Barcelona University (UB), where she lectures on labour law and social security law in the degree of Law and Labour Relation Studies. Her main areas of research are concerned with employment law and social protection in the European Union and Spain, especially from a gender perspective. She currently chairs the Equality Commission of the UB Law Faculty and is involved in organising the 'Feminist Analysis of Law' seminar, currently in its eighth session. In 2010, she led the research project 'A Review of Social Security Protection afforded to Single-Parent Families', on a grant from the Ministry of Labour and Immigration. Since 2011, she has been engaged in the research project 'One-parent families in the new century: Challenges and dilemmas in times of change'.

Belinda Smith is an Associate Professor in the Faculty of Law, University of Sydney. Her main field of research is anti-discrimination laws, with a focus on gender equality and workers with family responsibilities. In articles and chapters published in Australia, the United States and Japan she has explored alternative regulatory tools and frameworks for promoting equality. She has worked extensively on promoting reform of Australian anti-discrimination laws, served on the board of the Disability Discrimination Legal Centre and is a member of the editorial board of the *Australian Journal of Labour Law*. She is currently co-authoring a book with Associate Professor Beth Gaze on *Introduction to Equality and Discrimination Law in Australia* (Cambridge University Press, forthcoming).

Lucy A Williams is a Professor of Law at Northeastern University School of Law in the United States. She teaches in the area of social welfare law and civil litigation. An authority on social welfare law and low-wage labour, she has recently focused on judicial enforcement of social and economic rights. She is a co-director of the Program on Human Rights and the Global Economy and the Convener of the International Social and Economic Rights Project. She has published widely, including in the *Yale Law Journal*, the *Columbia Journal of Transnational Law*, the *Yale Law & Policy Review*, the *South African Journal on Human Rights* and the *Stellenbosch Law Review*. In 1994–1995, she was honored by the school as the Public Interest Distinguished Professor. In August 1994, she was appointed by President Bill Clinton to the three-year Advisory Council on Unemployment Compensation, which evaluated all aspects of the unemployment compensation programme and made policy recommendations to the President and Congress.

1

Introduction: Interpreting and Advancing Women's Rights to Social Security and Social Protection

BETH GOLDBLATT AND LUCIE LAMARCHE

INTRODUCTION

THIS COLLECTION PROVIDES a detailed examination of the human rights to social security and social protection as they pertain to women.[1] It brings together three broad areas of scholarship—social policy and development, law and human rights and gender/feminist studies. The chapters consider the content of the rights to social security and social protection and the relationship between these specific human rights and principles underlying human rights such as gender equality, participation and dignity. While women's poverty and exclusion is frequently examined outside a human rights framework, the contributors to this book see social protection as a women's right issue. Although women as a group are the focus, the intersections between gender and other categories of discrimination such as race, age, class, geographical location and family status are considered throughout the collection.

Alongside conceptual insights across the field of women's social security rights, the book analyses recent developments in international

[1] The chapters in this collection were first discussed at a workshop held at the International Institute for the Sociology of Law in Oñati, Spain on 6–7 June 2013. The workshop followed a webinar series in 2012, organised by the editors through the University of Ottawa Centre for Human Rights Research and Education, to highlight some of these issues for a wider audience. The webinar videos can be viewed at www.cdp-hrc.uottawa.ca?p=4575.

law and domestic law in a range of country settings.[2] It considers the International Labour Organization's (ILO) National Social Protection Floors Recommendation[3] and examines the work of the United Nations treaty bodies. It explores the different approaches to expansion of social protection in developing countries, with specific chapters on current legal developments in China, Chile and Bolivia. The debates around welfare conditionality in Conditional Cash Transfers Programmes, a central debate in social policy and development, are looked at through a gender lens. The book also considers the position of poor women, particularly single mothers, in developed countries (Australia, Canada, the United States, Ireland and Spain) facing the damaging consequences of recent welfare cuts following policy and legal reforms. It considers shifts in global discourse on the role of social policy and the way in which ideas of crisis and austerity have been used to undermine rights with harsh impacts on women.

The chapters in this collection engage with various frameworks for assessing social security law and policy from a women's rights perspective and for interpreting and advancing the rights of women in future social security and social protection measures.

This introductory chapter begins with a discussion of the global context of social security and social protection and its implications for the world's women. It then outlines the value of a gender lens in understanding social policy. Thereafter, the way in which social security and social protection are defined and understood within human rights is unpacked. The chapter then considers three possible ways of approaching the interpretation and development of the rights to social security and social protection. Finally, some of the major themes emerging from this collection are outlined with reference to the various chapters contained within the book.

THE CONTEXT

Social security and social protection are in the spotlight internationally, particularly in the recent context of financial crisis. In the developing world social protection is increasingly seen as a valuable mechanism to address

[2] The editors have not tried to present an exhaustive survey of different country experiences in this book. The choice of contributions reflect the following typology: (1) developing countries illustrating significant, recent progress, from a women's rights perspective (China and Bolivia); (2) a developing country where gender equity adjustments followed the brutal privatisation of the pension system (Chile); (3) countries that have been severely hit by recent austerity measures (Ireland and Spain); and (4) countries where the welfare system is being gradually dismantled (United States, Canada and Australia).

[3] ILO Recommendation R202: Social Floors Protection Recommendation (Recommendation Concerning National Floors of Social Protection) (101st Conference Session, Geneva, 14 July 2012).

poverty and generate development and growth. In the developed world, governments looking to limit state expenditure on social programmes are reducing their commitments to social security. These processes of building up and breaking down welfare systems are not operating in isolation from each other. Ongoing ideological challenges to welfarism in rich countries are proving influential in the shaping of new programmes in poor countries in some instances.[4] At the same time, strategies being tested in developing countries are making their way into some of the policies of the developed world.[5] Challenges to the universalism of social security and a growing use of conditionality in social assistance programmes are two of the concerning features of the current phase. At the same time, greater numbers of people are accessing social security than ever before with many beneficial initiatives emerging from around the world.

Women's place within social security and social protection is of increasing interest to international bodies, development agencies and states. There is a growing recognition that women are the best human investment in the development context. As a result, women are sometimes being asked to carry the burdens of development without protection of their interests and needs. For example, conditional cash transfers are often designed in a way that adds to the responsibilities of women and that reinforce the stereotype of mothers as the parents responsible for children.[6] While the more redistributive intuition and the focus on women behind current efforts seem valuable, what is often missing is a human rights approach that shapes and guides these interventions. The focus should not just be on women's *roles* in development, but also on women's *rights* in relation to social provision. A human rights approach to women's rights to social security and social protection provides an entitlement and accountability framework that guarantees not only a better balanced gender redistribution of resources but, also a less discriminatory and a more participatory one.

Not all developing countries are following the conditional cash transfer approach—some, like China, have chosen a social insurance model.[7] Others, such as India, have combined a focus on employment creation with social assistance or have, as in some Latin American countries, combined social assistance and social insurance models in expanding health and

[4] See Fredman, in this collection, who notes the introduction of 'workfare' in the United States (US) and elsewhere in the developed world that was the forerunner of conditional cash transfer programmes in developing countries. Also see Williams, in this collection, for some of the history behind this approach in the US.

[5] Fredman, in this collection, refers to a conditional cash transfer programme being run in the city of New York. Goldblatt, in this collection, refers to a programme that links social assistance payments to school attendance in parts of Australia.

[6] Fredman, in this collection, explains how conditional cash transfers designed to benefit poor women often impose duties on them in relation to children's school attendance or medical visits.

[7] Li, in this collection.

pension coverage.[8] Clearly, modern social protection schemes rely more and more on mixed models and the frontier between social security and social protection schemes is being blurred. [9] These models, some more inclusive than others, are not always designed with women's rights in mind. A gender rights perspective is necessary in order to evaluate how new social protection designs address economic redistribution together with human dignity, women's equal citizenship and the transformation of gender relations in society.

Alongside the growth in social protection programmes in the developing context are cutbacks to social security programmes in the context of austerity measures in developed countries. These often have the harshest impact on women, with single mothers a particularly vulnerable target group.[10] These cuts should be understood, similarly from a rights perspective, not just as economic decisions but also as potentially retrogressive violations of human rights, with specific gendered impacts.[11]

THE GENDER LENS

There is a rich engagement with issues of gender and social security. Scholars of social policy and development have produced sustained critiques of the welfare state in advanced economies[12] and of development and social programmes in developing countries.[13] They have pointed to

[8] Ossio Bustillos, in this collection, explains the significance for Bolivian women—including aboriginal women—of the *Renta Dignidad*, a universal pension programme. Arrellano Ortiz, in this collection, describes how Chile opted for a mixed model of contributory and non-contributory systems in order to produce more gender equity in relation to pensions.

[9] For a thorough consideration of recent social protection initiatives, see UN Development Programme (UNDP), *Sharing Innovative Experiences Volume 18: Successful Social Protection Floor Experiences* (New York, UNDP, 2011); and International Social Security Association (ISSA), *Social Security Coverage Extension in the BRICs: A Comparative Study on the Extension of Coverage in Brazil, the Russian Federation, India, China and South Africa* (Geneva, ISSA, 2013).

[10] Williams, in this collection, describes the highly disciplinary and gender discriminatory reality of social welfare programmes in the US. Murphy and Loftus, in this collection, echo a similar (though more recent) situation in Ireland.

[11] See Goldblatt, Murphy and Loftus and Otto, respectively, in this collection.

[12] Eg, Fraser, N, 'After the Family Wage: Gender Equity and the Welfare State' (1994) 22(4) *Political Theory* 591; Lewis, J, 'Gender and the Development of Welfare Regimes' (1992) 2(3) *Journal of European Social Policy* 159; Gordon, L (ed), *Women, the State, and Welfare* (University of Wisconsin Press, 1990); Orloff, AS, 'Gender in the Welfare State' (1996) 22 *Annual Review of Sociology* 51; Orloff, AS, 'Gendering the Comparative Analysis of Welfare States: An Unfinished Agenda' (2009) 27 *Sociological Theory* 317; Pateman, C, 'The Patriarchal Welfare State' in C Pateman (ed), *The Disorder of Women* (Cambridge, Polity Press, 1989) 179; and Sainsbury, D (ed), *Gendering Welfare States* (London, Sage, 1994).

[13] Razavi, S and Hassim, S (eds), *Gender and Social Policy in a Global Context: Uncovering the Gendered Structure of 'the Social'* (Basingstoke, Palgrave Macmillan, 2006). See Holmes, R and Jones, N, *Gender and Social Protection in the Developing World: Beyond Mothers and Safety Nets* (London, Zed Books, 2013); Kasente, D, 'Gender and Social Security Reform in Africa'

the inbuilt biases in many of these systems that are designed around the archetype of the male breadwinner. This conceptualisation of the welfare state has denied women's right to social citizenship largely based on their lack of income as a product of their caring responsibilities.[14] Women, who generally earn less and have more insecure employment, gain more limited access to social security benefits. The system designs do not attempt to undermine structural inequalities around access to employment and responsibilities for care and household labour—in many cases they reinforce these inequalities.[15] The initial Western-centric critique of the welfare state has joined a more universal one as successive generations of structural adjustments programmes and the neo-liberal agenda increasingly put women from the global south at higher risk of poverty. Women in all countries are facing challenges as increasing 'informalisation', 'flexibilisation' and other features of globalisation change the nature of work which is becoming ever more precarious. Attempting to ensure that gender is taken into account in the development of social protection programmes that address these conditions is a central concern for feminists working in this area.

Today, women from both the north and the south are in urgent need of social protection in a globalised world of increasing poverty where adverse roles are assigned to women by both the market and neo-conservative ideology. As Razavi proposes, engendering social protection in a contemporary context requires efforts to prevent, to manage and to overcome all situations that adversely affect people's well-being and living standards.[16] This requires the promotion of transformative social policies that leave nobody behind and do not discriminate on the basis of attachment to the formal labour market.[17] This is aligned with ideas of redistributive gender equality.[18] In many countries there have been efforts to bring workers in the

(2000) 53(3) *International Social Security Review* 27; Sabates-Wheele, R and Kabeer, N, 'Gender Equality and the Extension of Social Protection' (ESS Working Paper No 16, International Labour Organization, 2003); and Sen, G, *Engendering Social Security and Protection: The Case of Asia* (Friedrich-Ebert-Stiftung, August 2011), available at: library.fes.de/pdf-files/iez/08436.pdf.

[14] See Scott, J, Dex, S and Plagnol, AC, *Gendered Lives: Gender Inequalities in Production and Reproduction* (UK, Edward Elgar Publishing, 2012).

[15] Smith, in this collection, shows how the failure to factor in the care responsibilities of women in the Australian social security system, ensures ongoing inequality. Similarly, Pumar Beltrán, in this collection, shows how recent pension reform in a struggling Spain fails to undo the underlying inequalities facing women who have primary responsibility for household labour and care.

[16] Razavi, S, 'Engendering Social Security and Protection: Challenges for Making Social Security and Protection Gender Equitable' (Berlin, Friedrich-Ebert-Stiftung, Global Policy and Development Division, June 2011). See also Razavi, S et al, 'Gendered Impacts of Globalization: Employment and Social Protection' (UN Research Institute for Social Development (UNRISD) Research Paper No 3, Geneva, UNSRID, March 2012).

[17] As discussed in Mkandawire, T, 'Transformative Social Policy and Innovation in Developing Countries' (2007) *European Journal of Development Research* 19, 13.

[18] See Fredman, in this collection.

informal sector and the self-employed into contributory pension or health schemes. But it is of questionable value to continue to retain the attachment between social protection and work given the unpredictable and unstable nature of women's work in the informal sector. While social assistance programmes are essential to address gendered poverty, these must be accompanied by greater investment in public services.[19] At the same time, efforts to restructure work[20] and gender roles should occur alongside such programmes to encourage women's right to livelihood.

Legal scholars have documented the difficulties involved in challenging the inbuilt gender inequalities in welfare systems.[21] The fight against sex discrimination in the workplace has largely hidden the centrality of paid and unpaid caring and domestic work done by women that is both a cause and a source of women's poverty and exclusion. Greater accessibility to social security benefits without discrimination, such as pensions, may partly remove the consequences of assumed dependency of women on the male breadwinner, but it does not address the negative impact of the peripheral connection of women to formal work and their role in care, combined with the poverty trap into which they fall. Feminist legal theorists have recognised that formal equality measures are inadequate in addressing gender disadvantage in the workplace and within social security systems and have looked instead to more substantive approaches to tackle inequality.

Some feminists working in both law and social policy have argued that a human rights-based approach must be central to efforts to reshape social security and protection. A human rights perspective is also valuable in assessing the gender dimensions of existing social security policies and programmes to see whether these will lead to far-reaching improvements in the lives of women facing poverty and vulnerability. The focus on gender as it relates to the right to social security and social protection, considered by a small number of writers until now,[22] is the subject of this book.

[19] *Ibid.*

[20] Williams, in this collection.

[21] For examples in the European context, see Luckhaus, L, 'Equal Treatment, Social Protection and Income Security for Women' (2000) 139(2) *International Labour Review* 149; and Sohrab, J, *Sexing the Benefit: Women, Social Security, and Financial Independence in EC Sex Equality Law* (Aldershot, Dartmouth, 1996).

[22] These include: Darooka, P, 'Social Security: A Woman's Human Right' (PWESCR Discussion Paper, New Delhi, Program on Women's Economic, Social and Cultural Rights (PWESCR), 2 April 2008); Goldblatt, B, 'The Right to Social Security—Addressing Women's Poverty and Disadvantage' in B Goldblatt and K McLean (eds), *Women's Social and Economic Rights* (Cape Town, Juta, 2011); Luckhaus, above n 21; Lamarche, L, 'Le PIDESC, les femmes et le droit à la sécurité sociale: considérations et propositions pour un droit "universel" à la sécurité sociale' (2002) 14(1) *Revue Femme Droit* 53; and Raday, F, 'Article 11' in S Freeman et al (eds), *The UN Convention on the Elimination of All Forms of Discrimination against Women: A Commentary* (Oxford, Oxford University Press, 2012).

SOCIAL SECURITY AND SOCIAL PROTECTION AS RIGHTS

Social security is a basic human right found in numerous international human rights instruments, regional human rights instruments and in the constitutions of many states.[23] While there is no question of the existence of this fundamental right, it has been, until recently, somewhat undeveloped in the human rights field. The phrase 'social protection' which has gained in popularity over the past decade, also has its origins in foundational human rights instruments. The term appears in the Universal Declaration of Human Rights[24] while the word 'protection' is mentioned in relation to social security in the ILO's Declaration of Philadelphia.[25] The ILO has played an important role in setting standards for social security measures but these have only begun to have real relevance to the developing world over the last decade. Two key documents reflect a new interest, at the human rights level, in providing universal meaning to the right to social security. One is General Comment No 19, prepared by the United Nations Committee on Economic, Social and Cultural Rights (CESCR) in 2008, which provides a detailed interpretation of the right to social security in article 9 of the International Covenant on Economic, Social and Cultural Rights (ICESCR).[26] The other is ILO Recommendation No 202 on Social Protection Floors, which promotes the establishment of social protection floors as a fundamental element of national social security systems.[27] In addition to these important developments, the UN Special Rapporteur on extreme poverty and human rights, Magdalena Sepúlveda Carmona, has made a significant contribution to the elaboration of a principled human rights approach to social protection in addressing poverty and extreme poverty.[28]

[23] For an elaboration of the sources of the right see International Labour Organization (ILO), 'Social Security and the Rule of Law: General Survey Concerning Social Security Instruments in Light of the 2008 Declaration on Social Justice for a Fair Globalization' (Geneva, ILO, 2011).

[24] Universal Declaration of Human Rights (UDHR) (adopted 10 December 1948) UN Doc 217 A (III), art 25(2).

[25] International Labour Organization (ILO) ILO, *ILO Declaration Concerning the Aims and Purposes of the International Labour Organization (Declaration of Philadelphia)*, 10 May 1994, s III(f), available at: www.ilo.org/dyn/normlex/en/f?p=1000:62:0::NO:62:P62_LIST_ENTRIE_ID:2453907:NO#declaration.

[26] UN Committee on Economic, Social and Cultural Rights (CESCR), *General Comment No 19: The Right to Social Security (art 9)*, 4 February 2008, UN Doc E/C.12/GC/19.

[27] ILO Recommendation R202, above n 3. This is discussed by Lamarche, in this collection.

[28] Some of the key reports by Magdalena Sepúlveda Carmona, Special Rapporteur on Extreme Poverty and Human Rights, include: *Promotion and Protection of all Human Rights, Civil, Political, Economic, Social and Cultural Rights, Including the Right to Development*, 27 March 2009, UN Doc A/HRC/11/9 ('Cash transfer programmes'); *Final Draft of the Guiding Principles on Extreme Poverty and Human Rights, Submitted by the Special Rapporteur on Extreme Poverty and Human Rights* 18 July 2012, UN Doc A/HRC/21/39; *Report of the Special Rapporteur on Extreme Poverty and Human Rights*, 9 August 2013, UN Doc A/68/293 ('Unpaid care work').

In this collection the right to social security is understood as a legal guarantee (whether in the form of contributory, non-contributory or universal programmes), while social protection is the normative aim of this legal guarantee. Women require access to the benefits of an effective and equal social security regime in order to exercise their rights to social protection. Increasingly, social security is understood as entailing combinations of social insurance and social assistance.[29] This should also include measures to enable women's participation in work and society such as the provision of childcare and other necessary social services.

While the importance of social security as a human right is increasingly being recognised, the gender dimensions of this right are not always fully appreciated or explored. The contributors to this collection have identified the need to develop and interpret the right to social security through a gender lens. This will strengthen and enrich the right and give it greater application in shaping meaningful social protection measures for women and men throughout the world. The following section will consider possible ways of 'gendering' the right to social security.

FRAMEWORKS TO BRING GENDER INTO THE RIGHTS TO SOCIAL SECURITY AND SOCIAL PROTECTION

There are different ways of undertaking the task of 'gendering' the right to social security. Three are suggested here. The first is to locate the work within the equality guarantee and ensure that the right to social security is realised in a gender equal way. The second requires a systematic gender-based reformulation of the social security right by critiquing and reframing it in light of feminist theory to ensure that every aspect of the right takes account of gendered considerations and results in a right with a deeply gendered content. The third devises a human rights approach to social protection that mainstreams gender and includes a set of guidelines that tests compliance of social protection programmes with human rights obligations informed by a gender perspective.

[29] This is a shift from the historically worker-biased, contingency-based approach of ILO Convention C102: Social Security (Minimum Standards) Convention (Convention Concerning Minimum Standards of Social Security) (adopted 28 June 1952, entered into force 27 April 1955) that emerged from a social insurance model. There is a growing recognition that poverty and social exclusion are social risks/contingencies just as are the more traditional categories such as illness, disability, and so on.

The Equality Approach to the Social Security Right

This approach recognises that human rights will not in themselves ensure that women's needs and interests are addressed without further efforts to put these at the forefront and find ways of meeting them. It sees equality, which is both an underlying value and an operational human right, as the standard against which other human rights can be tested and reframed to ensure that they are not advantaging some over others. Equality, with a gender focus, requires that social security and protection rights contribute towards far-reaching, positive alterations to gender relations in society. This approach is taken by Fredman in her chapter in this collection[30] and followed and discussed in other chapters.[31] Fredman sees substantive equality as a multidimensional concept pursuing four overlapping aims of redistribution, recognition, transformation and participation.[32]

Applying this concept of equality to laws and policies that claim to advance the right to social security and protection means testing them against each dimension in turn, informed by a gendered understanding of inequality and how it is created and maintained.[33] Lessard's chapter focuses specifically on the dimension of participation as a core element of human rights protection.[34] This can be seen as an elaboration of an element of a substantive equality approach or as an additional approach to ensuring that gender is brought into discussion of social security and protection.

Gendering the Social Security Right

The second approach is part of a feminist project that aims to expand and redefine the content of international human rights and social and economic rights in particular.[35] Otto argues that:

> There is also the continuing need to take a dynamic and gender-inclusive approach to interpretation of the substantive articles of the *ICESCR*. Women should not always have to rely on the discourse of equality and non-discrimination to ensure their inclusion in the mainstream of the human rights paradigm. Rather, human rights must also be interpreted from women's perspectives ... the content of each *1CESCR* right must be understood so that it addresses women's actual needs

[30] Fredman, in this collection.

[31] Goldblatt, in this collection; and Murphy and Loftus, in this collection.

[32] Fredman, in this collection.

[33] For another equality based approach see Brodsky, G and Day, S, 'Denial of the Means of Subsistence as an Equality Violation' (2005) 2005 *Acta Juridica* 149.

[34] Lessard, in this collection.

[35] See the 'Montréal Principles on Women's Economic, Social and Cultural Rights' (2004) 26 *Human Rights Quarterly* 760.

> when they are interpreted or implemented ... gender-inclusive interpretation is itself an important means of achieving substantive equality for women.[36]

This approach draws on key feminist concepts in engaging in a process of reinterpretation of the right to social security and protection. It assumes that the right will generally be understood using a male standard for the default rights holder. It takes women's lives as the starting point and requires attention to context. In so doing it requires that women's agency and voice are central to responses that address their circumstances. It recognises that women are not a homogenous group and that attention must be paid to the intersections between categories of disadvantage along lines of gender, race, culture, age, religion, disability and others. Efforts to address the needs of women should be careful not to leave certain groups of women behind, thus consideration of marginalisation and vulnerability is crucial. The structuring of the world into public and private domains sees women's experiences being privatised, diminished and ignored. The division of labour and the structuring role of care shape women's experiences over the life course and distinguish them from men's. Thus, work in the home, the usual preserve of women, is not regarded as work that counts; subsistence work and work in family enterprises is also often unpaid for women and children; and women's work in the informal and formal sector is often located at the bottom of the hierarchy in terms of value and recognition. Subordination of women is deeply embedded in the power structures of society leading to violence and oppression in all spheres of life. The need to understand and respond to the damaging conditions faced by women requires a focus that goes beyond national boundaries and pays attention to global challenges and the interplay between the global, national and local.

A number of the chapters in the collection follow this approach in their interpretation of the right to social security. Some of the chapters combine this approach with a substantive equality focus—a hybrid of the first two approaches set out here.[37]

Mainstreaming Gender into the Human Rights Approach to Social Protection

As noted above, the UN Special Rapporteur on extreme poverty and human rights, Magdalena Sepúlveda Carmona, has contributed important thinking on the right to social security and social protection. She has also emphasised

[36] Otto, D, '"Gender Comment": Why Does the UN Committee on Economic, Social and Cultural Rights Need a General Comment on Women?' (2002) 14 *Canadian Journal of Women and the Law* 1, 51.

[37] Goldblatt, in this collection; and Murphy and Loftus, in this collection.

that social protection systems should actively promote gender equality and empower women. She brings in many of the lessons of feminist development theory alongside feminist perspectives on social policy in a robust approach to human rights.

Her 2009 report on social protection measures identifies key issues for consideration in designing policies that promote gender equality and human rights more generally.[38] Her 2013 report considers the rights dimensions of unpaid care work and its effects on women's exposure to poverty. In this report, she highlights how care work forces women into informal, unpaid or precarious employment and increases their risk of being deprived of decent social protection.[39] The Guiding Principles on Extreme Poverty and Human Rights adopted by the Human Rights Council in 2012 note that states have an obligation to target resources to the benefit of women, who make up a majority of the poor, including resources allocated to public services and social protection.[40]

Sepúlveda and Nyst's recent book[41] summarises the human rights approach and makes specific gendered recommendations for the compliance of social protection systems with international human rights obligations.[42] They propose that states recognise the multiple forms of discrimination that women experience and their different needs over the life cycle in the design of social protection systems. They stress the recognition of women's care roles and the need for the state to take responsibility together with society for care, while encouraging a greater role by men. Appropriate gender-sensitive services designed and provided by gender aware administrators must be ensured to address problems of women's access. Social protection programmes must take account of intra-household dynamics to ensure that women are reached and are benefiting. Meaningful participation of women in all stages of social protection programmes must be facilitated. Lastly, gender related data collection must occur to ensure monitoring and evaluating of social protection programmes.

This is a valuable set of recommendations for policy design that are framed within a human rights approach. They illustrate the close relationship between human rights, social policy and development and inform the interpretation of the rights to social security and protection with the corresponding aim of addressing gender discrimination and promoting gender equality.

[38] Sepúlveda, *Promotion and Protection of all Human Rights*, above n 28.

[39] Sepúlveda, *Report of the Special Rapporteur*, above n 28, at para 49.

[40] Sepúlveda, *Final Draft of the Guiding Principles*, above n 28, at para 31.

[41] Sepúlveda, M and Nyst, C, 'The Human Rights Approach to Social Protection' (Ministry for Foreign Affairs, Finland, 1 June 2012) 72.

[42] *Ibid*, at 36–37.

It should be noted that the three approaches set out above are not mutually exclusive—on the contrary, they are closely interrelated and lead towards the same goal of a gendered social security right that is socially, economically and politically transformative. There is a recognised principle of international human rights law that human rights are universal, indivisible, interrelated and interdependent.[43] Thus, non-discrimination and equality are closely linked to social security in a rights framework.[44] The interdependence of rights also means that other rights may have a strong bearing on the right to social security such as the right to dignity, the right to life, the right to an adequate livelihood and the right to work. The gender dimensions of all these rights should also be considered and developed, alongside the development of the rights to social security and social protection.

KEY THEMES OF THE BOOK

Various themes emerge across the chapters in this collection concerning: the relationship between work and social security; the participation of women in the design and implementation of social security and social protection programmes; austerity and crisis; intersectional discrimination; differing approaches to equality; and the need for a rights-based response to address women's circumstances through social security and social protection. These are briefly surveyed.

The problematic relationship between participation in the formal labour market and social security entitlement is a frequent concern in this book. Women's responsibilities for household labour and care limit their access to the labour market and weaken their employment opportunities. Lower earnings affect their pensions in many countries. While there are some positive examples of efforts to factor women's work history into account in setting pensions, most countries ignore this issue. Women are also being forced into the workforce through social security policies that fail to provide the necessary support for their care and household work. For the millions of women who work outside the formal labour market, social security is often limited and inadequate. Thus, social assistance that is both universal and unconditional is an urgent need for women around the world. This basic protection needs to be complemented with the provision of other social services such as childcare if societies are serious about the full and

[43] UN General Assembly, *Vienna Declaration and Programme of Action*, 25 June 1993, UN Doc A/CONF.157/23, Part 1, para 5, which says that 'All human rights are universal, indivisible and interdependent and interrelated'.

[44] See Liebenberg, S and Goldblatt, B, 'The Interrelationship between Equality and Socio-Economic Rights in South Africa's Transformative Constitution' (2007) 23 *South African Journal on Human Rights* 335.

equal inclusion of women. Positive examples of attempts to include women in social security schemes are found in Chile where pension reforms have made provision for foreign domestic workers;[45] and in Bolivia where the basic, universal pension system is finally reaching indigenous women.[46]

Another central theme is the participation of women in ensuring their rights to social security. Reforms to social security systems will not prove adequate if women are not involved in consultation around the design of these changes. In both their chapters, Lessard and Fredman argue that women's right to participation in policymaking is an essential component of their right to equality. In China, the lack of participation by women has led to protectionist measures for women that are not always appropriate or equality enhancing.[47] In Australia, the failure to consult adequately with indigenous communities has led to the external management of social security payments that harm women in these communities.[48] In Ireland[49] and Spain,[50] poor women have been required to take on the burdens of austerity through reduced social security without being involved at the national level or the European level in shaping less painful solutions. In other cases, such as the United States[51] and Canada,[52] women are simply excluded from the debate about social protection, since they are seen as part of the problem in countries where welfare cutbacks are designed to discipline poor women and turn them into precarious workers.

Many chapters in this book highlight the challenges of economic austerity following financial crisis accompanied by the growing dominance of neo-conservative ideology.[53] Both of these have resulted in measures that negatively impact women, particularly those who are already facing the challenges of poverty and care responsibility. The ideological arguments for reduced or reformulated social security reinforce negative stereotypes of poor women.

Discrimination against women on the basis of gender intersects with other forms of discrimination such as race, class, age, citizenship and family status and deepens the difficulties facing these groups of women within various social security systems. Many authors in this collection note the multiple and intersecting forms of discrimination against women in their different national contexts. The chapters on the United States, Australia and Canada in this collection highlight the harsh impact of policies underpinned by race inequality

[45] Arellano Ortiz, in this collection.
[46] Ossio Bustillos, in this collection.
[47] Li, in this collection.
[48] Goldblatt, in this collection.
[49] Loftus and Murphy, in this collection.
[50] Pumar Beltrán, in this collection.
[51] Williams, in this collection.
[52] Mosher, in this collection.
[53] See, in particular, Mosher, in this collection.

on poor women.[54] The challenges facing women migrant workers internal to China and from outside Chile, many of whom are from Bolivia, are discussed in some of the contributions.[55] The plight of single mothers trying to manage with inadequate social security and increasingly precarious work is the focus of a number of chapters.[56]

The evaluation of current developments presented in this book shows a variety of approaches to gender equality. In Chile, recent changes to the pension system rely more on the concept of equity than on gender equality.[57] Bolivia has introduced the *Renta Dignidad* universal pension programme which tackles the extreme poverty of a significant percentage of women without grounding its reform in a gender equality framework.[58] The Spanish example illustrates a struggle between formal equality between men and women and a more transformative understanding of gender equality in a context of austerity and within the scope of European law.[59] The case of China is interesting as it claims to have attained formal equality between men and women while recognising that women from rural areas have been left behind.[60]

What is clear from most of the contributions is the need for a principled, human rights approach to social security and social protection based on a single, universal standard. While contexts may differ, this principled approach can be used to challenge removal of existing benefits (such as in Australia, Spain or Ireland), the imposition of conditions for receipt of social benefits (such as in the United States and Australia and in Conditional Cash Transfer Programmes in many parts of the developing world) and the failure to extend new social security programmes to women on a substantively equal basis (such as in China and Chile). It is also clear from many of the chapters that advances in social security protections will not be adequate unless issues of care and labour market restructuring are addressed in all the societies under consideration. Without challenging assumptions and practices that make care the responsibility of women, the fundamental inequalities will remain. Related to this, if women are relegated to precarious and inadequate work, they will not be able to participate in the workplace or the community as equal members of society. Addressing these issues of work and care within and alongside the rights to social security and social protection is essential for women in every country

[54] See Goldblatt, Lessard and Williams, respectively, in this collection.
[55] See Arellano Ortiz, Li and Ossio Bustillos, respectively, in this collection.
[56] See Smith, Williams, Loftus and Murphy, Pumar Beltrán and Goldblatt, respectively, in this collection.
[57] Arrelano Ortiz, in this collection.
[58] Ossio, in this collection.
[59] Pumar Beltrán, in this collection.
[60] Li, in this collection.

in the world. Otto points out that this is not just a challenge within national boundaries but a transnational struggle as well.[61]

CONCLUSION

This introductory chapter has provided a brief discussion of the current context in which social security and protection are needed to address gendered poverty and disadvantage. It has looked at the way a gender lens informs our analysis of social policy and has outlined the human rights framework in which the rights to social security and social protection are located. It has set out three of the ways in which these rights might be interpreted and developed taking gender into account. Lastly, it has discussed the key themes that emerge in this collection with reference to the various chapters in this book.

[61] Otto, in this collection.

Part I

Gender Transformation: Equality and Participation

2

Engendering Social Welfare Rights

SANDRA FREDMAN*

INTRODUCTION

SOCIAL WELFARE RIGHTS have traditionally been premised on a particular understanding of gender relations, which privileged male breadwinners and relegated women to secondary status.[1] In recent years, however, the perception of women as secondary citizens in relation to welfare rights appears to have reversed. Because the evidence shows that women are likely to prioritise their children's welfare in using available resources, they are now seen as the main vehicle for poverty alleviation and therefore the main recipients of welfare rights. This is particularly true of Conditional Cash Transfer Programmes (CCTPs), which have become increasingly popular in many countries.[2] The World Bank describes such programmes enthusiastically as increasing women's bargaining power and agency,[3] and as reinforcing women's independence within the family.[4] Others, however, point out that these programmes are based on preconceptions of gender relations which differ very little from the preconceptions of their predecessors in the welfare field. Thus, Chant argues that putting women in 'the frontline of dealing with poverty'[5] reinforces

* Earlier versions of this chapter were presented at the Friedrich-Erbert-Stiftung conference on 'Engendering Social Protection' in Lusaka in November 2012 and at the IISL workshop in Oñati in May 2013. I am grateful to the participants and to Linda Richter and Beth Goldblatt for their helpful responses.

[1] Fredman, S, *Women and the Law* (Oxford, Oxford University Press, 1997); and Sepúlveda Carmona, M, Independent Expert on the Question of Human Rights and Extreme Poverty, *Promotion and Protection of all Human Rights, Civil, Political, Economic, Social and Cultural Rights, Including the Right to Development*, 27 March 2009, UN Doc A/HRC/11/9, para 69.

[2] Fiszbein, A, Schady, NR and Ferreira, FHG, *Conditional Cash Transfers: Reducing Present and Future Poverty* (Washington, DC, World Bank, 2009) 4.

[3] *Ibid*, at 9–10.

[4] See, eg, Sepúlveda Carmona, above n 1, at para 68.

[5] Chant, S, 'The "Feminisation of Poverty" and the "Feminisation" of Anti-Poverty Programmes: Room for Revision?' (2008) 43 *Journal of Development Studies* 165, 176.

gendered stereotypes about women's role and responsibility for children, while at the same time considerably increasing their burdens.

This chapter does not attempt to prescribe the ideal model for delivering the right to social welfare. Instead, my aim is to construct a way of evaluating social welfare programmes from the perspective of substantive equality. To do this, I draw on the four-dimensional model for substantive equality which I have developed in other contexts. Rather than collapsing substantive equality into equality of opportunity, equality of results, dignity or other single dimensional approaches, I argue that substantive equality should have four interrelated aims: (i) redressing disadvantage; (ii) addressing stigma, stereotyping, humiliation and violence; (iii) accommodating difference and transforming institutions; and (iv) facilitating participation.[6] The aim is to mainstream gender equality by assessing whether particular social welfare programmes fulfil these criteria for substantive equality, and by incorporating these perspectives into its design and modification.

This chapter begins with a brief look at the current context. The following section sketches the four-dimensional equality paradigm, while the final section illustrates this approach by considering examples drawn from CCTPs.

GENDERED POVERTY

Women's over-representation among the extreme poor[7] is not purely accidental. Instead, it is argued here that women's risk of poverty is specifically affected by their gender.[8] Whereas for men, this risk is predominantly connected to exclusion from the labour market, whether due to low skills, previous unemployment or lack of regional job opportunities, for women, these risks are compounded by other, gender-based factors. In particular, women's poverty is closely linked to their role in the family, especially their caring roles.[9] Unpaid caring roles can significantly limit women's access to decent paid work, leaving many women with no choice but to accept precarious and low-paid work.[10] Part-time work is particularly at risk of

[6] Fredman, S, *Discrimination Law*, 2nd edn (Oxford, Oxford University Press, 2011).

[7] See, eg, Sepúlveda Carmona, above n 1, at para 67.

[8] This section is taken from Fredman, S, 'Engendering Socio-Economic Rights' (2009) 25 *South African Journal on Human Rights* 1.

[9] Goldblatt, B, 'The Right to Social Security—Addressing Women's Poverty and Disadvantage' in B Goldblatt and K McLean (eds), *Women's Social and Economic Rights* (Cape Town, Juta, 2011) 35.

[10] Rosenblatt, G and Rake, K, 'Gender and Poverty' (London, Fawcett Society, 2003), available at: sedighedolatabadi.org/wp-content/uploads/2012/07/poverty-and-gender-000.pdf.

low pay;[11] yet part-time workers are predominantly women.[12] Women also predominate in the informal sector, especially in the lowest-paid segment—as homeworkers or industrial outworkers.[13] Caring roles have an impact on women's lifetime earnings, which in turn significantly affect pension entitlements. Furthermore, divorce, widowhood, separation and teenage motherhood are major triggers of women's poverty in a way they are not for men.[14] This is aggravated by a lack of power. For example, household income may bear no relation to women's poverty because women may not be able to access it.[15]

Women's poverty cannot therefore be characterised solely in terms of income poverty.[16] It has also to do with inequality in relation to time and labour input;[17] continuing discrimination in relation to property, succession and family law; customary practices such as 'property grabbing' from widows; inadequate education; exposure to gender-based violence and lack of full political participation.[18] Domestic violence and divorce are two of the biggest precipitants of women into poverty. Thus, as Brodsky and Day powerfully argue, 'poverty is a sex equality issue because women's poverty is a manifestation of persistent discrimination against women'.[19]

The gendered nature of women's poverty poses specific challenges for the right to social security. Benefits based on contributions over a full-time, continuous working life or conditional on an employment contract will exclude a large number of women, who need to reconcile caring work with paid work in the labour market. Universal cash transfers directly to women solve some of these problems: they are unrelated to working patterns or household income and are not subject to intra-household imbalances of power. Universal child benefit in the United Kingdom (UK), now under

[11] Hills, J et al, 'An Anatomy of Inequality in the UK: Report of the National Equality Panel' (London, Government Equalities Office, January 2010) 11–13.

[12] European Commission (EC), 'Report from the Commission to the Council, the European Parliament, the European Economic and Social Committee, and the Committee of the Regions: Equality Between Women And Men—2009' (Com(2009) 77 Final, Brussels, EC, 2009) 4; and Low Pay Commission, *National Minimum Wage: Low Pay Commission Report 2009* (Low Pay Commission, May 2009) 98.

[13] Employment Trends Team, International Labour Organization (ILO) *Global Employment Trends for Women* (Geneva, ILO, March 2009) 10–12; and The World Bank, *World Development Report 2012: Gender Equality and Development* (Washington, The International Bank for Reconstruction and Development/The World Bank, 2011) 79–80.

[14] Rosenblatt and Rake, above n 10, at 3.

[15] Chant, S, 'Rethinking the Feminisation of Poverty' (2006) 7 *Journal of Development and Capabilities* 201, 208.

[16] *Ibid*, at 174.

[17] *Ibid*, at 182.

[18] Fredman, S, 'Antidiscrimination Laws and Work in the Developing World: A Thematic Overview' (Background Paper for the World Development Report 2013).

[19] Brodsky, G and Day, S, 'Beyond the Social and Economic Rights Debate: Substantive Equality Speaks to Poverty' (2002) 14 *Canadian Journal of Women and the Law* 185, 189.

threat, has always been regarded in this light. However, cash transfers can only be palliative. Universal access to good quality public services such as health and education, free at the point of delivery; availability of childcare and flexible working; equal rights in relation to property and family law; minimum wage laws and a particular focus on the informal sector are all essential components of any strategy to address women's poverty.

SUBSTANTIVE EQUALITY AND ENGENDERING SOCIAL SECURITY

The great variety of social welfare systems and different contexts make it impossible to construct the perfect model. The aim of this section, instead, is to create a set of criteria to mainstream gender equality in the process of establishing, evaluating and modifying welfare rights. The founding premise is that welfare[20] is a human right. Welfare is not charity, nor development aid nor a reward for good behaviour. Welfare systems should therefore conform to the four human rights-based requirements set out by the Special Rapporteur for Extreme Poverty. First, there should be an adequate legal framework. Social welfare rights should not be delivered through discretionary policies or projects run through development agencies. Second, benefits should reach the most vulnerable. Third, there should be transparency, accountability and access to information. Fourth, there should be meaningful and effective participation by rights holders.[21]

These requirements are necessary but not sufficient to engender social welfare rights. As Chant argues, poverty alleviation measures will not achieve gender equality on their own.[22] Unless specific attention is paid to gender, social welfare rights risk reinforcing gender inequalities. Welfare systems should therefore aim to achieve substantive gender equality. In this section, I elaborate on the meaning of substantive equality in the gender context, before applying it to welfare rights.

The most basic conception of equality is that likes should be treated alike. This conception has an important role to play, particularly where women are expressly excluded from legal rights such as property or succession, or the suffrage, or where women are expressly discriminated against, such as in some systems of family law. However, there is a limit to the extent to which formal equality can address structural barriers. Treating likes alike requires a prior judgement that two people are relevantly alike: yet it is the very fact that women usually do not conform to male norms that leads

[20] In this context, welfare is synonymous with social security/social protection.

[21] Sepúlveda Carmona, above n 1, at para 3 ff; see also Standing, G, 'Behavioural Conditionality: Why the Nudges Must be Stopped—An Opinion Piece' (2011) 19(1) *Journal of Poverty and Social Justice* 27, 28.

[22] Chant, 'The "Feminisation of Poverty"', above n 5, at 182.

to gendered inequality. This is particularly true for many social welfare systems. Thus, the fact that contributions-based welfare rights are applied equally to both men and women does not mean that men and women are equal under such a system. Because women have interrupted working patterns or predominate in the informal sector, fewer women than men will be eligible for such rights. The notion that likes should be treated alike regardless of gender can also be antagonistic to the basic redistributive aims of welfare systems. As long as everyone is treated alike, it does not matter if they are treated equally well or equally badly. For example, the Court of Justice of the European Union upheld a complaint by a man that the fact that women qualified for pensions at a younger age than men constituted sex discrimination against men.[23] In response, many pension funds simply increased the pension age of women to that of men, a move which was upheld by the Court of Justice as compatible with the principle of equality.[24] The result was that men gained nothing and women were worse off. The like treatment principle is particularly problematic for affirmative action measures. Unless positive measures in favour of a disadvantaged group are specifically insulated against formal equality challenges, they risk breaching the equal treatment principle.

Substantive equality aims to go beyond like treatment. However, its precise meaning remains contested. One possibility is to focus on the results rather than the treatment, legitimating different treatment in order to achieve equal outcomes. This is an important means to address the ways in which women's disadvantage in the social welfare field can be reinforced by apparently neutral treatment as between men and women. Unequal outcomes become, in themselves, a breach of equality. This, however, does not address the question of when individual choices can legitimately lead to different results. A second option is to focus on equality of opportunity: by equalising the starting point, equality permits all to have equal opportunities, but individual choices, differing talents and other relevant differences mean that equality is compatible with diverse outcomes. Equality of opportunity is potentially a radical approach, requiring far-reaching change in social structures. However, it is more usually limited to removing 'demand side' barriers, such as recruitment measures based on nepotism or word of mouth. A third approach is to regard substantive equality as treating all with equal dignity.[25] This has the potential advantage of focusing attention on the ways in which social security systems can demean and humiliate beneficiaries. However, 'dignity' is an open-textured concept. It has just as often been used as a pretext for 'protecting' women's dignity by excluding

[23] Case 262/88 *Barber v Guardian Royal Exchange Assurance Group* [1990] IRLR 240.
[24] Case 408/92 *Smith v Avdel Systems Ltd* [1995] ICR 596.
[25] *Law v Canada (Minister of Employment and Immigration)* [1999] 1 SCR 497, para 51.

them from valuable opportunities in political life or the paid workforce as it has been to further equality.[26] It is also problematic if material disadvantage on its own is not viewed as a breach of dignity. Thus, the Canadian Supreme Court, in a case concerned with a welfare-to-work programme, held that the fact that welfare for younger beneficiaries was significantly lower than their older counterparts did not breach their dignity despite keeping them in severe poverty.[27]

This detachment of dignity from disadvantage has now been reversed[28] but it demonstrates strongly that using dignity on its own, without also referring to material disadvantage, is problematic. At the same time, a focus on material disadvantage may obscure the risk of stigma and intrusiveness that welfare systems carry with them. I have therefore developed a multidimensional concept of substantive equality which draws on all these insights, pursuing four overlapping aims.[29] First, it aims to redress disadvantage. A formal application of equality which leaves everyone equally badly off would not fulfil this dimension. This focus on disadvantage means that equality must address the impact of measures, even if they are neutral on their face. It also means that equality is not breached by measures which treat a disadvantaged group better than others to compensate for past disadvantage. The second aim of equality is to promote respect for dignity and worth, thereby redressing stigma, stereotyping, humiliation and violence because of membership of an identity group.[30] Third, equality should not exact conformity as a price of equality. Instead, it should accommodate difference and aim to achieve structural change. This captures the *transformative* dimension. Finally, substantive equality should facilitate full participation in society, both socially and politically. This is the *participative* dimension.

This multidimensional approach has specific resonance in relation to gender, as can be seen by looking at each dimension in more detail. I begin with the redistributive dimension. Rather than taking a symmetric stance, which outlaws differential treatment based on sex regardless of its effect on disadvantage, substantive equality focuses on the real problem, which is not the difference in sex, but the disadvantage associated with being a woman. This in turn requires a particularly gendered understanding of disadvantage. As we have seen, this encompasses more than mal-distribution of resources;

[26] See, eg, *Anuj Garg & Ors v Hotel Association of India & Ors* [2007] INSC 1226: AIR 2008 SC 663.

[27] *Gosselin v Quebec* 2002 [SCC] 84 (Canadian Supreme Court). Also see *Law v Canada*, above n 25; and Chant, 'The "Feminisation of Poverty"', above n 5.

[28] Chant, 'The "Feminisation of Poverty"', above n 5.

[29] Fredman, *Discrimination Law*, above n 6, at ch 1.

[30] Fraser, N and Honneth, A, *Redistribution or Recognition? A Political–Philosophical Exchange* (London, Verso, 2003) 1.

equality should also address the constraints which power structures impose on women.[31] For example, women who are trapped in the private sphere will suffer disadvantage in this sense even if they live in affluent households. Poverty for women also includes inadequate access to resources, lack of property rights, limited social participation and constraints on real choice.

Disadvantage can also be understood as a deprivation of genuine opportunities to pursue one's own valued choices. This draws on the insights of Sen[32] and Nussbaum's[33] 'capabilities' approaches, which stress the importance of considering the extent to which people are actually able to exercise their choices, rather than simply having the formal right to do so. Rather than seeing individuals as passive recipients of welfare, welfare rights should be aimed at enhancing capabilities, that is, enhancing the ability of women to be and do what they value. At the same time, choice itself can be problematic, since people often adapt their choices to their circumstances. Moreover, there are circumstances in which the concern is not solely to increase the range of feasible options but to address the disadvantage attached to the circumstances a person actually finds herself in. This dimension of substantive equality therefore requires particular attention to be paid to the ways in which social welfare rights impact on power relations, structural obstacles and burdens on women attached to traditional and stereotypical roles.

Even in its most expansive sense, disadvantage does not cover all the wrongs associated with inequality. Stigma, stereotyping, humiliation and violence on grounds of gender can be experienced regardless of relative disadvantage. Thus, the second main aim of substantive equality should be to promote respect for the equal dignity and worth of all. Equality attaches to all individuals, not because of their merit, or rationality, but because of their humanity.

In the context of social welfare rights, the particular value of this dimension of equality is to highlight the stigma associated with poverty as a harm in itself. Moreover, social welfare systems themselves can be designed in such a way as to be highly intrusive and demeaning. Basic means-testing on household income is in itself a lack of recognition of the individuality of each member of the household. The demonising of welfare recipients as lazy and scroungers in modern rhetoric is a further demonstration. This has been particularly true for single mothers in the United States (US), who

[31] Young, IM, *Justice and the Politics of Difference* (Princeton, Princeton University Press, 1990) 16.

[32] Sen, A, *Development as Freedom* (Oxford, Oxford University Press, 1999).

[33] Nussbaum, M, *Women and Human Development: The Capabilities Approach* (Cambridge, Cambridge University Press, 2000).

were specifically targeted by the introduction in 1996 of a welfare-to-work programme known as Temporary Assistance for Needy Families (TANF).[34]

The third dimension of equality—the transformative dimension—entails recognising and accommodating difference. It also entails changing underlying structures, rather than expecting individuals to conform. Traditionally, contributions-based welfare benefits systems have, as we have seen, required conformity to a male norm as a condition for equal treatment. Similarly, conditional programmes are premised on behaviour modification to fit the norm of a hard-working employee or a good parent. The transformative dimension requires welfare systems to accommodate difference. A gesture in this direction can be seen in the UK, where time taken out for pregnancy and maternity does not interrupt the continuity required for eligibility, and a fixed number of years can be 'added' for the purposes of pension entitlement. A transformative approach goes further than this; it requires the welfare systems to address rather than reflect the gendered power structures of society. For example, childcare could be guaranteed as part of the social protection floor; caring work by parents could be recognised as productive work, at least for the purposes of contribution criteria; and paid care leave could be provided for both mothers and fathers in both the formal and informal sectors.[35]

The fourth dimension relates to participation. Rather than the universal, abstract individual of formal equality, substantive equality recognises that individuals are essentially social. To be fully human includes the ability to participate on equal terms in community and society more generally. Thus, Young argues that the focus of theories of justice should be on structures which exclude people from participating in determining their actions.[36] Fraser puts particular emphasis on participation, regarding parity of participation as the normative core of her conception of justice, encompassing both redistribution and recognition without reducing either one to the other.[37] This dimension insists that welfare systems are responsive to women's voices. Welfare rights should also facilitate participation, both politically and socially. Conversely, cutbacks in welfare provision, as has happened in the UK as a result of recent austerity measures, have had a severe effect on women's ability to participate actively in the paid workforce, and in other

[34] Midgley, J et al, 'Welfare Reform in the United States: Implications for British Social Policy' (London, Centre for Analysis of Social Exclusion, London School of Economics, 2008).

[35] HRC Report draft recommendations, available at http://www.ohchr.org/en/issues/women/wgwomen/pages/wgwomenindex.aspx.

[36] Young, above n 31, at 31–32.

[37] Fraser, N, 'Social Justice in the Age of Identity Politics' in Fraser, N and Honneth, A, *Redistribution or Recognition? A Political–Philosophical Exchange* (London, Verso, 2003) at 36–77.

aspects of social and public life, because of their resulting re-privatisation of caring functions, the brunt of which are borne by women.

It should be emphasised that the gendered framework for evaluating social welfare rights needs to be sensitive to the great variety of women's experience, and in particular to the cumulative or synergistic disadvantage experienced by older women, girl children, ethnic minority women or women with disabilities. Moreover, gendered expectations of men also need to be scrutinised.

APPLYING THE FRAMEWORK: CONDITIONAL CASH TRANSFER PROGRAMMES

In this section, I use the gender equality framework to evaluate one of the most popular recent innovations in social welfare rights: the Conditional Cash Transfer Programmes (CCTPs) which have swept across South America, Mexico and parts of Africa and Asia. A similar programme has now been set up in New York.[38] These schemes are distinctive in that they specifically target women. But are they really as empowering as the World Bank report would have us believe?[39] This section does not attempt to come to a conclusion as to the many diverse such programmes which are now operating; rather, the aim is to illuminate ways in which the four-dimensional approach to equality outlined above could be used to evaluate such programmes in order genuinely to engender social welfare rights.

Cash transfer programmes are non-contributory benefits in the form of cash payments. They can come in a wide variety of forms: they can be universal or means-tested; they can respond to particular needs, such as old-age pensions, child benefits or disability benefits; or simply take the form of basic income. What is novel about conditional cash transfer benefits is that the transfer is conditional on the claimant fulfilling prescribed behavioural conditions, such as entering training programmes, seeking paid work, sending children to school or bringing children to health clinics. In the US, Canada, the UK and elsewhere, the focus has been on 'welfare-to-work' or, more frankly, workfare schemes that require beneficiaries to participate in defined work or undergo work-related training. The CCTPs in Latin America, Mexico and elsewhere have added a new kind of conditionality—the requirement to send children to school or attend child health clinics. In World Bank 'speak', CCTPs aim to incentivise the household to make

[38] Aber, L and Rawlings, LB, 'North–South Knowledge Sharing on Incentive-Based Conditional Cash Transfer Programs' (SP Discussion Paper No 1101, Social Protection and Labour, World Bank, January 2011) 1.

[39] Fiszbein et al, above n 2, at 1.

specified investments in the human capital of their children.[40] Such investments include the requirement to take their children for periodic check-ups or vaccinations, to attend perinatal care clinics, or to enrol their children in school. CCTPs therefore claim to achieve more than poverty alleviation. They also aim to break the inter-generational cycle of poverty by increasing investment in health and education. As Aber and Rawlings put it:

> The more traditional view of social assistance (transfers as a handout in times of need to alleviate poverty) has begun to evolve into a new view of social assistance as a dynamic where protection is complemented by dynamic, tailored support to develop the human capital needed to move out of poverty. The use of incentives to affect individual investments, spur effective practices among providers, and leverage mobility out of poverty are increasingly being applied within this new paradigm.[41]

CCTPs in Mexico known as *Oportunidades*, and in Nicaragua, known as *Red de Protección Social* (RPS), among others, have been hailed as particularly successful, promoted by the World Bank as models. *Oportunidades* provides a cash transfer representing an average of 19.5 per cent of household income. The grant is provided to women, but as a condition of receiving the grant, women must ensure school attendance, bring their children for health checks and attend workshops on health, nutrition and hygiene.[42] It is therefore designed to improve the health of young children and nutritional levels more widely, as well as ensure that children enrol and progress through school. Notably, in secondary school, girls receive a slightly higher grant than boys. A similar programme has now been instituted in New York City (NYC), which conditions cash transfers on family health and child education, but also builds in adult work or education.[43]

The World Bank concludes that such programmes have had positive effects on school enrolment and attendance,[44] and have led to increased visits to health service providers.[45] However, there is little sustained evidence of positive effects on outcomes such as school achievement or growth.[46] Thus, while CCTPs resulted in modest improvements in cognitive development

[40] *Ibid.* See Mosher, in this collection, for a discussion of the ideology and discourse of social investment.

[41] Aber and Rawlings, above n 38, at 1.

[42] Bradshaw, S, 'From Structural Adjustment to Social Adjustment: A Gendered Analysis of Conditional Cash Transfer Programmes in Mexico and Nicaragua' (2008) 8 *Global Social Policy* 188, 192.

[43] Aber and Rawlings, above n 38, at 14.

[44] Fiszbein et al, above n 2, at 16; and Sepúlveda Carmona, above n 1, at para78

[45] Molyneux, M, 'Mothers at the Service of the New Poverty Agenda: Progresa/ Oportunidades, Mexico's Conditional Transfer Programme' (2006) 40(4) *Social Policy and Administration* 425, 434; and Fiszbein et al, above n 2, at ix.

[46] Fiszbein et al, above n 2, at xii, 2.

among very young children, the World Bank report found 'no discernible effect on learning outcomes for children who benefited from CCTPs while they were of school age'.[47] Similarly, an early evaluation of the NYC programme found positive effects across economic and health outcomes such as reduced poverty and hardship, increased savings and use of bank accounts and increased receipt of Medicaid and dental care. However, there were few positive effects on education and employment outcomes.[48] One reason for this, as the Special Rapporteur points out, is that there is no accountability for the quality of the education: parents are bound to send their children to school regardless of the quality, and teachers know that the pupils are a captive audience.[49] Other constraints, such as poor nutrition, are not resolved by a cash transfer and can severely limit the extent to which CCTP beneficiaries can benefit from schooling. A similar picture emerges in relation to health. The World Bank report concludes that 'in a number of Latin American countries, where CCTPs have been implemented most extensively, malnutrition (particularly low height for age) remains stubbornly high'.[50] The only long-term study found no evidence that initial positive impacts were sustained over time.[51]

There are two factors which seem clear from the evidence. The first is that a major factor in achieving positive effects is the generosity of the cash transfer. The second is that effects depend heavily on the quality of the service.[52] Perhaps the most persuasive explanation for the absence of positive educational and health outcomes, despite compliance with the conditions, is that the quality of the service is so low that increased use yields very little benefit.[53] This suggests strongly that CCTPs should not displace proper investment in public services such as health and education, which should be of high quality and free at the point of delivery.

A key aspect of the vast majority of these programmes, particularly those in Mexico and Nicaragua, is the targeting of women as the recipients of cash transfers. This rests on mounting evidence that women are more responsible than men in the use of welfare payments and are more likely to use cash transfers for the benefit of their children.[54] However, correspondingly, it is women who are regarded as responsible for delivering the conditions

[47] *Ibid*, at 127.
[48] Aber and Rawlings, above n 38, at 14.
[49] Fiszbein et al, above n 2, at 145; and Sepúlveda Carmona, above n 1, at para 78.
[50] Fiszbein et al, above n 2, at 145–46.
[51] *Ibid*, at 151.
[52] *Ibid*, at 12.
[53] *Ibid*, at 21.
[54] *Ibid*, at 59.

attached to the transfers, particularly in relation to the health and education of the children in their care.[55] Molyneux describes *Oportunidades* thus:

> The responsible participants (mothers) receive their stipend conditional on fulfilling the duties laid out by the programme managers: this involves taking children for regular health checks, meeting targets for ensuring their children's attendance at school, attending workshops on health and programme coordinators' meetings, and contributing a set amount of hours of work to the programme, typically cleaning buildings or clearing rubbish. Failure to comply with the requirements can lead to being struck off the programme.[56]

In Nicaragua, the emphasis on mothers is even greater. Bradshaw cites the Inter-American Bank, which funds the programme, as stating that the targeting of women is 'motivated by the evidence that resources controlled by women translate into greater improvements in the well being of children and the family'.[57]

The evaluation of these programmes from a gender perspective reveals some contrasting perceptions. On the one hand, the World Bank suggests that CCTPs may have increased the bargaining power of women[58] and reports a decrease in the gender gap in school enrolment in countries such as Bangladesh, Turkey and Cambodia.[59] It also points to evidence suggesting that the imposition of conditions plays a role over and above the simple transfer of cash.[60] The Special Rapporteur, by contrast, points to the lack of clear evidence that conditionalities make a difference.[61] More broadly, Chant argues that by putting women in the front line in dealing with poverty,[62] women are being made to work for development, rather than development working for women.[63]

From the perspective of a human rights lawyer, it is difficult to come to clear conclusions on these claims. Instead, the question is how, if at all, to ensure that the design of such programmes incorporates a gender rights perspective and ultimately how to ensure that they fulfil the requirements of substantive gender equality outlined above. Below I sketch the ways in which the four-dimensional approach to equality outlined above could be used to evaluate such programmes in order genuinely to engender social welfare rights.

[55] Bradshaw, above n 42, at 191.

[56] Molyneux, above n 45, at 434.

[57] Bradshaw, above n 42, at 198, citing the Inter-American Development Bank (IADB), *La Red de Protección, Fase II: Inform de Evaluación* (Nicaragua, Social Protection Network, Phase II: Evaluation Report) (Washington, DC, IADB, 2003), author's translation.

[58] Fiszbein et al, above n 2, at xii.

[59] *Ibid*, at 19.

[60] *Ibid*.

[61] Sepúlveda Carmona, above n 1, at para 58.

[62] Chant, 'The "Feminisation of Poverty"', above n 5, at 176.

[63] *Ibid*, at 183.

Redressing Gender Disadvantage

Evaluating programmes from this perspective requires us to examine not just generalised distributive gains, but also the particular redistributive issues which affect women, such as the distribution of power within the family and the distribution of time. Both require careful evaluation. The World Bank report argues that 'attaching strings to the transfers by mandating specific human capital investments could strengthen the mother's bargaining position and reinforce her ability to shift household spending and time allocation decisions'.[64] However, there is also evidence suggesting that if women bring more resources into the family, men withhold more of their own resources for personal consumption.[65] Similarly, CCTPs might worsen time poverty, an aspect of poverty which is particularly gendered. A United Nations Development Programme (UNDP) study of 22 countries in both the developed and developing world found that women work more hours overall than men, and that for women, unpaid reproductive labour accounted for 66 per cent of their work, compared with 24–34 per cent of that of men.[66] Moreover 'the poorer the household, the longer women work'.[67] Given the extensive demands on women's existing time, conditions may well increase women's disadvantage by intensifying their burdens. Research into *Oportunidades* has shown that participating in the programme carries with it a high time burden, and that compulsory attendance criteria are problematic for women engaged in income generating activities. Women in female headed households and women engaged in productive activities have been found to be less likely to be beneficiaries,[68] or even ejected from the programme for non-fulfilment of the programme's criteria because of their commitments to productive and reproductive work.[69]

Clearly too, the amount of the cash transfer, and its net value to the woman once time burdens are accounted for, would make a difference to its effect. It is therefore important that claims to redress gender-based disadvantage through making mothers the recipients of cash grants should be supported by clear evidence that the transfer is indeed empowering. On the

[64] Fiszbein et al, above n 2, at 59.

[65] Bradshaw, above n 42, at 200.

[66] Chant, 'The "Feminisation of Poverty"', above n 5, at 179, citing Rodenberg, B, 'Gender and Poverty Reduction: New Conceptual Approaches in International Development Cooperation' (Reports and Working Papers 4/2004, Bonn, German Development Institute, 2004) 17.

[67] Chant, 'The "Feminisation of Poverty"', above n 5, at 179, citing Pineda-Ofreneo, R and Acosta, ML, 'Integrating Gender Concerns in Anti-Poverty Strategies' (2001) 5(2) *Public Policy* 1, 4.

[68] Bradshaw, above n 42, at 192.

[69] *Ibid*, at 192, citing Escobar, A and González de la Rocha, M, *Documento de Evaluación Cualitativa de Mediano Plazo del Programa Oportunidades en Zonas Rurales* (Evaluation Document: Medium Term Qualitative Evaluation of the Oportunidades Programme in Rural Areas) (Mexico, Instituto Nacional de Salud Pública, 2005) 56.

other hand, the imposition of conditions is by its nature disempowering. Empowerment in this context should include the enhancement of agency, based on improving the range of genuinely feasible choices open to women. Conditions could only empower a woman in this sense if they functioned as a way to achieve her own purposes in the face of resistance from her family. There is no evidence that this is how they function: instead, the evidence points, as we have seen, to limitations on choice and agency. Indeed, research seems to suggest that if empowerment of women is indeed the aim, it is far better achieved by giving resources to women without conditions. Thus, research by Patel et al into the Child Support Grant in South Africa, which until very recently had been unconditional, found that giving women resources enhanced women's power and control over household decision-making in financial matters, and general household spending in child well-being.[70] Similarly, a study in Malawi showed that girls who received unconditional cash transfers of the same monetary value had similar health and schooling outcomes as those receiving conditional transfers.[71]

This is not to say that there are not real benefits to the CCTP project. The gendered perspective argues that these benefits should be able to be delivered without deepening women's disadvantage in other ways. Moreover, CCTPs are focused on women as mothers: older women, childless women or older children are not covered. A gendered evaluation must take into account measures for these women.

Addressing Stigma, Stereotyping, Prejudice and Violence

At one level, these new approaches to the right to social security represent a welcome advance beyond the view that welfare recipients are passive beneficiaries of charity or of the largesse of the wealthy in society. Instead of the stigmatic portrayal of welfare recipients as parasites or scroungers, the aim is to empower individuals, to enhance their capabilities to find their own way out of poverty and to recognise their agency. This is reflected in the introduction of labels such as 'co-responsibility' and 'partnership' in relation to such schemes. Molyneux cites the *Oportunidades* website as proclaiming that '"co-responsibility" is an important factor in this programme, because families are expected "to take an active part in their own

[70] Patel, L et al, *The Gender Dynamics and Impact of the Child Support Grant in Doornkop, Soweto* (Johannesburg, Centre for Social Development in Africa, University of Johannesburg, 2012).

[71] Aber and Rawlings, above n 38, at 11, citing Baird, S, McIntosh, C and Ozler, B, 'Cash or Condition? Evidence from a Randomized Cash Transfer Program' (Policy Research Working Paper 5259, Washington, DC, The World Bank Development Research Group, Poverty and Inequality Team, March 2010).

development, and to move beyond the *asistencialismo* (philanthropy) and paternalism" that characterized earlier welfare systems'.[72]

Nevertheless, CCTPs score badly on this aspect of the substantive gender equality framework. The partner in co-responsibility is the mother because it is the mother who is assumed, and has been shown, to give the interests of the children top priority. As Bradshaw points out, 'this targeting rests on the explicit recognition of women's greater commitment to the well-being of their children'. Correspondingly, there is an 'implicit assumption that men and male heads do not show such commitment'.[73] Molyneux reiterates this point: 'With fathers marginal to childcare and further marginalized by the design of the programme, the state plays an active role in re-traditionalizing gender roles and identities'.[74] In Nicaragua, moreover, the RPS programme is expressly aimed at consolidating the family unit.[75]

This comes together with the assumption that without the conditions, women would not take the specified actions. As described by the World Bank, the aim of CCTPs is to target families who are under-investing in the human capital of their children. One reason why they are under-investing, on this view, is 'imperfect altruism'. The assumption that women's behaviour needs to be modified if they are not sufficiently altruistic is highly problematic. As Bradshaw points out in relation to the Nicaraguan programme:

> The RPS implicitly suggests that those women targeted need to learn to be better mothers, since transfers are dependent on their attending sessions focussed on better child care and family hygiene, as well as sessions on family planning.[76]

It is telling that the designers of the RPS decided to reduce the cash transfer in the second and third years of its three-year programme, on the basis that very little incentive indeed was needed to achieve a change in behaviour. Without the stigmatic assumptions about the behaviour of poor women, it might instead be argued that conditions are in fact unnecessary: women, given the appropriate capability set (such as good quality health clinics situated nearby) would make the best decisions for their children without the need for a condition.[77]

A further stigmatic aspect of CCTPs concerns the ways in which the conditionality is enforced. Molyneux reports that one of the major complaints of the Mexican recipients interviewed in her study was that targeting was arbitrary and opaque, and that means-testing generated lack of trust, social

[72] Molyneux, above n 45, at 434.
[73] Bradshaw, above n 42, at 191.
[74] Molyneux, above n 45, at 440.
[75] Bradshaw, above n 42, at 198–99.
[76] *Ibid*, at 199.
[77] *Ibid*, at 198.

divisions and feelings of envy.[78] This is even truer of the enforcement of conditionalities. There is a wide spectrum of enforcement: some programmes penalise lack of compliance severely, while others do not. A gender-based evaluation needs to consider the extent to which it is stigmatic and intrusive for the state to monitor women's behaviour sufficiently closely to determine whether they have met the conditions. As noted above, the very assumption that responsible actions would not be taken were it not for the cash incentive can be seen as stigmatic. While the cash transfer might be empowering, 'the imposition of conditions may unnecessarily undermine the individual's autonomy and assume that the poor cannot make rational choices that improve their livelihoods'.[79]

This is exacerbated by the ways in which conditional programmes inevitably increase discretionary powers of bureaucrats tasked with enforcement. Standing points out that in Brazil, 17,000 families qualifying for the Brazilian *Bolsa Família* 'are stripped of entitlement each month because a local official decides that they have acted incorrectly'.[80] There is little due process, and any rights of appeal are unlikely to be easily accessed or used. This increases the stigmatic nature of CCTPs. Welfare beneficiaries are rapidly transformed from rights holders to wrongdoers, and worse still, face sanctions without the usual due process afforded to other forms of wrongdoing, least of all those faced by the well off in society, whose tax avoidance is scarcely regarded as culpable. This also creates incentives towards corruption by those with power to provide the records (such as school attendance registers) necessary to fulfil the incentives.[81]

More fundamentally, it is doubtful whether conditionality can ever be regarded as compatible with human rights. The rights-bearer should not have to behave in a prescribed manner in order to 'earn' the right. While it is true that breach of the law can lead to loss of basic rights, such as freedom of movement, this can only take place after a proper trial has established illegal behaviour. If failure to send your child to school is regarded as a breach of the law, then criminal penalties should be evenly imposed on all wrongdoers, not just the poor. Conditional cash transfers transform welfare from a right to a reward. Instead, a gendered approach would regard the removal of benefits from the very poorest in society as a breach of the basic human right to welfare.[82]

Moreover, reasons for non-compliance may lie deep in the very structure of disadvantage which the programmes are aiming to address. As the

[78] Molyneux, above n 45, at 435.
[79] Sepúlveda Carmona, above n 1, at para 58.
[80] Standing, above n 21, at 32.
[81] *Ibid*, at 33.
[82] Standing, above n 21; and Sepúlveda Carmona, above n 1.

Special Rapporteur points out, girls might breach the condition of going to school because they are sexually harassed; pregnant women may fail to fulfil the conditions of attending health clinics because the service is so poor or clinics are so far away.[83] This is particularly true where conditions attach to women who are heads of their households. She concludes that if conditions are to be imposed, there should be a mechanism in place to help those who are not able to comply.[84]

The overemphasis on stigmatic assumptions about motherhood is most clearly evidenced by the fact that, in the design, implementation and evaluation of CCTPs, there has been a striking lack of attention to scientific advances on how to effectively incentivise behaviour.[85] On the other hand, the World Bank report acknowledges that one of the major reasons for including conditions is to convince voters that social welfare is not a handout. In other words, it is the stigmatic images of mothers as inadequate, lazy or insufficiently altruistic to which politicians are referring when promoting the condition. This is hardly a convincing justification.

The Transformative Dimension: Accommodating Difference and Addressing Structural Barriers

One of the key aspects of substantive equality is to move beyond the conformism inherent in the concept that likes should be treated alike. As we have seen, women's inability to conform to the male norm of continuous full-time paid employment has perennially disadvantaged them in the welfare system. Cash transfers have the potential to overcome this drive towards conformism. Given that they are not linked to past record in the employment market, they are capable of reaching women in the informal sector, women in precarious employment and women without access to income-generating activities. Universal child benefit in the UK has been a crucial source of income for women with children regardless of their role in the paid workforce.[86]

CCTPs go further than cash transfers and require behaviour modification on the part of families and particularly of women. The aim is claimed to be transformative, in that the expectation is that greater investment in human capital will prevent inter-generational transfer of poverty, and give poor families the opportunity to escape from poverty. However, there is a real risk that CCTPs have serious counter-transformative effects. As a start,

83 Sepúlveda Carmona, above n 1, at para 59.
84 *Ibid.*
85 Aber and Rawlings, above n 38, at 18.
86 Fredman, *Women and the Law*, above n 1.

CCTPs may become a substitute for investment in good service provision. The World Bank acknowledges that health and education provision are often dysfunctional.[87] Aber and Rawlings conclude that 'the introduction of CCTPs has not resolved longstanding issues of quality, efficiency and effectiveness within social sector ministries, across the myriad of often uncoordinated social assistance providers, and in often outdated and financially insolvent social insurance programs'.[88] As the Special Rapporteur points out, CCTP programmes might in fact be a disincentive to improve such services, since families are compelled to use them.[89]

Equally seriously, as we have seen, claims that CCTPs may change gender power relations within the family do not have a sound empirical basis. To the contrary, far from being transformative, CCTPs might entrench existing gender roles. As Bradshaw puts it: 'Targeting resources at women means that men's behaviour is implicitly recognised as problematic but is not addressed, while the personal deprivation suffered by women through their altruism is not problematized but explicitly reinforced as the social norm'.[90] A truly transformative approach would be that signalled by the Convention on the Elimination of All Forms of Discrimination against Women (CEDAW), which requires states to promote 'a common responsibility of men and women in the upbringing and development of their children'.[91]

The very fact that women are known to use resources for bettering their family should suggest that it is not here that conditions are needed. Instead, mandatory requirements should be directed at those who are least likely to fulfil expectations voluntarily—in this case, fathers. However, it is submitted that using conditionalities in this way carries costs which compromise any transformative potential. This is because the conditions are based on an assumption of 'misbehaviour' on the part of the welfare recipient, which in turn attributes responsibility and culpability to him or her, ignoring the fundamental structural constraints on both men and women living in poverty. This diverts attention from addressing the structural issues deterring people from pursuing the stated goals voluntarily. Poor schooling, lack of transport to school, risk of violence either in getting to school or at school are only a few examples of such structural issues from which CCTPs divert attention.

[87] Fiszbein et al, above n 2, at 24.
[88] Aber and Rawlings, above n 38.
[89] Sepúlveda, above n 1, at para 20.
[90] Bradshaw, above n 42, at 195.
[91] Convention on the Elimination of All Forms of Discrimination against Women (CEDAW) (adopted 18 December 1979, entered into force 3 September 1981) 1249 UNTS 13, art 5(b).

Participation

The participative dimension regards participants as agents rather than passive recipients and are therefore entitled to have a voice in the design, delivery and monitoring of programmes. As the Special Rapporteur stresses,

> due to the asymmetry of power between the beneficiaries of programmes and the authorities that administer them, beneficiaries are often unable to protect their rights. Without fair and effective mechanisms that enable beneficiaries to actively participate, CCTPs are vulnerable to political manipulation.[92]

She also argues that participation can improve the effectiveness and sustainability of programmes through feedback from its users; and to garner social and political support for cash transfer programmes.[93] Moreover, participation means more than just consultation. In the context of poor women, it is important to be sure that women's lack of voice in the family or community is taken into account. If there are already obstacles to participation for vulnerable groups, then it is easy for participation structures to give the impression of giving voice, while in practice reinforcing existing power structures. The Special Rapporteur suggests that, to compensate for asymmetries of power, participation should therefore include civil society organisations that can play a role in advocating the rights of beneficiaries, and not just beneficiaries themselves.[94]

Thus, a key factor in evaluating CCTPs should be to consider the extent to which recipients are given the opportunity to participate. Molyneux cites evidence suggesting that, despite claims that its aim was to function as a way of exercising civil and political rights and a means to achieve full citizenship, in the Mexican *Oportunidades* programme, participants were not given an active role in the design, management or evaluation of the programme.

Non-Conditional Cash Transfers

CCTPs can be contrasted with non-conditional cash transfers, such as the Child Support Grant (CSG) in South Africa. The CSG is a monthly, means-tested cash grant given to the primary carer of children under 18. There are now 10.7 million children who benefit from the grant, about 55 per cent of all South African children.[95] What stands out about this grant for our purposes is that it is deliberately targeted at the primary carer of the children, rather

[92] Sepúlveda Carmona, above n 1, at para 52.
[93] *Ibid*, at para 52.
[94] *Ibid*, at para 54.
[95] Patel et al, above n 70, at 1.

than at mothers, as one of the aims was to ensure that fathers or other male carers would also be eligible.[96] However, in practice as many as 96 per cent of beneficiaries have been women.[97]

Applying the four-dimensional evaluation to this grant yields a more optimistic picture for women than CCTPs. It appears to score reasonably well on the first dimension—that of redressing disadvantage. Patel et al found that women's agency was enhanced in relation to decision making in general household matters. Since women tended to use the money for communal household expenses and for children, food insecurity was decreased and children's well-being enhanced. They also found that the CSG, without any conditions attached, contributed to regular school attendance and performance. Caregivers were significantly more likely to engage with children through helping with schoolwork, playing or reading. Thus, disadvantage and the inter-generational transmission of poverty were interrupted. However, given the small size of the transfer, the extent of this improvement must inevitably be limited. Patel found that the cash transfer had no effect on improving service delivery, and at times had to be used to ameliorate poor delivery. Thus, from a gender perspective, it scores better on this dimension than its conditional competitors, but not necessarily than other alternatives, such as improved service delivery.

Unconditional cash transfers clearly score better on the second dimension, redressing stigma. There are no behavioural connotations, such as insufficient investment in human capital, or irresponsible parenting. Indeed, even in the absence of any conditionalities women tended to use the money for communal household expenses and for children. Thus, beneficiaries of the grants are regarded as genuine agents, whose choices are trusted. In addition, at least in principle, it reduces the risk of gender stereotyping by naming the recipient as the primary caregiver rather than the mother.

The CSG, however, does not score well on the transformative dimension, although for different reasons from its conditional competitor. This is, first, because, despite its gender neutral approach, experience shows that it has not in practice changed the gender division of roles. Indeed, as Patel shows, it has on occasion led to fathers withdrawing even further from responsibility for maintenance of their children, on the grounds that it is a substitute for maintenance payments. Although a small number of fathers are now claiming the benefit, transforming gender roles is a challenging task. Second, it has not had the effect of transforming service delivery, particularly in relation

[96] The original aim was to 'follow the child'. While it was about including men it was also about including other female carers because it was known that many children lived away from the mother. Lund, F, *Changing Social Policy: The Child Support Grant in South Africa* (Cape Town, HSRC Press, 2008) 52–53.

[97] Vorster, J and de Waal, L, 'Beneficiaries of the Child Support Grant: Findings from a National Survey' (2008) 20(2) *The Social Work Practitioner Researcher* 233.

to addressing the needs of women; although it might have mitigated the effects. Thus, cash transfers clearly need to be complemented by other measures.

The CSG seems to score reasonably well on the participative dimension, in the sense that Patel found that women recipients were able to participate in community activities. It is not clear, however, whether and to what extent it enhances their voice in the community.

CONCLUSION

This chapter has aimed to create a framework of substantive gender equality which can be used specifically to engender social welfare rights, using CCTPs as an example of how this might work. A truly gendered perspective means that a welfare programme should address all four dimensions of the multidimensional model of substantive equality advocated here. It must focus on alleviating gender-based disadvantage as well as poverty per se. It must address the specifically gendered stigmatic and prejudicial consequences for women. It must ensure the voices of the women are clearly heard and taken into account. Finally, it must ultimately address the structural causes of inequality rather than either requiring women to conform to the male norm, or cementing gender-based stereotypes of caring roles.

At the same time, a gender perspective should not obscure the reality of poverty for both men and women. The answer is not necessarily to shift responsibility to women, but to universalise the burden through state provision of services. Real substantive equality is most likely to be achieved, not through making women bear the burden of breaking the inter-generational cycle of poverty, but through universal, free access to good quality state schools, health clinics and other essential services.

3

Participatory Inclusion and Women's Rights to Social Security

HESTER LESSARD*

INTRODUCTION

WHAT IS ENTAILED in the participative dimension of the human right to social security?[1] Commitments of various sorts to participatory inclusion have been a common feature of international development agendas since the mid 1980s.[2] As one writer puts it, '[p]articipation has become development orthodoxy'.[3] In this context, critics have observed two contradictory threads in the discourse of participation, one prioritising citizen engagement and enhanced democracy and the other driven by neo-liberal objectives to reduce state support for rights to well-being.[4] Further, there has been some attention in the development literature to issues that pertain specifically to barriers to women's participation.[5] As participatory inclusion becomes a persistent theme in the delineation of international human rights, some of these same issues stand to be explored

* I would like to thank Lucie Lamarche and Beth Goldblatt for organising the workshop at which this chapter was first presented and for their editorial direction and leadership. Thanks are also owed to the participants for their helpful comments and insights. Finally, Doris Buss generously found time to provide me with invaluable feedback for which I am very grateful. All errors, misframings and misconceptions are of course my own.

[1] I am using the phrase 'social security rights' broadly to encompass social and economic rights.

[2] Hickey, S and Moran, G, 'Towards Participation as Transformation: Critical Themes and Challenges' in S Hickey and G Moran (eds), *Participation: From Tyranny to Transformation?* (London, Zed Books, 2004) 3.

[3] Cornwall, A, 'Whose Voices? Whose Choices? Reflections on Gender and Participatory Development' (2003) 31 *World Development* 1325.

[4] Dagnino, E, 'We All Have Rights ... But: Contesting Concepts of Citizenship in Brazil' in N Kabeer (ed), *Inclusive Citizenship* (London, Zed Books, 2005) 150, 160–61.

[5] Cornwall, 'Whose Voices?', above n 3; Gujit, I and Shah, MK (eds), *The Myth of Community: Gender Issues in Participatory Development* (London, Intermediate Technology Publications, 1998); and Mohanty, R, 'Gendered Subjects, the State and Participatory Spaces: The Politics of Domesticating Participation in Rural India' in A Cornwall and VS Coelho (eds), *Spaces for Change?* (London, Zed Books, 2007).

in relation to human rights frameworks and processes.[6] A central theme of this chapter is the relationship between participatory values, social movements (in particular women's movement actors) and international human rights discourses (in particular rights to social and economic security).

As the introduction to this volume observes, recent political attention and support at the international level for creating a social protection floor has opened up space for discussion of a human rights approach to social protection and security. Although rights discourses are, of course, open to capture by neo-liberal agendas, to the extent that social and economic rights envision a central role for the state, they offer a counter to neo-liberal approaches framed as social risk management or social investment, the latter placing primary reliance on markets to deliver 'the goods'.[7] Critical feminist engagement with these trends has focused on the importance of engendering social security rights, including assessing, from the perspective of women and of concerns about women's substantive equality, the robustness and efficacy of the participative dimension of programmes aimed at providing social protection. For example, Sandra Fredman has developed a four-dimensional model of substantive equality that she uses to assess social welfare programmes, such as conditional cash transfers, that have recently gained currency internationally and are widely touted as enhancing women's well-being.[8] The fourth prong of Fredman's model relates to participation and asks whether 'welfare systems are responsive to women's voices'.[9] In this chapter, I propose to focus on the significance and nature

[6] Eg, the Office of the UN High Commissioner for Human Rights points out that the right to participate can be found in the International Covenant on Civil and Political Rights (ICCPR) (adopted 16 December 1966, entered into force 23 March 1976) 999 UNTS 171, art 25; the International Covenant on Economic, Social and Cultural Rights (ICESCR) (adopted 16 December 1966, entered into force 3 January 1976) 999 UNTS 3, arts 13(1), 15(1); the Convention on the Elimination of Discrimination Against Women (CEDAW) (adopted 18 December 1979, entered into force 3 September 1981) 1249 UNTS 13, art 7; the Convention on the Rights of the Child (CRC) (adopted 20 November 1989, entered into force 2 September 1990) 1577 UNTS 3, art 12; the *Declaration on the Right to Development*, UN General Assembly Resolution 41/128, 4 December 1986, UN Doc A/RES/41/128, arts 1(1), 2, 8(2); the *Declaration on the Rights of Indigenous Peoples*, UN General Assembly Resolution 61/295, 2 October 2007, UN Doc A/RES/61/295, arts 5, 18, 19, 41; and United Nations Office of the High Commissioner for Human Rights, 'Participation of Persons Living in Poverty' (*Office of the High Commissioner for Human Rights*), available at: www.ohchr.org/EN/Issues/Poverty/Pages/ParticipationOfPersonsLivingInPoverty.aspx.

[7] Razavi, S, 'Engendering Social Security and Protection: Challenges for Making Social Security and Protection Gender Equitable' (Berlin, Friedrich-Ebert-Stiftung, Berlin, Friedrich-Ebert-Stiftung, June 2011) 3; Holmes, R and Jones, N, *Gender and Social Protection in the Developing World: Beyond Mothers and Safety Nets* (London, Zed Books, 2013) 22–27.

[8] Fredman, in this collection.

[9] *Ibid*; see also Baker, J et al, *Equality: From Theory to Action* (Basingstoke, Palgrave Macmillan, 2004) 38–39, 96–117, for a framework that has an explicitly participative dimension and is relied upon by Murphy and Loftus, in this collection; and Sheppard, C, *Inclusive Equality: The Relational Dimensions of Systemic Discrimination in Canada* (Montréal, McGill-Queens Press, 2010) whose conception of inclusive equality is rooted in participatory values.

of this commitment to participatory inclusion as a core element of human rights protection, as well as the political and strategic challenges participatory approaches pose when extended to diverse and differently positioned women.

My discussion is divided into three parts. I will begin by examining three key places where participation is recognised as a component of an internationally recognised right to social security: the deliberations of the Committee on Economic, Social and Cultural Rights (CESCR) under the International Covenant on Economic, Social and Cultural Rights (ICESCR),[10] in particular, General Comment 19: The Right to Social Security (article 9);[11] the Montréal Principles;[12] and the Report of the Special Rapporteur on Extreme Poverty and Human Rights, Magdalena Sepúlveda Carmona (EPHR Report 2013).[13] In the next part, I will explore critiques of how participatory rhetoric, along with the companion discourses of human rights and democracy, has been appropriated in ways that are ideologically suspect by powerful international institutions. The final part then turns to empirical questions, drawing on legal and social science literature. First, I examine how women's groups take up the language of human rights at the grass roots level, how the tension between different cultural life worlds and the universalist language of human rights is negotiated and how the reverse process, namely of human rights language incorporating a range of culturally embedded conceptions of well-being, might be envisioned. Second, I look at feminist work that analyses models of participation from the perspective of women's engagement.

RECOGNITION OF THE PARTICIPATIVE DIMENSION OF RIGHTS TO SOCIAL SECURITY

The existing regime of international human rights law displays some support for the notion that participation should be a key element in the articulation of rights to social security. In this first part, I canvass the ICESCR and its interpretation by the CESCR, the Montréal Principles and reports by the Special Rapporteur on Human Rights and Extreme Poverty.

[10] ICESCR, above n 6.

[11] UN Committee on Economic, Social and Cultural Rights (CESCR), *General Comment No 19: The Right to Social Security (art 9)*, 4 February 2008, UN Doc E/C.12/ GC/19.

[12] 'Montréal Principles on Women's Economic, Social and Cultural Rights' (2004) 26 *Human Rights Quarterly* 760, 762.

[13] Report by M Sepúlveda Carmona, Independent Expert on the Question of Human Rights and Extreme Poverty, *Promotion and Protection of all Human Rights, Civil, Political, Economic, Social and Cultural Rights, Including the Right to Development,* 11 March 2013, UN Doc A/HRC/23/36 (EPHR Report).

The text of the ICESCR predominantly conceives of rights in terms of the distributive paradigm of justice.[14] Social and economic rights—to work, social security, protection of the family, an adequate standard of living, freedom from hunger, physical and mental health and education—are presented as addressing basic needs, providing services and ensuring humane and safe conditions. Indeed, the positioning of concerns about democracy in the ICESCR's limitation provisions (articles 4 and 8), reinforces a broader orthodoxy, reflected in many domestic constitutions in the West, that rights are opposed to democracy, indeed that rights pose a 'counter-majoritarian difficulty'.[15] Thus, it is not surprising to find in the ICESCR a conceptual structure that would seem to eliminate a conception of rights that weaves democratic values into the right itself. In addition, numerous commentators attribute the silence on democracy in United Nations instruments to the polarised politics of the Cold War era.[16]

Despite these conceptual and historical features, Richard Burchill argues that the guarantee of the right to self determination in article 1 of the ICESCR 'suggests that the principles behind it, the ability of individuals to participate collectively in determining their lives, are directly applicable to the rights in the Covenant as the process of self-determination will include economic and social aspects'.[17] Moreover, Burchill offers a comprehensive review of instances in which the CESCR, in a number of its General Comments, clearly supports the elaboration of the content of ICESCR rights in a manner that incorporates the more foundational principle of participatory inclusion. For example, Burchill notes that the CESCR has mentioned the importance of participation in relation to the rights to housing, water, food, health and intellectual property as well as in relation to specific social groups, including women, indigenous peoples, persons with disabilities and the elderly.[18] The Committee has also observed that because

[14] Young, IM, *Justice and the Politics of Difference* (Princeton, Princeton University Press, 1990) 16–18.

[15] Bickell, A, *The Least Dangerous Branch: The Supreme Court at the Bar of Politics*, 2nd edn (New Haven, Yale University Press, 1986) 16–23.

[16] Franck, T, 'The Emerging Right to Democratic Governance' (1992) 86 *American Journal of International Law* 46, 49; Marks, S, *The Riddle of All Constitutions: International Law, Democracy, and the Critique of Ideology* (Oxford, Oxford University Press, 2000) 31–32; and Burchill, R, 'Democracy and the Promotion and Protection of Socio-Economic Rights' in MA Baderin and R McCorquodale (eds), *Economic, Social and Cultural Rights in Action* (Oxford, Oxford University Press, 2007) 363. Note that in more recent years, the silence regarding democracy has been broken. See, eg, the *Inter-American Democratic Charter 2001* OAS Doc. OEA/SerP/AG/Res.1 (2001), 28th Spec Sess, OAS Doc. OEA/Ser.P/AG/Res.1 (XXVIII-E/01) (OAS General Assembly) (11 September 2001), 40 ILM 1289 (2001). The *Charter* contains stirring commitments to democracy but its role, if any, remains largely rhetorical. See, Rudy, T, 'A Quick Look at the Inter-American Democratic Charter of the OAS: What is it and is it Legal?' (2005) 33 *Syracuse Journal of International Law and Commerce* 237.

[17] Burchill, *ibid*, at 375–76.

[18] *Ibid*, at 376–77.

the structural adjustment measures imposed by international financial organisations potentially implicate social and economic rights, steps should be taken to ensure widespread participation, through means in addition to voting in elections, by those affected, in particular by the poor.[19]

Burchill's argument finds some further support in the CESCR's General Comment 19: The Right to Social Security (article 9) (the Comment), issued in 2007 and not included in his survey. Although the Comment, like the ICESCR itself, adheres largely to a distributive conception of social security entitlements, participation is explicitly highlighted as a component of the right in several places. However, the participation envisioned is fairly minimal and cautious. Specifically, paragraph 26 asserts that 'beneficiaries of social security schemes must be able to participate in the administration of the social security system' of states. It then elaborates participation in terms of a right to 'seek, receive and impart information'. There is an obligation to provide a monitoring process with a participation component in paragraph 46, but it is limited to the situation where third parties operate social security schemes. The section of the document on implementation and enforcement asserts in paragraph 63 that the Committee, in assessing state fulfilment of obligations, will examine compliance with democratic principles. There is no elaboration of what this entails, however. Finally, paragraph 72 advises that states 'may find it advantageous' to put in place a legislative framework that 'might include' a commitment to collaborate 'with civil society, the private sector and international organizations' as well as national monitoring mechanisms. In sum, although these references reflect a relatively weak conception of participation, they reinforce Burchill's thesis that participation is a persistent theme in the CESCR's General Observations.

Consistent with this stance, the CESCR's own procedures include measures aimed at broadening participation. The CESCR made it clear early on that the point of the periodic reporting process set up to implement the ICESCR is to 'facilitate public scrutiny of government policies'.[20] The CESCR, in 1988, became the first UN treaty committee to allow formal written interventions by NGOs in the periodic reporting process; the Committee takes the interventions seriously, often using them to form the basis of questioning of states parties.[21] Another innovation is the Committee's day of general discussion, held at each of its sessions in order to elaborate the normative content of the rights within its mandate

[19] *Ibid*, at 377.

[20] UN Committee on Economic, Social and Cultural Rights (CESCR), *General Comment No 1: Reporting by States Parties*, 27 July 1981, UN Doc EN/1989/22.

[21] Alston, P, 'The Economic Rights Committee' in P Alston (ed), *The United Nations and Human Rights* (Oxford, Clarendon Press, 1988) 473, 501.

and assist with the drafting of General Comments.[22] States parties as well as a range of non-state entities, including experts drawn from the NGO community, are invited to participate.[23]

Although results from these NGO interventions before the CESCR in general have been disappointing in terms of producing changes in governmental behaviour, there are other valuable aspects of the process as it now stands. First, there is evidently a willingness on the part of the CESCR to meaningfully include voices 'from below' in the process of articulating the rights in the ICESCR.[24] Second, inclusion in the formal reporting process under international conventions creates an opening that potentially can be levered to address constraints on participation at the local level. Third, the formal reporting process, in some contexts, provides significant 'networking connections and collaboration opportunities' for NGOs and community groups.[25]

The next two international sources I examine envision a much more fully realised participation entitlement. The Montréal Principles (the Principles), adopted unanimously in 2002 by a group of feminist activists and thinkers, articulate a set of interpretive guidelines and principles aimed at elaborating on, from a women's equality perspective, the ICESCR guarantees of equality and non-discrimination in relation to economic, social and cultural rights. While generated outside the formal apparatus of the UN system, the Principles represent an informed engagement by feminists with experience of the potential and shortcomings of the ICESCR regime. As such, the Principles provide a benchmark, shaped by feminist insights, against which to measure the robustness of more formal commitments and interventions.

The Principles are quite explicit on their face with respect to women's entitlement to participation. Paragraph 25, in the section on Legal Obligations, asserts that 'states and inter-governmental bodies must ensure

[22] *Ibid*, at 491.

[23] *Ibid*, at 493–94, 501; and Otto, D, '"Gender Comment": Why Does the UN Committee on Economic, Social and Cultural Rights Need a General Comment on Women?' (2002) 14 *Canadian Journal of Women and the Law* 1, 16.

[24] Alston, above n 21, at 500.

[25] Krommendijk, J, 'Just "A Little UN Committee" or Important Policy Driver? The Impact and Effectiveness of the CEDAW Committee in New Zealand' (Tijdschrift voor Genderstudies, Maastricht, Maastrict Centre for Human Rights, 13 February 2013), available at: papers.ssrn.com/sol3/papers.cfm?abstract_id=2216605. Although Krommendijk's analysis is largely of the effectiveness of Concluding Observations under CEDAW, his remarks about the character of human rights treaty obligations and reporting processes apply more generally. *Ibid*, at 13; see also Petersen, CJ and Samuels, H, 'The International Convention on the Elimination of All Forms of Discrimination Against Women: A Comparison of its Implementation and the Role of Non-Governmental Organizations in the United Kingdom and Hong Kong' (2002–03) 26 *Hastings International and Comparative Law Journal* 1, 32–41 for an account of relatively successful networking and lobbying efforts by women's movement NGOs spurred by Hong Kong's report to CEDAW.

that women can and do participate fully in the formulation, development, implementation and monitoring of economic, social and cultural programs and policies'.[26] It goes on to clarify that this inclusion should also apply where such initiatives 'aim to eliminate their gender specific disadvantages' and where responsibility for service delivery has been delegated to non-state actors.[27]

The most vigorous articulation of the entitlement to participation and of the mechanisms and approaches required to realise a meaningful right is found in the work of Magdalena Sepúlveda Carmona, the Special Rapporteur on Human Rights and Extreme Poverty appointed by the UN Human Rights Council. Her report, *Guiding Principles on Extreme Poverty and Human Rights* sets out participation and empowerment as foundational principles, elaborated in terms that clearly envision the 'participation of persons living in poverty at all stages of the design, implementation, monitoring and evaluation of policies that affect them'.[28] The document also stipulates that indigenous peoples should be able to participate through 'their own representative institutions' with respect to 'the use of their lands, territories and resources',[29] and that implementation and monitoring regimes should be reviewed through a 'participatory and gender-sensitive process'.[30]

A subsequent report by Carmona, the EPHR Report 2013,[31] enlarges the focus on participation. Carmona identifies lack of participation as the cause of poverty rather than simply its consequence, thereby shifting the distributive paradigm significantly and putting questions of participation at the very core of a right to social security.[32] The EPHR Report 2013 highlights issues of power and domination both between and within groups, and provides a nuanced analysis of power asymmetries and 'elite capture' at the community level.[33] It explicitly condemns tokenistic processes, demands an expansive rather than minimal, electoral conception of participation[34] and notes barriers created by time constraints, lack of resources, transportation costs, childcare and other familial obligations, work obligations and linguistic, educational and literacy challenges.[35] It identifies state actors as

[26] 'Montréal Principles', above n 12, at para 25.
[27] *Ibid*.
[28] UN Human Rights Council, *Final Draft of the Guiding Principles on Extreme Poverty and Human Rights, Submitted by the Special Rapporteur on Extreme Poverty and Human Rights*, 18 July 2012, UN Doc A/HRC/21/39, para 38.
[29] *Ibid*, at para 40.
[30] *Ibid*, at para 104.
[31] Sepúlveda Carmona, above n 13.
[32] *Ibid*, at para 14; see Young, above n 14, at 22–23.
[33] Sepúlveda Carmona, above n 13, at paras 12, 16, 44, 47.
[34] *Ibid*, at para 26.
[35] *Ibid*, at para 43.

primarily responsible for rights protection and therefore for ensuring full participation. As a consequence, it stipulates in relatively concrete terms key features of that responsibility such as conducting a gender analysis and providing the option of women only spaces,[36] taking account of work patterns of migrant workers,[37] using culturally appropriate spaces and approaches[38] and where necessary, conducting capacity building workshops in advance.[39]

The EPHR Report 2013's elaboration of participation as a component of a right to social security provides a useful jumping off point for examining more practical issues. However, before doing so, it is important to place the heightened attention to participation in international human rights discourses in the context of the more longstanding deployment of discourses of democracy and participation in the fields of international law, development and poverty alleviation.

DEMOCRACY, PARTICIPATORY RHETORIC AND HUMAN RIGHTS: CONTRADICTIONS AND CRITIQUES

Democratisation, although a latecomer to the discourse of international law in comparison with human rights, has taken on the stature of a 'leading principle',[40] causing one writer to observe that 'democratization has supplanted modernization as the discourse of transformation in the Third World and, therefore, as the driving ideology behind international law as the law that governs the relations between the West and the Third World'.[41] Democracy in this conjuncture is understood in a way that views human rights protection as a signature feature of a democratic order.[42] There are two facets of this expansion of 'democracy talk' that critical scholars have highlighted as requiring scepticism, if not outright rejection. One relates to the imposition of a historically specific conception of liberal democracy on non-Western societies and raises concerns about 'liberal democratic jihad'.[43] The critique is aimed at scholarship that, in the wake of the end of the Cold War, argued that the dissipation of Cold War conflict opened up the

[36] *Ibid*, at para 49.
[37] *Ibid*, at para 56
[38] *Ibid*, at para 55.
[39] *Ibid*, at para 56.
[40] Burchill, above n 16, at 362.
[41] Rajagopal, B, *International Law from Below: Development, Social Movements, and Third World Resistance* (Cambridge, Cambridge University Press, 2003) 136.
[42] *Ibid*, at 137; see also Mutua, MW, 'The Ideology of Human Rights' (1996) 36 *Virginia Journal of International Law* 589, 601–07.
[43] Marks, S, 'What Has Become of the Emerging Right of Democratic Governance?' (2011) 22(2) *European Journal of International Law* 507, 513 citing Roth, BR, 'Popular Sovereignty: The Elusive Norm' (1997) 91 *American Society of International Law Proceedings* 363, 368.

way to international acceptance of a Western derived right to democratic governance.[44] However, this optimistic vision of Western conceptions of liberal democratic constitutional forms has since been severely sidelined by the post-9/11 security agenda and the backlash against the US pursuit of 'regime change' in the name of democracy.[45]

The second facet relates to the economy. Here critics raise concerns about the neo-liberalisation of democracy and human rights.[46] Rajagopal, for example, argues that democracy, human rights and participatory values have been taken up by key international actors resulting in 'intense management of resistance movements, wholesale "modernization" (read westernisation) of political and economic structures in the Third World and a tremendous expansion in the size and power of international institutions'.[47] A key instrument deployed in this regard is the Poverty Reduction Strategy Paper (PRSP) which has become almost universal as a condition of international development aid.[48] Unlike the previous generation of structural adjustment measures, the PRSP approach treats participation as a 'core element'.[49]

Critics see this resort to participation as continuous with, rather than disruptive of, colonialism. Historically, colonial powers used local participation as a way to reduce costs and stifle opposition.[50] Cornwall describes efforts by international financial institutions to facilitate participation by the poor as 'the latest example of this well worn strategy'.[51] Some also argue that participation within the PRSP framework is a 'highly manipulated form of public consultation' that in many instances actually 'stifles democratic policy development'.[52]

[44] Franck, above n 16, is generally credited with providing an influential version of this argument in relation to international law and relations; see also Marks, *The Riddle of All Constitutions,* above n 16. For a more far-reaching and controversial version of this claim, see Fukuyama, F, *The End of History and the Last Man* (New York, Free Press, 1992).

[45] Marks, 'the Emerging Right', above n 43, at 514; Dean, J, *Democracy and Other Neo-Liberal Fantasies* (Durham, Duke University Press, 2009) 75; see also D'Aspremont, J, 'The Rise and Fall of Democratic Governance in International Law: A Reply to Susan Marks' (2011) 22(2) *European Journal of International Law* 549.

[46] Dean, above n 45, at 76; Marks, 'the Emerging Right', above n 43, at 517–19.

[47] Rajagopal, above n 41, at 137.

[48] Brown, D, 'Participation in Poverty Reduction Strategies: Democracy Strengthened or Democracy Undermined?' in S Hickey and G Moran (eds), *Participation: From Tyranny to Transformation?* (London, Zed Books, 2004) 237.

[49] *Ibid*, at 238.

[50] Cornwall, A, 'Making Spaces, Changing Places: Situating Participation in Development' (IDS Working Paper 170, Brighton, Institute of Development Studies, October 2002) 12.

[51] *Ibid*; see also Cooke, B, 'Rules of Thumb for Participatory Change Agents' in S Hickey and G Moran (eds), *Participation: From Tyranny to Transformation?* (London, Zed Books, 2004) 42–55. Cooke traces the use of participation to maintain existing power relations back to New Deal practices directed by US authorities at indigenous peoples. The practices were explicitly borrowed from British colonial practices of indirect rule. *Ibid*, at 45–47, 51–52.

[52] Brown, above n 48, at 241, 244.

The role of NGOs in relation to participation also arises in the critiques of participatory development initiatives. NGOs have been identified as the key institutional mechanism for the manipulation of participation in pursuit of neo-liberal poverty reduction[53] and privatisation agendas. Dagnino, writing about Brazil, observes that privatisation strategies involve a selective reliance on NGOs, because of their 'technical competence and social insertion', as ideal partners for the delivery of privatised services for the needy, while others, such as some trade unions and landless movements, that 'remain organised and combative' are criminalised.[54]

Despite the seriousness of these critiques, many of their authors refrain from a wholesale rejection of democracy, participatory values and the role of NGOs in progressive struggles. Rather, most arrive at a position where, as in the case of the language of human rights itself, they identify an inevitable, ongoing contradiction between progressive and oppressive uses of democracy and participation discourses.[55] Thus, it is important to continue to map the more progressive, counter-hegemonic conceptions of democratic participation at play. Bill Cooke, for example, despite a pessimistic view of the future of participatory development, advises moving forward by rejecting neo-liberal instrumentalism. To this end, he suggests separating the term 'participatory' from the term 'development' to generate more emancipatory conceptions.[56] In addition, NGOs, in particular NGOs that pursue rights-based approaches, are viewed by some as offering an effective means of locating issues of poverty within a political rather than economic framework.[57] Rajagopal invokes what he dubs the 'new cosmopolitanism' as a locus of resistance to the bureaucratisation of democracy for neo-liberal economic purposes.[58] He argues for drawing on social movement voices—activists, organisations, NGOs, academics and scholars—to bring a social movement perspective to international law. In doing so, Rajagopal envisions an encounter in which an alternative 'legal and regulatory architecture' is generated, 'not only from the space-based "universal" discourses of globalisation, marketisation, democracy, and rights, but also from the concrete and place-based cultural and political practices of social

[53] Townsend, J et al, 'The Role of the Transnational Community of Non-Government Organizations: Governance or Poverty Reduction?' (2002) 14 *Journal of International Development* 829, 833.

[54] *Ibid.*

[55] Baxi, U, 'Voices of Suffering and the Future of Human Rights' (1998) 8 *Transnational Law and Contemporary Problems* 125, 128–29.

[56] Cooke, above n 51.

[57] Hickey, S and Moran, G, 'Realizing Transformative Participation in Practice: State and Civil Responses' in S Hickey and G Moran (eds), *Participation: From Tyranny to Transformation?* (London, Zed Books, 2004) 159, 164–65.

[58] Rajagopal, above n 41, 155–56.

movements'.[59] This brings us to the central questions for this chapter. How is the turn to participation in the context of human rights frameworks experienced? What does it mean and require from the perspective of women?

PARTICIPATORY INCLUSION AND WOMEN'S RIGHTS TO SOCIAL SECURITY

This part is divided into two sections. In the first I draw on the human rights 'from below' literature to examine the empirical processes by which rights frameworks are taken up by grass roots women's groups. In particular, I am interested in the way in which this research maps the cross-cultural encounter between diversely positioned women and the liberal language and ideals of universally framed human rights. For this I turn to ethnographic work on the 'vernacularisation' of human rights generated by Sally Engle Merry and associated researchers. Typically the vernacularisation process is not formally structured as an opportunity for participation in deliberation on the meaning of human rights, but rather occurs in the course of NGO or civil society activism around pressing social issues. However, much of the 'from below' literature argues that our conceptions of human rights must be expanded beyond formal deliberations to encompass grass roots engagement with human rights of the type analysed in the studies of vernacularisation. Thus, this work provides insight into how a range of women's groups participate in giving meaning to, and transforming, the content of human rights.

In this first section, I also borrow the concept of 'jurisgenesis' from US constitutional law scholarship to conceptualise the other (and less successful) half of the process: namely, the taking up of local knowledge and conceptions of well-being by the decision-makers and institutions that constitute the architecture of international human rights. In short, the work on jurisgenesis argues that the meanings generated through the less visible and informal processes by which human rights concepts are vernacularised, often in conjunction with social movement activism, can be directed into the formal channels for deliberation on rights. In the second section, I turn to the literature on participation in the development field to examine strategic challenges and approaches to including women and persons living in poverty in participatory processes.

[59] *Ibid*, at 169.

Participation in Human Rights 'From Below': Vernacularisation and Jurisgenesis

The notion of 'law from below' challenges the assumption, in the specific context of law and legal forms, that globalisation is a top-down process of disseminating ideas and models from west to non-west, global north to global south, international to domestic, or global to local. The political point is to disrupt the 'common sense' that top-down dissemination of neo-liberal ideas and models of governance by powerful institutional actors is impossible to contest or resist. Instead, the 'strategy of counter-hegemonic globalisation and its legal counterpart, subaltern cosmopolitan legality' is invoked.[60] The latter is described as a 'perspective or approach' rather than a theory with distinct substantive components.[61] This is because of the wide-ranging plurality of 'forms of resistance and embryonic legal alternatives'.[62] Nonetheless, theorists have identified three distinguishing features of subaltern cosmopolitan legality, all of which pertain to the relationship between social movements and rights. The first is to examine the connections between illegal, non-legal and legal strategies when studying grass roots struggles for social change. The second is the significant role that broad-based political mobilisation plays in rights-based strategies. The third is the multi-scalar approach of social movements seeking to address injustice and suffering at the community level.[63] The concepts of vernacularisation and jurisgenesis discussed below describe phenomena in relation to social movement engagement with human rights in the way envisioned in the 'from below' literature.

Sally Engle Merry has coined the term 'vernacularisation' in work that focuses on the deployment of human rights language and ideas in struggles by women to improve their well-being and security in a range of different locales in both the global north and south. Vernacularisation describes the process whereby human rights ideas are appropriated and translated to fit local situations and cultural expectations.[64] The translators are usually persons who occupy the 'middle'—who are conversant in the international discourse of rights, are part of a relatively elite network of activists and NGOs and, as well, are fluent in the languages, structural conditions and cultural practices and norms of the particular locale. Although Merry

[60] De Sousa Santos, B and Rodriguez-Garavito, CA, 'Law, Politics, and the Subaltern in Counter-Hegemonic Globalization' in B De Sousa Santos and CA Rodriguez-Garavito (eds) *Law and Globalization from Below: Towards a Cosmopolitan Legality* (Cambridge, Cambridge University Press, 2005) 8.

[61] *Ibid*, at 13.

[62] *Ibid*, at 12.

[63] *Ibid*, at 15–17.

[64] Merry, SE, *Human Rights and Gender Violence: Translating International Law into Local Justice* (Chicago, University of Chicago Press, 2006) 219.

and affiliated researchers have 'mapped' this middle space of activism and translation,[65] here I focus on work concerning the way rights are taken up in their vernacular form by a range of women's groups.[66]

Appropriation and translation occur on a spectrum according to locale: from resistance, to avoidance, to background feature and to affirmation. For example, where there is very little or only superficial reliance on human rights at the community level, community organisations nevertheless may seize on opportunities to work with more committed transnational human rights activists who act as 'translators'. In the process, the grass roots groups contribute valuable experiential knowledge and insights.[67] In other situations, beneficiaries of the vernacularisation of human rights may take up rights language very explicitly and, in some situations, become active vernacularisers themselves.[68]

The translation process, as Merry and her co-researchers describe it, often constitutes an inter-cultural encounter. It does not entail a transformation of human rights norms, but rather their 'repackaging' in 'culturally resonant wrappings', and with changes that reflect local 'structural conditions' and appropriately tailored target groups.[69] For example, in Hong Kong,

> [s]helters focus on getting Hong Kong women into public housing while Delhi and Beijing activists find the concept of shelters less valuable since finding housing outside the family is virtually impossible ... Victims of domestic violence in the United States are typically intimate partners ... whereas in China they are typically members of an extended household of several generations but not necessarily in intimate relationships.[70]

Nor does translation fundamentally transform local norms and practices. Instead, human rights typically add another layer of meaning, one which may be in tension with local norms but which does not displace them.[71]

[65] Merry, SE, 'Transnational Human Rights and Local Activism: Mapping the Middle' (2006) 108 *American Anthropologist* 38.

[66] Merry, *Human Rights and Gender Violence*, above n 64; Mujica, RA and Meza, MC, 'Women's Rights in Peru: Insights from Two Organizations' (2009) 9 *Global Networks* 485; Liu, M, Hu, Y and Liao, M, 'Travelling Theory in China: Contextualization, Compromise and Combination' (2009) 9(4) *Global Networks* 529; Rajaram, N and Zararia, V, 'Translating Women's Human Rights in a Globalizing World: The Spiral Process in Reducing Gender Injustice in Baroda, India' (2009) 9(4) *Global Networks* 462; Rosen, MS and Yoon, DH, '"Bringing Coals to Newcastle"? Human Rights, Civil Rights and Social Movements in New York City' (2009) 9(4) *Global Networks* 529–53; Merry, SE and Rosen, MS, 'Law From Below: Women's Human Rights and Social Movements in New York City' (2010) 44(1) *Law Society Review* 101.

[67] Merry, *Human Rights and Gender Violence,* above n 64, at 215; see also Levitt, P and Merry, S, 'Vernacularisation on the Ground: Local Uses of Global Women's Rights in Peru, China, India and the United States' (2009) 9 *Global Networks* 441, 448.

[68] Levitt and Merry, above n 67, at 450.

[69] Merry, *Human Rights and Gender Violence*, above n 64, at 220.

[70] *Ibid.*

[71] *Ibid*, at 219–20.

Thus for a Hawaiian woman, redefining the experience of unwanted sex as rape and a violation of bodily security 'is layered over other frameworks, such as fair treatment by kinsmen'.[72] At the far end of the spectrum, resistance occurs where human rights values are too deeply at odds with local values. This occurred, for example, with respect to women in Lima, Peru who rejected initiatives by a local feminist NGO encouraging them to embrace their sexuality and to adopt perspectives that were viewed as anti-male.[73]

Crucially, Merry observes that although human rights frameworks are voluntarily appropriated rather than imposed, the translation process is, for the most part, one way. In other words, 'international perspectives are translated "down" more than grass roots perspectives are translated "up"'.[74] A significant consequence of this disconnect on the way 'up' is that, at the level of committee deliberations, cultural practices and norms are viewed as the 'problem'; they are understood within the simplified binary of liberal modernity/patriarchal tradition, rather than as dynamic frameworks and 'wrappings' that can offer alternative conceptions of justice and well-being to the language of rights. Indeed, the latter, Merry argues, is better understood as a fluid 'cultural practice' rather than 'a form of global law that imposes rules'.[75]

The predominantly one-way process of translating down, then, needs to be transformed into a two-way process in order for vernacularisation and participation to mean something other than convenient ways to facilitate implementation of norms and models derived from Western influenced international institutions. As discussed earlier, this latter instrumental conception of participation is deployed, for instance, by the World Bank to obtain 'buy in' for development initiatives. A more robust, substantive conception of participation demands a model and understanding of rights premised on what Reva Siegel describes as the jurisgenerative role of social movement and grass roots engagement with respect to rights. Siegel argues that mobilisations around rights 'incubate normativity' and are jurisgenerative in the sense that they do not merely supplement more official or judicial interpretations, but that they themselves claim authorship and ownership of those interpretations and their governing texts.[76] Although Siegel confines her conception

72 *Ibid*, at 219.

73 Levitt and Merry, above n 67, at 451.

74 Merry, *Human Rights and Gender Violence*, above n 64, at 216.

75 *Ibid*, at 131–32, 228. Note that Merry's analysis is aimed at committee deliberations under CEDAW.

76 Siegel, R, 'The Jurisgenerative Role of Social Movements in United States Constitutional Law' (Yale Law School, for publication with the papers of the Seminario en Latino América de Teoria Constituional y Politica, Oaxaca, 10–12 June 2004) 15, available at: www.law.yale.edu/documents/pdf/Faculty/Siegel_Jurisgenerative_Role_of_Social_Movements.pdf); see also Siegel, R, 'Constitutional Culture, Social Movement Conflict and Constitutional Change'

of jurisgenesis to American constitutional culture,[77] a more cosmopolitan understanding of jurisgenesis and grass roots voices is reflected in the central place given to political mobilisation in the articulation of rights by subaltern legal scholars.[78] In the next section, I look in more detail at markers of meaningful participatory spaces in order to identify, in more concrete terms, key elements in the design of frameworks that genuinely seek to foster the jurisgenesis of human rights norms by women's groups and activists.

Including Women

In this final section, I draw on the critical participatory development literature, in particular its feminist variant, to identify some of the features of participatory structures aimed at facilitating 'bottom-up' participation by women. Most of this literature focuses on invited spaces, namely those to which an official actor, usually but not necessarily government, invites others to participate and which is therefore, to a significant extent controlled and shaped by the invitor.[79] As such these spaces differ from those that are the focus of the vernacularisation literature. First, they are more formally and explicitly organised with the primary goal in mind of providing opportunities for participation. Second, they are *not* organised around the purpose of directly engaging with aspects of human rights other than in an indirect or attenuated way. Nevertheless, the discussion of participation in this context offers a wealth of insights into the design features of participatory frameworks. As my discussion unfolds, I will relate those aspects that are aimed at facilitating participation by women to the commitments set out in the CESCR's General Comment 19, the Montréal Principles and the EPHR Report 2013 discussed earlier. My point is not to provide a comprehensive analysis but rather to urge more attention to the critical literature on participatory development in thinking about the participative dimension of an engendered right to social security.

A useful starting point for assessing participatory inclusiveness in invited spaces is the framework provided by Bettina Von Lieres and David Kahane.[80]

(2006) 94 *California Law Review* 1323. Siegel takes the term 'jurisgenesis' from Robert Cover who used it to describe the way in which law takes its meaning from the normative universe generated by collective, social interactions, rather than the other way around; see Cover, R, 'The Supreme Court, 1982 Term—Foreword: Nomos and Narrative' (1982) 97 *Harvard Law Review* 4.

[77] Siegel, 'Constitutional Culture', above n 76, at 1328–30.

[78] De Sousa Santos and Rodriguez-Garavito, above n 60; Rajagopal, above n 41.

[79] Cornwall, *Making Spaces*, above n 50, at 17.

[80] Von Lieres, B and Kahane, D, 'Inclusion and Representation in Democratic Deliberations: Lessons from Canada's Romanow Commission' in A Cornwall and VS Coelho (eds), *Spaces for Change?* (London, Zed Books, 2007) 131.

Writing in the context of the participation of indigenous people and groups in a national consultative process on health care in Canada, Von Lieres and Kahane posit that meaningful participation is directly related to three features in the design of invited spaces: reflexivity, recursivity and the potential for separate spaces.[81] The first two—reflexivity and recursivity—apply across a number of contextually diverse circumstances while the third—separate spaces—is a recurrent theme in the literature on women's participation. I will elaborate briefly on the first two and then finish with a more extended discussion of the third.

Reflexivity concerns the extent to which a framework gives participants 'a deliberative say in defining the terms of their participation, the issues they will address, and the form deliberation will take'.[82] Recursivity, refers to the extent to which participation takes place from the beginning (contemplating a fully reflexive set of preliminary steps), through to the end (contemplating involvement in accountability structures where there is ongoing implementation). Both go to the extent and degree of control ceded to participants within the invited spaces of deliberation over law and policy. Of the three key documents discussed earlier, only the EPHR Report 2013 is vigorously reflexive, noting that mechanisms for coordinating participation, for example, identifying stakeholders, should themselves be participatory, and that advance meetings should be held in order to reach agreement on 'parameters, goals, purposes and scope' as well as '[a]cceptable forms of facilitation, chairing and leadership'.[83] Additionally, the Report's operational framework recommends that states 'involve people living in poverty in setting the agenda and goals for participatory processes'.[84]

Both the Montréal Principles and EPHR Report 2013 assert the need for a recursive approach extending from design right through to monitoring of implementation.[85] The EPHR Report 2013 is perhaps more explicit in clarifying that participation should extend from the discussion of the reflexive issues noted above as well as to agenda setting and articulation of purposes.[86] In contrast, the CESCR General Comment 19 contemplates only information exchange. This level of participation has been characterised as tokenistic to the extent that there are no further mechanisms for participation in accountability or monitoring regimes.[87] The latter are

[81] *Ibid*, at 133.
[82] *Ibid*.
[83] Sepúlveda Carmona, above n 13, at paras 48, 62.
[84] *Ibid*, at para 86(f)(i).
[85] 'Montréal Principles', above n 12, at art 25; *ibid*, at paras 86(a), (f).
[86] Sepúlveda Carmona, above n 13.
[87] Arnstein, S, 'The Ladder of Participation' (1971) 35(7) *Journal of the American Institute of Planners* 216. Arnstein's typology for assessing participation is relied upon by Cornwall, 'Whose Voices?', above n 3, and Gujit and Shah, above n 5.

absent from General Comment 19 except where third parties deliver social security services.[88]

The third feature in Von Lieres and Kahane's framework is the availability of separate spaces. I would suggest rephrasing it in expanded terms as consideration of the spatial–temporal matrix. I do so because it is important to include temporal as well as spatial aspects and their interactions and, more particularly, to problematise separate spaces. This third, spatial–temporal feature gets more deeply into the politics of difference.

With regard to temporal aspects, a number of analyses have observed the importance of being sensitive to the way in which timing and duration of meetings impact on women.[89] Also, a constant theme is the need to approach participation of women and other marginalised voices as a long-term project, involving often significant amounts of advance work building capacity and trust as well as returning repeatedly to issues of reflexivity and representation as the process unfolds.[90] While 'catalytic moments' are important to push transformation forward, 'the processes of social justice might often be temporally lengthy and grinding rather than explosive'.[91] Finally, it is important to integrate into a participatory process sensitivity to multiple and overlapping temporalities—sometimes tied to different spaces, sometimes to external events like elections.[92]

Spatial concerns—and the resort to separate space strategies—raise particularly complex issues of cultural norms regarding public expression, safety and intersectionality. Ranjita Mohanty's study of women participants in three kinds of invited spaces in Rajasthan, India is particularly instructive. In the area of her study the population consists largely of scheduled castes and tribes who live in 'a context marked by extremes of poverty and exclusion'.[93] In addition, participation took place within the framework of a legal commitment to affirmative action aimed at the inclusion of women. In all three spaces, Mohanty found that women were formally present but experienced 'multiple doses of humiliation, discrimination and exclusion'.[94]

[88] CESCR, above n 11, at para 46.

[89] Gujit, I and Shah, MK, 'Waking Up to Power, Conflict and Process' in I Gujit and MK Shah (eds), *The Myth of Community: Gender Issues in Participatory Development* (London, Intermediate Technology Publications, 1998) 1, 15; Cornwall, 'Whose Voices?', above n 3, at 1330, drawing on Aggarwal, B, 'Re-sounding the Alert—Gender, Resources and Community Action' (1997) 25 *World Development* 1373–80.

[90] Gujit, I et al, 'Agreeing to Disagree: Dealing with Gender and Age in Redd Barna Uganda' in I Gujit and MK Shah (eds), *The Myth of Community*, above n 89, 228, 240–41; Humble, M, 'Assessing PRA for Implementing Gender and Development' in Gujit and Shah, ibid, at 35, 42; and Gujit and Shah, 'Waking Up to Power', above n 89, at 17.

[91] Hickey and Moran, 'Towards Participation', above n 2, at 3, 16.

[92] *Ibid*.

[93] Mohanty, above n 5, at 77.

[94] *Ibid*, at 93.

In the space of an elected local council with places reserved for women, women candidates were selected by male members of their families. They were not discouraged from attending but if they did, were treated with indifference.[95] On a resource management committee structured as a community–government partnership, despite formal inclusion, women were excluded from attending until it was time to assign tasks. In short, they were treated as labourers rather than decision-makers.[96] At a child development centre, women were present as workers and beneficiaries. A small core of workers experienced some agency and voice but most of the women using the space were treated as mothers, a 'domesticated, conflict free identity valued by society and their families'.[97] Mohanty observes that the fact that the state, in the face of this 'empty' participation by women, assumed the role of neutral facilitator in effect worsened the situation by treating the pattern of dominance as invisible. She concluded that official invited spaces for participation, even with a legal commitment to inclusion of women, are *not* sufficient by themselves as a starting point for building a meaningful participatory regime.

In the face of such deeply embedded barriers, many argue for a strategy of providing separate spaces to facilitate participation. Von Lieres and Kahane link the need for separate spaces to situations in which a group, because of its vulnerability within existing social and political relations, needs to develop its position without the requirement for translation or the pressure to present a common front. For example, in the context of indigenous people in Canada, it permits discussion of positions that do not have to be explained and justified in terms that majority or more privileged groups will understand and accept.[98] This same point is made in relation to the need for separate spaces for women.[99] Furthermore, several studies argue that the availability of separate spaces is crucial in situations where cultural norms render women's participation transgressive. In this situation, separate spaces are important not only to provide a safe space for women to articulate their input, but, as a prelude to participatory engagement in merged spaces, for capacity building.[100] For this purpose, a long-term strategy is required, often one that engages NGOs or social movement groups in the

[95] *Ibid*, at 87.
[96] *Ibid*, at 87–88.
[97] *Ibid*, at 89.
[98] Von Lieres and Kahane, above n 80, at 143.
[99] Mohanty, above n 5, at 93; Shah, MK, '"Salt and Spices": Gender Issues in Participatory Programme Implementation in AKRSP, India' in I Gujit and MK Shah (eds), *The Myth of Community: Gender Issues in Participatory Development* (London, Intermediate Technology Publications, 1998) 243, 245–46.
[100] Cornwall, 'Making Spaces', above n 50, at 1333.

capacity building project.[101] Safety, however, although secured in the short term by separate spaces, may be compromised later. Cornwall tells of one situation in which women, who were emboldened to speak out publicly by a comparatively sophisticated and multilayered reliance on separate space strategies, subsequently experienced serious backlash in the form of domestic violence and divorce.[102]

Similarly, intersectionality issues are both partially addressed and rendered more problematic by separate space strategies. On the plus side, Von Lieres and Kahane invoke the importance of separate spaces in terms of allowing for a fuller range of complexity and diversity of views within the group in question.[103] However, questions of power and silencing are by no means solved and, in some cases, may be exacerbated by separate spaces. Feminists point out that separate spaces, although they may empower women, can sometimes simply empower the more privileged women within the group. For example, in one project involving women-only participatory spaces, older women took control and assigned younger women chores at times that excluded their participation.[104] Furthermore, while separate spaces may facilitate a greater diversity of views within the group, the lines of separation, as much intersectionality theory tells us, are themselves problematic. First, the 'assumption of female solidarity' may undermine the agency of women who choose to 'pursue goals based on other lines of connectedness and difference'.[105] Second, equating gender difference with women may exclude other dimensions of gender oppression and exclusion.[106] Cornwall, arguing for a more inclusive understanding of gender, notes the absence of 'the voices of marginal men, and their gender issues and gender concerns'.[107] She cites a Ugandan process in which, exceptionally, 'some men spoke about their gendered vulnerabilities' in relation to their poverty, lack of education and employment, causing some of them to move in with older women as concubines.[108] Responses to these complexities have included combining a separate space strategy with an ongoing discussion of representation in relation to an 'issues matrix'. The objective is to remain open to a continuous remapping of the groupings in separate

[101] *Ibid*, at 1333; Mohanty, above n 5, at 93. Note that Mohanty advises that the solution is not simply more NGO created separate spaces which would risk bypassing the state, but a strategy that coordinates NGO work with interventions in state-created spaces.

[102] Cornwall, *Making Spaces*, above n 50, at 1333–34 citing Mukasa, G, 'Gender and Participation: The Case of Redd Barna, Uganda' (unpublished MA thesis, Brighton, Institute for Development Studies, 2000).

[103] Von Lieres and Kahane, above n 80, at 143.

[104] Cornwall, *Making Spaces*, above n 50, at 1334.

[105] *Ibid*, at 1330.

[106] *Ibid*, at 1328

[107] *Ibid*, at 1337.

[108] *Ibid,* in relation to a Ugandan Participatory Poverty Process (UPPAP).

spaces.[109] Such an approach is grounded in a contextualised relational, rather than categorical, understanding of identity and intersectionality, one that takes account of ever shifting political dynamics.[110] A relational approach is also crucial to the inclusion of a range of gender identities, such as intersex and transgendered persons.[111]

Of the three documents discussed earlier, only the EPHR Report 2013 refers to the provision of separate spaces. It recommends that states take 'pro-active measures' to ensure women's participation, especially poor women, by, 'for example implementing women-only participatory spaces or providing childcare facilities'.[112] The EPHR Report 2013 also highlights the need for capacity building and the importance of the role of NGOs, recommending that states allocate resources for, among other things, 'long term funding for capacity building in disadvantaged communities'[113] as well as more generally to 'include capacity-building activities in participatory processes'.[114] It also notes the need to support civil society organisations by protecting them from retaliation and by recognising their rights to participate as well as by providing for 'financial and logistical assistance', especially where they have 'long term partnerships with people living in poverty'.[115]

These issues concerning timing and temporalities as well as the meaning and experience of separate and merged spaces do not lend themselves to a formulaic set of guidelines. Rather, what is required is an ongoing sensitivity to contextually specific issues of power and voice; a commitment to building participatory spaces and capacity over the long term; and an understanding of identities that is intersectional but also profoundly relational and situational. The latter requires a focus on localised and shifting patterns of exclusion rather than the identity harms of decontextualised individuals.[116]

[109] Gujit et al, 'Agreeing to Disagree', above n 90, at 238–39.

[110] Cornwall, A, 'Gender Participation and the Politics of Difference' in I Gujit and MK Shah (eds), *The Myth of Community: Gender Issues in Participatory Development* (London, Intermediate Technology Publications, 1998).

[111] Huq, S, 'Confronting our Prejudices: Women's Movement Experiences in Bangladesh' in A Cornwall, S Corrêa and S Jolly (eds), *Development with a Body: Sexuality, Human Rights and Development* (London, Zed books, 2008) 181, 185.

[112] Sepúlveda Carmona, above n 13, at para 86(c)(vii).

[113] *Ibid*, at para 86(b)(iii).

[114] *Ibid*, at para 86(f)(iii).

[115] *Ibid*, at para 86(g).

[116] Cornwall, Corrêa and Jolly, above n 111, at 46, for example, advises commencing by exploring local models of difference and how difference is spatialised both within and across identity categories such as male and female. *Ibid*, at 54–55; Gujit et al, 'Agreeing to Disagree', above n 90, describe how five different separate participatory spaces based on gender and age were initially resorted to, including one for children, but then reconfigured halfway through the project after a 'merged' meeting that dealt with issues of representation and management.

CONCLUSION

The rhetoric of participation has an undeniable allure, promising in the context of human rights a set of guarantees that are shaped and constantly reinvigorated by the experiences of those for whom they are designed. The work on vernacularisation provides helpful insights into how the tensions between the universalist premises of human rights discourse and alternative conceptions of well-being are being negotiated in a range of different cultural contexts by women's groups and human rights activists. However, this work also makes obvious the need to complement this largely 'top-down' phenomenon with a 'bottom-up' process in order to achieve participation that is meaningful and that enhances citizenship agency or self-government rather than simply governability. The framework for rights to social security found in the ICESCR and in the deliberations of the CESCR is sympathetic to a participative approach to rights, and the CESCR reporting process is itself open to a wide range of actors and interventions. In addition, feminists working in the human rights arena consistently press for participatory approaches to rights. However, as the critical literature on participatory development points out, the language of participation, empowerment and democracy is easily co-opted by neo-liberal agendas and rendered 'empty' for women and other marginalised voices, despite their formal inclusion. The EPHR Report 2013 provides a nuanced elaboration of what a participatory approach to human rights to social security in the context of extreme poverty might look like and how specific barriers to women's agency might be addressed. However, more work needs to be done, especially on the complex challenges presented by the temporal and spatial dimensions of participation as experienced by women in different situations. The critical feminist literature in the participatory development field offers a rich set of insights to draw upon in that work.

Finally, firmer, more explicit recognition of the jurisgenerative character of women's movement actors' engagement with rights—at both domestic and international levels—is required to ensure that participatory rhetoric and principles are not deployed instrumentally, to manage and diffuse resistance, but rather creatively, to generate a discourse of rights rooted in local knowledge and histories as well as human rights ideals. The dialogic process of generating meaning by connecting the voices of women in political struggles to formal human rights processes is likely to be messy, uncertain, and rife with 'normative incompleteness'.[117] The promise is deeply compelling, however: namely to affirm women's standing—epistemologically as knowers, legally as persons and politically as citizens—while securing their material well-being.

[117] Goodale, M, 'Introduction: Locating Rights, Envisioning Law Between the Global and the Local' in M Goodale and SE Merry (eds), *The Practice of Human Rights: Tracking Law Between the Global and the Local* (Cambridge, Cambridge University Press, 2007) 26.

Part II

Gender, Poverty and Rights in Global Perspective

4

Unpacking the ILO's Social Protection Floor Recommendation from a Women's Rights Perspective

LUCIE LAMARCHE

INTRODUCTION

AROUND THE WORLD, women represent the majority of the poor and of the extremely poor. The gendered aspect of poverty can largely be explained through examination of patriarchy, culture, gender stereotypes, extreme capitalism, under-development (or mis-development) and women's family and community responsibilities. The twentieth century witnessed the development of national social security and social protection[1] mechanisms aimed at providing financial, social and public services to address social risks. Those developments were captured in the International Labour Organization's (ILO) Social Security (Minimum Standards) Convention, 1952 (No 102).[2] In reality, the social security programmes that developed according to the principles of ILO Convention No 102 were never universal, neither did they adequately address all women's needs, nor respect the principle of gender equality.

The increased presence of women in the formal labour market (as well as their important contributions through domestic production and reproduction) has not greatly modified the prevailing assumptions about their role in a liberal economy. Their wages are lower than those of men; their contributions to social security schemes are put at risk by interrupted patterns of work and intra-household economic tensions; and their disproportionate participation in the precarious and informal labour market

[1] For discussion of the distinction between social security and social protection, see Goldblatt and Lamarche, in this collection.

[2] ILO Convention C102: Social Security (Minimum Standards) Convention (Convention Concerning Minimum Standards of Social Security) (adopted 28 June 1952, entered into force 27 April 1955).

often keeps them at a distance from social security benefits. In addition, the division of family and community responsibilities between men and women has only slightly changed over time. In less developed countries, women still shoulder a largely disproportionate burden of the reproductive and domestic work.

That being said, we have recently witnessed a global change in social and development policy, which is largely premised on the recognition of women's 'role' in a global economy.[3] Following the brutal era of the Washington Consensus and structural adjustment policies, women became visible in a very specific way. Razavi[4] and others suggest that a liberal perspective on the new economy calls for human and social investments. In terms of this ideology, 'investing in women' (and in their children) promotes social cohesion and facilitates economic transition. It claims to address women's needs and facilitates their integration in the formal economy. The new global social policy agenda aims at managing women's poverty, extreme poverty and social exclusion as matters of economic risk to be alleviated.

However, social security and social protection are more than just economic policies. They are rooted in a human rights framework which is embedded in many international human rights instruments. The right to social security is currently in the process of being en-gendered, notably by human rights treaty bodies such as the UN Committee on the Elimination of Discrimination against Women (CEDAW) and the UN Committee on Economic, Social and Cultural Rights (CESCR). Their analysis takes into account the interdependence of the gender equality standard and of the human right to social security.

In addition to being understood as a human right, the universal dimension of the right to social security has also been reaffirmed as such. In 2007, the CESCR adopted General Comment No 19 on the Right to Social Security.[5] Further, the UN Human Rights Council Special Rapporteur on extreme poverty, Magdalena Sepúlveda Carmona, submitted, in 2010 and in 2012, important reports that promote a human rights approach to social

[3] For a presentation of recent developments, see UN Development Programme (UNDP), *Sharing Innovative Experiences Volume 18: Successful Social Protection Floor Experiences* (New York, UNDP, 2011); International Social Security Association (ISSA), *Social Security Coverage Extension in the BRICs: A Comparative Study on the Extension of Coverage in Brazil, the Russian Federation, India, China and South Africa* (Geneva, ISSA, 2013).

[4] Razavi, S, *Engendering Social Security and Protection, Challenges for Making Social Security and Protection Gender Equitable* (Berlin, Friedrich-Ebert–Stiftung, Global Policy and Development Division, June 2011). See also Razavi, S et al, 'Gendered Impacts of Globalization: Employment and Social Protection' (UN Research Institute for Social Development (UNRISD) Research Paper No 3, Geneva, UNRISD, March 2012).

[5] UN Committee on Economic, Social and Cultural Rights (CESCR), *General Comment No 19: The Right to Social Security (art 9)*, 4 February 2008, UN Doc E/C.12/GC/19.

protection.[6] These initiatives, inspired by recent national policies aimed at fighting poverty, revisit old assumptions about the scope of social security schemes as worker-oriented rather than being provided for all citizens and also challenge their historically un-gendered approaches.

This chapter pays attention to the most recent initiative that contributes to the global fight against poverty: the ILO Recommendation concerning National Floors of Social Protection, 2012 (No 202).[7] The ILO, as a specialised UN agency, has been closely involved in the debate surrounding the fight against poverty. It took leadership in promoting the Decent Work for All Agenda in 2001.[8] ILO Recommendation No 202 is the result of a decade of intense institutional activity. Despite the significance of the Recommendation, this chapter will show how remarkably un-gendered it is.[9]

The first section of this chapter discusses the issue of the historical gender deficit and of the gender bias present in the ILO's normative work with regard to social security. It surveys the organising principles of ILO Convention No 102, the major social security instrument of the ILO. It then analyses how, over the decade between 2001 and 2011, the ILO came to acknowledge the need and the right of every person to basic social protection. In doing so, room was made to explore the gender dimensions of social security, and gender equality was understood substantively. Unfortunately, these positive developments are not reflected in the recently adopted Recommendation No 202.

The second section of this chapter examines the discussion that led to the adoption of the text of the Recommendation. The first part looks at the 2011 Report submitted to the International Labour Conference by the ILO Committee of Experts on the Application of Conventions and

[6] M Sepúlveda Carmona, Independent Expert on the Question of Human Rights and Extreme Poverty, *The Contribution of Social Protection Measures in Achieving Millennium Development Goals (MDGs)*, 9 August 2010, UN Doc A/65/259; M Sepúlveda Carmona, Independent Expert on the Question of Human Rights and Extreme Poverty, *Final Draft of the Guiding Principles on Extreme Poverty and Human Rights, Submitted by the Special Rapporteur on Extreme Poverty and Human Rights*, 18 July 2012, UN Doc A/HRC/21/39. For further discussion of the Recommendations promoted by the Special Rapporteur, see Goldblatt and Lamarche, in this collection.

[7] ILO Recommendation R202: Social Floors Protection Recommendation (Recommendation Concerning National Floors of Social Protection) (101st Conference Session, Geneva, 14 July 2012).

[8] International Labour Office, *Report 1(A): Report of the Director-General: Reducing the Decent Work Deficit—a Global Challenge* (International Labour Conference, 89th Session, Geneva, ILO, 2001). See also World Commission on the Social Dimension of Globalization, *A Fair Globalization: Creating Opportunities for All* (Geneva, International Labour Organization, 2004).

[9] A fact recently acknowledged by the ILO itself. See International Labour Office (ILO), *The Strategy of the International Labour Organization—Social Security for all—Building Social Protection Floors and Comprehensive Social Security Systems* (Geneva, International Labour Organization, 2012) para 30.

Recommendations (CEACR). The second part of the section unpacks, article by article, the text of the Recommendation as well as the amendment process that led to the final text. The conclusion is quite pessimistic, as it finds that ILO Recommendation No 202 is mainly driven by liberal economic considerations. As a consequence, women are not given visibility and are simply lumped within the broad category of 'vulnerable persons' in need of basic social protection.

The conclusion affirms that ILO Recommendation No 202 is neither gender specific nor gender inclusive. It is simply un-gendered. Such a conclusion is surprising, and even disconcerting considering the evolution of both the global women's rights regime, including an encompassing right to gender equality, and the recent more gender aware interpretation of the human right to social security by some of the other UN bodies.

THE HISTORICAL GENDER DEFICIT OF THE RIGHT TO SOCIAL SECURITY[10]

The right to social security is guaranteed by article 22 of the Universal Declaration on Human Rights (UDHR)[11] and by article 9 of the International Covenant on Economic, Social and Cultural Rights (ICESCR).[12] The universal language is nevertheless tainted by implicit assumptions about the roles assigned, de facto and de jure, to both men and women in the household and, more generally, in the global economy. For example, article 11 of the ICESCR provides for the right of everyone to an adequate standard of living for himself and his family.[13] Women, in the context of the drafting and of the adoption of both the UDHR and the ICESCR, are clearly asked to give way to men and/or the family, as the rights holder. The industrial welfare state developed social security schemes based on such assumptions. Either women were to behave like male workers of the industrial sector, or would be considered as wives of such workers, the unstated meaning of which was that they were dependants carrying on the bulk of domestic and unpaid work. In addition, men or women elsewhere in the world who carried out productive activities outside the formal economy were simply rendered

[10] This section is partly drawn from Lamarche, L, 'Le Pacte International relatif aux droits économiques, sociaux et culturels, les femmes et le droit à la sécurité sociale: des considérations et des propositions pour un droit "universel" à la sécurité sociale' (2002) 14 *Canadian Journal of Women and the Law/Revue Femmes et Droit* 53.

[11] Universal Declaration of Human Rights (UDHR) (adopted 10 December 1948) UN Doc 217 A (III), art 9.

[12] International Covenant on Economic, Social and Cultural Rights (ICESCR) (adopted 16 December 1966, entered into force 3 January 1976) UN Doc 993 UNTS 3, art 9.

[13] *Ibid*, at art 11.

invisible. The only, but nevertheless important, explicit protection granted to women was, at the time, maternity related.[14]

ILO Social Security (Minimum Standards) Convention, 1952 (No 102) came into force in 1955.[15] Parts II to X of the Convention set out the scope of protection and the level of coverage, which are different according to the nature of each risk: medical care (Part II); sickness benefit (Part III); unemployment benefit (Part IV); old-age benefit (Part V); employment injury benefit (Part VI); family benefit (Part VII); maternity benefit (Part VIII); invalidity benefit (Part IX); and survivor's benefit (Part X). At a minimum, a ratifying state must commit itself to addressing three of the risks belonging to a group of five: unemployment, old age, employment injury, invalidity and survivor's benefits. Maternity and family benefits do not belong to the core group of risks to be addressed by members when they choose to ratify the Convention.[16] The structure of Convention No 102 essentially puts women in the position of benefiting from rights deriving from their marital attachment to the male worker.[17]

ILO Convention No 102 provides for a domestic floor of coverage determined in relation to a percentage of insured workers and a minimal level of benefits. This rule operates on a 'risk-by-risk' basis. For example, article 27 of the Convention[18] (Part V: old-age benefit) states that the persons protected shall comprise prescribed classes of all employees *or* prescribed classes of the economically active population constituting not less than 20 per cent of all residents *or* all residents whose means do not exceed limits prescribed. Such a determination should not lead to protection lower than 30 per cent of the wages of a labourer,[19] or 40 per cent[20] in the case of a pensioner with a wife of pensionable age.[21] ILO Convention No 102 mainly offers a system aimed at protecting classes of employees through contributory social insurance. When the coverage addresses the needs of all residents, a lower level of benefits is then provided.

The technique that characterises ILO Convention No 102 (percentage of covered populations of workers or of residents) was not the one promoted by the International Labour Bureau which, at the time, aimed for universal

[14] See UDHR, above n 11, at art 25(2); and ICESCR, above n 12, at art 10(2).

[15] At the time, only European countries and Israel had ratified ILO Social Security (Minimum Standards) Convention, 1952 (No 102). In 1980, 31 states had ratified it. The total number of ratifications is now 49. ILO Convention No 102 is thus not considered a highly ratified Convention.

[16] See ILO Convention C102, above n 2, at art 2(a)(ii).

[17] Interestingly, art 1 of ILO Convention C102, above n 2, provides for a definition of the terms 'wife', 'widow' and 'child', but not of the term 'husband'.

[18] ILO Convention C102, above n 2, at art 27.

[19] A labourer is a person deemed typical of unskilled labour in manufacture of machinery other than electrical machinery. ILO Convention C102, above n 2, at art 66(4).

[20] The percentage varies according to the risk and to the composition of the family. See chart in ILO Convention C102, above n 2, at art 67.

[21] See ILO Convention C102, above n 2, at arts 66 and 67.

coverage comprising both categories of workers and of residents.[22] Further, as opposed to what is often said, ILO Convention No 102 does not rely solely on contributory social insurance schemes. Article 71 of the Convention states:

> The cost of the benefits provided in compliance with this Convention and the cost of the administration of such benefits shall be borne collectively by way of insurance contributions or taxation or both in a manner which avoids hardship to persons of small means and takes into account the economic situation of the Member and of the classes of persons protected.[23]

ILO Convention No 102 has clearly influenced the unfolding of social security schemes in the developed and industrial world.[24]

As women increasingly entered the formal labour market in developed countries in the 1960s and 1970s, they realised that maternity and care constituted systemic obstacles to equal treatment. This was in addition to the general undervaluing of their work, which is either the result of biased perceptions of women's work, or of clear discrimination in wages, in the case of equal and equivalent work. Of course, such analysis prevails for developed countries. Linda Luckhaus analysed the progress accomplished in Europe in regard to gender equality at work. In an article published in 2000, she concluded that if greater access to social security benefits was provided without discrimination, such as by way of pensions,[25] this would partly remove the consequences of assumed dependency of women on the male breadwinner.[26] She noted however, that this would not address the

[22] International Labour Office (ILO), *Report IV(1), 335 and IV(2), 3 and 366: Minimum Standards of Social Protection* (International Labour Conference, 34th Session, Geneva, International Labour Organization, 9 June 1951). For a detailed analysis, see Lamarche, L, *Perspectives Occidentales du Droit International des Droits Économiques de la Personne* (Brussels, Bruylant, 1995) 345.

[23] ILO Convention C102, above n 2, at art 71.

[24] Other ILO Conventions shall also be considered in this discussion, namely: ILO Convention C121: Employment Injury Benefits Convention (Convention concerning Benefits in the Case of Employment Injury) (adopted 8 July 1964, entered into force 28 July 1967); ILO Convention C128: Invalidity, Old-Age and Survivors' Benefits Convention (adopted 29 June 1967, entered into force 1 November 1969); and ILO Convention C130: Medical Care and Sickness Benefits Convention (Convention concerning Medical Care and Sickness Benefits) (adopted 25 June 1969, entered into force 27 May 1972).

[25] One can also consider ILO Convention C183: Maternity Protection Convention (Convention Concerning the Revision of the Maternity Protection Convention (Revised)) (adopted 15 June 2000, entered into force 7 February 2002); and ILO Convention C175: Part-Time Work Convention (Convention Concerning Part-Time Work) (adopted 24 June 1994, entered into force 28 February 1998).

[26] Luckhaus, L, 'Equal Treatment, Social Protection and Income Security for Women' (2000) 139(2) *International Labour Review* 149. See also International Labour Organization (ILO), *Report III Part IV(B): Equality in Employment and Occupation* (International Labour Conference, 83rd Session, Geneva, ILO, 4 June 1996).

negative impact of the peripheral connection of women to informal work and to care. For Luckhaus, formal equality, as a legal norm, does not necessarily engender social security. Luckhaus considered substantive gender equality as a standard that secures income for women and promotes their citizenship. This perspective on women's work and relationship to care responsibilities has, in more recent years, been accepted at the global level.

In the decade preceding the adoption of the 2000 Millennium Development Goals, social security experts called for urgent reforms of social security and social protection domestic schemes. This came from the realisation that the majority of the world's population was excluded from any kind of protection. Women being the poorest of the poor were further identified as a group at high risk. In 1995, the International Association for Social Security (IASS) summarised the challenges then confronting social security: lack of accessibility; privatisation; impact of structural adjustments programmes; and increased dependency of all persons on informal economic activities. This diagnosis was offered by the IASS in the context of a growing concern for poverty all around the world.[27] The ILO was not left out of this discussion. In 1996, Wouter Van Ginneken, then of the social security division of the ILO, revisited the defeated aspiration of the International Labour Office for universal coverage of social security. On the one hand, he promoted a system that would address the need for universal income replacement guarantees and, on the other, proposed a basket of priority needs to be addressed universally: medical care; survivor's benefits; invalidity benefits; and (although with a bit less enthusiasm) maternity and family benefits.[28]

Efforts like those of Van Ginneken, or of the late Roger Beattie,[29] led to a general discussion on the topic of poverty alleviation through social security at the 89th session of the International Labour Conference in 2001.[30] The Committee on Social Security presented a report to the Conference which promoted social security for all. This report was adopted.[31] The Committee

[27] International Social Security Association (ISSA), 'Report of the Director General: Developments and Trends in Social Security 1993–1995 Part 1: Social Security in the 1990s: the Imperatives of Change' (1996) 49 *International Social Security Review* 5.

[28] Van Ginneken, W, 'Social Security for the Informal Sector: Issues, Options and Tasks Ahead 1996' (Geneva, ILO, May 1996) The Interdepartmental Project on the Urban Informal Sector (1994/95) Working Paper, available at: www.ilo.org/public/libdoc/ilo/1996/96B09_156_engl.pdf.

[29] Beattie, R, 'Social Protection for All: But How? Special Issue: Social Policy and Social Protection' (2000) 139 *International Labour Review* 129.

[30] International Labour Organization (ILO), 'Examination of the Report of the Committee on Social Security' (International Labour Conference, 89th Session, Geneva, ILO, 5–21 June 2001).

[31] International Labour Organization (ILO), 'Report of the Committee on Social Security: Issues, Challenges and Prospects' (International Labour Conference, 89th Session, Geneva, ILO, 2001).

of the Conference then reached a consensus and adopted 21 conclusions.[32] The ILO stated that its concern for social security was firmly grounded not only in the social security conventions that members had adopted, but also in the ILO's own Declaration of Philadelphia and in the Decent Work Agenda.[33] The first conclusion reached by the Committee was the need to give urgent consideration and high priority to the need for all to access social security. This is captured in conclusion 2, stating that full social security coverage supports economic development if it provides health care, income security and social services. Conclusion 7 states that although social security should be coordinated with assistance to find employment, it should never encourage benefits lower than the amount needed in order to protect an adequate standard of living. Conclusion 8 of the 2001 Consensus provides for a comprehensive definition of gender equality with regard to social security. According to the Committee, gender equality should be able to ensure equitable outcomes (of social protection) for all women.

Looking at that era retrospectively, we note that one of the main preoccupations of the Committee, and of the International Labour Conference, was to reach those relying on the informal economy to make a living. Bringing the informal sector within the realm of the formal is often referred to as part of the solution towards achieving better social protection coverage. Implicit in this analysis lies the assumption that the more formal workers the economy can generate, the more those workers will contribute to social security schemes. Such an assumption replicates some of the causes of women's exclusion from social security schemes. The fact that women are overburdened by their domestic and care responsibilities is not seriously considered.

Nevertheless, from a women's rights perspective, the willingness of the International Labour Conference to consider social security as a human right and to root it both in the UDHR and the Philadelphia Declaration was a positive development.[34] The Global Campaign on Social Security and Coverage for All was then launched in 2003.[35] Further, the adoption by the CESCR of General Comment No 19 on the Right to Social Security[36] would flesh out the meaning of this development within a rights framework.

[32] International Labour Office, *Social Security: A New Consensus* (Geneva, International Labour Organization, 2001).

[33] The extension of social security is one the four pillars of the ILO Decent Work Agenda. The four pillars are: jobs creation; guarantees of rights at work; extension of social security; and promotion of social dialogue. International Labour Organization (ILO), 'Decent Work Agenda', available at: www.ilo.org/global/about-the-ilo/decent-work-agenda/lang--en/index.htm.

[34] ILO, *Social Security: A New Consensus*, above n 32, refers twice to social security as a human right.

[35] International Labour Organization (ILO), 'Global Campaign on Social Security and Coverage for All', available at: www.ilo.org/public/english/protection/socsec/pol/campagne/.

[36] *General Comment No 19*, above n 5, at paras 9–28.

More or less a decade separates the adoption by the ILO Conference of the *Social Security—A New Consensus* Report and ILO Recommendation No 202. During this decade, significant efforts were made all over the world towards addressing poverty. Cash transfer programmes (sometimes conditional), employment guarantee programmes, tax incentives and universal basic income security measures, as well as others were introduced and experimented with. Some of the human rights treaty monitoring bodies began to assess such programmes from a gender equality perspective.[37] They sought to understand how these 'new' programmes might negatively impact on women, sometimes by overburdening them with correlative duties. Special Rapporteur Magdalena Sepúlveda Carmona has also addressed this issue forcefully.[38]

One could reasonably expect that during this same decade the ongoing work that lead to the adoption in 2012 of ILO Recommendation No 202 would reflect upon the risks of social protection programmes that may not be designed within a human and women's rights framework. In addition, it would consider the special needs of women, without oversimplifying the issue of the relationship of women to the informal sector economy and to unpaid and domestic productive and reproductive activities. The next section will demonstrate that this is not the case.

THE ILO RECOMMENDATION CONCERNING NATIONAL SOCIAL SECURITY FLOORS, 2012 (NO 202): WHERE DID ALL WOMEN GO?

This section of the chapter looks at the process that led to the adoption of ILO Recommendation No 202 in June 2012. The first part examines the period from 2001 to 2011, which followed the adoption by the ILO of a benchmark document entitled *Social Security—A New Consensus*.[39] The consensus was about the need to provide basic social protection for all, including basic health care, basic income benefits and social services. Although each of those components does strongly address women's needs, the discussion reveals a very light concern for women's rights, including their right to gender equality. Women mainly fall into the ungendered category of the poor and of the vulnerable, in need of social protection.

The second part of this section analyses, article by article, the tensions surrounding the elaboration of the final draft of the Recommendation to

[37] See Otto, in this collection.
[38] Sepúlveda, *Final Draft of the Guiding Principles*, above n 6.
[39] ILO, *Social Security: A New Consensus*, above n 32.

be submitted to the International Labour Conference in June 2012. This analysis demonstrates the ambiguities of the three-dimensional scope of the Recommendation: social protection, social development and economic development. Such ambiguities led to an increased commodification of social protection, with unfortunate consequences for women's rights because of women's specific relation to non-commodified activities and to paid employment. Women's needs and rights were not clearly addressed—despite the final text of the Recommendation's reliance on strong assumptions about women's roles in a liberal and global economy.

The Social Security and Social Protection Discussion 2001–11: When the Universal Makes Women Differently Invisible

The ILO Committee of Experts on the Application of Conventions and Recommendations (CEACR) presented to the International Labour Conference of 2011 the results of the General Survey concerning social security instruments.[40] This Report is entitled *Social Security and the Rule of Law* and Part II of the Report is written under the heading 'Towards a Rights-Based Approach to Social Security'. This precise wording was not designed to trigger a debate about the rule of law, but to underline the urgent need to look at social protection from a human rights perspective as well as from the perspective of the added value of a human rights framework. Accordingly, the Report requires respect for certain standards, including the need for legal rules and the principle of non-discrimination in the design of social protection schemes. However, the focus on non-discrimination in social protection did not in itself provide a gender lens.

According to the CEACR, the relevant ILO standards needed to be supplemented by a new high-impact instrument setting down the obligation of the state to provide a set of basic benefits to all residents, which would be acceptable to all Member States.[41] The CEACR had in fact started to provide guidance to Member States in that regard, structuring its observations around indicators and accountability processes.[42] The CEACR

[40] International Labour Office, *Report III (Part 1B): Report of the Committee of Experts on the Application of Conventions and Recommendations—General Survey Concerning Social Security Instruments in Light of the 2008 Declaration on Social Justice for a Fair Globalization: Social Security and the Rule of Law* (International Labour Conference, 100th Session, Geneva, International Labour Organization, 2011).

[41] *Ibid*, at para 31.

[42] See, eg, International Labour Office, Committee of Experts on the Application of Conventions and Recommendations (CEACR), *Report III (Part 1A): Observation, Plurinational State of Bolivia* (International Labour Conference, 100th Session, Geneva, ILO, 2011) 893 ff, available at: www.ilo.org/wcmsp5/groups/public/---ed_norm/---relconf/documents/meetingdocument/wcms_151556.pdf.

General Survey of 2011[43] also acknowledges that there is now a movement towards greater recognition of the essential role of social rights and of the right to social security as a human right,[44] and that such recognition creates an interaction between international social security law and human rights law, which substantiates the human right to a minimum standard of protection.[45] In making such a statement, the CEACR relies on the ILO Declaration on Social Justice for a Fair Globalization, 2008.[46]

The CEACR is well positioned to witness the deep transformations of social programmes around the world. In its 2011 Report, it recognises that the biggest challenge facing the extension of social protection worldwide is the increasing informality of national economies, especially in middle and low-income countries, which leaves major parts of the population without any social security protection. The CEACR then links this informality and the move by many countries towards universal social security coverage, giving priority to achieving universal access to health care and universal pension schemes.[47]

In the 2011 debate, the idea of engendering social protection received very light attention on the part of the CEACR or from the International Labour Conference. In fact, the Report gives the impression that the CEACR is looking somewhere else for answers:

> The Committee believes that these provisions of Convention No 102 and subsequent Conventions should be adapted to the needs of modern social security administration and the ILO's more recent policy guidance on gender equality so as to strengthen the outgoing efforts to increase the level of ratification of Convention No 102. One way of doing so would be a limited revision of the Convention by the International Labour Conference or the adoption of a Protocol to the Convention to integrate gender-sensitive language and adapt the definition of the standard beneficiary to the present realities. Another way would be for the Committee of Experts to provide an interpretative declarative statement on the adaptation of certain provisions of the Convention. The Governing Body also has the possibility of reviewing the report forms related to social security Conventions with a view to simplifying and updating the monitoring criteria and requests for statistical data related to the definition of the standard beneficiary. Of course, any adaptation or language change in the provisions of the Convention should not lead to any reduction in the level of benefits guaranteed by Convention No 102.[48]

[43] International Labour Office, *General Survey*, above n 40.

[44] *Ibid*, at para 155.

[45] *Ibid*, at para 159.

[46] International Labour Organization (ILO), *Declaration on Social Justice for a Fair Globalization* (adopted by the International Labour Conference at its 97th Session, Geneva, 10 June 2008, available at: www.ilo.org/global/resources/WCMS_099766/lang--en/index.htm.

[47] International Labour Office, *General Survey*, above n 40, at para 313.

[48] *Ibid*, at para 631.

Only in a footnote included in the Report do we find a quote from the UN CEB (Chief Executives Board for Coordination) that obliquely suggests what an engendering process of the right to social security may look like:

> The United Nations System Chief Executives Board for Coordination (CEB) suggests that a social protection floor should consist of two main elements that help to realize respective human rights: (1) services: geographical and financial access to essential services (such as water and sanitation, health, and education); and (2) transfers: a basic set of essential social transfers, in cash and in kind, paid to the poor and vulnerable to provide a minimum income security and access to essential services, including health care.[49]

Services and transfers are essential components of a social security floor that factor in women's needs and promote gender equality. As stated in Conclusion 8 of the 2001 *New Consensus* Report, gender equality should guarantee equality of outcomes. The 2011 CEACR Report is not as explicit about this requirement.

Although some palpable tensions around the idea of a new instrument guaranteeing a social protection floor to all were obvious, the CEACR felt the need to outline such programmes in a way that would impact on ILO member obligations and responsibilities. The envisaged instrument on the social security floor was to seek to close the gap and ensure coverage for all persons, and to be in line with the human rights-based approach and with the principle of non-discrimination. It was also to institute a system based on sound governance, accountability and transparency, with effective supervisory mechanisms and safeguards against inappropriate or non-transparent uses of social security funds. The CEACR also took into account the need to consider the distinctive structural realities of less-developed economies.[50]

Following the CEACR 2011 Report, the ILC created the Committee for the Recurrent Discussion on Social Protection.[51] The report of this Committee clearly indicates that the extension of social security coverage mobilises social assistance programmes, as well as social insurance ones, and recalls that they must be human rights based. This implies that strategies must be guided by principles of sustainability, adequacy and a focus on outcomes as well as on progression towards the levels provided for under

[49] *Ibid*, at para 295, fn 262. See Somavia, J, Director General, ILO, Chair of the High-Level Committee on Programmes, 'The Global Financial Crisis and its Impact on the Work of the UN System' (UN CEB (Chief Executives Board for Coordination) Issue Paper, 2009) 20, available at: www.un.org/ga/econcrisissummit/docs/CEB_Paper_final_web.pdf.

[50] International Labour Office, *General Survey*, above n 40, at para 628.

[51] International Labour Office, *Report of the Committee for the Recurrent Discussion on Social Protection Floor* (International Labour Conference, 100th Session, Geneva, International Labour Organization, 2011).

ILO Convention No 102.[52] The Committee states that social protection is a human right, a social need and a pillar of economic development.

The Committee of the Conference reconvened in May 2012 with the intention of submitting a draft Recommendation to the Conference in June 2012.[53] Clearly, there was no support for the idea of a new Convention. The Recommendation would also reflect upon another consensus: it would promote the immediate obligation of all members to establish and to maintain a floor of social protection, as well as the one to progressively provide higher levels of protection to as many people as possible.

The universal requirement of social protection was clearly the object of a consensus in 2011. Yet such consensus distinguishes itself from that of 2001 with regard to gender, as the Drafting Committee received no guidance at all from the CEACR 2011 Report accepted by the Conference. This decade of evolution took the project of engendering social security in another direction: the minimalist one. In sum, from being treated as 'dependents' under the regime of ILO Convention No 102, women were to be considered as belonging to the anonymous sub-group of the poor and of the extremely poor.

The next subsection focuses on the negotiation process that led to the final text of the Recommendation, as submitted for adoption at the International Labour Conference in 2012.[54] It unpacks, article by article, how the gender dimension of the right to social security has been forgotten along the way.

The Adoption of the ILO Recommendation Concerning National Floors of Social Protection: An Un-Gendered Process

As the Committee started its discussion about the draft Recommendation proposed by the International Labour Bureau in May 2012, the Bureau summarised the remaining difficulties as follows: should the Recommendation use the language of 'benefits' or of 'guarantees' when talking about social protection? How much discretion should be given to members when implementing a social protection floor?[55] What exactly should be the scope of the

[52] *Ibid*, at paras 36–38.

[53] International Labour Office, *Report of the Committee for the Recurrent Discussion on Social Protection Floor* (International Labour Conference, 101st Session, Geneva, International Labour Organization, 2012).

[54] The reader who wishes to compare the text submitted to the Committee by the International Labour Bureau in 2012 with the one of the Recommendation as finally adopted in 2012 will find the 2012 proposal at International Labour Office, *Report IV (2B): Social Protection Floors for Social Justice and a Fair Globalization* (International Labour Conference, 101st Session, Geneva, International Labour Organization, 2012).

[55] Bangladesh maintained all through the discussion that the position of national levels of development and circumstances should be given some consideration in the text of the Recommendation: International Labour Office, *Recurrent Discussion* (2012), above n 53.

expression 'all' when saying that social protection coverage for all persons was to be made available?[56]

Equally, some government members insisted on the need to address the issue of employment activation measures as a social security issue.[57] Denmark, for example, announced that it would propose language aimed at improving the wording of the Recommendation in relation to employment policies, to the sustainability of social security regimes and to their affordability.[58] In addition, Denmark and other EU members effectively implied throughout the process that mature social security systems, as well as their more recent transformations, fell outside the scope of the future Recommendation, which was a Recommendation for the 'poor'. The agreed triple aim of the proposed Recommendation (social security as a human right and an economic and social necessity for development and progress) was generating some tension among the members of the Drafting Committee. While some developed countries tried to transform the Recommendation into an employment activation tool, some emergent countries such as Brazil were working at securing the universal dimension of a social protection floor for all, as well as seeking to have their different national strategies recognised as tools for social protection.

Finally, the formal–informal labour sector debate was another dividing line between groups of countries. Such tensions dominated the debate, and, as so often happens when the focus is on the economic, the situation of women in regard to the accessibility, sufficiency and adequacy of social protection mechanisms received close to no attention. The only reference made to women in the opening discussion of the Committee was by Canada, who reminded all parties (workers, employers and government representatives) of the relevance of gender considerations, without providing further

[56] *Ibid*, at para 9.

[57] For a discussion about employment activation measures, see Aber, L and Rawlings, LB, 'North–South Knowledge Sharing on Incentive-Based Conditional Cash Transfer Programs' (SP Discussion Paper No 1101, Social Protection and Labour, World Bank, January 2011); and Bonoli, G and Natali, D, *The Politics of the New Welfare State* (Oxford, Oxford University Press, 2012).

[58] International Labour Office, *Recurrent Discussion* (2012), above n 53, at para 19. Denmark received direct demands for clarifications from the CEACR in 2007 and 2011. They concerned the modifications to national social security programmes and, namely, the privatisation of the workers' compensation programme and the entry in force of a more stringent rule of reasonable work to be quickly accepted by the newly unemployed. Such changes led the CEACR to wonder if such transformations were in line with ILO Convention C102, above n 2, and ILO Convention 168. See also International Labour Office, Committee of Experts on the Application of Conventions and Recommendations (CEACR), 'Direct Request: Social Security (Minimum Standards) Convention, 1952 (No 102): Denmark' (International Labour Conference, 101st Session, 2011), available at: www.ilo.org/dyn/normlex/en/f?p=1000:13100:0::NO:13100:P13100_COMMENT_ID:2699202.

explanation.[59] ATD Quart Monde, a non-status NGO, was the only NGO to make an explicit reference to women and caregiving responsibilities.[60]

The Preamble of Recommendation No 202

The Preamble of Recommendation No 202 (as adopted by the Conference in June 2012) reflects the consensus reached in 2011 by the Committee. The first paragraph of the Preamble states that social security is a human right. However, along with employment promotion, it is equally introduced as an economic and social necessity. Denmark fought for separating the first and second paragraphs of the Preamble. At that point, no member of the Committee raised the question of the relationship, at the global level, between women and formal employment, or between women and all other productive activities.

According to the Preamble of Recommendation No 202, social security serves many purposes: it is an investment in people; a facilitator for structural economic adjustments; a stimulator of aggregate demand in times of crisis (and beyond) (paragraph 3); and a support to the formalisation of work (paragraph 4). The employers group expressed some reservations about such an optimistic programme, which had some impact on the ultimate wording. For example, the fourth paragraph of the Preamble now reads, 'help stimulate aggregate demand' instead of 'maintain' such demand. The employers group also did not consider social security to be an automatic stabiliser in times of economic crisis and transitional economy. Again, the implicit characterisation of women is a 'male' one, as the Preamble promotes the image of a global labour force aiming for the formal labour market, without further consideration for their other responsibilities or constraints. Not only is such characterisation globally wrong, as the informal sector will not simply disappear, but, in addition, it neglects to assess the specific impacts on women belonging to a sector that only reluctantly receives the attention of ILO members.

A tension also arose over the text of the sixth paragraph of the Preamble as to whether formal employment and social security are mutually supportive, or whether formal employment is a guarantee of a more sustainable social security system. Employers were sceptical, and some African countries clearly opposed this proposal.[61] This unresolved issue reinforces the point that women left outside the formal sector are seen as risks to the sustainability of social protection systems.

Also worth noting is the third paragraph of the Preamble, which concerns the social dimensions of social security. Social security is presented as a

[59] International Labour Office, *Recurrent Discussion* (2012), above n 53, at para 23.
[60] *Ibid*, at para 47.
[61] *Ibid*, at paras 140–53.

tool for the prevention and reduction of poverty, inequality, social exclusion and social insecurity and for the promotion of equal opportunity and gender and racial equality. If Canada succeeded in introducing into this paragraph the notion of gender equality (the initial proposal talked about gender equity), it is the Latin American group and Brazil that proposed the addition of racial equality.[62] No discussion about the intersectional nature of social exclusion and discrimination, in the case of women, was initiated by any party to the discussion.

In conclusion, the Preamble of ILO Recommendation No 202 shows quite eloquently that a vague allusion to gender concerns and a strong affirmation of social security as a human right do not magically provide the means for the effective en-gendering of women's right to social security.

The Objectives, the Scope and the Principles of the Recommendation

Article 1[63] of Recommendation No 202 provides for a social security protection floor designed around two objectives: the immediate and horizontal (extension of coverage) obligation of members to provide a basic social protection floor (article 1(a)); and the progressive and vertical (increase in level of coverage) obligation of members to ensure higher levels of social security to as many people as possible (article 1(b)). Here, the principle of universality was secured, although the employers group tried to limit the scope of the progressive vertical effect to persons in need.[64] In the case of developed countries this would have equated to a severe regression for women as a social protection floor would have been guaranteed only to women 'in need', seen as an undefined and un-gendered (or invisible) vulnerable group of poor persons.

After a discussion and the subsequent defeat of some proposed amendments, it was agreed in article 2[65] of the Recommendation that a national social protection floor would provide legal guarantees aimed at the alleviation of poverty, vulnerability and social exclusion.[66] Such language must be read in conjunction with the Chapeau of article 3,[67] which reiterates the overall and primary responsibility of the state in giving effect to the Recommendation. This amended Chapeau was the initiative of the Worker Vice-Chair, and is highly welcomed considering that social security is recognised as a human right in the Preamble of the Recommendation.[68] It is even

[62] *Ibid*, at para 75.
[63] ILO Recommendation R202, above n 7, at art 1.
[64] International Labour Office, *Recurrent Discussion* (2012), above n 53, at paras 226–48 for the debate.
[65] ILO Recommendation R202, above n 7, at art 2.
[66] International Labour Office, *Recurrent Discussion* (2012), above n 53, at para 249.
[67] ILO Recommendation R202, above n 7, at art 3.
[68] International Labour Office, *Recurrent Discussion* (2012), above n 53, at para 281.

more useful as the discussion inside the Committee showed severe reservations from some members and the employers group towards 'guarantees of social protection'.

A basic social protection floor is, according to article 3, governed by 18 principles. The principles are largely drawn from the text of General Comment No 19 adopted by the UN Committee on Economic, Social and Cultural Rights,[69] although this was not explicitly acknowledged in the discussion by the ILO Drafting Committee. This is especially true of paragraphs (a) (universality of benefits), (b) (entitlement to benefits provided for by law), (c) (adequacy and predictability of benefits) and (d) (non-discrimination, gender equality and responsiveness to special needs of benefits) of article 3.

The Worker group felt the need to propose paragraph (f) of article 3 (respect for rights and dignity of persons). They believed such an amendment would qualify the nature of the services offered under the umbrella of social protection.[70] For example, the quality of public services is as important as their availability. Also, paragraph (k) was amended in order to qualify the nature of the sustainability that social protection floor programmes should guarantee, and to make sure that social justice and equity would then be considered.[71] Brazil proposed the addition of paragraph (o) to article 3 which stresses the need for an efficient and accessible complaint and appeal procedure.[72] Clearly, such successful amendments created a stronger link between the right to social security, as guaranteed by article 9[73] of the ICESCR and ILO Recommendation No 202. The Worker Vice-Chair did an impressive job of securing human rights language in article 3. Her only reservation was about paragraph (r) which provides for consultation beyond the usual ILO tripartite participation, but she was quickly reminded that this broadening of parties had been agreed upon.

The Worker group was also successful with their proposition to amend paragraph (n) of article 3 in order to add the adjective 'public' before 'services'. Public services are important for women and are now considered a principle governing the implementation of social protection floors. Read in conjunction with paragraph (e), which makes social inclusion of persons in the informal sector another principle, one can at least say that an implicit and indirect consideration is given to gender in the final text of the Recommendation.

[69] *General Comment No 19*, above n 5; Part XI of ILO Convention C102, above n 2, is also relevant as far as it provides for periodical and predictable social security payments.

[70] International Labour Office, *Recurrent Discussion* (2012), above n 53, at para 335.

[71] *Ibid*, at para 423.

[72] *Ibid*, at para 310.

[73] ICESCR, above n 12.

Article 4[74] of the Recommendation is the backbone of this instrument. Members are to establish (as quickly as possible) and maintain a social protection floor comprising basic social security guarantees. Such guarantees should 'ensure at a minimum, access to essential health care, basic income security and access to goods and services, defined as necessary at the national level'. Zimbabwe tried to introduce the notion of differential development of social security floors based on national levels of development, but it was defeated.[75]

No proposal aimed at echoing article 3(n), in which access to high quality public services is described as a principle of the social protection floor, was introduced under article 4. Considering, again, the essential relation of women to public services of quality, this omission can be considered a missed opportunity. Accordingly, a reasonable interpretation of both article 3(n) and 4 of the Recommendation could be that the need for a basic income confirms the nature of essential services, such as health care, as market goods. The CESCR's General Comment No 19 on the Right to Social Security does not, of course, consider public services as the only and exclusive way to protect, to promote and to fulfil the right to social security. Yet a gender analysis of such a right shows, without a doubt, the relevance of such public delivery from a gender perspective. Thus, article 4 of ILO Recommendation No 202 may privilege an economic reading of social goods that does not well serve the principles of the right to social security enunciated in article 3 of the same instrument.

Article 5[76] of the Recommendation defines the core content of a national social protection floor programme which must include: essential health care (defined as a set of goods and services—not necessarily public) including maternity care (paragraph (a)); basic income security for children providing access to nutrition, education, care and other necessary goods and services, as defined nationally (paragraph (b)); basic income security for persons in active age incapable of earning sufficient income, in particular in cases of sickness, unemployment, maternity and disability (paragraph(c)); and basic income security for older persons. Only one amendment to the text of paragraph (a) was introduced by the Worker group, and accepted. It provides that essential health care, including maternity care, must be available, accessible, acceptable and of sufficient quality.[77] This represents a significant gain for women, from a human rights standpoint.

[74] ILO Recommendation R202, above n 7, at art 4.

[75] International Labour Office, *Recurrent Discussion* (2012), above n 53, at para 507.

[76] ILO Recommendation R202, above n 7, at art 5.

[77] International Labour Office, *Recurrent Discussion* (2012), above n 53, at para 550. The Worker group here made an explicit reference to General Comment No 14—*The right to the highest attainable standard of health (article 12 of the International Covenant on Economic,*

Article 6[78] provides that members should ensure basic social security guarantees to all residents and children, as defined in national laws and regulations. Brazil made an 'on record' intervention, making the point that article 6 should be understood as covering all migrant workers, which in Latin America is highly relevant considering the substantial number of women employed as domestic workers in neighbouring countries.[79]

Article 8[80] of the Recommendation provides for further considerations by members on implementing a social protection floor programme. Paragraph (a) states that health care services, if not free, should not cause hardship for persons in need nor increase the risk of poverty. The Worker group succeeded in introducing an amendment that provides for free pre-natal and post-natal care for the most vulnerable.[81] We can certainly celebrate this amendment, which is also the only specifically gender-based requirement provided for by Recommendation No 202. Yet there are also reasons to worry. On the one hand, this provision speaks only to the biological attributes of poor women and not to the broader need for free health services for poor women facing other medical issues. On the other, access to free services depends, as provided for in paragraph (b) of article 8, on national poverty lines that the same Worker group expressed suspicions about. Indeed, and as stated by this group, national poverty lines are constructs intended to show that governments are dealing with poverty when in reality they can be manipulated by simply lowering the poverty line.[82]

Article 9[83] of Recommendation No 202 looks at the methods for delivering social security guarantees and specifies that members should consider different approaches with a view to implementing the most effective combination. If article 5(a) states that essential health care, including maternity care, must be available, accessible, acceptable and of sufficient quality, paragraph (2) of article 9 only states that Members 'may' consider offering child and family, disability, old-age, survivor's and employment benefits. In addition, paragraph (2) of article 9 also considers employment guarantees as potential benefits,[84] and specifies that all benefits can be delivered in cash

Social and Cultural Rights), Committee on Economic, Social and Cultural Rights, August 2000, Doc NU E/C.12/2000/4.

[78] ILO Recommendation R202, above n 7, at art 6.

[79] International Labour Office, *Recurrent Discussion* (2012), above n 53, at para 585. On the issue of social security coverage and migrant workers, see Lamarche, L, 'The Social Protection of Temporary Migrant Workers: An Evolutionary Process' (Social Science Research Network, 9 July 2013), available at: papers.ssrn.com/sol3/papers.cfm?abstract_id=2291582.

[80] ILO Recommendation R202, above n 7, at art 8.

[81] International Labour Office, *Recurrent Discussion* (2012), above n 53, at para 600.

[82] *Ibid*, at para 629.

[83] ILO Recommendation R202, above n 7, at art 9.

[84] International Labour Office, *Recurrent Discussion* (2012), above n 53 at para 702. India presented, as an example, the Mahatma Gandhi National Rural Employment Guarantee Act

or in kind. In other words, although social security is a human right, the combined reading of articles 5 and 9 of the Recommendation indicates that the essence of a social protection floor is a mix of accessible, essential health care and basic 'cash transfer' income, determined according to a national poverty line. Other benefits, in cash or in kind, are optional. Nowhere in the discussion was the impact of this minimalist (but nevertheless essential) anti-poverty strategy on women even considered.

Article 10[85] of Recommendation No 202 enumerates considerations that members should take into account when designing and implementing a national social protection floor programme. Paragraphs (a), (b) and (c) illustrate how fragile the consensus between members is. Countries from the north insisted on including active employment measures under the umbrella of social benefits and services, thereby promoting employment in the formal sector as the best way for an individual to protect the household against social risks.[86] While other countries, such as Brazil, asked their fellow members from the Committee not to shy away from a list of strategies that also consider the promotion of all productive activities.[87] Finally, paragraph (c) of article 10, while acknowledging the fact that coordination between all kinds of policies enhances formal employment,[88] also enumerates a list of social goods[89] that can be guaranteed through the implementation of a social protection floor, in coordination with other policies, including: income generation, education, literacy, vocational training, skills; and also employability that reduces precariousness and promotes secure work[90] within a decent work framework. Often though, women do need those 'other policies' in order to exercise all their human rights; and often, such policies can be considered as necessary social goods. The dichotomy between employment policies, as stated in paragraph (a), and 'other' policies, enumerated in paragraph (c), creates a restrictive environment for social protection floors that are respectful of all women's rights. In other words, does Part II of ILO Recommendation No 202 provide for any other guarantee for women than the guarantee of being a bit less poor for as long as they are considered in need? How can such an interpretation be congruent with the principles enumerated in article 3 of the same document and with CESCR General Comment No 19?

(MGNREGA). The United States supported India in an amendment that introduces 'employment guarantees' in art 9(2).

85 ILO Recommendation R202, above n 7, at art 10.

86 International Labour Office, *Recurrent Discussion* (2012), above n 53, at para 719, Canada.

87 *Ibid*, at para 731.

88 Described by Chile as the opposite of undue competitive advantage.

89 International Labour Office, *Recurrent Discussion* (2012), above n 53, at para 766, Brazil.

90 Described as the opposite of precarious.

The Extension of National Social Security Strategies

Articles 13 to 18[91] of Recommendation No 202 provide for national strategies for the extension of social protection floors. Article 13(1) reads as follows:

> (1) Members should formulate and implement national social security extension strategies, based on national consultations through effective social dialogue and social participation. National strategies should:
>
> (a) prioritize the implementation of social protection floors as a starting point for countries that do not have a minimum level of social security guarantees, and as a fundamental element of their national social security systems; and
>
> (b) seek to provide higher levels of protection to as many people as possible, reflecting economic and fiscal capacities of Members, and as soon as possible.[92]

Some interesting discussion occurred around this wording. Namely, the amendment proposed by EU members to article 13(b) which reads: 'reflecting economic and fiscal capacities of Members, and, as soon as possible'.[93] Discussion also occurred around the defeated amendment that intended, in paragraph (b), to restrict the members' obligation to seek to provide 'higher levels of protection to as many people as possible', only to those in need.

Social security extension strategies are obviously not stressed as strongly as the social protection floor provided for in Part II of the Recommendation, and this emphasises again the strong belief of ILO members that social security is above all guaranteed through contributory schemes. For example, article 14(c) states that when seeking to close gaps between covered and uncovered groups, members may consider extending the existing contributory schemes to all concerned persons with contributory capacity.[94] Article 15,[95] which states that extension strategies should apply to persons both in the formal and informal sectors, must be read in this context.[96]

Article 16[97] closes the commitments under Part III of Recommendation No 202, by stating that social security extension strategies should ensure support for disadvantaged groups and people with special needs. An amendment by the Worker group was withdrawn. It read as follows: 'Social Security systems should recognize care work and provide rights and incentives

91 ILO Recommendation R202, above n 7, at arts 13–18.

92 *Ibid*, at art 13(1).

93 International Labour Office, *Recurrent Discussion* (2012), above n 53, at para 896. To be read with art 13(a) where the verb 'prioritise' is used.

94 International Labour Office, *Recurrent Discussion* (2012), above n 53, at para 951. India believes it includes the workers of the informal sector who can contribute.

95 ILO Recommendation R202, above n 7, at art 15.

96 The coverage of the informal sector and the reaffirmation of the need to reinforce the growth of the formal sector is the result of amendments proposed by both Argentina and Zimbabwe. International Labour Office, *Recurrent Discussion* (2012), above n 53, at para 1005.

97 ILO Recommendation R202, above n 7, at art 16.

for more gender equal sharing of care responsibilities'.[98] This last minute attempt to capture the complexity of women's right to social security, but only under the heading of extension strategies, speaks for itself. Women's care and reproductive work remains unexplored territory within the ILO.

Monitoring Recommendation No 202

Article 21[99] of ILO Recommendation No 202 sets out the obligation for members to collect and analyse social security data. Almost 20 years after the Fourth World Conference on Women (1995), it took a proposal introduced by the Worker group, USA and Australia[100] to add to this commitment the words 'in particular by gender'. Further, some members even expressed doubt that such an obligation exists in international law.[101]

In conclusion, one could say that the global economy did not need ILO Recommendation No 202 in order to contribute to the global trend represented by cash transfer programmes to benefit the poorest, including women. In most cases such transfers already give minimal access to necessary goods, thus constituting a national social protection floor. In addition, ILO Recommendation No 202 is not a convention and is thus not considered binding on ILO members.

However, there are concerns around Recommendation No 202 that should elicit greater condemnation. This Recommendation confirms women's unequal role in the 'precarious' global economy, rather than contributing to the understanding of women's rights, including their right to social security. If anything, it neglects to take into account what it means to be a poor woman. This is because ILO Recommendation No 202 amalgamates all poor persons into one category that can be broadly described as the 'vulnerable ones'. The question thus becomes, do poor women have more than poor rights? Based on recent work from UN treaty bodies, the answer is positive. Yet why is it that such progress is not reflected in the work of a specialised agency such as the ILO, but for a list of principles enumerated in article 3 of the Recommendation?

My hypothesis is that the heritage of the ILO with regard to social security constitutes a significant obstacle to the engendering of the right to social security. Contributory social insurance regimes are still the dominant paradigm. The formal sector of employment remains the reference model. Further, women, if not mothers, wives or widows, are expected to fulfil their citizenship in behaving like male workers from developed countries. In other words, women are just differently invisible. The idea of analysing

[98] International Labour Office, *Recurrent Discussion* (2012), above n 53, at para 1053.
[99] ILO Recommendation R202, above n 7, at art 21.
[100] International Labour Office, *Recurrent Discussion* (2012), above n 53, at para 1097.
[101] *Ibid*, at para 1099.

the impact of and providing direction for the new cash and in kind social transfer programmes on women (as one example where such a role is needed to address gender equality in the developing world context) seems to be beyond the reach of the ILO.

CONCLUSION

ILO Recommendation No 202 is neither gender inclusive nor gender specific. It does not address, but for one important issue—free pre-natal and post-natal health care—the structural inequalities that women are victims of in a globalised and 'new' economy. Further, it assumes that poor women should simply be treated like poor men, with a bit of financial help. Yet, as the work of Special Rapporteur Sepúlveda Carmona has shown,[102] women are not equally situated with men even with regard to universal basic cash transfers. Violence, racism, corruption, intra-household dynamics and dominant local power relations negatively impact on women's access to such benefits. Punitive measures attached to conditional cash transfers often carry consequences that are exclusive to women as mothers. Finally, in the paradigm proposed by ILO Recommendation No 202, care and domestic responsibilities that women carry remain unaddressed.

In addition, the Recommendation fails to address in a non-contradictory fashion the issue of public services, which are so crucial to women's equality. After all, it may be that the ILO CEACR was right when it stated in its 2011 Report[103] that policy guidance on gender equality and social security is required.[104] Such guidance does exist, as UN treaty bodies are now simultaneously addressing the issue of gender equality and of women's right to social security in their concluding observations as well as in adopted general comments and observations.[105] The ILO needs to incorporate this advice into its body of standards.

[102] Sepúlveda, *The Contribution of Social Protection*, above n 6; and Sepúlveda, *Final Draft of the Guiding Principles*, above n 6.

[103] International Labour Office, *General Survey*, above n 40.

[104] *Ibid*, at para 631.

[105] See Otto, in this collection, but also note her critiques of the equality approach of some of the treaty bodies.

5

Social Protection in China: Is there a Gender Equality Problem?

MANKUI LI*

INTRODUCTION

HUMAN BEINGS HAVE been working tirelessly since the very beginning to create an affluent society in which human needs will be met, decent work can be guaranteed and in the worst cases of unfortunate events, normal life can be restored. Confucius, arguably the most famous philosopher from China, shed some light on this ideal society. His version of the ideal society is referred to as 'The Great Together', in which the Great Way is practised:

> Thus people do not treat only their parents like parents, nor do people treat only their sons like sons. That makes the aged have the appropriate last years, those in their prime have the appropriate employment, and the young have the appropriate growth and development. Elderly men with no spouses, widows, orphans, elderly people without children or grandchildren, the handicapped, the ill—all are provided for ... This is called the 'Great Together'.[1]

One indispensable element of the concept of an ideal society is social security and social protection for all. The level of social security in society is generally determined by its level of economic development. For example, in

* I would like to thank Lucie Lamarche and Beth Goldblatt for their support in writing this chapter. I would also like to thank Katherine Lippel, Sandra Fredman and Lucy Williams for their invaluable comments on the draft chapter.

[1] This famous remark is quoted from the chapter on Etiquette ('Li Yun') in the book on Etiquette ('Li Ji'). There are different translations of this remark. The quote in this chapter is based on the one translated by Feng Xin-ming, available at: www.tsoidug.org/Literary/Etiquette_Great_Together_Simp.pdf.

ancient times there were only simple and limited disaster relief and poverty alleviation measures available.[2]

Social Protection in the Command Economy Era

As with many other countries in Asia, China started its modern social security programmes after the Second World War.[3] After the founding of the People's Republic of China in 1949, China implemented a Soviet-type command economy under which the state rigidly controlled economic activities, including the production and supply of goods through directives and commands.[4] The de facto lifetime employment and the disappearance of unemployment, though criticised by many as lacking flexibility, served to ensure access to employment opportunities and services. Associated with the command economy was the strategy of rapid industrialisation, which was comprised of heavy industries in the cities and an extraction of agricultural surplus from the peasantry.[5] The *hukou* (household registration) system was introduced to support this strategy. It served as a central instrument of the command system, established for this big push industrialisation.[6] As observed by the Canadian Immigration and Refugee Board: 'Traditionally, there were numerous social benefits and privileges associated with an urban *hukou*, including the provision of basic food, better employment, higher incomes, subsidised housing, the right to free education, medical care, social security and pensions'.[7] Its explicit intention was to discourage or restrict the 'rural-to-urban migration'.

For social protection in the urban sector, mechanisms applied to workers differed between the public and 'private' sector. For workers in the public sector, a 'safety net' was gradually formed, which required the government, as the employer, to provide financial support for various benefits, taken from general tax revenue, and also to directly manage the programmes.[8]

[2] Zheng, G, *Social Security: Concept, Institution, Practice and Deliberation* (Beijing, Commercial Press, 2000) 113.

[3] International Labour Organization (ILO), Asia–Pacific Regional High-Level Meeting on Socially-Inclusive Strategies to Extend Social Security Coverage: New Delhi, India, 19–20 May 2008 (Social Security Policy Briefings Paper 6, Geneva, ILO, 2008).

[4] See Naughton, B, *Growing out of the Plan: Chinese Economic Reform 1978–1993* (Cambridge, Cambridge University Press, 1995) 26–32; and Li, Y, 'Command Economy and Economic Reform in China' (2008) 8 *China Development Observation* 30, 30–31.

[5] Chan, K, 'The Household Registration System and Migrant Labour in China: Notes on a Debate' (2010) 2 *Population and Development Review* 357, 357.

[6] *Ibid*, at 358.

[7] Immigration and Refugee Board of Canada, *China: Reforms of the Household Registration System (Hukou) (1998–2004)* (Ottawa, Immigration and Refugee Board of Canada, February 2005), available at: www.refworld.org/docid/4305fbc04.html.

[8] See Zheng, G, *The Development of a Social Security System with Chinese Characteristics* (Beijing, China Labour and Social Security Press, 2009) 72.

For workers in the private sector, China established an 'all-in-one' labour insurance regime in 1951, which included many elements of modern social security, such as workers' compensation, sickness benefits, old-age pension and maternity benefits. In the rural sector, under the collectivisation policy of the 1950s, the unique production mode offered another kind of 'ration system'. This system performed a certain 'social protection' function through the de facto rural collective guarantee system, most notably the 'barefoot doctors' system.[9] In addition, a social assistance programme, known as the rural 'Five Guarantees' was established. This programme provided material assistance in the form of room, board, clothing, medical care, funeral expenses and compulsory education for minors. Those assisted included the elderly, persons with disabilities, minors, widows and widowers without children who were unable to work and had no source of income.

In 1969, at the peak of the Cultural Revolution, this traditional social security system was downgraded into a private 'enterprise-guarantee system' in the urban sector. In the rural sector, rural collectives were struggling, depending on their available fiscal space, to provide minimum medical care to their members and some material assistance to those who had lost their earning capacity. At this time there was an alarming drop in the government's accepted responsibility with regard to social security. The government passed its duty on to enterprises in the urban sector and to rural collectives in the rural sector. People's access to social security service was at stake.

Social Protection in the Reform Era

From 1978, a series of reform measures was phased in to grow the economy and improve the standard of living. The market oriented reform and rural-to-urban migration of this period led to a collapse of the traditional system and to the privatisation of social security. For a long time since, both urban residents and rural residents have had to pay for essential services, such as medical care, housing and education, out of their own income. To further aggravate the problem, the prices of these services have continually skyrocketed. Massive rural-to-urban migration has also added to the complexity of the issue.

Gradually, the government has begun to realise the importance of allowing the people of China to share the fruits of the country's development.[10] As such, social security has begun to be given more weight within the

[9] See Anonymous, 'Briefing Rural China: Missing the Barefoot Doctors' *The Economist* (London, 13 October 2007).

[10] See 'Full Text of Hu Jintao's Report at the 18th Party Congress' *English News* (17 November 2012), available at: news.xinhuanet.com/english/special/18cpcnc/2012-11/17/c_131981259.htm.

government's agenda. The economic aggregate and the increase and scale of tax revenue have provided fiscal space for a full-fledged social security system, and the transformation of the economy towards domestic consumption growth has raised the urgent need for putting in place a social security scheme.[11] It is worth noting that there have been some attempts to reformulate the social security system, though on a relatively small scale, while simultaneously carrying out market-oriented economic reform. For example, as part of the 'employment-contract-reform' package, some pilot unemployment insurance and retirement pension programmes were established to reduce the repercussions of these reforms. Other social security programmes, including workers' compensation, maternity insurance, medical insurance and social assistance programmes were re-established in the context of a market economy. Social insurance programmes, which are designed for economically active groups, form the central pillar of the system, while social assistance programmes designed for non-worker residents supplement social insurance programmes. Together, they form a social safety net, which caters for the needs of industrial society.[12] It might be helpful to note that there are different social insurance programmes for workers in the public and private sectors. These operate based on different principles, and the level of benefits for workers in the public sector is higher than those in the private sector.

Nascent Social Protection Floor

Compared with social insurance programmes, social assistance has largely lagged behind. Before 2002, there were only scattered social assistance programmes, such as the urban minimum living standard guarantee, which provided only very weak social protection to urban non-worker residents. These programmes occasionally assisted rural residents as well, for example, in relation to disaster relief or under the Five Guarantees. Hence, the process of putting in place a social protection floor in China is essentially a process of extending social security coverage to non-worker residents. The three key elements of the Chinese social protection floor are the Minimum Living Standard Guarantee Scheme, the Basic Medical Insurance Scheme and the Basic Old-Age Pension Scheme.

China established its Urban Minimum Living Standard Guarantee Scheme in 1999 in order to provide assistance to poor households in urban areas, and to ensure that they do not fall below the minimum standard of living.

[11] See Zheng, G, 'Reform and Future Development of Social Security in China' (2010) 5 *Journal of Renmin University of China* 2, 3.

[12] United Nations Development Programme (UNDP), *Sharing Innovative Experience Volume 18: Successful Social Protection Floor Experiences* (New York, UNDP, 2011).

This standard is a tax financed minimum subsistence guarantee. In 2007, the coverage of the minimum standard of living guarantee was extended to include rural residents by establishing a separate but similar Rural Minimum Living Standard Guarantee Scheme. The Rural New Cooperative Medical Scheme was established in 2002, targeting rural residents. In 2007, a pilot Urban Basic Medical Scheme was established to provide basic health care for non-worker residents (including college students) in urban areas, exploring viable ways to realise full coverage for urban non-worker residents. The New Rural Pension Scheme was introduced in 2009 as the replacement for the old voluntary rural pension scheme, whose membership had stagnated since the late 1990s due to its reliance on personal contributions and an absence of supporting policies.[13] For urban residents, the New Urban Pension Scheme was introduced in 2011 in order to provide a minimum level of income security for urban non-worker residents. This social protection floor contains within it a basic set of rights and transfers that enables and empowers every citizen in China with a minimum level of essential goods and services.

The Social Insurance Act 2010, which is the milestone legislation for the Chinese social security system, came into force in July 2011 and set the tone for future development.[14] The Act reaffirms that it is the responsibility of the government, not the employers or rural collectives, to establish social insurance programmes, to properly administer them and to provide financial support in cases of deficiency or other need. Hence, in recent years we have witnessed a clear trend of 'upward movement', with the government accepting once again its duty to provide the social security benefits it had previously passed on to enterprises and/or rural collectives. This legislation not only establishes social insurance programmes for workers, but also regulates the basic medical insurance and basic pension scheme for urban and rural non-worker residents. It encourages provincial jurisdictions to merge the basic medical insurance programmes for urban residents and rural residents into one, and also to merge the basic pension schemes for urban and rural residents in order to promote equity between them. Therefore, the coverage of basic medical insurance and basic pensions are extended to urban and rural non-worker residents who are not formally employed. This practice challenges the perception of a binary division, ie, social insurance applies exclusively to those whose employment is 'formal', while social assistance relates only to those lacking formal employment.[15]

[13] International Social Security Association (ISSA), *Social Security Coverage Extension in the BRICS: A Comparative Study on the Extension of Coverage in Brazil, the Russian Federation, India, China and South Africa* (Geneva, ISSA, 2013).

[14] *Ibid*, at 110.

[15] See Report of the Advisory Group chaired by Michelle Bachelet, Convened by the International Labour Organization (ILO) with the Collaboration of the World Health Organization, *Social Protection Floor: For a Fair and Inclusive Globalization* (Geneva, ILO, 2011).

THE CHINESE PRACTICE OF GENDER EQUALITY

According to international human rights instruments, everyone has the right to social security. This means that all persons should be covered by social security systems—especially individuals belonging to the most disadvantaged and marginalised groups.[16] Interpreted from a gender perspective, social security rights shall be guaranteed without discrimination based on gender, because 'it is not possible—because it is not acceptable—to speak of social inclusion and dignity without ensuring that it covers women as well as men'.[17] Thus, it would be premature to comment on China's efforts in building a social protection floor before evaluating the overall status of women in China and their access to social protection.

The History of Women's Oppression

Like many other countries, China has, in the past, treated unfairly women whose role was once solely restricted to internal family affairs. Women's role in the family had been regarded as a matter of course, and as suited to both men and women.[18] The idea that women were inferior to men was deeply rooted in traditional Chinese culture. One can easily find old sayings to this effect in the ancient literatures, such as 'a good woman is one who knows nothing', and 'only women and narrow-minded persons are difficult to get along with'.[19] Women's oppression was a part of Chinese history. As admitted by the Chinese government itself, 'Chinese women were long subject to humiliation and brutal oppression in a feudal and, subsequently, semi-feudal, semi-colonial society'.[20]

The 'traditional' division of labour required women to stay at home doing chores and taking care of the whole family, while their male counterparts were supposed to financially support the family by undertaking remunerated work. Instead of recognising women's equal rights, the rulers at that time, through feudal rituals and laws, confirmed and reinforced the

[16] UN Committee on Economic, Social and Cultural Rights (CESCR), *General Comment No 19: The Right to Social Security (art 9)*, 4 February 2008, UN Doc E/C.12/GC/19.

[17] International Labour Organization (ILO), 'Introduction—Social Policy and Social Protection' (2000) 2 *International Labour Review* 113, 115.

[18] Zheng, D, 'On Social Justice and Gender Equality' (2010) 1 *Journal of Huazhong University of Science and Technology* 96, 97.

[19] Verse 25, Chapter 17 of *Analects of Confucius* (*Lun Yu*).

[20] UN Committee on the Elimination of Discrimination Against Women, *Consideration of Reports Submitted by States Parties Under Article 18 of the Convention on the Elimination of All Forms of Discrimination Against Women: Third and Fourth Periodic Reports of States Parties—China*, 10 June 1997, UN Doc CEDAW/C/CHN/3-4, available at: www.un.org/womenwatch/daw/cedaw/cedaw20/china.htm.

unequal relationship between men and women.[21] Chinese society at that time was male dominated. There was no gender equality from the modern feminist perspective.

Women's Liberation and Gender Equality

The rise of the Communist Party brought some change to this bitter history. In order to win the communist victory, the Communist Party had to unequivocally advocate for women's liberation in order to acquire the maximum support of the Chinese people, including Chinese women.[22] After the Communist Party came to power in 1949, it consolidated its efforts towards women's liberation by passing the Basic Law (later, the Constitution), declaring that women enjoy the same rights as men in political, economic, cultural, educational, social and family life. This basic principle was further corroborated by specific pieces of legislation, on matters such as marriage and divorce, and land distribution. Women were encouraged to actively participate in social production. However, these new laws and policies on women's liberation and gender equality were in fact designed as a means to meet the needs of nation building and development, rather than the goal of female empowerment.[23]

The Cultural Revolution took gender equality to an extreme, as seen in examples such as the uniform colour and style of the popular outfit for both women and men, and slogans such as 'whatever men can do, women can do too', which used men as the yardstick to evaluate women.[24] This approach was visible even before the Cultural Revolution. According to some scholars, in the period from 1949 to 1976, Chinese women were being liberated as a collective group; socialised to be 'half of the sky', equal in all aspects with men, included even in the jobs that required the most arduous physical labour.[25] This approach was gender blind in the way that it refused to acknowledge difference on the basis of gender in order to mobilise and motivate women to join in productive work. To some scholars, the official classification of the Maoist approach to mobilising women is 'Marxist maternalist', because it sought to achieve gender equality by

[21] See Liu, W, 'Remarkable Historical Transformation of Women's Status in New China' 2010 17(5) *Journal of Contemporary Chinese History* 41, 41.

[22] Zhou, J, 'Keys to Women's Liberation in Communist China: An Historical Overview' (2003) 5(1) *Journal of International Women's Studies* 67, 69.

[23] Zhang, Y, 'Gender Equality Policy and Status of Women after Founding of People's Republic' (1996) 2 *Journal of China Women's College* 37, 38.

[24] Li, Y, 'Women's Movement and Change of Women's Status in China' (2000) 1 *Journal of International Women's Studies* 30, 31.

[25] Lin, J, 'Chinese Women under the Economic Reform: Gains and Losses' (Summer 2003) *Harvard Asia Pacific Review* 88, 90.

drawing women into remunerated labour, while continuing to attend to their reproductive health and unquestioned role in maintaining the family.[26] Under this gender blind approach, the explicit articulation of gender difference was certainly lessened,[27] but with an inadvertent by-product, being that Chinese women experienced rapid progress in terms of gender equality during the Cultural Revolution.[28]

Progress on Legislating Gender Equality

Even though many scholars argue that drastic changes had a mixed and inconsistent impact on the women's movement and women's status in China,[29] few would deny that China made important steps in legislating gender equality, that is, de jure (or formal) equality, and promulgating the notion that women were equal to men.[30] Various pieces of legislation have played a pivotal role in promoting gender equality in China. Besides the Land Reform Act 1950, the Marriage Act 1950 and the Election Act 1954, there are many other laws which were introduced during this period that touched upon gender equality, or were even dedicated to gender equality. The Protection of the Rights and Interests of Women Act 1992 was promulgated in 1992, and amended in 2005, to promote equality between men and women. It reaffirmed the government's commitment to safeguarding women's equal rights with men in every aspect. The Act is dedicated, in its Chapters 2 to 7 respectively, to women's equal political, cultural and educational rights, labour and social security rights, property rights, personal rights and equal rights in marriage and family affairs. The subsequent Labour Act 1994 explicitly provides that women have the same employment rights as men, and makes gender a prohibited ground of discrimination. In addition, its pay equity, or equal pay provisions are of great significance in terms of gender equality. In 2007, China passed the Employment Promotion Act, which includes a chapter on equal employment opportunities. Again, gender discrimination is explicitly prohibited; it would now seem that gender equality has become a self-evident principle in the Chinese legislative process.

[26] See Hershatter, G, *Women in China's Long Twentieth Century* (California, University of California Press, 2007) 60.
[27] *Ibid*, at 45.
[28] Li, 'Women's Movement', above n 24, at 33.
[29] *Ibid.*
[30] Hershatter, above n 26, at 63.

China's Attitude Towards International Obligations

In the international arena, after an initial hesitation in recognising international human rights instruments, the Chinese government has gradually changed its attitude towards women's rights. In an effort to integrate itself into the international community, China launched the Reform Movement.[31] As early as 1980, China ratified the Convention on the Elimination of All Forms of Discrimination against Women[32] (CEDAW), which is the key international human rights instrument dedicated to women's rights. Further, China signed in 1997, and ratified in 2001, the International Covenant on Economic, Social and Cultural Rights[33] (ICESCR). Article 3 of the ICESCR provides the equal right of men and women to the enjoyment of all economic, social and cultural rights. In 1998 China signed the International Covenant on Civil and Political Rights[34] (ICCPR). Articles 3 and 26 of the ICCPR provide equal rights of men and women to the enjoyment of all civil and political rights, and prohibition of discrimination based on gender. China's top legislature is yet to ratify the ICCPR (at the time of the writing of this chapter) due to discrepancies with China's domestic laws with regard to provisions on the 'most serious crimes' for the death penalty (article 6(2)), arbitrary arrest and detention (article 9) and the right to a fair trial (article 14).[35] The delay in ratifying this Covenant has nothing to do with gender considerations. In addition, China has ratified the ILO's Equal Remuneration Convention[36] (C100) and the Discrimination (Employment and Occupation) Convention[37] (C111), which are listed by the ILO as fundamental Conventions. China's engagement with international human rights treaties reflects the government's commitment to human rights and bears witness to China's largely responsible attitude to international obligations.[38] Since then, China has been constantly mainstreaming a gender perspective into major legislations, policies and programmes to implement and realise its commitments and obligations on gender equality under

[31] Zhou, above n 22, at 70–71.

[32] Convention on the Elimination of All Forms of Discrimination against Women (CEDAW) (adopted 18 December 1979, entered into force 3 September 1981) 1249 UNTS 13.

[33] International Covenant on Economic, Social and Cultural Rights (ICESCR) (adopted 16 December 1966, entered into force 3 January 1976) 993 UNTS 3.

[34] International Covenant on Civil and Political Rights (ICCPR) (adopted 16 December 1966, entered into force 23 March 1976) 999 UNTS 171.

[35] Lee, K, 'China and the International Covenant on Civil and Political Rights: Prospects and Challenges' (2007) 2 *Chinese Journal of International Law* 445, 457.

[36] ILO Convention C100: Equal Remuneration Convention (adopted 29 June 1951, entered into force 23 May 1953).

[37] ILO Convention C111: Discrimination (Employment and Occupation) Convention (Convention Concerning Discrimination in Respect of Employment and Occupation) (adopted 25 June 1958, entered into force 15 June 1960).

[38] Lee, above n 35, at 445.

various international human rights instruments. According to the United Nations Development Programme, China ranks thirty-fifth in the Gender Inequality Index 2011, out-performing the overall Human Development Index ranking of 101.[39]

SPECIAL PROTECTION AND SUBSTANTIVE EQUALITY

Fredman's Four-Dimensional Model as a Test[40]

The above-mentioned pieces of legislation, usually written in gender neutral language, are about formal recognition of gender equality, and have been especially instrumental in dismantling express legal prohibitions relating to gender.[41] China also has gender specific laws and regulations accommodating women's special physiological conditions and redressing the inequalities in practice.[42] These laws, concerning 'special protection' for women, are designed to promote de facto (or substantive) equality. Few people in China would challenge or question these protective laws, as they understand that the realisation of gender equality 'requires more than formal legal recognition of equality between the sexes'.[43] Sandra Fredman's four-dimensional model of substantive equality, ie, redistribution, recognition, transformation and participation,[44] will be used here to test the compatibility of China's special protection laws with substantive equality.

The Redistributive Dimension

In China, special protection for women stems from Acts relating to working conditions in which female workers are entitled to special labour protection, especially in terms of occupational health and safety protection. These special protection mechanisms mainly include protection prohibiting women from certain categories of jobs; protection during menstruation, gestation, maternity and breastfeeding periods; protection of interests regarding maternity; and protection of interests regarding career development. The first two types of these legislative protections form the core of this special

[39] United Nations Development Programme (UNDP), *Human Development Report 2011: Sustainability and Equity: A Better Future for All* (New York, UNDP, 2011).

[40] Fredman, in this collection.

[41] See Fredman, S, *Discrimination Law*, 2nd edn (Oxford, Oxford University Press, 2011) 6; and Fredman, in this collection.

[42] Zhang, above n 23, at 38.

[43] 'Montréal Principles on Women's Economic, Social and Cultural Rights' (2004) 26 *Human Rights Quarterly* 760.

[44] See Fredman, above n 41, at 25–33.

protection.[45] The fact that China creates special protection legislation for female workers reflects its intention and commitment to correct the cycle of disadvantage experienced on the basis of gender. This echoes the redistributive dimension of Fredman's four-dimensional model.

The Recognition Dimension

Chapter 7 of the Labour Act 1994 is dedicated to the special protection of women, and elaborates the various protective measures to be put in place. Article 59 prohibits female workers from working in mines, underground workplaces and certain jobs with a physical labour intensity above Grade IV. Article 60 prohibits female workers in the menstruation period from working in elevation, low temperature, cold water and certain jobs with a physical labour intensity above Grade III. Article 61 prohibits female workers in the gestation period from performing certain work with a physical labour intensity above Grade III, and other jobs specified by regulations. For those female workers in their third trimester of pregnancy, overtime work and night shifts are prohibited. Article 63 prohibits female workers who are breastfeeding infants up to one-year-old from performing certain work with a physical labour intensity above Grade III, and other jobs specified by regulations, with overtime work and night shifts also prohibited. Remarkably for a statute that generally lacks specificity, there are four articles in the Labour Act 1994 (articles 59, 60, 61, 63) setting out prohibitions, and the Act authorises further limitations to be set by other rule-making bodies.[46] The State Council (the equivalent of Cabinet) released Regulations on Labour Protection for Female Workers 1988, further detailing protective measures. Accordingly, the Ministry of Labour issued Regulations on the Scope of Employment Prohibited for Female Workers in 1990 to supplement the aforementioned legal instruments. These three legal instruments now define the special labour protection for female workers in China, along with the newly released Special Regulations on Labour Protection for Female Workers 2012. The 2012 Regulations impose a new obligation on employers to prevent harassment towards their female employees. To some extent, this conforms to the recognition dimension of substantive equality in the sense that it aims to eradicate harassment and violence and promote dignity and respect.

[45] Guo, H and Wang, H, 'Negative Effect Analysis and the Resolution of Special Protection for Women's Labour Rights' (2009) 4 *Journal of Hebei University* 38, 38.

[46] Cooney, S, Biddulph, S and Zhu, Y, *Law and Fair Work in China* (New York, Routledge, 2013) 64.

The Transformative Dimension

Both Chapter 7 of the Labour Act 1994 and the Regulations on Labour Protection for Female Workers 1988 provide that female workers are entitled to no less than 90 days' maternity leave. There is no reference to parental leave in these two pieces of national legislation, though some provincial legislation provides that female workers in need can apply for parental leave of up to one year with 75 to 80 per cent salary, subject to management's approval. Given the way that this parental leave is framed, only female workers will be entitled to it, and must prove that they face a realistic difficulty in rearing children.

Another gender-specific mechanism that has been established is the differing mandatory retirement ages for women and men, ie, 60 for men and 50 or 55 for women.[47] The predominant underlying reason for this is the protection of female workers, based on the implicit presumption that work is an obligation and is tedious.[48] Under the above-mentioned 'Marxist maternalist' model,[49] besides their roles in remunerated labour, women are also expected to play a major role in maintaining the family. Therefore, retiring five or even 10 years earlier than their male counterparts means that women are eligible for pension benefits at an earlier age and can then focus on their role in the family. This is regarded by many men and women in China (as high as 44 per cent according to one survey) as a special protection for women.[50]

Aimed at realising substantive equality, the protective legislative measures are designed in ways that take women's socially constructed disadvantage into account, and secure for women the equal benefit, in real terms, of existing laws and measures.[51] In China, as stated in the legislation itself, these protective measures are designed to reduce and overcome the special disadvantages faced by women in the workforce due to their physiological characteristics, and to protect their health.

In scholarly works, special protection is defined as protection specially designed to accommodate female workers' tasks along with the needs of maternity and rearing children.[52] Arguably, this reflects the popular thinking

[47] Brown, RC, *Understanding Labour and Employment Law in China* (New York, Cambridge University Press, 2010) 142.

[48] Pan, J, 'Gender Interests in the Old-age Social Insurance System' (2002) 2 *Social Sciences in China* 118, 127.

[49] Hershatter, above n 26, at 60.

[50] Liu, B, Guo, L and Hao, R, 'Why Are Men or Women For or Against Same Age Retirement?' (2011) 3 *Collection of Women's Studies* 22, 27.

[51] 'Montréal Principles', above n 43.

[52] Ye, J and Zhang, Z, 'General Introduction into Special Labour Protection for Female Workers' in D Yang and J Guo (eds), *Theory and Practice on Protection of Women's Rights and Interests in Contemporary China: Survey on the Implementation of CEDAW in China*

in China on special protection for women. To an extent, it allows the female workers to deviate from the dominant (male) norms in the workplace, and changes the existing institutions to accommodate the different needs of female workers. In this sense, it conforms to the transformative dimension of the four-dimensional model of substantive equality.

The Participation Dimension

International human rights instruments, for example CEDAW, allow for special measures aimed at protecting maternity and temporary special measures intended to accelerate de facto equality between men and women, which are not considered to be discriminatory. However, from the point of view of workplace equality, the Chinese model of 'special protection' for women might be problematic; some of its elements are characterised by several anomalies and anachronisms.[53] Substantive equality does not necessarily entail different treatment for women and men in every circumstance; rather it requires re-examination and assessment of the adequacy of existing measures against the background of women's actual conditions.[54] Therefore, for pregnant and breastfeeding women, due to their special conditions, certain special labour protection and maternity leave provisions can be justifiable. This can fall within the category of special measures aimed at protecting maternity under CEDAW, which mandates that, 'States Parties shall take appropriate measures … To provide special protection to women during pregnancy in types of work proved to be harmful to them'.[55] Hence, these measures do not constitute discrimination per se. Yet for other women special labour protection can reinforce their traditional role as the primary caregiver, for example, when it is provided to accommodate women's needs in rearing children. These measures require further justification or clear scientific evidence, if there is any, on safety and health concerns, or concerns about fertility, and why they should apply differently to men and women. The decision to exclude women from certain categories of 'hazardous' employment could be viewed as unacceptable by many people, especially westerners, and as discriminatory in nature, even if the alleged purpose is to provide proper protection for women.

Other special protection mechanisms carry with them the same problem. The lower mandatory retirement ages for women, as have been contested

(Beijing, China Workers' Press, 2001) 142; Wang, Q, *Labour and Employment Law* (Beijing, Law Press China, 2008) 135; and Lin, Y, 'Problems on Special Labour Protection for Female Workers and Countermeasures' (2011) 11 *Law Magazine* 59, 59.

[53] See Cooney, Biddulph and Zhu, above n 46, at 63.
[54] See 'Montréal Principles', above n 43.
[55] CEDAW, above n 32, art 11(2) d.

in South Africa and the EU, could be discriminatory to men for whom access to pension rights at an earlier age is of growing importance.[56] This is evident against the background of the unique 'intergenerational division of labour', being when young working couples have to count on their parents to take care of their children.[57] It can also, by obliging women to retire five or even 10 years earlier, reinforce the traditional division of labour between women and men, and the gender-based stereotype that women will not be committed to their career. Further, parental leave that is only available to female workers as a special protection misinterprets the nature of parenthood, which is a joint responsibility. By granting parental leave only to female workers, it not only reinforces gender-based stereotypes and traditional roles, it also creates a 'legitimate' excuse for men to delegate their share of parenthood onto their female partners. These mechanisms fail to accelerate de facto equality between men and women; they offer inappropriate special protections, which only serve to reinforce and exacerbate existing patterns of disadvantage suffered by women.

The Chinese approach to special protection draws some criticism. The UN Committee on the Elimination of Discrimination against Women expressed its concern that '[The Chinese] Government's approach to the implementation of the Convention has an apparent focus on the protection of women rather than on their empowerment … Likewise, labour laws and regulations overemphasize the protection of women'.[58]

Under the fundamental principle of gender equality, states must not only adopt measures of protection, but also take positive measures in all areas so as to achieve the effective and equal empowerment of women.[59] The language used in Chinese laws to refer to special protection, ie, 'prohibit' or 'oblige' instead of 'rights' or 'choice', reflect the embarrassing lack of empowerment of women in China. The decision to remove and exclude female workers from certain employment is not made by women themselves and serves to hinder women's participation in the decision-making process. This chapter will not discuss political participation in China, which differs greatly from other countries, though it is worth noting that China scores

[56] Fredman, above n 41, at 21.

[57] In China, the focus of older adults' lives after retirement will switch from work to family with the majority of older adults playing the role of caregiver rather than care recipient. See Liu, Q and Ke, W, 'Survey and Reflection on the Current Situation of Older Caregivers in Jinan' (2010) 3 *China Journal of Social Work* 201, 201–17.

[58] See UN Committee on the Elimination of Discrimination Against Women, *Report of the Committee on the Elimination of Discrimination Against Women Twentieth Session*, 4 May 1999, UN Doc A/54/38, para 280.

[59] UN Human Rights Committee (HRC), *General Comment No 28: Article 3 (The Equality of Rights Between Men and Women)*, 29 March 2000, UN Doc CCPR/C/21/Rev.1/Add.10.

badly in terms of the participation dimension of Fredman's concept of substantive equality.

Reflection on China's Approach

'Special protection' without empowerment can have a series of repercussions for women, including infringement of their equal employment rights, gender segregation by occupation and fewer social security benefits.[60] Its adverse impact on access to social protection will be discussed in the next section. Some Chinese feminist scholars argue that it would be better to reconceptualise the objectives of these legal protections, replacing the various limitations on women's work with a system of entitlements rather than restrictions, established by reference to research rather than presuppositions.[61] One possible way to do so would be by adding 'empowering elements' into legal protections by giving women the right to decide whether or not they need the protection. The preventive reassignment for pregnant and breastfeeding workers in other countries may provide some clues.[62] It has been shown, after several decades of application, that 'the balance sheet for the right to protective reassignment seems positive for female workers, both directly and indirectly'.[63]

According to CEDAW, protective laws shall be reviewed periodically in light of scientific and technological knowledge and shall be revised, repealed or extended as necessary. In China, the different mandatory retirement ages were established in 1978, and are still effective; the most 'recent' special labour protection was established in 1988, and had been effective through 2012. These protective pieces of legislation have not been reviewed periodically in any sense. In order to update these protective measures, the State Council released the Special Regulations on Labour Protection for Female Workers 2012 which replaced the Regulations on Labour Protection for Female Workers 1988. Annexed to these new Regulations is the new list on the scope of prohibited employment for female workers, replacing the old Regulations on the Scope of Employment Prohibited for Female Workers 1990. The current list of prohibited employment is shorter than the old one. This can be seen a positive step forward in China toward empowerment for women.

[60] Guo and Wang, above n 45, at 38–39.

[61] See Cooney, Biddulph and Zhu, above n 46, at 64.

[62] See, eg, *An Act Respecting Occupational Health and Safety*, RSQ, c S-2.1, ss 40–48.

[63] Lippel, K, 'Preventive Reassignment of Pregnant or Breast-Feeding Workers: The Québec Model' (1998) 2 *New Solutions* 267, 276.

CHALLENGES FOR WOMEN'S ACCESS TO SOCIAL PROTECTION IN CHINA

In the fields of employment and social security, as in other fields, gender equality has long been a self-evident principle in China. The gender neutral language used in relevant legislation indicates that women's equal right to the enjoyment of social security rights has gained formal legal recognition in China. However, even with the help of protective legislation, women are still not on the same footing as men in terms of access to social protection in China; women are facing considerable challenges and obstacles in their pursuit of equal access to social protection.

Challenges Caused by Unfair Employment Practice

Some of these challenges and obstacles are rooted in the de facto unfavourable treatment of women in employment practice. Though in China the fine line between social insurance and social assistance has been crossed by the fact that non-worker residents are also covered by social insurance, namely, medical insurance and the pension scheme, the level of benefits under these social insurance programmes is much lower than those of workers. That said, the level of social protection in China is still largely attached to employment conditions. If women remain the disadvantaged group in employment practice and in the labour market, then they are destined to have less favourable social protection than their male counterparts.

In China, due to the scope of prohibited employment for female workers, the scope of allowable employment for women is narrower than that available to men. This practice unquestionably restricts and limits available employment opportunities for women, though the government and many others still argue that it is a 'protection' for women against hazardous work environments. Even if one admits that this is a form of 'special protection', one must bear in mind that this protection is not without a price, being loss of employment opportunities for women. There is a prevailing stereotype among employers and the general public that women will invest less in human capital and that their career choice will be influenced by their family commitments.[64] This creates a tendency to prefer men over women in the labour market.

The 'special protection' model exacerbates this tendency. The Committee on the Elimination of Discrimination against Women in its report was critical when it said that 'An overemphasis on the protection of, rather than equal

[64] See Yu, S, 'Comparative Study of Anti-Employment Discrimination Laws' (2005) 1 *China Law Science* 129, 130.

opportunities for, women in the labour market perpetuates stereotypes and creates additional obstacles for women competing in a market economy'.[65]

Under the 'special protection' model, employers are obliged to provide most of the special protection for female workers, such as occupational health and safety protection, parental leave and job accommodation for pregnant or breastfeeding female workers. Even if some of these protections, for example, benefits during maternity leave (replacement wage paid by maternity insurance), are not directly provided by employers, they will still affect employers' businesses and productivity. For pregnant or breastfeeding female workers, due to the restrictions on the types of work they are allowed to perform, their employers will have to reassign the work to other workers, causing inconvenience from the perspective of management. In the case of maternity leave, employers have to look for temporary replacement workers during maternity leave (and perhaps also parental leave) to avoid any interruption in their business operation. In short, the special protections add up in such a way that they may adversely influence employers' competitive edge in the market. For employers, one way to avoid incurring the 'extra' expenses on special protection for female workers is to recruit fewer female workers, or not to recruit women at all. The discrimination suffered by female workers in the labour market is the natural result of employers' pursuit of profit maximisation.[66]

The laws on gender equality, targeting mainly 'visible' or direct gender discrimination,[67] do little to stop this discrimination from happening. In a survey on the employment of college graduates conducted in 2010, 68.98 per cent of the employers set specific requirements on gender (most often, the requirement is for males).[68] This result is not surprising to legal scholars in China, as laws only make generalised policy statements that employers shall not engage in any discrimination based on gender, yet lack specificity on the elements of gender discrimination, the burden of proof and similar details.[69] Though the laws make clear that any person who feels aggrieved by employment discrimination can seek remedies by filing a lawsuit, few victims who have actually filed such lawsuits were awarded with remedies.[70]

[65] See *Report of the Committee*, above n 58, at para 296.

[66] See Cai, H, '"Discrimination" in Laws on Anti-Gender Discrimination in Employment: An Economic Perspective' (2005) 8 *Jiangxi Social Science* 150, 155.

[67] See Yue, C and Liu, L, 'Embarrassing Laws Countering Against Employment Discrimination in China' (2011) 7 *Tribune of Social Sciences* 245, 247.

[68] See Constitutionalism Research Institute of China University of Political Science and Law, 'Report on the Survey on Employment Discrimination Encountered by College Graduates' *China Science Daily* (Beijing, 3 August 2010) A3.

[69] See Lin, J, 'On Legal Regulation of Employment Discrimination in China' (2006) 5 *Henan Social Science* 16, 18.

[70] Jiang, Y and Song, Y, 'On the Remedy Approaches of Employment Discrimination' (2012) 1 *Journal of China Institute of Industrial Relations* 58, 59.

Without any operational policies for judges, the generalised legislative language cannot be reduced to concrete judicial practice;[71] the remedy is no more than a hollow promise. The 'special protection' model and the dysfunctional laws against gender discrimination do not stop employers from circumventing the restriction and prohibition imposed by those laws. The prevalent direct and indirect discrimination against women reduces their chance of employment and their labour participation rate. According to the Information Office of the State Council, in 2004 'the number of female workers in urban work units stood at 42.27 million, accounting for 38.1 per cent of the national total'.[72]

This will have repercussions for women's access to social protection, as fewer women than men will have access to relatively high levels of social protection under the social insurance programmes for workers. In addition, due to the fact that workers' contributions and benefits under social insurance programmes are calculated based on their individual salary (payroll from the perspective of employers), the widening gender wage gap (women's wages are only 60.2 per cent of men's wages)[73] which is the result of gender discrimination, will also reduce the level of protection for female workers.

Challenges Posed by the Social Protection System

The remaining challenges and obstacles are caused by the social protection system itself. Though China adheres to the principle of gender equality in providing social protection for all, the lack of existence or flawed design of some mechanisms will have disparate impacts on women, preventing them from having equal access to social protection.

In China, the maternity insurance programme has long been uniquely designed with women-specific benefits: to provide maternity protection for female workers and the unemployed wives of male workers. Under the maternity insurance programme, services like attended births and income replacement during maternity leave are included. However, the limited coverage of maternity insurance has disparate impacts on female workers. Though it has the same compulsory nature as other social insurance programmes, the inspection and enforcement efforts in ensuring employers' participation are relatively relaxed. Compared with 252 million workers covered by medical insurance, only 139 million are covered by maternity

[71] Wang, B, 'On Problems in Judicial Remedies for Employment Discrimination and their Resolution' (2009) 11 *Forward Position* 52, 52.

[72] Information Office of the State Council of the People's Republic of China (IOSC), 'Gender Equality and Women's Development in China' (Beijing, IOSC, August 2005), available at: www.china.org.cn/e-white/20050824/.

[73] Women's Federation and Statistics Bureau of Guangdong Province, 'Third Provincial Survey on Women's Social Status' *Guangzhou Daily* (Guangzhou, 2 March 2012) 12.

insurance, according to statistics from 2011.[74] Due to China's 'unique' way of interpreting 'mandatory nature', that is, default employers who do not participate will have to pay the benefits to their employees, the limited coverage restricts female workers' access to maternity protection under the maternity insurance programme.

Given the fact that maternal and child mortality rates in China are at the global intermediate level and are far behind those in many developed and relatively developed countries,[75] cash transfer programmes should prioritise children under the age of five and pregnant women, in efforts to reach children at an early age.[76] However, there are almost no child benefits in terms of social transfer in cash or in kind to ease the burden of rearing newborn children in China. The absence of such benefits, which when disbursed directly to households and to women themselves can elevate women's social status and allow them to exert more control over how household income is spent,[77] means that a possible chance for gender empowerment is lost. Women can barely find sufficient social services to support them. The lack of public day care centres and nurseries forces a parent, most often the mother, to take care of their children with the help of their parents, thus preserving the still prevalent 'traditional' family model. In this respect, China still lags far behind its obligations under CEDAW:

> States Parties shall take appropriate measures … To encourage the provision of the necessary supporting social services to enable parents to combine family obligations with work responsibilities and participation in public life, in particular through promoting the establishment and development of a network of child-care facilities.[78]

In addition, parental leave, framed as a 'special protection' for female workers (compared with no leave), is only 'available' to female workers and not to their husbands. This runs counter to the requirement in the ICESCR gender equality clause, ie, parental leave must be provided equally for both

[74] National Bureau of Statistics of China, 'Statistical Communiqué on the 2011 National Economic and Social Development' (National Bureau of Statistics China, 22 February 2012), available at: www.stats.gov.cn/english/NewsEvents/201202/t20120222_26575.html.

[75] Ministry of Health of People's Republic of China (MHC), UN Children's Fund (UNICEF), the World Health Organization (WHO) and UN Fund for Population Activities (UNFPA), 'Joint Review of the Maternal and Child Survival Strategy in China' (Beijing, MHC, UNICEF, WHO and UNFPA, 2006), available at: www2.wpro.who.int/NR/rdonlyres/E6C29183-BC8E-4DEF-9A50-3606032E8CB4/0/MaternalandChildSurvivalStrategyinChinaENG.pdf.

[76] See The Save the Children Fund (SCF), 'Social Protection and Child Survival' (London, SCF, 2010), available at: south-south.ipc-undp.org/index2.php?option=com_sobi2&sobi2Task=dd_download&fid=170&format=html&Itemid=137.

[77] See Report of the Advisory Group, above n 15.

[78] CEDAW, above n 32, art 11(2)c.

men and women.[79] This certainly acts as a restraint on female workers, as it reinforces the stereotype and traditional assignment to women of the role of primary caregiver for children, which restricts women's freedom of movement and consequently their access to paid employment and education.[80]

The pension scheme design—especially the different and lower mandatory retirement ages for female workers—also runs contrary to women's equal access to social protection. The current retirement ages, being 60 for male workers, 55 for female workers in managerial roles, and 50 for those in non-managerial roles, were created in the context of a command economy. At that time, the pension was more like a non-contributory defined-benefit system, under which retirees could claim pension benefits from employers (most were state-owned enterprises). The income replacement rate can be as high as 90 per cent,[81] regardless of work history. By allowing female workers to retire five or even ten years earlier while claiming the same pension benefits, can provide a protection for female workers. However, it violates the obligation under the ICESCR's gender equality clause (article 3) in relation to the social security rights clause (article 9), which requires, inter alia, the equalisation of the compulsory retirement age for both men and women.[82] The fundamental reform to the pension system, as part of the overall reform towards a market economy, relates the work history to benefits. The current pension system is a hybrid of a defined-contribution system and a defined-benefit system, under which workers' contribution records, based on the years of work they have completed, will influence the level of benefits they can access after retirement. Under the current system, lower retirement ages for female workers means shortened working careers and shortened contribution histories, which not only deprives the senior female workers of the right to work, but also results in fewer pension benefits.[83]

Other challenges include the portability of social security benefits among different programmes. As mentioned earlier, even under basic pension systems, there are three sub-programmes for different groups within the population: one for workers including migrant workers; one for non-worker urban residents; and one for non-worker rural residents. This segmented system creates a unique problem for migrant workers, who contribute to the basic pension programme for workers, but still 'belong to' the rural areas where they were originally from under *hukou* system. This begs the question: can they carry the contribution records under the one for workers

[79] UN Committee on Economic, Social and Cultural Rights (CESCR), *General Comment No 16: The Equal Right of Men and Women to the Enjoyment of All Economic, Social and Cultural Rights (art 3 of the Covenant)*, 11 August 2005, UN Doc E/C.12/2005/4.

[80] See 'Montréal Principles', above n 43.

[81] Zheng, G, *Study on Social Security in China* (Wuhan, Hubei People's Press, 1994) 122.

[82] ICESCR, above n 33.

[83] Lin, J, 'On Legal Regulation', above n 69, at 18.

over to the one for rural residents? Though the government sought to solve this problem by devising some rules on such a transfer, the chaotic situation and lack of coordination among different jurisdictions at this initial stage so far can still only disadvantage migrant workers, including migrant female workers.

Possible Reform Measures

These challenges and obstacles will adversely influence the effectiveness of the social protection system and will test China's ability to ensure women's equal access to social protection. In tackling these challenges and obstacles, China needs to take into consideration their root causes, and accordingly, attack on two fronts. That is, the 'special protection' model and discrimination in employment practice on the one hand, and the flawed design of the social protection system on the other. The compatibility of existing models of 'special protection' with the current market economy settings should be critically evaluated; its pros and cons for women's equal access to social protection should be objectively analysed. China should step up its efforts in combating gender discrimination in employment, and should launch more women-empowering programmes in order to realise gender equality. In addition, China should also further improve its social protection mechanisms, by detaching social protection from employment conditions and reforming the segmented nature of the social protection system.

6

Evaluating Reforms for Bolivian Women's Rights to Social Security and Social Protection

LORENA OSSIO BUSTILLOS*

INTRODUCTION

THE PLURINATIONAL STATE of Bolivia[1] is the second poorest country in South America after Paraguay.[2] In 2002, the infant mortality rate was 59 deaths per 1000 live births in urban areas, and higher still in rural areas, where the rate is 96 deaths per 1000 live births. For indigenous people the rate is substantially higher than for non-indigenous people; being 87 deaths per 1000 live births for the former and 45 deaths per 1000 live births for the latter.[3] The poverty level in Bolivia has reduced significantly since 2007, from 60.1 per cent to 45 per cent in 2011.[4] Bolivia's population reached 10,027,254 people according to the 2012 census,[5] with a life expectancy at birth of 65 years for men and 69 years for women.[6] The

* The author would like to thank Lucie Lamarche and Beth Goldblatt for their comments.

[1] *Estado Unitario Social de Derecho Plurinacional Comunitario* (Plurinational State of Bolivia), abbreviated herein as Bolivia due to space limitations.

[2] United Nations (UN), *Statistical Yearbook for Latin America and the Caribbean* (Chile, UN, 2013) 75, available at: www.eclac.org/publicaciones/xml/5/51945/1Primeras_paginas.pdf.

[3] Organización Panamericana de la Salud/Organización Mundial de la Salud, *Boletin epidemeológico. Análisis Coyuntural de la Mortalidad en Bolivia*, Vol 23 No 2 June 2002, quoted in Organización Panamericana de la Salud, *Perfil de los sistemas de Salud de Bolivia* (Washington 2007) 11.

[4] *Una década de análisis y propuestas por una vida digna*, Revista Fundación Jubileo Noviembre-no 27, Diciembre 2013, 22, available at: www.jubileobolivia.org.bo/publicaciones/revista-jubileo.html.

[5] Instituto Nacional de Estadística, *Principales Resultados del Censo Nacional de Población y Vivienda 2012 (CNPV 2012)*, Julio 2013, available at: www.eldeber.com.bo/2013/2013-07-31/resultadosCenso2012.pdf.

[6] For the period from 2010 to 2015, see Bolivia, Instituto Nacional de Estadistica, *Proyección de las esperanzas de Vida al Nacer por sexo y períodos según región y departamento, 2000–2030*, available at: www.ine.gob.bo/indice/visualizador.aspx?ah=PC20131.HTM.

differences between the Altiplano plateau, valleys and plains in Bolivia are also reflected in the life expectancy; in the poorest region of high land, for example, the mining department of Potosí, the life expectancy for men is 60 and 64 years[7] for women. Inequalities between rural and urban populations are extremely high, which is why the internal migration from rural to urban centres is increasing. However, social mobility in rural areas is less available for indigenous women than it is for indigenous men. For indigenous women who migrate to the cities, employment opportunities remain limited to working at local market places or in domestic employment. Bolivia submitted its fifth and sixth Periodic Reports to the CEDAW Committee in December 2013.[8] In this Report, Bolivia recognised the important development gap between urban and rural women and between indigenous and non-indigenous women. Further, Bolivia explained the significant role of domestic activities and of the informal sector for women and for indigenous women.[9] According to the 2009 International Labour Organization (ILO) study, employees engaged in a formal employment relationship represent only 25 per cent of the total population and work primarily in urban areas.[10] Self-employed, domestic and rural workers are then excluded from any compulsory social security scheme.

That being said, Bolivia is a prosperous country and one consequence of this prosperity over the last few years[11] has been the remarkable reduction of global poverty by almost 15 points. Nevertheless, it is important to consider that state intervention remains a crucial factor in the reduction of poverty. Since 2006, Bolivia has implemented different cash transfer

[7] *Ibid.*

[8] UN Committee on the Elimination of all Forms of Discrimination against Women (CEDAW), Bolivia, *Examen de los informes presentados por los Estados partes en virtud del articulo 18 de la Convencion sobre la eliminacion de todas las formas de discriminacion contra la mujer—Informes periodicos quinto y sexto combinados que les Estados partes debian presentar en 2011*, Un Doc CEDAW/C/BOL/5-6, 12 December 2013.

[9] *Ibid*, at para 9.

[10] International Labour Organization, Committee of Experts on the Application of Conventions and Recommandations (CEACR), Observation—Bolivia, *Social Security (Minimum Standards) Convention, 1952 (No 102)*–2011, available at: www.ilo.org/dyn/normlex/en/f?p=1000:13100:0::NO:13100:P13100_COMMENT_ID:2699200.

[11] The recent 'International Monetary Fund Report' evaluated positively the yearly economic growth average of Bolivia of 5% between 2006 and 2013, despite the world economic crisis. Its projection estimates that extreme poverty is expected to decrease from 37.7% to 24.1% in 2015. Following this data projection, one of the Millennium Development Goals, to reduce the percentage of extreme poverty by half will be reached; the declaration was based on data from 1996. The source of prosperity has certainly stemmed from high oil prices, from the privatisation of state-owned enterprises and from the renegotiation of international contracts resulting in better conditions and in some cases the re-nationalisation of these enterprises. International Monetary Fund, *IMF Mission Concludes Article IV Consultation Visit to Bolivia*, Press Release No 13/455, 18 November 2013, available at: www.imf.org/external/np/sec/pr/2013/pr13455.htm.

programmes which benefit 36.5 per cent of the population. This percentage is composed of targeted groups. *Bono Juancito Pinto,* created in 2006, improves access to education by providing annual school vouchers to children attending public schools up to grade eight and covers 17.7 per cent of targeted groups. *Bono Juana Azurduy*, another cash transfer programme, provides financial support to mothers, conditional on their attendance at state health centres for pre-natal and post-natal checkups; this programme covers 17.7 per cent of targeted groups. Rural women are four times more likely to die during childbirth or due to complications after birth than urban women. This reflects, among other things, the lack of access to hospitals in rural areas. The cultural practices of indigenous women in giving birth at home may also increase the risk. However, the results of *Bono Juana Azurduy* show that it is possible to reduce female mortality at childbirth not only by providing cash as an incentive to use health services, but also by making access to physicians a real possibility.

Finally, *Renta Dignidad*, a programme introduced in 2007, provides a non-contributory basic pension to those over 60 who have no other source of income, and tops up the pensions of those who benefit from some kind of contributory pension, although the amount is too small to guarantee a decent standard of living. This last measure covers 9.3 per cent of all targeted groups in Bolivia. *Renta Dignidad* is an improvement on the *Bonosol* pension programme introduced in 1996. Those three cash transfer programmes were preceded in 2002 by the creation of a universally accessible health care programme for mothers and children (SUMI), and in 1998 by a programme of the same nature for elderly persons over 60 years of age who were deprived of other insurance (SMVG). In this last case, the contributory annuity (estimated at US$56) is paid by both the National Treasury and the municipalities.

According to the Committee of Experts on the Application of Conventions and Recommendations (CEACR) the health system in Bolivia remains very segmented.[12]

This chapter explores the recent reform of social protection and social security in Bolivia with a gender lens. It pays special attention to the universal pension system, known as *Renta Dignidad.* The first part recalls the constitutional history and evolution of social protection in Bolivia; the second part presents the case of pension in relation to gender; and finally, the last part analyses the gender impact of Renta Dignidad. It is followed by some preliminary conclusions.

[12] CEACR, above n 10.

THE CONSTITUTIONAL HISTORY OF SOCIAL PROTECTION IN BOLIVIA

The History of Unequal Treatment

The legal history of social legislation in Bolivia has demonstrated different socio-political aims since its foundation in 1825. Zacher offers a broad definition of such aims, being the assurance of a life of human dignity for everyone, the reduction of differing levels of material conditions and the relief or control of economically determined dependence.[13] The first liberal Constitution drafted by Simon Bolivar[14] and approved by the Bolivian assembly in 1826, expressed socio-political aims for achieving social equality through the granting of freedom to persons confined in slavery[15] and through the abolishment of special taxes for the indigenous population.[16] The first Constitution is considered a liberal Constitution for the guarantees that it conceded, granting essential levels of human rights protection and social aid for the poor and socially excluded.

Yet women and the indigenous population, who were not considered citizens at that time, were protected in a paternalistic and charitable way. Further, according to the decision of the President of the new Bolivian Republic, article 83(16) of the Constitution of 1826 provides pensions for the military and their families. From the beginning, the history of the constitutional rules of Bolivia reveal legal privileges given to certain sectors or categories of workers, like the military, that still require justification in regard to the principle of equal treatment.

The Bolivian Constitution of 1938 is known as the Social Charta. After the Chaco War between Bolivia and Paraguay (1932–35), an internal political debate began in Bolivia over the nationalisation of the mining enterprises and the social function of property. This resulted in the new Bolivian Constitution of 30 October 1938, which included a constitutional chapter on modern social rights. Article 122 of this Constitution stipulated that a law should regulate a mandatory scheme for sickness, accidents, unemployment, invalidity, old age, maternity and death, and also included other social benefits such as protection of employees, particularly women

[13] Zacher, H and Ross, RB, *Social Legislation in the Federal Republic of Germany* (London, Bedford Square Press, 1983) 9.

[14] At the Congress of Angostura in 1819, Simón Bolívar introduced the term 'social security': *Simón Bolívar: Obras Completas, Volume III* (Lex, La Habana, Cuba 1950) 683.

[15] Art 11 of the first Bolivian Constitution grants freedom to those in slavery. However, this art adds that they still have to stay in the house of their Lords until a law regulates their status. The first law for the protection of rights of employees was passed on 16 November 1896, with the obligation to provide a labour contract and, in case of sickness, to guarantee free health care.

[16] See art 153 of the first Bolivian Constitution. This art was derogated in the next Constitution of 1834.

and children. Article 130 stated for the first time at a constitutional level that social assistance is a function of the state which must be regulated by law, and that social assistance for health care is mandatory and compulsory.

The level of a country's industrialisation, expansion of industries and formal work goes hand in hand with the development of a contributory social security scheme. A lack of industrialisation presents a serious hazard for a landlocked country such as Bolivia, despite its abundance of natural resources (gas, lithium and water). In addition, the poor level of coverage by contributory social security in Bolivia is also explainable by the fact that only about 15 per cent of the population (especially women) belong to the formal sector economy.[17]

Conceptualisation

In Bolivia, the terms 'social security' and 'social insurance' refer to contributory systems. Social assistance benefits are not recognised as such, although more recently the SUMI and SMVG programmes have drawn on universal and non-contributory design.

In the actual context, the evocation of the right to a state of well-being is one that subsumes technical notions such as the nature of social security regimes. Accordingly, it provides an opening for more non-contributory and universal solutions. Law No 300, enacted 15 October 2012,[18] provides a definition of social protection. In a wider sense, the objectives of the public policies in Bolivia are the intercultural terms of *Vivir Bien* and *Madre Tierra*. These terms include all forms of social protection required for an equal society, based on justice and solidarity without social classes, without any kind of poverty and in harmony with mother earth. The efforts to include a new conception of the state which incorporates the principles and values of the indigenous people in the Plurinational State of Bolivia are remarkable but still in progress. Such efforts do not clearly address gender issues, with only a reference in Law No 300 to women as a group to be privileged above others when land is distributed.[19] The principle of gender equality cannot be found under the notion of equal society and *Vivir Bien*.

[17] The highest coverage of the economically active population (EAP) at 1980 began notably to decrease and fell by 18.6% to 11.9% in 1985, when state participation in the mining companies was reduced and public enterprises were closed and the labour law act was changed by decree. Unidad de Análisis de políticas sociales y económicas- Ministerio de Planificación del Desarrollo Estado Plurinacional de Bolivia 2013, 22, available at: www.udape.gob.bo/evaluaciondeimpacto/12_Documento_Impacto%20Renta%20Dignidad.pdf.

[18] Gaceta Oficial de Bolivia No 431 NEC, *Ley Marco de la Madre Tierra y Desarrollo Integral para Vivir Bien*, 15 October 2012.

[19] *Ibid*, at art 28(2).

Bolivia is also a very violent society for women. After Haiti, Bolivia is the country in the region with the most sexual violence against women. Abortion remains a criminal offence in Bolivia, although a recent decision of the Bolivian Constitutional Plurinational Court declared that women have a right to access medical services for abortion when pregnancy is the result of rape, and do not have to wait for a criminal conviction of the assaulter to be granted this access.[20] This judgment has been criticised by some conservative sectors of Bolivian society.[21]

The impunity for perpetrators of sexual violence against women in Bolivia remains very high, with only 0.04 per cent of all cases of sexual violence against women resulting in a judicial sentence. To combat this, Law No 348[22] was enacted in 2013 to guarantee women a life without violence and includes the new offence of femicide, defined as the murder of women, which is punishable with a prison sentence of 30 years. The mitigation of the punishment for murder in an emotional situation was removed, which had previously been used primarily to the benefit of men. In addition, special Law 243[23] was enacted in 2012 to protect women in political positions from harassment. It is important to consider the context of Bolivian society and the lack of protection from the state for women, in order to analyse the special field of social security and social protection and the development of legislation.

Article 67 of the new Constitution of Bolivia of January 2009 recognises the right to grow older in dignity and to lead a quality life characterised by human warmth. The concepts of dignity and human warmth are subject to constitutional interpretation and could, therefore, be considered as principles and not as subjective rights. Furthermore, article 45 of the Constitution provides for everybody the right to social security. This guarantee is not conditioned by means-tested measures. Section 45(IV) states that it is the responsibility of the state to provide universal and equitable social security to all and section 45(VI) prohibits the privatisation of social security in Bolivia.

Finally, the Constitution of Bolivia guarantees women's right to equality (article II(I)) and prohibits all forms of discrimination (article 14(II)). However, the gender gap remains very high in Bolivia and influences

[20] Bolivia, Tribunal Constitucional Plurinacional, SC 0206/2014, 5 February 2014, available at: www.tcpbolivia.bo/tcp/sites/default/files/images/comunicados/ABORTO2.pdf.

[21] Barrios, F La Razón, available at: www.la-razon.com/opinion/columnistas/Licencia-aniquilar-vida_0_2012798739.html.

[22] Gaceta Oficial de Bolivia No 494 NEC, *Ley integral para garantizar a las mujeres una vida libre de violencia*, 9 March 2013.

[23] Gaceta Oficial de Bolivia No 376 NEC, *Ley contra el acoso y violencia politica hacia las mujeres*, 21 May 2012.

the challenges attached to realising women's right to social security and protection, especially in regard to pensions.

THE EVOLUTION OF SOCIAL SECURITY AND PENSIONS IN BOLIVIA

Bolivia's provision of public pensions dates from the early 1900s, yet its social security system was not actually set up until after the Constitution of 1938. Implementation began with the promulgation of the first, and still valid, Social Security Code on 14 December 1956. The code was a public pension system with defined contributions pensions. This was a legal innovation in Bolivia that was directly connected to the ILO Social Security (Minimum Standards) Convention No 102.[24] The structure of the Social Security Code covers three areas: social insurance, families and a housing allowance scheme. Bolivia ratified Convention No 102 on 31 January 1977, during the period of governance by the military dictatorship of General Hugo Banzer Suarez. Twenty years later, under President Gonzalo Sanchez, the social security system saw radical change and, with the technical assistance of the World Bank, was transformed in 1997 into a new social security scheme (individualised and privatised pension funds). On 29 November 1996, Law No 1732[25] was enacted, and the old pay-as-you-go (PAYG) pension system as well as 38 complementary pension funds, were replaced with obligatory social insurance, which provided pre-funded, individual accounts under private management by the pension fund administrators (AFPs). Article 22 of Law No 1732 established the Fund of Individual Capitalisation and the Fund of Collective Capitalisation, both linked with Law No 1544 on Privatisation (called Capitalisation in Bolivia).[26]

The private system integrated all previous pension schemes; charged the lowest administrative fees in Latin America; reinforced the relationship between the contribution and pension levels; and achieved one of the highest regional capital accumulations relative to GDP. Conversely, it failed to

[24] ILO Convention C102: Social Security (Minimum Standards) Convention (Convention Concerning Minimum Standards of Social Security) (adopted 28 June 1952, entered into force 27 April 1955).

[25] Gaceta Oficial de Bolivia No 1962 NEC, *Ley de Pensiones (The Pensions Act)*, 29 November 1996.

[26] The structural reforms of the pension system were carried out during the first presidency of Sanchez e Losada (1993–97) against the backdrop of Washington Consensus-type reforms. Accordingly, the largest state-owned enterprises in Bolivia were privatised. The partial (51%) capitalisation of *Yacimientos Petroliferos Fiscales Bolivianos* (YPFB), the state oil and gas companies, was implemented by Law No 1544 (Gaceta Oficial de Bolivia No 1962 NEC, *Ley de capitalización*, 21 March 1994). This process was further extended to the partial privatisation of five nationally-owned industries: *Empresa Nacional de Electricidad*, ENDE (electricity); *Empresa Nacional de Telecomunicaciones*, ENTEL (telecommunications); *Lloyd Areo Boliviano*, LAB (airlines); *Empresa Nacional de Ferrocarriles*, ENFE (railroads); and EMV (tin/antimony).

increase the coverage of the economically active population (EAP) (one of the two lowest in Latin America); lacked social solidarity (partly contributed to by the state with *Bonosol*); expanded gender inequalities; failed originally to guarantee the minimum pension and compensation for previous contributions (both added later with restrictions); provided very low benefits; abolished social participation in the system administration; and eliminated the employer's contribution.

The female share in total affiliation rose slightly from 33.6 per cent to 35.4 per cent in the years between 1999 and 2010, whereas the female proportion of the EAP was significantly smaller than that of the male population and decreased from 11.6 per cent to 10.6 per cent between 1999 and 2005, becoming the lowest in Latin America.[27] The average monthly income gap between women and men expanded by 91 per cent in the period from 2000 to 2009, from US$65 to US$103. The percentage distribution of contributions by gender in 2003 was 66 per cent for men and 34 per cent for women and deteriorated to 73.4 per cent and 26.6 per cent respectively in 2010. Average female pensions in 2010 were lower than for men; depending on the type of pension they ranged from 39 per cent to 86 per cent of the average male pension.[28]

In private systems women receive lower pensions than men because of family-related non-employment periods, in which gainful employment is completely given up for child raising or caregiving responsibilities. This plays a major part in women's employment biographies. Contrary to public systems, in private systems there are no compensated exits from the labour market to raise children. Further, women have a lower contribution density than men due to pension calculations being based on the funds accumulated in the individuals' account, and sex-differentiated mortality tables. Having a lower capitalised fund and a higher life expectancy results in women's annuity being lower than that of men.The proportion of elderly females receiving any type of pension fell from 23.7 per cent in 1995 to 12.8 per cent in 2007, but the proportion covered by the *Renta Dignidad* was 54 per cent in 2008. The privatised pension system has brought more disadvantages, especially for women. In contrast to other Latin American countries, the change of system was mandatory in Bolivia, leaving no option for choosing better conditions and lacking a minimum pension. This sytem was introduced several years later under the next government.

[27] Asociación Internacional de Organismos de Supervisión de Fondos de Pensiones (AIOS), *Boletín Estadística* (AIOS 1999–2011), available at: www.aiosfp.org/estudios_publicaciones/estudios_pub_boletin_estadistico.shtml.

[28] Government of Bolivia, Instituto Nacional de Estadistica, Autoridad de Fiscalización y Control de Pensiones y Seguros, 2011, available at: www.ine.gob.bo/indice/EstadisticaSocial.aspx?codigo=30501.

In 2010, the Plurinational Assembly approved the new Law of Pensions that changed the 1997 pension rules, although the different former systems did not immediately disappear as this transition will certainly take years.[29] The new system is comprised of three branches: (a) contributory pensions for old-age-disability-survivor pensions which are financed by contributions alone; (b) semi-contributory pensions which cover the same risks but are financed by contributions and a new solidarity fund; and (c) non-contributory pensions for *Renta Dignidad*.

The legal reform maintained the special regime for the armed forces administration of the military scheme (COSSMIL). Workers in mining, metallurgy and under insalubrious conditions that contributed to the closed public system can retire at age 56; and for each year of work, one year of contribution is reduced, for up to five years, allowing retirement at age 51. On the other hand, the reform equalised the previously different ceilings between pensioners of the closed public system (14 times the minimum wage) to those in the private system (60 times the minimum wage).

The important changes include a new social model, which will improve the low pensions through a *Fondo Solidario* (Solidarity Fund). It is called *Fondo Solidario* because it applies a mechanism for redistribution of income, in that those women or men who earn more will offset those with a low-income salary. The objective is to extend the coverage of the social security system, especially to independent workers. A minimum of 10 years of contributions is required to accede to the pension.

This law reduces the age at which entitlement to a pension is triggered from 60 to 58. The explanation given by the government concerning gender equality refers to the special treatment that the pension provides to mothers. To compensate women for the time devoted to raising their children, the pension reform allows insured mothers with 10 years of contributions, paid into either the old public system, the private system, or the new system, to reduce the age at which they will be entitled to a pension by one year for each child born alive, with a three-year maximum reduction. On the other hand, a widow pensioner loses this benefit if she remarries or is a cohabiting spouse. There was a proposal to include a clause which obliged the affiliated spouse to contribute in favour of the unaffiliated partner (*aporte conyugal*) in order to cover housewives. This clause, however, was eliminated due to opposition from trade unions and consequently is not present in the final law. As a result of the pension reforms, women's share of pensions has increased slightly: in total, affiliates to the contributory programme rose from 34.6 per cent to 35.4 per cent in the period between 2007 and 2012, and, in total, contributory pensions rose from 17 per cent to 18 per cent between 2007 and 2010.

[29] Gaceta Oficial de Bolivia No 201 NEC, *Ley de pensiones*, 10 December 2010.

THE IMPACT OF *RENTA DIGNIDAD* ON GENDER EQUALITY

Universal Old-Age Pension: *Renta Dignidad*

The *Renta Dignidad*, with different titles in the past (*Bonosol, Bolivida*), in contrast to other cash transfer programmes, like *Bono Juancito Pinto* or *Bono Juana Azurduy de Padilla*, has been part of a historical and political process.[30] This is evidenced by the fact that it has remained in place despite changes to governments that represented different ideological positions, from the 'neo-liberal' period to the Social Communitarian State in Bolivia. Even though the domestic resources for financing the *Renta Dignidad* have changed over these different political periods, there has been no discussion or debate around the justification given for the provision of this social benefit. The social mobilisation againt the central government's decision came later from the universites and regions in the form of discussion of the new redistribution of direct tax on hydrocarbons (impuesto directo a los hidrocarburos, IDH) through an executive decree.

The *Renta Dignidad* benefits 1,023,612 citizens over the age of 60 in urban and rural areas, which is 9.3 per cent of the Bolivian population.[31] Of this total, 67 per cent are concentrated in three regions (La Paz, Cochabamba and Santa Cruz); 83 per cent do not have another pension; and 17 per cent do.

Law No 3791[32] regarding the universal old-age pension, *Renta Dignidad*, or dignity income, was enacted on 28 November 2007. It established the monthly payment of 200 Bolivian Boliviano (Bs), approximately US$28 (or Bs 2400 per year, approximately US$340) for all resident citizens over 60 years of age, who were not already receiving a contributory pension or income from the state (civil servants); and for those receiving a pension, a payment of 75 per cent of the monthly payment mentioned, equalling Bs 150, approximately US$21 (or Bs 1800 per year, approximately US$255). With Law No 378,[33] enacted on 16 May 2013, the amount was increased by Bs 50 approximately US$7, to the monthly payment of approximately US$35, or Bs 3000 per year, approximately US$425. For those receiving a pension, the restriction of 75 per cent was revoked, so they now receive

[30] Müller, K, 'Contested Universalism: From Bonosol to Renta Dignidad in Bolivia' (2009) 18(2) *International Journal of Social Welfare* 163.

[31] Government of Bolivia, Ministerio de Economía y Finanzas Públicas, *Población beneficiada con la transferencias directas condicionadas a diciembre 2013*, 30 December 2013, available at: medios.economiayfinanzas.gob.bo/MH/documentos/RAF/2014/Enero2014/Bonos_280114.pdf.

[32] Gaceta Oficial de Bolivia No 3046 NEC, *Ley de la Renta Universal de Vejez (Renta Dignidad)*, 28 November 2007.

[33] Gaceta Oficial de Bolivia No 525 NEC, *Ley de la Renta Universal de Vejez (Renta Dignidad)*, 16 May 2013.

Bs 2400 per year, approximately US$340. The monthly sum of *Renta Dignidad* is 10 per cent of the average contributory pension. In 2012, the minimum pension in the contributory branch equalled the national minimum wage (US$145) and the contributory pension 60 times that minimum wage (US$8700), both high for Bolivia, whereas the semi-contributory pension may be lower than the minimum wage and has a maximum of US$376.

According to articles 8 and 9 of Law No 3791, the Universal Old-Age Pension Fund was created to finance the payment of this benefit. The fund is made up of 30 per cent of the resources of the Hydrocarbon Direct Tax, the prefectures, the Indigenous Fund and The National General Treasure (TGN) and the dividends from capitalised public enterprises. Article 7 provides that the payment of *Renta Dignidad* is to expire after a year passes where the amount is not collected. The sentence: 'this right to this benefit is guaranteed' was added by executive decree.

The Executive Decree of Law No 3791[34] concerning the *Renta Dignidad*, enacted in December 2007, improves the security of the payment from the government's perspective, as it regulates the madatory registration data of beneficiaries and establishes the mandatory requisite identity document (different from a birth certificate). It also provides for the payment of funeral expenses, stipulating an allowance of Bs 1800, approximately US$254, for the year 2008. Payments to those without another pension are made by financing institutions and mobile units of the armed forces in rural areas without banking subsidiaries, whereas to those with pensions from the AFPs, payments are made by insurance companies and COSSMIL.[35]

In the Context of the Informal Economy

The link between the gender impact of legal reforms on social security for women working in the informal sector and for indigenous women is not easy to make, and this is not only due to a lack of data. If we focus on the conceptualisation of work in the informal economy being like an occupation in the labour market but without access to social security benefits, then most self-employed women in Bolivia, selling for example products at local markets, live without social insurance. Therefore, the non-contributory old-age pension scheme has the positive impact of reducing extreme poverty

[34] Geceta Oficial de Bolivia No 3052 NEC, *Reglamento a la Ley No 3791 de 28 noviembre de 2007, de la Renta Universal de Vejez (Renta Dignidad) y los Gastos Funerales*, 29 December 2007.

[35] Estado Plurinacional de Bolivia, Vice Ministerio de Pensiones y Servicios Financieros (VMPSF) (2012), *Boletín Mensual del Sistema de Pensiones*, 7/78 (September 2012), available at: medios.economiayfinanzas.gob.bo/VPSF/documentos/Boletines/2012/Binder78tuc.pdf.

in rural areas. This political measure enjoys broad support throughout the Bolivian population, yet the social inequity persists.

Two-thirds of the labour force in Bolivia are virtually uncovered or covered only by voluntary affiliation. There is an important distinction beteen affiliation and contribution. The EAP data,[36] based on affiliates, has steadily climbed and is about three times that based on contributors. For data based on affiliation, it is sufficient to be affiliated and to pay one contribution. According to survey data concerning all social security schemes, EAP coverage in Bolivia based on contributions was 15 per cent per cent in 2007.[37] Within Latin America, Bolivia had the lowest coverage.[38] Voluntary affiliation of self-employed and other informal workers is discouraged by imposing upon them a total contribution of 14.42 per cent of their income. The agricultural seasonal workers are given the choice to affiliate either as self-employed or as wage earners.

Bolivian women have a considerably lower share of salaried work than men, but the opposite holds true in the informal sector, with virtually all domestic employees being women. For domestic workers, there is only optional social security coverage available and it is difficult to enforce. The following figures do seem to point to a certain improvement in the gender data:[39] in 1999, the proportion of men employed in the informal sector was 58 per cent, while for women this was 70 per cent. Eight years later, official data showed that 44.2 per cent of men worked in the informal sector, while for women this was 56.5 per cent. Thus, the high percentage of women in the informal sector is explained not only by the lack of formal employment positions held by women, but also by women's preference for flexibility regarding working times.[40] Even though, according to some Bolivian studies the gender gap in formal employment has narrowed in recent years, further interpretation of this data reveals that the stereotype of the traditional role of women has not really been questioned.

Findings from a number of studies[41] on land ownership in communities on the Altiplano plateau in Bolivia indicate indirectly that *Renta Dignidad*

[36] Estado Plurinacional de Bolivia, Instituto Nacional de Estadística, Autoridad de Fiscalización y Control de Pensiones y Seguros, 1998–2011, available at: www.ine.gob.bo/indice/EstadisticaSocial.aspx?codigo=30501.

[37] Mesa-Lago, C, *Reassembling Social Security: A Survey of Pension and Health Care Reforms in Latin America* (Oxford, Oxford University Press, 2008).

[38] Picado Chacón, G and Durán Valverde, F, *República de Bolivia: Diagnóstico del Sistema de Seguridad Social* (Lima, International Labour Organization, Oficina Sub-Regional para los Países Andinos, 2009).

[39] Data from Evia, JL and Pacheco, N, 'Bolivia' in *Sector Informal y Políticas Públicas en América Latina* (Río de Janeiro, KAS-SOPLA, 2010).

[40] *Ibid*, conclusions from the study.

[41] The results of the study entitled '*Los nietos de la Reforma Agraria: acceso, tenencia y uso de la tierra en el Altiplano de Bolivia*' ('The grandsons of the Agrar Revolution: Access, Tenure and Use of the high land in Bolivia' (our translation) (Urioste F de C, M, Fundacion

has substantial positive impacts on a wide range of variables. We can conclude that due to the complexity of land ownership in rural areas, not only do indigenous mothers and daughters depend on men, who typically work the land, but further the whole family as a unit (*peon*) depends on the 'white' owner of the individual property,[42] and therefore the *Renta Dignidad* is a source of self-determination for elderly women.

Non-contributory pension programmes reduce poverty among the elderly and their households; enable investment in human and physical capital within beneficiary households increasing the income of the household to 20.7 per cent and per capita consumption to 15.4 per cent;[43] strengthen intergenerational solidarity and transfers; insure poorer rural communities against the adverse effects of agricultural reform; and encourage local economic activity. Nevertheless, indigenous elderly women still face multidimensional discrimination. For example, in the Aymara and Quechua culture, coming of age is considered to be achieved when the union equivalent to marriage is formalised in the indigenous community. The access to land inherited by a woman in some indigenous communities first takes place after she gets married. Most women in rural areas do not have identity documents or even birth certificates; therefore, they neither have access to basic health insurance nor to *Renta Dignidad*. They do not have the political space for decision making, and they also face cultural and language barriers. In Bolivia there are only 43 public retirement homes, 20 of which are in La Paz, while the rest of the country has only one or two in each administrative district. There are no common standard rules for the national operation of these public retirement homes; many of them look after poor women with some level of incapacity.

CONCLUSION

In Bolivia, those with limited coverage under the social security scheme, in terms of pensions and health protection, are primarily self-employed domestic workers (the large majority of whom are women) and rural workers

Tierra, Bolivia, 2005)) showed that, between 1953 and 1992, 10% of the beneficiaries (66,325 men) of the national land endowment received 30% (13 million hectares) of the distributed land area. Until 1978, 96% of the total land area restored was individual property, while the outstanding 4% was collective property (which means indigenous property).

[42] Based also on the study 'Saneamiento en su laberinto' ('Reorganization in its Labyrinth') (Fundacion Tierra, Bolivia, 2005) 70.

[43] This is only evidenced for urban areas, Estado Plurinacional de Bolivia, Ministerio de Planification del Desarrollo, Unidad de analiss de Politicas sociales y Economicas, *El impacto de la Renta Dignidad: Política de Redistribución del Ingreso, Consumo y Reducción de la Pobreza en Hogares con Personas Adultas Mayores*, La Paz 2013, 88, available at: www.udape.gob.bo/evaluaciondeimpacto/12_Documento_Impacto%20Renta%20Dignidad.pdf.

(the large majority of whom are indigenous people). The creation of a social security system was, and remains focused on covering the employed workers (the large majority of whom are men), benefiting from formal employment and working, essentially, in urban enterprises.

Bolivia has administered different pensions systems over a short period of time that have made significant differences to women. The first pay-as-you-go (PAYG) pension system provided some advantages for women, giving consideration to their particular roles as mothers and wives, although a small percentage of women benefited from such pensions. Through the private pension systems, a type of gender neutral equality has been adopted that reformulates the pension system and changes the entitlements previously only available to men, so that they are conferred on both men and women. However, the formally equal access to pension benefits with the individual accounts produced disadvantages for women, because differences were not taken into account. By contrast, entitlements created by *Renta Dignidad*, based on citizenship and residence, have been of particular importance to women in Bolivia and are a result of formally equal access to newly available social benefits. Entitlements based on citizenship neutralise the influence of strong patriarchal and traditional cultural patterns adopted in rural areas and could reduce discrimination suffered by rural as opposed to urban populations.

7

Recent Coverage Developments in Social Security Protection for Chilean Women

PABLO ARELLANO ORTIZ

INTRODUCTION

THE CHILEAN PENSION system has been strongly criticised since its very beginning. Following the Chilean model, many Latin American and eastern European countries have privatised their pension systems as well.[1] In 1980, the Pinochet regime created a system of retirement pensions based on individual capitalisation of retirement accounts invested with private pension fund managers. The system essentially functions as a 'compulsory private savings programme'. All new workers entering the workforce are required to contribute at least 10 per cent of their wages to an account of their choosing, and self-employed workers were offered the same option. Other workers were given the possibility of joining the new system and to move their accumulated pension contributions to an individualised account. However recent developments have confirmed that today the privatisation of systems is in retreat.[2]

For the purposes of this chapter, social security will be understood as

> an integrated set of principles, rules and institutions of state management, that aim to provide protection to the people against the contingencies or states of need (social risk) through benefits (social transfers) in cash or in kind, contributory or

[1] See Arellano Oritz, P, 'Protection of Old Age in Chile' in U Becker, F Pennings and T Dijkhoff (eds), *International Standard-Setting and Innovations in Social Security* (The Netherlands, Kluwer Law International, 2013).

[2] Calvo, E, Bertranou, F and Bertranou, E, 'Are Old-Age Pension System Reforms Moving Away from Individual Retirement Accounts in Latin America?' (2010) 39(2) *Journal of Social Policy* 223.

non-contributory funding, whose administration can be public and/or private. The state must ensure a minimum of protection to its population.[3]

From its beginning, social security coverage provided by the Chilean pension fund model has had several serious issues in terms of compliance with international standards. The International Labour Organization's (ILO) Committee of Experts on the Application of Conventions and Recommendations (CEACR) has noted, for several years, the key issues that need to be reformed. The conclusions of the Conference Committee on the Application of Standards recalled in 2001 that the Chilean case had been examined in 1987, 1993 and 1995, and had been the subject of three representations.[4] Today there is one more representation, presented by the College of Teachers of Chile AG specifically concerning the 'historic debt'.[5]

[3] Cifuentes Lillo, H and Arellano Ortiz, P, 'Derecho a la Seguridad Social y la Protección por Pensiones de Vejez, Invalidez y Sobrevivencia en Chile' in I Rojas Miño (ed), *Cincuenta Años de la Sociedad Chilena de Derecho del Trabajo y de la Seguridad Social: Homenaje* (Santiago, Legal Publishing, 2011) 186.

[4] International Labour Organization (ILO), *Report of the Committee set up to examine the Representation Submitted by the National Trade Union Coordinating Council (CNS) of Chile under article 24 of the ILO Constitution, Alleging Non-Observance by Chile of International Labour Conventions Nos 1, 2, 24, 29, 30, 35, 37, 38 and 111 (Vol LXXI, 1988, Series B, Supplement 1)*; *Report of the Committee Set Up to Examine the Representation Alleging Non-Observance by Chile of the Old-Age Insurance (Industry, etc) Convention, 1933 (No 35) and the Invalidity Insurance (Industry, etc) Convention, 1933 (No 37) Submitted Under Article 24 of the ILO Constitution by the College of Teachers of Chile AG* (GB.271/18/1 and GB.274/16/4, 1999); *Report of the Committee Set Up to Examine the Representation Alleging Non-Observance by Chile of the Old-Age Insurance (Industry, etc) Convention, 1933 (No 35), the Old-Age Insurance (Agriculture) Convention, 1933 (No 36), the Invalidity Insurance (Industry, etc) Convention, 1933 (No 37) and the Invalidity Insurance (Agriculture) Convention, 1933 (No 38), Made Under Article 24 of the ILO Constitution by a Number of National Trade Unions of Workers of the Private Sector Pension Funds (AFPs)* (GB.273/15/4 and GB.277/17/5, 2000); *Report of the Committee Set Up to Examine the Representation Alleging Non-Observance by Chile of the Old-Age Insurance (Industry, etc) Convention, 1933 (No 35), and the Invalidity Insurance (Industry, etc) Convention, 1933 (No 37), Made Under Article 24 of the ILO Constitution by the College of Teachers of Chile AG* (GB.292/17/1 and GB.298/15/6, 2006).

[5] International Labour Organization (ILO), *Representation Alleging Non-Observance by Chile of the Old-Age Insurance (Industry, etc) Convention, 1933 (No 35), and the Invalidity Insurance (Industry, etc) Convention, 1933 (No 37), Made Under Article 24 of the ILO Constitution by the College of Teachers of Chile AG* (GB.308/7, 2010 and GB.310/18/3, 2011). The ILO Governing Body decided that the representation was receivable and to establish a committee to examine the representation. The issue of the 'historic debt' of social security results from the failure of the Chilean government to take into account part of the remuneration of nearly 80,000 teachers for the purposes of calculating the right to a pension. In November 2009, the government's refusal to acknowledge the 'historic debt' prompted a national strike by teachers and internal political conflict.

However, the most important statement on compliance with international standards was made by the ILO's Governing Body in March 2000.[6] It resulted in the following recommendations being made concerning the Chilean situation: (i) that the pension system established in 1980 by Law Decree No 3.500,[7] as amended, should be administered by non-profit-making organisations; (ii) that representatives of the insured should participate in the administration of the system under conditions determined by national law and practice; and (iii) that employers should contribute to the financing of the insurance system. These recommendations remain valid for Chile even after the 2008 reform,[8] and they were repeated in the CEACR reports in 2010[9] and 2011.

The recommendations were made in relation to the problems of coverage as provided by the Chilean model. These problems have been repeated in many of the countries that have adopted the Chilean model. In Chile, the objective of privatisation has failed to create uniformity and extension of pension coverage. In addition, it has not always been well suited to the cultures of the countries in which it has been implemented. Some of these problems were solved by the 2008 reform, which introduced solutions to coverage gaps through major initiatives in the area of the self-employed, and also in the protection of women. The reform of 2008 introduced a new non-contributory set of benefits that completely changed the Chilean framework, but that also, at the same time, confirmed the fact that the pension funds and their contributory schemes play an important role in coverage. The non-contributory measures introduced will be described and then a reference to the amendment introduced for the pension funds will be made.

This chapter focuses on the protection of women after the 2008 reform. Women in Chile face difficulties including: reduced participation in the labour market (only 38 per cent of Chilean women are employed); lower salaries (women receive a 30 per cent lower salary than men in the same position); and the focus on the family required by women during certain periods of their lives. These factors have combined to create an inequality of

[6] International Labour Organization (ILO), *Report Of The Committee Set Up To Examine The Representation Alleging Non-Observance By Chile Of The Old-Age Insurance (Industry, etc) Convention, 1933 (No 35), The Old-Age Insurance (Agriculture) Convention, 1933 (No 36), The Invalidity Insurance (Industry, etc) Convention, 1933 (No 37), and the Invalidity Insurance (Agriculture) Convention, 1933 (No 38), Made Under Article 24 Of The ILO Constitution By A Number Of National Trade Unions Of Workers Of The Private Sector Pension Funds (AFPS)* (GB.277/17/5, 2000).

[7] Law Decree No 3.500 *OJ 1980-11-13*.

[8] These arguments are developed in Arellano Ortiz, P and Cifuentes Lillo, H, 'Legislación Chilena de Pensión e Indicaciones de la Comisión de Expertos de la OIT' (2010) 1(1) *Revista Chilena de Derecho de Trabajo y de la Seguridad Social* 123.

[9] See ILO, above n 6.

old-age pension benefits for women in comparison to the male population. Before the 2008 reform, the only existing measures in favour of women were a lower retirement age of 60 and a survivor's pension in the case of widowhood. It should be noted that the objective of these measures was never to create equality between men and women.

In this context, the 2008 reform establishes two categories of measures to expand coverage for women. The first category includes general measures which predominately benefit women. This category includes the 'basic solidarity pension' and the 'solidarity-based top-up benefit'; two assistance measures that have the goal of extending coverage provided by pensions. Estimates suggest that approximately 60 per cent of beneficiaries of these measures are women. According to other estimations, 250,000 women who have no right to any other pension will receive the basic solidarity pension and 30,000 more the solidarity-based top-up benefit.

The second category is aimed more specifically at the protection of women under the relevant contribution mechanisms. The measures that fall under this category benefit women directly and try to re-establish a balance between the savings of men and women. They are called 'gender equity measures' within the reform.

This chapter first analyses the general non-contributory measures introduced by the 2008 reform, and then the specific measures adopted in favour of women. Second, the situation of the family in relation to social security in Chile is examined. This is followed by some overall conclusions.

INTRODUCTION OF A NON-CONTRIBUTORY MECHANISM: TOWARDS A UNIVERSAL EXTENSION OF COVERAGE

In her 2006 campaign, former President Michelle Bachelet (re-elected in December 2013) proposed a reform of the pension system. As a result, one of her first decisions upon taking office was to appoint an advisory board to discuss this matter, known as the Marcel Commission.[10] The proposals developed by this Committee were included in a legal project drafted by the end of 2006,[11] presented to Parliament in 2007, promulgated on 17 March 2008, and entering into force on 1 July 2008.[12]

[10] See 'Consejo Asesor Presidencial para la Reforma Previsional, [Comision Marcel]' (Congreso Nacional de Chile, 2006), available at: www.bcn.cl/carpeta_temas_profundidad/temas_profundidad.2007-09. See also Delano, M, *Reforma Previsional en Chile. Protección Social para Todos* (International Labour Office, 2010).

[11] Government of Chile, Legislative Session 130, January 2008, Boletin 4742-13, *Sistema de pensiones solidarias.*

[12] Law No 20.255, OJ 2008-03-17. On this law see Walker, F and Cifuentes, H, 'Aspectos Generales de la Ley que Establece una Reforma Previsional' (2008) *Revista Laboral Chilena* 88; see also, Walker, F and Cifuentes, H, 'Principales Aspectos Institucionales del Proyecto de Ley que Perfecciona el Sistema de Pensiones' (2007) 154 *Revista de Economía y Administración* 58.

The solidarity pension scheme introduced by the reform consolidated, harmonised and improved the regime of basic pensions and the regime of minimum guaranteed pensions that existed before the full enforceability of Law 20.255.[13] These mechanisms suffered, as they were heavily dependent on the government budget and the availability of resources, which exhibited a large deficit in coverage, and were not designed to give rights but only to confer conditional benefits. The new non-contributory mechanism provides two types of benefits through a legal rights-based approach: one for those who lack contributory capacity, the basic solidarity pension, and another for those with a very limited contributory capacity, the solidarity-based top-up benefit.

The Basic Solidarity Pension

The basic solidarity pension is financed by the state general budget, which means that it is a non-contributory mechanism, and is managed by the Instituto de Previsión Social (IPS). This new mechanism of the Chilean pension system[14] offers a solid foundation for the protection against the associated risks of old age. This reform established a minimum pension for a large majority of Chileans and benefits are aimed at those who meet certain criteria: the elderly; those of low socio-economic status; and those resident during a specified period. Those who meet the conditions benefit from a basic solidarity pension financed by the state, known as a non-contributory pension. To qualify for a basic solidarity pension, people must meet the following criteria:

1. They have no right to a pension under any regime.
2. The person is at least 65 years old, the current legal retirement age for men. For women, the legal retirement age is 60 years, so for a woman to receive the benefit she must wait five years longer than if she had retired under a contributory pension fund mechanism. However, this chapter would argue that this measure is to prevent age discrimination and that the retirement age of women will increase to 65 in the near future.
3. The person is part of a family group belonging to the poorest 60 per cent of the population.
4. The person can prove residence in the Chilean national territory for at least 20 years, either continuously or intermittently, of which four of the years were during the five years preceding the application of the solidarity pension. This criterion of residence creates a link between the

[13] *Ibid.*

[14] Mesa-Lago, C, 'La Protection Sociale au Chili: des Réformes Pour Plus de Justice' (2008) 147(4) *Revue internationale du travail* 428; and Walker and Cifuentes 'Aspectos Generales', above n 12; Walker and Cifuentes 'Principales Aspectos', above n 12.

> benefit and Chilean citizenship. This is even more so as foreigners that have resided in Chile for 20 years are also entitled to receive the benefit. No doubt this represents important progress in terms of the extension of social protection. This period of 20 years' residence counts from the time the individual reaches 20 years of age, except for those who qualify as being without resources, for whom this period is counted from the date of birth.[15]

The amount of basic solidarity pension from 1 July 2009 has been 75,000 Chilean pesos (CLP),[16] and cannot be combined with another pension from another pension regime. The pension is automatically adjusted at 100 per cent of the variation in the consumer price index (IPC) as determined by the Chilean National Statistics Institute. The first adjustment was applied from 1 July 2009.

The Solidarity-Based Top-Up Benefit

This was the second benefit added to the system by the reform in the form of a monthly contribution.[17] The objective of this benefit is to supplement the amount of pension provided under Law Decree No 3500[18] of 1980 when they fall below a certain income level, according to the rules of the Decree.

To be eligible for this provision the law has established the following conditions:

1. The person must be entitled to a pension or pensions contained in Law Decree 3500.
2. The amount of pension should be less than the maximum value of a pension solidarity top-up. In fact, it is a top-up variable with a variable amount.
3. The person must comply with all conditions required to access the basic solidarity pension, for example, be at least 65 years old, be part of a family group belonging to the poorest 60 per cent of the country and prove a period of residence. The residency requirement is met when the applicant is able to prove 20 years of contributions.

[15] In the case of former exiles who benefit from Law No 18.994 OJ 1990-08-20, it has been established that time spent abroad was nevertheless counted, Law No 20.255, above n 12, at art 5.

[16] There was a transitional period from 1 July 2008 until 30 June 2009, during which the amount of the pension was 60,000 CLP; see Law No 20.255, above n 12, at art 13, para 1, of Title VIII, 'Transitional Provisions of'.

[17] Mesa-Lago, above n 14; and Walker and Cifuentes, 'Aspectos Generales', above n 12; Walker and Cifuentes 'Principales Aspectos', above n 12.

[18] Law Decree No 3.500, above n 7.

The solidarity top-up will be the sum obtained when the other pension or pensions that the applicant has received are deducted from the pension. The solidarity top-up is gradually decreased when it reaches an amount equal to or greater than 255,000 CLP.[19] The top-up is adjusted to the IPC in the same way as the basic solidarity pension.

This top-up has been designed with a dual purpose: first, to relieve the middle class which cannot afford to save more than they are legally obliged to and is why they have been frequently excluded from protection; and second, to allow all those excluded to finally have a pension, even if their savings are limited. This type of mechanism can also be seen as consisting of public and private actors. It is a unique benefit in that one part comes from the state (the top-up) and the other part from the funds accumulated in the AFP (*administradoras de fondos de pensiones*).

These provisions show that universalism has finally become an element of the Chilean social security system. Universalism can be understood as the achievement of the coverage of all persons under the particular legislation. Phrased differently, it covers all those in need due to a specific social risk. The 2008 reform transformed the Chilean pension system into a completely hybrid system that claims to offer universal coverage to the entire population; it is hybrid in its administration, its funding and the benefits it offers. The reform can be reflected in the following graph.

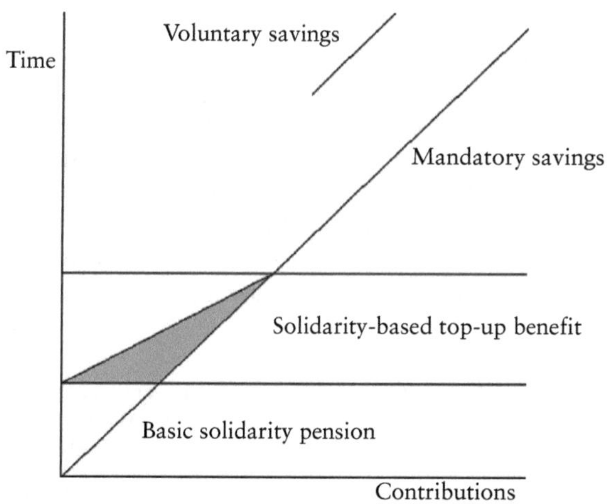

Graph 1: Chilean Pension System: Time Versus Contributions[20]

[19] This amount corresponds to the provision after the period of transition reached on 1 July 2011, as set out in Law No 20.255, above n 12, art XIII, para 1, of Title VIII 'Transitional Provisions of', amended by Law No 20.366, OJ 27-07-2009.

[20] Arellano Ortiz, P, *Universalisme et Individualisme dans le Régime des retraites, l'exemple du Chili* (Paris, L'Harmattan, 2012).

MEASURES IN FAVOUR OF WOMEN: EQUITY MEASURES

The measures established in favour of Chilean women were adopted with the aim of achieving equity. However, this notion is unknown in Chilean legal culture. Nevertheless, the semantic discussion about the qualification of the measure can be allocated second place, due to the result of the measures introduced that place women in a better position and provide them with better benefits.

Equity or '*Igualdad*'?

It appears necessary to point out that Chilean lawmakers do not provide a definition of equity. However, this approach might be taken from the following definition: 'loosening and modifying law considering special circumstances; reasonable moderation in the application of the law'.[21] In this context, it can be observed that the terminology used by the Chilean lawmakers differs from that used in European countries, where the principle of equality is applied. On the one hand, the Chilean doctrine does not pay attention to the equality standard in the context of compulsory pension schemes, while European legal analysis often scrutinises equality in relation to complementary schemes. On the other hand, Chilean law pragmatically tries to correct the harmful effects of the compulsory contribution system. Thus, while the scheme takes a step away from a formal equality test, it takes a step towards real equality considering the concrete situation of the individual. 'Equity' measures generally aim at the female population in this way.

The influence of Anglo-Saxon terminology is notorious. The term 'equity' belongs to the theory of justice by Rawls, which does not necessarily fit with the culture of Chilean law. The influence of this author is extensive and has been the subject of study in numerous countries, including France.[22] The quest for a term of equal consideration in law is met in Spanish by

[21] Cornu, G, Association Henri Capitant, *Vocabulaire Juridique*, 8th edn (France, Presses Universitaires de France, 2007) 367. In French: atténuation, modification apportées au droit, à la loi, en considération de circonstances particulières; modération raisonnable dans l'application du droit.

[22] To read more on this question, see: *La France de l'an 2000: Rapport au Premier Ministre de la Commission résidée par Alain Minc* (Paris, Editions Odile Jacob, 1994); Luckhaus, L, 'Égalité de traitement, Protection Sociale et Garantie de Ressources pour les Femmes' (2000) 139 *Revue internationale du Travail* 163; Moreau, MA, 'Les justifications des discriminations' (2002) 12 *Droit Social* 1112; Lhernould, JP, 'L'Égalité des sexes dans les régimes privés de pension' (2004) 11 *Droit Social* 1000; Michelet, K, 'Les incertitudes liées à la question de l'égalité entre hommes et femmes' (2004) 9 *Revue de Droit Sanitaire et Social* 560; Zarca, A, 'Le Conseil d'État, le Traité CE et l'égalité des rémunération entre hommes et femmes: À propos de l'Arrêt D'Amato du 29 décembre 2004' (2006) 1 *Droit Social* 82; Lanquetin, MT, 'L'Égalité de traitement entre les hommes et les femmes en matière d'emploi et de travail: À propos de la Directive 2000/54 CE du 5 juillet 2006' (2007) (7–8) *Droit Social* 861; Zaidman, C, 'L'individualisation des droits réduit-elle les inégalités hommes/femmes?' (1998) 6 *Droit Social* 591.

the term *igualdad.* But the concept of *igualdad* in law has a very specific meaning depending on the position of a person under law. Taking from a variety of legal cultures, a distinction can be made, for example, between *igualdad real*, *igualdad formal* and *igualdad ante la ley* (before the law).[23] In Chile, such distinctions are of lesser value when considering social security and pension issues from a gender perspective. This is not to say that the case law of the European Court of Justice or European law is seen in Chile as irrelevant, but clearly, when the time comes to search for more gender equality in matters related to social security, the notion of equity dominates the debate in Chile.

The Equity Measures

The 2008 Chilean reform that introduced basic pension protection and non-contributory benefits as well as top-up benefits also provides the following 'equity' measures.

Economic Benefit per Child

The reform grants all women the right to receive a benefit for each child they have given birth to or adopted. Hence, this right benefits both biological and adoptive mothers. The benefit is included in the individual account at the age of 65.

Here, it is necessary to mention that one of the measures rejected by the government was the adjustment of retirement ages to be the same for both sexes. The different retirement ages for men (65) and women (60) for some constitute a problem in terms of equality. The measures which were finally adopted should be seen as a first step towards adjusting the retirement age. However, the ageing of the Chilean population is likely to lead, sooner rather than later, to further reform increasing the age of retirement for both sexes.

A woman who has worked and has been able to save some money will retire at the age of 60, but when wanting to receive the benefit per child she will have to wait until the age of 65. Indirectly this measure creates an incentive for women to remain in the labour market for longer. On the other hand, the only option for women who have not accumulated enough money by the age of 60 or even 65 will be to wait until 65 to apply for a solidarity (non-contributory and universal) pension.

The benefit consists of 10 per cent of 18 times the amount of the minimum income as defined at the moment when the child was born. This benefit is applicable to all women retiring after 1 July 2009.

[23] For an analysis of French law, see: Rivero, J, 'Rapport sur les notions d'égalité et de discrimination en droit public français' in *Travaux de l'Ass H Capitant* (Dalloz, 1965).

Women who are affiliated with the compulsory scheme under Law Decree No 3.500 of 1980,[24] and those who benefit from a basic solidarity pension or a survivor's pension, must present an application to the Institute of Social Security (Instituto de Previsión Social) in order to receive their benefit. The corresponding amount will be deposited into their individual capitalisation account or added to the corresponding benefits.

This benefit per child increases the amount of solidarity payment—be it the basic solidarity pension or the solidarity-based top-up benefit. Women who wish to receive this benefit must prove they are Chilean residents under the same conditions as those outlined for a solidarity pension.

This measure clearly factors into the cost of pensions a gender equality dimension, or a consideration of de facto equality (*igualdad real*), as it considers the reality of motherhood. However, from the moment of its introduction, the pension system has been linked to a public pro-natal policy as much as to the need of women for a decent pension.

Economic Compensation in the Case of Divorce or Marriage Annulment

Another measure that has tried to establish some balance between men and women consists of calculating compensation payments using the accumulated amounts in the capitalisation accounts of both spouses in cases of divorce or annulment of marriage. The idea behind this measure is to divide the pension benefits between the spouses. The pension has been accumulated throughout the marriage; hence the woman should receive a share corresponding to her participation in the acquisition of these rights.

This measure also marks the demise of the 'male breadwinner' model, and accounts for the civil law principle of the equality of the spouses in marriage. The reform considers the contributions made by the women during the marriage, echoing again the notion of de facto or real (as opposed to formal) equality. Before the reform it was not possible to realise any transfers between the individual pension accounts of spouses, and the contribution periods during the marriage were not compensated at the moment of the divorce or marriage annulment. Legislation on Chilean civil marriage, which was only recently adapted to include divorce, contains provisions regulating the compensation between spouses in the form of compensation payments made due to damages suffered by one spouse, resulting from his or her exclusive availability for the needs of the common household.

Law No 20.255[25] of the 2008 pension reform establishes that, in the case of divorce or marriage annulment, the judge may order a transfer of funds from the individual capitalisation account of one of the spouses to

[24] Law Decree No 3.500, above n 7.
[25] Law No 20.255, above n 12.

the other's account. If there is no other individual capitalisation account, the transfer will go to a voluntary capitalisation account, which is opened specifically for this purpose. The amount transferred may not exceed 50 per cent of the funds accumulated during the marriage. In this context, the Superintendent of Pensions plays a technical role, and informs the court as well as regulating the procedures of this transfer.

In cases where a spouse is a dependent worker, she will have an individual account into which the savings will go. However, in a case where the spouse is a 'homemaker', she is unlikely to have an individual account since she is not mandatorily required to affiliate with the AFP. In this case, she will open an individual account as a voluntary affiliate and the funds will go into this account. Thus, not only women with dependent jobs have access to this measure, but also women who may never have worked. Economic compensation of retirement pensions in cases of divorce or marriage annulment are to be applied to all procedures initiated after the seventh month following the publication of the law: this being 1 October 2008.

Survivor's Pension

For a long time, the right to social security considered women as beneficiaries of a widow's pension derived from a man, which was never offered to men in the opposite case, unless the man was handicapped. This position of weakness was improved by assistance policies aimed at women as the main beneficiaries.

When acknowledging the differences in protection between men and women, the duration of the marriage is often omitted. This has negative consequences for men, as they have to finance a survivor's pension in favour of their wives. The consequences for women are more positive, as the mere fact of marriage influences their level of income and compensates any lack of contributions and later pension payments.

Coverage provided by this survivor's pension is more important for women than for men. As Law Decree No 3.500 indicates,[26] a woman receives a survivor's pension when she becomes a widow if the marriage was celebrated at least six months before the death of her husband, or at least three years before if the husband was already receiving an old-age or disability pension. There is no time period defined for cases where the woman is pregnant or they have children in common. On the other hand, the husband only receives a survivor's pension if he is handicapped.

It is important to point out that both women and men must pay a commission to the pension fund AFP, which covers the disability and survivor's pensions. This commission is independent of the beneficiary's gender, but in

[26] Law Decree No 3.500, above n 7.

total more men benefit from AFP pensions. The amount of the commission is the same for both sexes, which can be interpreted as a manifestation of formal equality before the law. A factor that at first sight should have benefited women in fact turns out to be a disadvantage over time.

Another example that illustrates a stereotyped approach of social protection before the 2008 reform concerns men as widowers. Handicapped widowers could receive similar benefits to widows, but contributions made by married women could not benefit their non-handicapped husbands if the wife dies first.

The 2008 reform modifies article 5 of Law Decree No 3.500 of 1980, and as of 1 October 2008 creates the right to a survivor's pension in favour of the surviving husband, handicapped or not, if he is the father of the woman's child or children and is responsible for these children. This modification of the law constitutes another step towards the formal equality of rights for men and women in matters related to social security. In order to benefit from this pension the husband must fulfil a condition of minimum marriage duration with the deceased spouse, identical to the one valid for women, meaning a minimum of six months before the death of the spouse or three years where the deceased spouse was handicapped.

FAMILY OR 'FAMILY GROUP?'[27]

The ILO Declaration of Philadelphia[28] (1944), annexed to its Constitution, suggests a connection between the family and the need for social security. Article I of the Declaration reaffirms the fundamental principles on which the organisation is based: among such principles section (a) of article I states that labour is not a commodity and section (c) affirms that poverty anywhere constitutes a danger to prosperity. In relation to social security, the 10-point action programme provided for at article III of the Declaration includes the following:

> (f) extend social security measures in order to guarantee basic income to those who need it and provide complete medical assistance; (g) adequately protect the life and health of workers; (h) protect childhood and maternity; (i) provide food, housing, recreational and cultural opportunities.[29]

[27] This section is taken from Arellano Ortiz, P, 'La Noción de Familia en Seguridad Social: Aporte a la Discusión del Proyecto de Ley Sobre el Acuerdo de Vida en Pareja' (April 2012) *Revista Laboral Chilena* 54.

[28] International Labour Organization (ILO), *ILO Declaration Concerning the Aims and Purposes of the International Labour Organization (Declaration of Philadelphia)*, 10 May 1994, available at: www.ilo.org/dyn/normlex/en/f?p=1000:62:0::NO:62:P62_LIST_ENTRIE_ID:2453907:NO#declaration.

[29] *Ibid*, at art III.

Those elements of the programme outlined in the Declaration of Philadelphia highlight the fact that social security is not only about the worker, but that it also covers all persons in need, whether or not they belong to the model of the male breadwinner and his family. In the last decade, social security for *all* has become the main goal of the right to social security.

Following the Declaration of Philadelphia, the adoption in 1952 of ILO Social Security (Minimum Standards) Convention No 102[30] seems logical. This Convention today remains the main reference for social security and reflects essentially a compromise between the Bismarckian system of social insurance reserved to the workers and the Beveridge model of universal social security. Being a convention of its time, it is based on the male breadwinner model,[31] which was the prevailing model of society and protection against social risks. It was also understood that through the 'working man' social security benefits are extended to the other members of society: women and children.[32] Women were essentially seen as 'the wife of'.[33] Thus, women appear as widows. However, it considers the model of the male breadwinner as a fiction of sorts, which allows determining the amount of benefits in different countries, thus establishing a point of comparison.[34]

Today an important number of women work and represent a major source of income for their families, not to mention the women who raise their children alone.[35] Equality between sexes has become an important political goal in many countries.[36] In the European Union, for example, mechanisms in favour of the equal treatment of female and male employees clearly reflect this evolution.[37] If the male breadwinner model was dominant in the 1950s and 1960s when social security emerged, the situation

[30] ILO Convention C102: Social Security (Minimum Standards) Convention (Convention Concerning Minimum Standards of Social Security) (adopted 28 June 1952, entered into force 27 April 1955).

[31] Arellano Ortiz, P, 'Reflexiones Sobre las Evoluciones Recientes en Materia de Protección de Riesgos Sociales a Nivel Internacional' (2010) 17(2) *Revista de Derecho Universidad Católica del Norte* 167.

[32] Esping-Andersen, G, 'The Sustainability of Welfare States into the 21st Century' in R Vij (ed), *Globalisation and Welfare: A Critical Reader* (New York, Palgrave Macmillan, 2007) 52.

[33] Lamarche, L, 'The Right to Social Security as a Human Right Guaranteed by the Covenant on Economic, Social and Cultural Rights: The Time has come to think about it' in A Chapman and S Russell (eds), *Core Obligations: Building a Framework for Economic, Social and Cultural Rights* (Antwerp, Intersentia Uitgevers NV, 2001).

[34] Arellano Ortiz, 'Reflexiones Sobre', above n 31.

[35] Pennings, F and Schulte, B, 'Some Current Points of Discussion Concerning Social Security Conventions' in F Pennings (ed), *Between Soft and Hard Law; The Impact of International Social Security Standards on National Social Security Law* (New York, Kluwer International Law, 2006) 43. See also Lamarche, above n 33, at 90.

[36] Reynaud, E, 'The Right to Social Security: Current Challenges in International Perspective' in E Riedel (ed), *Social Security as a Human Right Drafting a General Comment on Article 9 ICESCR—Some Challenges* (London, Springer, 2007).

[37] Pennings and Schulte, above n 35, at 46. See also, Pumar Beltrán, in this collection.

now is totally different, although the model of the male breadwinner still plays an important role. Reality often reflects the dynamic of two breadwinners frequently including a dominant male one. Hence, and to stay with the private law discussion, the contract between spouses is not only a matter of distribution of wealth, but is now also one of economic protection within the family.

One has also to consider the fact that the so-called male breadwinner model built in developed countries has not, as one might expect, extended itself to developing countries. For some, this becomes clear through the fact that its origins lie in the industrial model, which today corresponds neither to so-called developed nor so-called developing countries.[38] Furthermore, it must be noted that in developing countries the informal economy has grown rapidly,[39] suggesting first that the labour market grew, and second that the market structure is different from the one in developed countries.

Chilean legislation, through Law 20.255 on pension reform[40] departs not only from the male breadwinner model, but also from the classical understanding of a family or of a household. It establishes the solidarity pension system and determines that these benefits are conditioned by belonging to a 'family group'. This notion is quite interesting, as it is a determining criterion when defining the beneficiary of a pension. The concept of a 'family group' in article 4 states that, under the law, the family is comprised of individuals united by ties of kinship or the existence of common children, living on the family budget. The person applying for the benefit may include or exclude family members depending on whether or not they participate in the economic situation of the family.[41]

This definition shows a shift away from the classical definition of family, as determined by civil marriage. Traditionally civil rights consider the concept of family in connection to parenthood and parental authority, and always under the contract of civil marriage. The family is hence a juridical notion, but it is also a notion based on fact.[42] The family group becomes a cultural phenomenon, going beyond kinship through blood relations. The 2008 pension reform allows us to include the common law partner in the definition of family; something previously unthinkable in conservative societies dominated by a civil law tradition.

[38] Supiot, A, 'Esquisse d'un Accord-Cadre relatif à l'extension de la protection sociale' (September 2006) 1271 *Semaine Sociale Lamy Supplément* 91.
[39] Reynaud, above n 36.
[40] Law No 20.255, above n 12.
[41] Walker and Cifuentes, 'Aspectos Generales', above n 12, at 88–127.
[42] Garcia, K, 'Le Droit du travail et la famille' (2009) 1 *Droit Social* 13.

This definition of the family group may give rise to a wider debate on the familiarisation or individualisation[43] of protection, especially when talking about social assistance mechanisms like the 'Chile Solidario' programme. The individualisation of contribution-based rights has existed in Chile for almost 30 years. However, it is nothing more than the manifestation of a subjective right derived from the contract with the pension fund AFP. True individualisation implies that the individual, not the affiliated member nor the citizen, has determined social rights which are specifically defined according to the individual's needs. The step away from the familiarisation of rights towards their individualisation may mean that we are questioning the family.[44] This may have important consequences for the legislation of a country as conservative and committed to its traditions as Chile.

That being said, the family situation may be considered, in certain circumstances, as an acceptable differentiation criterion. The law may, for example, introduce differences in the treatment of employees depending on their family situation. As an example, in France, the duration of maternity leave is longer for those workers who are caring for two children.[45] There is hence a close relation between social rights and the family,[46] and when the family is a direct beneficiary of employment protection mechanisms and social risks, social security rights of the family consider the professional situations of its members.

CONCLUSION

The set of measures on social fairness introduced by the 2008 reform try to correct the pension system in order to make it more universal. Generally, it is less favourable for women, who at times are subject to direct compensation and policies. The new measures show that even under a juridical system of formal equality, a new movement can favour measures of positive discrimination.

In fact, these measures are inspired by the acknowledgment of de facto gender discrimination and the need to correct it. Yet each of these measures is based on the sex of the individual and excludes the other. On the surface, the 2008 pension reform shows the will not to continue the application of the formal sex equality standard that has prevailed and to adopt de facto equality measures concerning gender, though the concept of discrimination

[43] Lanquetin, MT, 'Principe d'égalité entre hommes et femmes: individualisation des droits en matière de protection sociale' in *Mélanges en l'Honneur de Jean-Maurice Verdier, Droit Syndical et Droit de l'Homme à l'Aube du XXI siècle* (France, Dalloz, 2001) 413.

[44] *Ibid.*

[45] Baron, P and Rigaud, D, 'Égalité de traitement et rémunérations complémentaires' (2006) 1579 *Semaine Sociale Lamy* 5, 28.

[46] See Garcia, above n 42, at 12.

(particularly indirect discrimination and positive discrimination) might lead to profound changes in social protection, especially in terms of retirement.

Women now see the benefit of new mechanisms which tend to improve their situation based on the logic of pension funds: the economic benefit per child and compensation in the case of divorce. These are positive discrimination measures that increase women's savings and consequently their future old-age pensions. However, these measures are aimed at certain groups of women: mothers and (ex-) wives.

A third measure which the reform adds in regard to the equality of access to pensions is the opening of the survivor's pension to men. This measure, which does not affect women, remains within the framework of the logic of formal equality.

The model of the male breadwinner is not an exclusive reference and may be adjusted to new realities. Social security must adapt to the cultural realities of each society and find mechanisms which allow coverage of all its members. If civil marriage is not enough, new mechanisms must be found so that all individuals living under the same roof are protected.

At this stage, the question as to whether certain categories of women are protected or not can be raised. In this sense, women domestic workers hold a particular status in Chilean labour law. They are considered as dependent workers. However, the difficulties of controlling labour and social security laws in the private sphere of domestic work often results in the non-payment of social security contributions for domestic workers. The measures exposed in this chapter help to extend coverage to this group of women when informality prevails.

Another category of women that draws attention is that of migrant workers. In general, these women are covered by general labour legislation as nationals. In relation to social security coverage, and old-age risk in particular, the situation is quite different. If migrant women workers have dependent work, they must contribute to their individual capitalisation accounts at the AFP of their affiliation. They need to save as much as Chilean nationals in order to obtain an old-age pension. If migrant women do not have a formal job or have not saved enough in their accounts, they may benefit from the measures explained in this chapter. There is no limitation based on nationality; however the solidarity pensions require a residency period of 20 years in Chile. For the contributory benefits from the AFP, there is a possibility through social security agreements for recognition of periods of contribution in third countries.[47] Nevertheless, the possibility

[47] For social security agreements in Chilean legislation see Arellano Ortiz, P, 'Trabajadores Migrantes y Seguridad Social: Aproximación Nacional e Internacional a Los Mecanismos de Protección que Otorgan Continuidad a Sus Prestaciones, I Parte' (2013) 3(6) *Revista Chilena de Derecho de Trabajo y de la Seguridad Social* 87.

of the portability of non-contributory benefits has not yet been developed in Chilean legislation.

In conclusion, it can be said that simple measures like the ones adopted in the context of the 2008 pension reforms in Chile may have a huge impact on the female population and can be proof of how—in order to advance social protection—social security mechanisms can be made more gender inclusive.

Part III

Markets, Employment and Welfare: Poor Women in Rich Countries

8

Rethinking Social Protection Beyond Waged Work: A United States Perspective

LUCY A WILLIAMS

INTRODUCTION

SOME SOCIAL WELFARE programmes in the United States (US) have achieved notable, if imperfect, successes for certain individuals, particularly those with strong ties to waged work. For example, Social Security[1] can be credited with a central role in the huge reduction of elder poverty in the US over the past 50 years. However, as a whole, US social welfare policy has failed to eliminate poverty, and it continues to victimise or ignore certain social groups (single mothers in particular, and men and women in secondary labour markets generally, especially immigrants and people of colour).

The US has the largest number of poor people and the largest gender gap of those in poverty since the US official poverty standard was devised. It has the highest poverty rate for female-headed households among 22 'wealthy' nations and has the largest gender gap for single people among 23 'wealthy' nations. This is not the result of women failing to contribute to society. Quite aside from their work contributions outside formal waged employment, ie, both within the household and in the informal economy, ie, market relationships that are on the edge of or outside the system of legal regulation, they are largely participating in mainstream, paid labour markets. Rather, the gender poverty gap is the result in part of

[1] Note that people in the United States commonly use the term 'Social Security' not as a generic reference to social protection programmes in general, as do some authors in this book, but rather to reference the federal retirement income programme for individuals with a long-term tie to waged work established in 1935 under the Social Security Act of 1935, Pub L No 74-271, 49 Stat 620, 42 USC A § 301 et seq. Assistance to people with disabilities was added to this programme in 1956.

legal constructions that (1) fail to take account of dual labour markets that force poor women into secondary labour market jobs which provide little stability for family caregiving and job retention; and (2) fail to recognise the waged work of poor women, largely in the secondary labour market, as 'work' at all in defining eligibility for and administering both short-term and long-term social assistance through the Unemployment Insurance and Social Security programmes.

A majority of social assistance programmes in the so-called developed world are based on the assumption that most people will earn income in relatively stable, long-term paid employment. This paradigm is central to explaining the inadequacy of modern social welfare policy in confronting gendered poverty. This chapter places these issues within a US context. In the first section, I describe the current status of gendered poverty in the US. In the second section, I briefly recount the historical context in which to understand the current situation and discuss how legal institutions contributed to it. In the third section, I attempt to move the analysis of gendered poverty beyond one centred on waged work—an emphasis that was always problematical and is now doubly so in light of the dilemmas posed by the decline of vertical economic integration and of the internal labour market. I also argue that human rights discourse, while helpful, ultimately provides us with limited purchase on the critical problems that must be addressed to eliminate gendered inequality.

GENDERED POVERTY IN THE UNITED STATES: A STATISTICAL OVERVIEW

It is an embarrassment in 2013 to write a chapter that exposes the extent of poverty in one of the richest nations in the world, and even more so to expose the continuing gendered bias contained in the US legal structure providing for social protection.

The US currently has the largest number of people living in poverty in the half century since poverty has been measured in this country.[2] US Census data for 2010 reflect that 46.2 million people in the US were living in poverty.[3] Even taking into account the population increase over those years, the

[2] The Census Bureau began tracking poverty data in 1958, although the methodology for calculating the poverty measure for the US was not officially adopted until 1969. The thresholds are updated each year to account for inflation, but otherwise have not changed. Analysts have criticised the thresholds as being too low and out of date as they were based on multiplying the 1955 US Department of Agriculture 'thrifty food plan' by three.

[3] DeNavas-Walt, C, Proctor, BD and Smith, JC, of the US Department of Commerce, US Census Bureau, 'Income, Poverty, and Health Insurance Coverage in the United States: 2010' (Washington, DC, Current Population Reports, US Government Printing Office, September 2011), available at: www.census.gov/prod/2011pubs/p60-239.pdf.

2010 Census data indicate that this is the highest overall poverty *rate* in the US, 15.1 per cent, since 1993.[4] The poverty report for 2011 indicated only a slight drop to 15.0 per cent.

There have been large gender gaps in poverty rates every year since the official poverty standard was created. A report prepared by Legal Momentum[5] based on the 2011 US Census Bureau data revealed deep gender gaps in poverty rates even when factors such as work experience, education or family structure are taken into account. Overall, women were 34 per cent more likely to be poor than men, an increase from the 29 per cent gender poverty gap in 2010.

Table 1: Poverty Rates for Adult Women and Men in 2011[6]

	Women	Men	Increased incidence of poverty among women compared with men %
All adults (18 or above)	14.6	10.9	34
Age 65 or above	10.7	6.2	73
Single parents	40.9	21.9	87
Worked	8.0	5.8	38
Not high school graduate	33.2	23.7	40
High school graduate only	17.4	12.4	40
College less than 4 years	12.6	9.2	37
College 4-year degree	5.4	4.8	13

In comparative studies among wealthier countries, the US ranks highest statistically regarding female poverty and the gender poverty gap. Two Luxembourg Income Study Working Papers analysed data relating to this phenomenon. One—which defined poverty as an income less than 50 per cent of the median income and was based on national income surveys conducted in the early 1990s—found that, of 22 countries studied, the US had the highest poverty rate for female-headed households: 30.9 per cent

[4] *Ibid.*

[5] Legal Momentum is the successor to the National Organization for Women Legal Defense and Education Fund founded in 1970.

[6] Table drawn from: Legal Momentum, The Women's Legal Defense and Education Fund, 'Women's Poverty in the United States, 2011: Poverty Rate Remains High, Gender Poverty Gap Grows' (New York, Legal Momentum, September 2012), available at: www.legalmomentum.org/our-work/women-and-poverty/resources--publications/latest-poverty-data.pdf.

compared with the 10.5 per cent average for the group.[7] The second study, reporting on poverty rates for single people in 23 high-income countries, found that the US had the largest gender poverty gap.[8] A third study, conducted by Legal Momentum in the mid-2000s, concluded that the poverty rate for single mothers in the US was almost twice that of the other 15 high-income countries canvassed.[9]

The high poverty rate for lone mothers translates into significant child poverty as well. In 2011, more than one in five children in the US lived in a family with income under the official poverty level ($22,350 for a family of four).[10] For children under the age of six, 24.5 per cent, or 5.8 million, lived in poor families, and of these, 2.8 million children lived in 'deep poverty'—a term used for households living under 50 per cent of the federal poverty level.[11]

The rhetoric driving much of the social assistance law and policy in the US is that poor women, particularly poor single mothers, are responsible for their own poverty because they are lazy and not willing to engage in waged work. However, studies reflect significant waged work participation on the part of poor women. Again, looking at comparative data, one study in the mid-1990s of lone mothers in eight wealthy countries who were in waged work (either full or part-time) documented a 69 per cent waged work rate for lone mothers in the US as opposed to the 49 per cent average employment rate for single mothers in the other seven countries.[12] Another study documented that single parent poor households in the US averaged 1087 annual hours of work in 2000, almost twice the average of 582 in six

[7] Pressman, S, 'Explaining the Gender Poverty Gap in Developed and Transitional Economies', September 2000, Luxembourg Income Study Working Paper No 243, available at: www.lisdatacenter.org/wps/liswps/243.pdf.

[8] Wiepking, P and Maas, I, 'Gender Differences in Poverty: A Cross-National Research', October 2004, Luxembourg Income Study Working Paper No 389, available at: www.lisdatacenter.org/wps/liswps/389.pdf. However, in six of the countries, single men actually had somewhat higher poverty rates than single women.

[9] Legal Momentum, The Women's Legal Defense and Education Fund, 'Poverty Rates for Single Mothers are Higher in the US than in Other High-Income Countries' (New York, Legal Momentum, June 2011), available at: www.legalmomentum.org/sites/default/files/reports/single-mothers-poverty-higher-us.pdf.

[10] Gabe, T, 'Welfare, Work, and Poverty Status of Female-Headed Families with Children: 1987–2011' (CRS Report for Congress CRS R41917, Washington, DC, January 2013) (on file with author).

[11] DeNavas-Walt, C, Proctor, BD and Smith, JC, of the US Department of Commerce, US Census Bureau, 'Income, Poverty, and Health Insurance Coverage in the United States: 2011' (Washington, DC, Current Population Reports, US Government Printing Office, September 2012), available at: www.census.gov/prod/2012pubs/p60-243.pdf.

[12] Hakovirta, M, 'The Income Sources of Single Parents: A Comparative Analysis', November 2001, Luxembourg Income Study Working Paper No 282, Table 3, available at: www.lisdatacenter.org/wps/liswps/282.pdf. The other countries were Australia, Denmark, Finland, Germany, the Netherlands, Norway and the United Kingdom.

other countries.[13] The percentage of never-married mothers who were in waged work rose to a high of 76 per cent in 2000 and since that time has fallen considerably.[14]

The current recession has had a particularly harsh job loss impact on less educated mothers who are most likely to need cash assistance. However, this job loss appears to be overwhelmingly driven by the poor state of the economy rather than by any lack of desire for employment on the part of the mothers. In fact, among women with a high school education or less, single never-married mothers are just as likely to be employed as their childless peers.[15]

Yet, as noted by several of the chapters in this book,[16] lone mothers seeking to earn wages are often frustrated by barriers contained in the legal and social structure of low-wage labour markets. The working conditions are so precarious, when combined with the demands of single parenting, as to guarantee that many low-wage working mothers will regularly cycle through periods of unemployment.

At the same time, the share of those 'disconnected' from either social assistance or wage work has also increased. Significantly, in 2010 and 2011, 38 per cent of poor lone mothers were neither in waged work nor receiving cash assistance; the comparable figure for 1995 was 16 per cent.[17]

Nearly a half-century after President Lyndon Johnson's 'war on poverty',[18] poverty is rampant and stubbornly enduring in the US, and it has a disproportionate, devastating impact on women and children. The question is why?

SOCIAL WELFARE POLICY IN HISTORICAL CONTEXT

Background before the 1996 Personal Responsibility and Work Opportunity Reconciliation Act

US social welfare programmes are funded both through payroll tax contributory schemes and non-contributory programmes relying on general

[13] Smeeding, T, 'Poor People in Rich Nations: The United States in Comparative Perspective', October 2005, Luxembourg Income Study Working Paper No 419, Table 6, available at: www.lisdatacenter.org/wps/liswps/419.pdf. The other countries included Austria, Belgium, Canada, Germany, the Netherlands and Ireland.

[14] Trisi, D, 'The Myth that Single Mothers Don't Work', Center on Budget and Policy Priorities, 9 October 2012, available at: www.offthechartsblog.org/author/trisi.

[15] *Ibid.*

[16] See Smith, Pumar Beltrán, Goldblatt, Murphy and Loftus and Mosher, in this collection.

[17] Gabe, above n 10, Figure 11, 26.

[18] See Edelman, PB, 'Toward a Comprehensive Antipoverty Strategy: Getting Beyond the Silver Bullet' (1993) 81 *Georgetown Law Journal* 1697, 1710–19.

taxation.[19] From their inception, these programmes have been imbued with assumptions regarding class, race and gender and, with but one time-limited exception,[20] have always contained significant gaps in cash assistance coverage. US thinking about social welfare derives from the Elizabethan Poor Laws—concepts of control by local cities and towns rather than by provinces or nations,[21] family responsibility, residency and elite definitions of who is worthy or unworthy were central to the framing of US social welfare policy. Historically, US social welfare policy has been based on the theory that poverty is caused by individual human failure and a deficit of 'traditional' family values. As will be seen below, a special theme based on the political influence of the Southern States was that all programmes of social protection were consciously designed to maintain the power of the white plantation system elite and the domination of this group over African-American people.[22]

To comprehend social protection or social welfare programmes in the US, one needs to understand the somewhat unique structure of US federal–state relationships. In brief, some social welfare programmes are established by the Federal government and funded entirely from federal revenues (although such programmes may be administered by State governments); some are established entirely by the Federal government but funded primarily through payroll taxes (these, too, may be administered at state level); some are 'joint federal–state' programmes funded primarily through payroll taxes but have both state and federal involvement in determining substantive eligibility criteria; some are 'joint federal–state' programmes that are jointly funded and established by the Federal and State governments; and others are entirely state programmes. This somewhat unusual structure of social welfare programmes results from a lack of coherent overarching planning about or national commitment to addressing poverty. The legal foundation of each programme determines the relative influence and control of the Federal and State governments over the eligibility criteria and benefit levels and the extent of discretion that the individual states can exert.

Regardless of a programme's legal foundation, the vast majority of US social welfare programmes, particularly those that provide cash assistance, have always been connected with labour markets. Eligibility for programmes

[19] My primary focus in this chapter is on social assistance, although I describe certain connections with the US social security, unemployment insurance and pension systems that are relevant to the gender poverty analysis.

[20] The Federal Emergency Relief Act 1933 provided cash relief through a programme for all needy unemployed persons and their dependants. Pub L No 73-15, ch 30, § 4(a), 48 Stat 57.

[21] Note the continuation of this local control in the exclusion of African-Americans and local discretion in social welfare programmes discussed below.

[22] See Linder, M, 'Farm Workers and the Fair Labor Standards Act: Racial Discrimination in the New Deal' (1987) 65 *Texas Law Review* 1335.

such as Social Security and Unemployment Insurance is directly tied to one's earnings record and often requires a substantial history in waged work. But, in addition, means-tested or needs-based social assistance programmes[23] have always been significantly linked to low-wage labour markets, although the connection is often not reflected in the stated goals of the programme.

Importantly, public provision for poor women and children has historically reflected a tension between the conflicting imperatives of family care and waged work. Consider, for example, the predecessors to the first federally sanctioned social assistance programmes for single parent families enacted in 1935 (Aid to Dependent Children), the 'Mother's Pensions' or 'Widow's Pensions' Acts introduced in numerous states in the early twentieth century. One goal of these programmes was to provide cash assistance to enable single mothers to fulfil the 'woman's role' of homemaker, rather than placing their children in institutions. To avoid the stigma of immorality attached to unmarried mothers or deserted wives, the proponents of these programmes highlighted an image of the 'worthy, white widow'. Programmes were highly discretionary, allowing localities to exclude 'immoral' women and women of colour.[24] In 1931, only 3 per cent of recipients of mother's pensions were African-American.[25]

Yet, even for a 'deserving' woman eligible for such assistance, the benefit amount was so low that in order to survive, she (and often her children) either had to do paid labour or to attach themselves to a male breadwinner, or both. It was always a feature of US social assistance programmes that poor women needed to seek additional income by, for example, laundering, sewing or taking in boarders. However, whenever a single mother *did* do waged work, usually in the informal economy, she was stigmatised and moved into the category of a 'bad' mother. Thus, poor women faced irreconcilable pressures: they were expected not to earn, yet they were required to earn; they were expected to be chaste, yet needed to find a man; they were expected to care for their children, yet they were forced to leave their children to perform paid labour.

The Social Security Act of 1935, which enacted Social Security, Unemployment Insurance and Aid to Dependent Children (ADC), primarily funded benefits based on past earnings tied to the model of a stable,

[23] I use the term 'social assistance programmes' to refer to programmes that are means-tested or needs-based as opposed to those where eligibility is based on a sufficient tie to waged work or to a categorical eligibility such as veteran's status.

[24] Gordon, L, *Pitied, But Not Entitled: Single Mothers and the History of Welfare, 1890–1935* (New York, The Free Press, 1994) 27. The National Congress of Mothers, in lobbying for mother's aid, initially framed the programme as providing support for mothers of 'the race' (*ibid*, at 62–63); See also Bell, W, *Aid to Dependent Children* (New York, Columbia University Press, 1965) 29–31, 34–35.

[25] Gordon, above n 24, at 48; See below n 33, for examples of racist implementation after the Social Security Act was enacted.

long-term workforce. Social Security was a federal programme funded through employee/employer payroll taxes; Unemployment Insurance was a federally authorised programme funded primarily through an employer payroll tax but in which the states had wide discretion to set eligibility criteria; and only the smallest programme, ADC, was funded through federal and state general tax revenues.

The three programmes also incorporated values and assumptions supportive of racial domination. As will be seen, racial values interact in complicated ways with the work/family gender analysis that follows below. President Franklin D Roosevelt was forced to compromise with Southern congressmen in order to get their votes.[26] In terms of the federally authorised Social Security programme, Southern congressmen defeated proposed statutory language that would have protected African-Americans from discrimination in eligibility for old-age pensions.[27] They used their clout in Congress to exclude domestic and agricultural employees—the vast majority of Southern African-American workers—from eligibility for federal Social Security, fearing that if elderly African-Americans provided financial assistance for younger African-Americans, the latter would then become less pliant field workers.[28]

In terms of the dependent children's programme, which subsequently became the Aid to Families with Dependent Children (AFDC) programme covering parents as well,[29] the legislative history of the Social Security Act[30] allowed the states, which administered the programme, to establish or administer eligibility criteria which intentionally excluded African-American single mothers from the AFDC rolls (or to administer the rules in ways that accomplished the same racial-gender exclusion).[31] For example, Georgia implemented a presumption that fieldwork was available for all 'appropriate' persons during the cotton-chopping season, a practice that was eventually held unconstitutional at the height of the civil rights movement of the 1960s.[32] Some states conditioned eligibility upon the sexual morality of AFDC mothers through 'suitable home' or 'no man-in-the-house' rules and applied those rules almost exclusively to African-American

[26] Linder, above n 22, at 1351.

[27] Douglas, PH, *Social Security in the United States: An Analysis and Appraisal of the Federal Social Security Act* (New York, McGraw-Hill, 1939) 87, 101.

[28] Social Security Act 1935, ch 531, Title II, § 210(b)(1)–(2), 49 Stat 620, 625; See Williams, L, 'The Ideology of Division: Behavior Modification Welfare Reform Proposals' (1992) 102 *Yale Law Journal* 719, 723.

[29] Public Welfare Amendments 1962, Pub L No 87-543, § 104(a)(3), 76 Stat 172.

[30] HRRep No 615, 74th Cong, 1st Sess 24 (1935); S Rep No 628, 74th Cong, 1st Sess, 36 (1935) ('[The State] may, furthermore, impose such other eligibility requirements—as to means, moral character, etc—as it sees fit'.)

[31] Bell, above n 24, at 34–35.

[32] *Anderson v Burson*, 300 F Supp 401 (ND Ga 1968).

women.[33] Childcare for employed African-American women in Mississippi was not considered an issue because 'Negro mothers always had farmed out their children to neighbours and relatives'.[34] In seven Southern States, the number of African-Americans in the AFDC caseload was considerably smaller than the child population as a whole, and in 1938 Georgia granted benefits not based on need, but on a fixed ratio of African-American and white recipients.[35] As one Southern field supervisor reported:

> The number of Negro cases is few due to the unanimous feeling on the part of the staff and board that there are more work opportunities for Negro women and to their intense desire not to interfere with local labour conditions. The attitude that 'they have always gotten along', and that 'all they'll do is have more children' is definite ... There is hesitancy on the part of lay boards to advance too rapidly over the thinking of their own communities, which see no reason why the employable Negro mother should not continue her usually sketchy seasonal labour or indefinite domestic service rather than receive a public assistance grant.[36]

However, in the 1960s and 1970s, the civil rights and welfare rights movements achieved the inclusion of many who had been previously excluded from the original programmes. At the same time, aggressive lawyering on behalf of poor people removed many of the administrative barriers used to keep African-American women off the AFDC rolls. As a result, the number of African-Americans on the AFDC rolls increased by approximately 15 per cent between 1965 and 1971. In addition, by 1971, only 4.3 per cent of AFDC recipients were widows.[37] In other words, the image of the 'worthy, white widow', which had formed the basis of much support for the Mother's Pensions Acts and AFDC, was eroding.

[33] Alabama denied AFDC payments to the children of a mother who cohabited in or outside her home with any single or married able-bodied man; in Louisiana, any home in which an illegitimate child was born subsequent to the receipt of public assistance was considered unsuitable, and benefits were denied. *King v Smith* 392 US 309 (1968) 311, 322. The use of these behavioural rules to keep African-Americans and children of unwed mothers off the welfare rolls is well documented. See Reich, CA, 'Midnight Welfare Searches and the Social Security Act' (1963) 72 *Yale Law Journal* 1347; Reich, CA, 'Individual Rights and Social Welfare: The Emerging Legal Issues' (1965) 74 *Yale Law Journal* 1245, 1246–51; Piven, FF and Cloward, RA, *Regulating the Poor: The Functions of Public Welfare* (London, Tavistock Publications Limited, 1971) 138–45; Katz, MB, *The Undeserving Poor: From the War on Poverty to the War on Welfare* (New York, Pantheon Books, 1989) 253; and Abramovitz, M, *Regulating the Lives of Women: Social Welfare Policy From Colonial Times to the Present* (Boston, South End Press, 1989) 318–19, 323–27.

[34] Mississippi State Advisory Committee to the US Commission on Civil Rights, 'Welfare in Mississippi' (Mississippi, Mississippi State Advisory Committee to the US Commission on Civil Rights, 1969) 31.

[35] Bell, above n 24, at 34–35.

[36] *Ibid*, citing Larabee, MS, 'Unmarried Parenthood under the Social Security Act' (National Conference of Social Work Proceedings, New York, 1939).

[37] Rein, M, *Dilemmas of Welfare Policy: Why Work Strategies Haven't Worked* (New York, Praeger, 1982) 6.

Not surprisingly, with this shift in composition of the single mother population came the first federal work programme for single parents.[38] As seen in the above quote, African-American women had frequently been expected to participate in waged work rather than to abide by the 'domestic code' of serving as a homemaker.[39] The Work Incentive (WIN) programme, enacted in 1967, required all 'appropriate' (a term left unspecified in the statute) AFDC recipients to register for work programmes. But it was a relatively small programme in terms of funding and coverage, and the larger context of providing family support continued as a guiding principle of AFDC.[40] In 1988, the Family Support Act (FSA) amended the AFDC programme to emphasise both waged work and education, including programmes of higher education, as ways to improve a family's financial situation. Indeed the FSA required that, by 1995, 20 per cent of mentally and physically able AFDC recipients with children over three were to be participating in educational and training programmes.[41]

Finally, between 1987 and 1996, the Federal government processed numerous 'waivers' of federal eligibility criteria, thereby allowing the states to 'condition' benefit eligibility on specific behaviours or actions of single mothers.[42] Under the joint federal–state nature of the AFDC programme, states were not allowed to vary the categorical eligibility standards[43] established by the Social Security Act.[44] However, with a waiver, AFDC benefits could be partially or totally withheld if, for example, a child had too many school absences or failed to maintain a certain grade average; if a child was not immunised or did not get regular medical care; if a poor family moved from one state to another that provided a higher benefit amount;[45] or if a

[38] Social Security Amendments 1967, Pub L No 90-248, Title II, 81 Stat 821, 877–921 (1967) (repealed 1996). A work requirement had been present since 1961 for AFDC-Unemployed Father (later Unemployed Parent) two-parent households, because one parent would still be a full-time caretaker. Social Security Act 1935, Pub L No 87-31, Title IV, § 407(2)(B), 75 Stat 75, 84 (1961).

[39] For a discussion of the domestic code, see Handler, JF and Hasenfeld, Y, *The Moral Construction of Poverty* (California, SAGE Publications, 1991) 22–26.

[40] For a more extensive discussion of the WIN programme see *ibid*, at 138–42.

[41] Family Support Act 1988, Pub L No 100-485, 102 Stat 2343; see discussion of the historical progression in AFDC law for welfare recipients to obtain higher education, particularly college degrees, in Davis, MF, 'Learning to Work: A Functional Approach to Welfare and Higher Education' (2010) 58(1) *Buffalo Law Review* 147.

[42] See generally Williams, 'The Ideology of Division', above n 28; Bennett, S and Sullivan, K, 'Disentitling the Poor: Waivers and Welfare' (1993) 26 *Michigan Journal of Law Reform* 741; and Williams, L, 'The Abuse of Section 1115 Waivers: Welfare Reform in Search of a Standard' (1994) 12 *Yale Law and Policy Review* 8.

[43] Categorical eligibility standards determine whether an applicant falls within the group or 'category' intended to be covered by the programme, rather than whether the applicant is financially eligible; eg, in AFDC, there must be a child in the home, there usually must be an absent parent, etc.

[44] *King v Smith* 392 US 309 (1968) 333.

[45] This provision was found to be unconstitutional in *Saenz v Roe* 119 S Ct 1518 (1999).

woman already receiving AFDC became pregnant. These 'waivers' presaged the Conditional Cash Transfers now much touted by the World Bank discussed in other chapters in this volume.[46] As Lamarche notes, giving authorities power over poor women by conditioning subsistence benefits on prescribed behaviour can easily produce more exclusion than inclusion.[47]

The 1996 Personal Responsibility and Work Opportunity Reconciliation Act

The tenor of the programme for lone mothers, which had been evolving over decades, changed dramatically in 1996 when Congress passed the Personal Responsibility and Work Opportunity Reconciliation Act (PRWORA).[48] Among other changes, PRWORA repealed AFDC and replaced it with the Temporary Assistance to Needy Families (TANF) programme. The slogan of 'end welfare, work first' is driving the social welfare debate in several Western countries. In the US, however, the legacy of profound racism and a political culture that had long demonised social welfare produced two major provisions in PRWORA relating to mandatory work programmes and the role that mainstream, paid labour markets would now play in US policy regarding subsistence provision for single mothers and their families.

First, states must require significant percentages of primarily single mothers who receive TANF to participate in designated work activities for 30 hours a week.[49] Virtually all forms of education and job or skills training, ie, activities that would contribute to the upward mobility of single mothers, are excluded from the definition of 'core work activity' for the purposes of fulfilling the states' mandate regarding work participation.[50] The US Department of Health and Human Services' final rule implementing the 2005 reauthorisation of TANF expressly excludes from the definition of 'core work activities' all jobs and skills training directly related to employment, education directly related to employment and secondary school completion.[51] In addition, activities that would address barriers to employment, such as mental health treatment or rehabilitation services, count towards work participation only under the category of 'job readiness assistance', which many states limit to six weeks in any given year.[52] Finally, the 2005

[46] Goldblatt and Lamarche, Fredman, Goldblatt, in this collection.
[47] Lamarche, in this collection.
[48] Pub L No 104-193, 110 Stat 2105, 42 USC § 601 et seq.
[49] 42 USC § 607(c)(1); 45 CFR § 261.31(a)(1).
[50] 42 USC § 607(c) and (d).
[51] 45 CFR § 261.31(b) and (c).
[52] Center on Budget and Policy Priorities (CBPP) and the Center for Law and Social Policy, *Implementing the TANF Changes in the Deficit Reduction Act*, 2nd edn (Washington, DC, CBPP, February 2007) 17.

reauthorisation work-participation rules focus on measuring attendance at countable work activities and primarily have the effect of increasing the paperwork burden on both clients and the administrative agency personnel. But the programme includes little or no monitoring of the effectiveness of the programmes or investigation of questions such as whether employment programmes are actually getting people into jobs; whether the jobs are ones that improve the families' financial status; whether the jobs are better than those mothers could have found on their own, and so on.[53]

The numbers of AFDC, now TANF, recipients in college fell from 172,176 in 1996 to 58,055 in 1998.[54] Some states were able to maintain discretion to allow recipients to attend higher education through the so-called 'Maintenance of Efforts' (MOE) dollars that they were required to allocate as a condition of receiving federal TANF funds.[55] This option was eliminated by the Deficit Reduction Act of 2005.[56]

Second, the PRWORA places a five-year, lifetime limit on receipt of social assistance benefits by most claimants. Participation in work-requirement programmes does not extend the limit.[57] Many states impose an even shorter lifetime limit on eligibility. This restriction on the period of time a single mother and her family can receive governmental cash assistance rests on the assumption that mainstream, paid labour markets can and will provide adequate family support at all other times. The lifetime limit introduced by PRWORA is a modern reincarnation of the Elizabethan notion that poverty is caused by human failure. The assumption is that any person can escape poverty by individual effort and participation in waged work. Despite all of the evidence to the contrary, PRWORA presupposes that the US has an institutional structure in place that guarantees that any single parent breadwinner can acquire subsistence income by formal sector paid labour.

Beyond these onerous requirements, TANF benefits are woefully insufficient. In every state, the benefit level is half or less than half of the poverty level. Prior to 1996, federal AFDC appropriations were based on a matching-grant system: simply put, the Federal government would match the amount that the state allocated. While never automatically adjusted for inflation, the federal allocation would increase if a state chose to increase benefits. As enacted in

[53] US Government Accountability Office, 'Temporary Assistance for Needy Families: Implications of Recent Legislative and Economic Changes for State Programs and Work Participation Rates' (GAO-10-525, Report to Congressional Requesters, May 2010).

[54] Greenberg, M, Strawn, J and Plimpton, L, 'State Opportunities to Provide Access to Postsecondary Education Under TANF' (Washington, DC, Center for Law and Social Policy, February 2000) 40.

[55] Greenberg, M, 'The TANF Maintenance of Effort Requirement' (Washington, DC, Center for Law and Social Policy, 2002).

[56] Pub L No 109-171, 120 Stat 4 (2006).

[57] 42 USC § 608 (a)(7) (2003); 45 CFR § 264.1 (a)(1).

1996, the federal TANF appropriation is a 'block-grant' or fixed amount. Since 1996, the real value of the allocated grants has declined by 32 per cent due to inflation.[58]

Finally, the PRWORA eliminated the long-standing federal mandate that states may not alter the categorical eligibility criteria contained in the Social Security Act. This allows states to impose multiple conditions for TANF eligibility without obtaining approval of or 'waiver' from the Federal government. States now have wide discretion to impose conditions on the receipt of TANF and failure to comply with these conditions can result in partial or total ineligibility for even the insufficient benefit amount allocated.

The result is that from 1996 to 2009, the share of poor children in the US receiving TANF fell from 62 per cent to under 23 per cent.[59] Despite increasing unemployment and poverty, the percentage of single mother families receiving TANF fell from 16 per cent in 2001 to 10 per cent in 2010,[60] and single mother families accounted for over 75 per cent of the 171,000 families in the US officially counted as homeless.[61] Unlike countries where authors in this book note that women are 'now seen as the main vehicle for poverty alleviation and therefore the main recipients of welfare rights'[62] or 'the best human investment in all development contexts'[63] the United States expects a single mother to obtain subsistence benefits for her family largely through waged work.

The Interaction between TANF, Unemployment Insurance and Social Security

Yet, while assuming that single mothers should participate in mainstream, formal sector waged work and that earnings from paid labour will provide

[58] Lower-Basch, E, of the Center for Law and Policy, 'Hearing on Waiving Work Requirements in the TANF Program' (Testimony to the Subcommittee on Human Resources, Committee on Ways and Means, US House of Representatives, 28 February 2013) 8.

[59] Lower-Basch, E, 'Goals for TANF Reauthorization' (Center for Law and Social Policy, 6 February 2013), relying on figures through 2006 from Crouse, G et al of the US Department of Health and Human Services, 'Indicators of Welfare Dependence, Annual Report to Congress' (Washington, DC, US Department of Health and Human Services, 2008). Values for 2009 are calculated based on CPS poverty data and HHS caseload data.

[60] Women's Legal Defense and Education Fund, 'Single Mothers Since 2000: Falling Farther Down' (New York, Legal Momentum, January 2011), stating that rates are calculated from the data reported by the Census Bureau in the annual report 'Table C8. Poverty Status, Food Stamp Receipt, and Public Assistance for Children under 18 Years by Selected Characteristics (year)', available at: www.census.gov/population/www/socdemo/hh-fam/cps2010.html.

[61] US Department of Housing and Urban Development, 'The 2010 Annual Homeless Assessment Report to Congress' (US Department of Housing and Urban Development, Office of Community Planning and Development, 2010), available at: www.census.gov/population/www/socdemo/hh-fam/cps2010.html.

[62] Fredman, in this collection.

[63] Goldblatt and Lamarche, in this collection.

adequate income for family support, key US contributory and insurance based social welfare programmes, such as Social Security and particularly Unemployment Insurance, treat poor mothers and many other formal sector low-wage workers as 'non-workers'. Far from fulfilling the stated objective of giving poor women dignity, the legal constructions of 'worker' reposition poor women who work as 'non-workers', thereby stigmatising them as dependent and lazy.

As in most Western nations, US law employs the category of 'worker' for purposes of determining eligibility for benefits under programmes such as Unemployment Insurance (UI). However legal discourse is based on a deeply embedded, 'bright-line' dichotomy between formal sector wage workers and welfare recipients. As a result, many people who work fall into the legal definition of 'non-worker'. Under UI's division of authority as a joint federal–state programme, states may establish many of their own eligibility standards. Based on an antediluvian male breadwinner model, virtually all of the states impose minimum earnings requirements that privilege higher earning employees and those in long-term stable jobs. By discounting recent earnings for eligibility purposes, these programmes tend to exclude those in precarious, secondary labour market jobs who move in and out of waged work. Many states' programmes effectively exclude part-time workers or those looking for part-time work, rendering single mothers struggling to maintain the balance between family care and waged work ineligible. Others disqualify waged workers who leave their jobs because their employer unilaterally assigns them to work on night shifts or during hours for which they have no childcare. Rules in many states disqualify workers fired because they miss work due to caregiving necessities, or because they are fleeing abusive relationships. These and similar rules exclude low-wage workers, including significant numbers of single mothers, as a result of which such workers are rendered ineligible for unemployment insurance.[64] Many single mothers who move from welfare to precarious

[64] Eg, two-fifths of high-wage unemployed receive UI, as compared with fewer than one-fifth of low-wage unemployed (note that 60 per cent of low-wage workers are women). Lovell, V and Hill, C, 'Fact Sheet: Today's Women Workers: Shut Out of Yesterday's Unemployment Insurance System' (Washington, DC, Institute for Women's Policy Research, May 2001). Women are four times more likely to be working part-time during their prime earning years than men, and 25 US states deny UI benefits to part-time workers. National Employment Law Project (NELP), 'Why Unemployment Insurance Matters to Working Women and Families: An Important Tool in the Work–Family Balance' (New York, NELP, 2004), available at: nelp.3cdn.net/160e9cc27e3f2a6d6e_bwm6b5dz6.pdf. Because, at the time of that study, only 15 states allowed individuals who must leave their employment because of compelling family circumstances to receive UI benefits, women who leave are 32 per cent less likely than men to receive benefits. *Ibid*. See also O'Leary, CJ and Kline, KJ, 'UI as a Safety Net for Former TANF Recipients: Final Report' (Washington, DC, US Department of Health and Human Services, Assistant Secretary for Planning and Evaluation, ASPE Project HS-05-001, March 2008) (showing that of TANF leavers who become unemployed and apply for UI benefits, only 36

waged work, and then lose their jobs precisely because the employment is precarious, find that they are *ineligible* for UI benefits and have no choice but to reapply for TANF. Indeed, unemployed women are about 10 per cent less likely than men to receive UI benefits because of outdated eligibility rules that disproportionately disqualify women,[65] and in 41 of the 50 U.S. states, men are more likely to receive UI than women.[66]

In one study of women-maintained families in which the mother was employed for at least three months, almost three times as many families turned to welfare as turned to UI.[67] Another study of 1200 single mothers who received welfare for at least two months in a 24-month period showed that 43 per cent also worked for pay, averaging just about half-time hours.[68] However, only 11 per cent of those who worked later qualified for UI. They returned to welfare having no choice but to use AFDC/TANF as their substitute 'unemployment insurance'. By denying many low-wage earning mothers transitional support when they become unemployed, UI law *constructs* them as persons who are 'not attached to the labour force', that is, as social deviants who cause their own poverty by refusing to work and who therefore are unworthy of assistance from society. They are then viewed as 'dependent' on the state; meanwhile the economic dependency of workers on precarious employment that is a structural feature of low-wage labour markets is rendered invisible.[69]

A notable achievement of the Obama Administration was the incorporation of incentives for states to revise their UI laws in the American Recovery

per cent will be eligible due to non-monetary reasons, such as having left work 'voluntarily' because they were required to change to a job shift for which they did not have childcare). There is no data available after the changes made pursuant to the American Recovery and Reinvestment Act 2009 discussed below.

[65] US Department of Labor, Employment and Training Administration (2007), 'Percent Distribution of Characteristics of the Insured Unemployed, Report for Calendar Year 2006', available at: www.workforcesecurity.doleta.gov/unemploy/chariu.asp and analysed in Lovell, V, Institute for Women's Policy Research, 'The Unemployment Insurance Modernization Act: Improving UI Equity and Adequacy for Women' (Testimony before the House Ways and Means Committee, Subcommittee on Income Security and Family Support, Hearing on Modernizing Unemployment Insurance to Reduce Barriers for Jobless Workers, 19 September 2007).

[66] Stettner, A, 'What is UI Modernization and Why is it Important?' (National Employment Law Project, May 2008).

[67] Pierce, DM, Statement of the Women and Poverty Project, 'Wider Opportunities for Women' to the National Advisory Council on Unemployment Compensation, 11 May 1993 (on file with author); Spalter-Roth, R, Hartmann, H and Burr, B, *Income Security: The Failure of Unemployment Insurance to Reach Working Mothers* (Washington, DC, Institute for Women's Policy Research, 1994).

[68] Spalter-Roth, R, Hartmann, H and Burr, B 'Income Insecurity: The Failure of Unemployment Insurance to Reach Working AFDC Mothers' paper presented at the Second Annual Employment Task Force Conference (1994) 2.

[69] Likewise eligibility for Social Security benefits is based on an even more substantial tie to waged work than UI.

and Reinvestment Act of 2009 (ARRA), commonly known as the 'Obama stimulus package'.[70] The ARRA provided up to $7 billion to states in order to encourage them to make specific reforms before August 2011 that would provide coverage for workers previously excluded from the programme. States could receive one-third of their allocated funding simply by adopting the procedure (known as 'the alternative base period') of considering a claimant's most recent earnings in determining eligibility.[71] This method of calculating labour market attachment, and therefore entitlement to UI, makes it easier for unemployed people who frequently cycle in and out of waged work to qualify for benefits. A state could receive the additional two-thirds of its allocated funding by adopting any two of four reform initiatives: allowing benefits to workers who are only available for part-time work; allowing workers to qualify for benefits if they had to leave their job for a 'compelling family reason'; providing an additional six months of benefits to laid-off workers who enrol in state approved education or training programmes; and offering additional allowances for unemployed workers caring for dependent children.[72] However, Congress in the ARRA did not make these reforms mandatory. In a spectacle of bizarre political posturing, the Governors in 12 states forfeited that 'tainted' Obama funding by refusing to implement any of these reforms; five others drew down only partial funding.[73] Since the supplemental funding programme ended in August 2011, three States—Kansas, North Carolina and Tennessee—have repealed all or part of the initiatives they adopted.

Now that TANF caps the number of years a person may receive benefits over the course of a lifetime, the option to return to TANF when a single mother is not eligible for UI becomes unavailable at a certain point. Regardless of an individual's desire and efforts to remain in waged work, when the cap is reached, poor single mothers and their families are ineligible for further social assistance and often for UI. These women bear no responsibility for the revolving door nature of precarious employment, and obviously they lack the power to restructure low-wage labour markets. The interaction between law and labour market patterns quite likely explains the increase from 16 per cent in 1995 to 38 per cent in 2010 and 2011 of those 'disconnected' from (not receiving or participating in) either social assistance or waged work.[74]

[70] American Recovery and Reinvestment Act 2009, Pub L No 111-5 § 2000, 123 Stat 115.

[71] *Ibid*, at § 2003 (a)(1)(C)(i), 123 Stat 440.

[72] *Ibid*, at § 2003(a)(3), 123 Stat 440–41.

[73] National Employment Law Project, 'Modernizing Unemployment Insurance: Federal Incentives Pave the Way for State Reforms' (Briefing Paper, May 2012), available at: nelp.3cdn.net/a77bc3b5988571ee4b_dfm6btygh.pdf.

[74] A 2011 study that compared UI and AFDC/TANF receipt in a pre-reform period (1990–94) and post-reform period (2001–05) showed no increase in low-educated single mothers receiving UI, but a significant drop in that same group receiving TANF. Shaefer, HL, Wu, L

Looking Forward

As is evident from the chapters included in this collection, the flaws of US social welfare policy appear in local variation in most modern systems. They can be traced back to a fundamental design feature. The problem is not just that social welfare policy is built on the foundation of formal sector waged work, but rather, that it is anchored in a *historically specific image or understanding* of formal sector waged work. Almost all of our social welfare programmes take for granted the white, male, breadwinner model. In its mid-twentieth-century incarnation, the male breadwinner model was in turn intimately connected with a distinct paradigm of paid employment, what labour and employment law scholars have recently come to call the 'standard employment contract'.[75] The standard employment contract, whether a product of legislation, private law, collective bargaining and/or social practice, assumed a stable, long-term commitment to one employer over a lifetime, with decent wages, some job security and protections against unfair treatment at work. (In the non-union sector in the US, job security protections were much weaker than elsewhere in the industrial world.) In the US, this type of paid employment traditionally provided a system through which employees' health care, vacation leave, retirement and other benefits were delivered. Of course, millions of employees never enjoyed the standard employment contract; segmentation is a pronounced feature of US labour markets. Nevertheless, the standard employment contract served as the paradigm that framed most of US social policy, particularly Social Security and Unemployment Insurance. The policymakers who designed AFDC were disingenuous or in denial about, or simply oblivious to the contradiction that the programme provided inadequate subsistence benefits to single mother families while at the same time expecting women to stay in the home. More recently, TANF quite openly relies on the premise that poor single mothers can and must obtain and maintain stable, long-term, sustainable employment, despite the precarious reality and gendered nature of the low-wage labour market. Little effort has been made to provide realistic opportunities for education to increase the human capital of poor and uneducated single mothers that might enable them to move into primary labour market jobs. The US social welfare policy systematically disenfranchises women, minorities, immigrants and others who do not have

and Phillips, E, 'Unemployment Insurance and Low-Educated Single Working Mothers Before and After Welfare Reform' (Upjohn Institute Policy Paper No 2011–007, Kalamazoo, MI, WE Upjohn Institute for Employment Research, 2011).

[75] Stone, KVW and Arthurs, H, 'The Transformation of Employment Regimes: A Worldwide Challenge' in KVW Stone and H Arthurs (eds), *Rethinking Workplace Regulation: Beyond the Standard Contract of Employment* (New York, Russell Sage Foundation, 2013) 2.

primary sector employment and/or who are not attached to someone with access to primary sector employment.

Much has been written by US feminists in recent years about the problem of balancing work and family life. Sadly, as I have discussed elsewhere,[76] this work has focused on middle-class and affluent women. It addresses issues of great importance, such as the glass ceiling, equal pay for equal work and family and medical leave, but it is oblivious to and thereby renders invisible the issues of foremost concern to poor women.[77]

Progressives committed to guaranteed social assistance, equality and dignity have proposed, advocated for and on rare occasions have actually seen policymakers adopt interesting policy innovations and reforms. As much as I value and support these efforts, they typically suffer from a conceptual limitation. The instinct is to see the long-term problem as one of *including* vulnerable and excluded groups in generous social welfare programmes. An example in the European Union is the complex of proposals to award social drawing rights to caregivers and to increase female-friendly direct granting to households.[78] Given the current political context in the US, progressives can only fantasise about the coming of a day when it will even be plausible to submit such proposals to Congress. A shining beacon of reform in the US is the important but modest example of the ARRA which provided temporary funding to encourage states to make gender and low-wage friendly improvements in their UI statutes (which would make a form of cash assistance available to single mothers who exceed the TANF time limit). However, the ARRA was an accomplishment of the halcyon days of President Obama's arrival in office; it is not likely to be repeated in the near future.

We should support these efforts wholeheartedly, but with caveats. Efforts to improve conditions for poor women by achieving greater *inclusion* in existing models of social protection are not without their problems. They sometimes legitimate political pressures to privatise the welfare system by treating the family as the primary delivery unit. Given the uneven division of labour prevalent within families, this approach can have the perverse effect

[76] Williams, LA, 'Poor Women's Work Experiences: Gaps in the 'Work/Family' Discussion' in J Conaghan and K Rittich (eds), *Labour Law, Work, and Family* (Oxford, Oxford University Press, 2005) 195.

[77] See, eg, Williams, JC, *Reshaping the Work-Family Debate: Why Men and Class Matter* (Cambridge, MA, Harvard University Press, 2010).

[78] Fultz, E, 'Pension Crediting for Caregivers: Policies in Finland, France, Germany, Sweden, the United Kingdom, Canada, and Japan' (Washington, DC, Institute for Women's Policy Research, 2011); and López, J, Chacartegui, C and Cantón, CJ, 'Social Rights in Changing Labor Markets: Caring for Caregivers in the European Union' in KVW Stone and H Arthurs (eds), *Rethinking Workplace Regulation: Beyond the Standard Contract of Employment* (New York, Russell Sage Foundation, 2013) 333–50.

of reinforcing traditional gender roles and of making social reproduction even more dependent on women workers' 'second shift' at home.[79]

However, I join those who increasingly argue that social welfare systems must be entirely re-imagined and redesigned. The problem runs deeper than achieving greater inclusion. The fact is that the economic and social assumptions on which the admirable aspects of the post-Second World War welfare regime were based are now unravelling. The new economy of the twenty-first century is leaving behind the 'industrial' model of production and work organisation—mass production of relatively uniform items in large, vertically integrated businesses; stable, employer attached and site attached careers at work for at least one family member; and internal labour markets, gradually rising wages and implicit promises that employees who acquire firm-specific skills and stay the course with their employer will be relatively protected at the end of their working careers.[80]

To a greater or lesser extent, this model of wealth production and work organisation is in decline all over the world, and certainly in the US. As Stone and Arthurs have described, globalisation, technology and new management strategies have all contributed to the demise of the standard employment contract model.[81] The paradigm of the future appears to involve unstable, mobile, intermittent employment; vertical disintegration; global production chains;[82] rising competition from the BRICs;[83] a huge gap between knowledge-based jobs and low-wage service jobs; permanent economic insecurity; and, at least in the US, the disappearance of collective bargaining and stable public sector employment. The very categories of 'employer' and 'employee' are becoming more attenuated as the years go by.[84] Many of the social welfare benefits associated with job tenure are being diminished or lost as these changes in the structure of waged labour occur.

In other words, the time is long past when it is enough to address the dilemmas of social protection solely within the frame of widening inclusion of those groups previously excluded, such as single mothers, in our social welfare scheme. The structure on which the social welfare policy

[79] Otto, in this collection.

[80] Klare, K, 'The Horizons of Transformative Labour and Employment Law' in J Conaghan, RM Fischl and K Klare (eds), *Labor Law in an Era of Globalization: Transformative Practices and Possibilities* (Oxford, Oxford University Press, 2002) 3; Stone and Arthurs, above n 75, at 1–10; and Pumar Beltrán and Mosher, in this collection.

[81] Stone and Arthurs, above n 75, at 4–5.

[82] See generally Kaplinsky, R and Morris, M, 'A Handbook for Value Chain Research', available at: www.prism.uct.ac.za/Papers/VchNov01.pdf.

[83] 'BRICs' refers to Brazil, Russia, India, China and South Africa. These are so-called developing nations distinguished by large, internationally competitive, fast-growing economies and significant influence on regional and global affairs.

[84] See Klare, above n 80.

and institutions of the twentieth century were based is disintegrating. This makes it urgent to address the question of whether the models of social welfare policy invented by progressives in the twentieth century will remain relevant as the twenty-first century progresses. This conceptual agenda involves at least two very difficult institutional challenges.

First, we must devise new ways of *funding* social welfare programmes. The twentieth-century method was one or another variation on the payroll tax, which is essentially a device to siphon off a portion of the wealth created in industry at the moment of payment between employer and employee. The rise of the new economy, new forms of production and new forms of work organisation require the invention of creative mechanisms to draw off a portion of wealth production to fund social welfare programmes. Second, in my view, social welfare design in the twenty-first century must de-emphasise categorical eligibility rules and move towards universal access.

In other words, even if the political climate trended enduringly in a progressive direction, reform requires us to address very complicated and nuanced questions of institutional design. I readily concede that I do not have the answers to these questions, but we must begin by understanding the nature and scope of the challenge that we must address.

Human rights discourse can make an important contribution to our work in that endeavour, but I believe that the human rights approach will ultimately run up against limitations. The strength of human rights discourse is twofold: (1) it is a powerfully resonant and mobilising rhetoric that articulates the moral imperative of guaranteeing a decent livelihood for all and exposes the gendered inequality of the current structure; and (2) it shifts the discourse from a waged work and individual responsibility frame to social understandings based on universal needs and entitlement in which society has a responsibility to address the subsistence needs of all. Its weakness, however, is that beyond abstractions (the right of all people to equal respect and concern of the state, the right of everyone to live in dignity, for example), it tells us precious little that we need to know in order to address the institutional design challenges indicated above. The strength and attractiveness of the human rights approach is discursive, but human rights thinking gives us very little analytical purchase on questions of social organisation. For example, human rights thinking cannot tell us much about how to construct new social welfare policies detached from earnings history in waged work in stable employment, or how to construct and finance universal social assistance. Human rights discourse helps us to see the need for and the urgency of universal social assistance, but not very much about how to deliver it. Courts and legislatures in countries with constitutions containing progressive social and economic rights provisions face difficult decisions about how to stretch limited resources to build housing, deliver water, medical care, construct schools and so on. Human rights discourse affirms that all of these are important and should be legally required, but it gives little guidance on how to set priorities and how to create institutional systems that produce results on the ground. Decisions of this kind are not merely 'technical' questions; they implicate controversial choices that will generate different distributive outcomes for different groups in society. So while I am very committed to the dissemination of human rights discourse and particularly to sophisticated development of social and economic rights thinking, we should be sceptical about embracing the human rights framework as a magic bullet. Focusing on human rights discourse takes the debate about social welfare policy and programmes away from a now disintegrating waged work model, but it must be supplemented with other bodies of knowledge and forms of social enquiry if we are to face the hard questions of institutional design that those of us committed to gender and income/asset equality must address.

9

Human Capital and the Post-Scripting of Women's Poverty

JANET E MOSHER

INTRODUCTION

A SIZEABLE SCHOLARSHIP tracks the influence of neo-liberalism on Canadian social policy. Beginning in the 1970s and marking a break from the post-Second World War welfare state and ideals of social citizenship, the Canadian State staged a retreat from its responsibility for the provision of a range of social supports and in the place of many social entitlements, installed new duties.[1] This reconfigured social landscape implicated a wide swathe of social life, from childcare to unemployment insurance, to labour regulation and social assistance. Neo-liberalism's footprint brought into relief a pronounced shift to reliance upon the market to meet social needs, together with a corresponding valorisation of individualism and self-sufficiency (particularly through an emphasis on waged work).

In so doing, neo-liberalism simultaneously marked the disappearance of women within social policy. The responsibilised, self-sufficient and starkly individualistic subject central to neo-liberalism obscured social relations, including those entailed in the labour of social reproduction (primarily performed by women). Indeed, the very concept of social groups, central to both identity formation and to practices of oppression, receded into the background, as did the aspiration of equality.[2] As Martha McCluskey has

[1] See generally Banting, K, 'Do We Know Where We Are Going? The New Social Policy in Canada' (2005) 31 *Canadian Public Policy* 421; McKeen, W, 'The National Children's Agenda: A Neoliberal Wolf in Lamb's Clothing' (2007) 80 *Studies in Political Economy* 151; Jenson, J, 'Lost in Translation: The Social Investment Perspective and Gender Equality' (2009) 16 *Social Politics* 446; and Rittich, K, 'Social Rights and Social Policy: Transformations on the International Landscape' in D Bark-Erez and AM Gross (eds), *Exploring Social Rights: Between Theory and Practice* (Oxford, Hart Publishing, 2007).

[2] See Young, IM, *Justice and the Politics of Difference* (Princeton, Princeton University Press, 1990) on social groups and oppression; and Brodie, J and Bakker, I, *Where are the Women? Gender Equity, Budgets and Canadian Public Policy* (Ottawa, Canadian Centre for Policy Alternatives, 2008) on the disappearance of women in social policy.

so poignantly illustrated, neo-liberalism moved social rights not only off the table, but off the wall.[3]

More recent developments in social policy, frequently associated with a modernising of social architecture and often described as a 'social investment' paradigm, reflect a cluster of common concepts and practices: activation (understood almost exclusively as waged work); an orientation towards the future; investments (in human capital development in particular); and an expectation of social returns on investments.[4] These developments were heavily influenced by the Organisation for Economic Co-operation and Development (OECD), commencing in the late 1990s, although Canada was a 'relative late-comer' to the social investment alter.[5] While some social investment paradigms invoke a notion of constant investment in the ongoing development of the human capital necessary to meet the rapidly changing needs of a global, knowledge-based economy, the implementation of 'investment' policies in many jurisdictions—Canada included—has focused heavily upon children, in what some term a 'starting gate' model.[6] Although the goals associated with social investment frequently include social inclusion, disrupting the intergenerational transmission of poverty, and securing populations against the risks of contemporary economies, significant questions have been raised about the extent to which actual 'investment' practices have kept pace with this rhetoric.[7]

There is widespread agreement that the social investment paradigm shares much in common with neo-liberalism, yet views vary about the extent of its departures from central neo-liberal tenets. Some regard social investment as reflecting a renewed role of the state in preparing citizens for labour market participation over the life course and as such, demonstrating a shift towards increased state responsibility. Others see social investment

[3] McCluskey, MT, 'Efficiency and Social Citizenship: Challenging the Neoliberal Attack on the Welfare State' (2003) 78 *Indiana Law Journal* 783, 791; and Dobrowolsky, A and Jenson, J, 'Shifting Representations of Citizenship: Canadian Politics of "Women" and "Children"' (2004) 11 *Social Politics* 154, 155 conclude that neo-liberalism 'sidelined talk of social rights and spending and made equality claims for adults difficult to sustain'.

[4] See Banting, above n 1; Dobrowolsky and Jenson, above n 3; and Jenson, J and Saint-Martin, D, 'Building Blocks for a New Social Architecture: The LEGO™ Paradigm of an Active Society' (2006) 34 *Policy & Politics* 429.

[5] Williams, C, 'Asset-building Approaches and the Search for a New Social Policy Architecture in Canada' in J Robson and P Nares (eds), *Wealth and Well-Being/Ownership and Opportunity: New Directions in Social Policy for Canada* (North York, Social and Enterprise Development Initiatives, 2006) 54.

[6] McKeen, W, 'Diminishing the Concept of Social Policy: The Shifting Conceptual Ground of Social Policy Debate in Canada' (2006) 26 *Critical Social Policy* 865.

[7] See Jenson, 'Lost in Translation', above n 1, at 447; McManus, R, 'Work–Life Balance: A Case of Technical Disempowerment?' (2009) 16 *Social Policy* 111; and Simon-Kumar, R, 'The Analytics of "Gendering" the Post-Neoliberal State' (2011) 18 *Social Politics: International Studies in Gender, State and Society* 441.

discourses and practices as neo-liberalism hidden behind a soft cloak, or as a 'wolf in lamb's clothing'.[8] Yet others point to the dark underbelly of a paradigm heavily reliant on the market as the principle source of well-being and that dehumanises citizens by reducing them to assets in which investments are made and from whom returns in productivity and profits are expected. Given a labour market that increasingly offers only precarious work and which casts off many who seek to participate—a casting off which is not indiscriminate but which tracks race, gender, newcomer status and (dis)ability—those who 'fail' to be self-sufficient will be, like bad debt, written off and abandoned.[9]

There are also significant differences in views about the implications of the social investment paradigm for women, social security and gender equality. In some states, such as Canada, gender continues to be obscured, while in others the emergence of the social investment paradigm has been accompanied by the reinsertion of gender in social policy.[10] Jenson argues persuasively, however, that gender has reappeared in a manner incompatible with feminist analysis of the state.[11] She poses a series of important questions about the social investment paradigm, among them:

> [D]oes the social investment perspective offer an approach to gender relations that responds to women's equality claims and ambitions for full citizenship rights? Do the child-centered and human capital foci of the social investment strategy reinforce an agenda for gender equality?[12]

In what follows I take up these questions—as well as the related question of how social investment strategies impact women's right to social security—in the context of social assistance in one Canadian province, Ontario.[13] I briefly track the impact of neo-liberalism on social assistance policy in Ontario, and the corresponding disappearance of women, caring labour, social relations and social rights. However, my focus is primarily upon developments over the past half a dozen years, a time when Ontario crafted its first poverty reduction strategy, and pursuant to that strategy, embarked on a review of social assistance programmes. Poverty reduction and social

[8] McKeen, 'The National Children's Agenda', above n 1. See also Coulter, K, 'Women, Poverty Policy, and the Production of Neoliberal Politics in Ontario, Canada' (2009) 30 *Journal of Women, Politics & Policy* 23; and Simon-Kumar, above n 7.

[9] Green, DA, 'A Cautionary Discussion About Relying on Human Capital Policy to Meet Redistributive Goals' (2007) 33 *Canadian Public Policy* 397.

[10] Jenson, 'Lost in Translation', above n 1; and Simon-Kumar, above n 7.

[11] See Jenson, J, 'Writing Women Out, Folding Gender In: The European Union "Modernises" Social Policy' (2008) 15 *Social Politics* 131.

[12] Jenson, 'Lost in Translation', above n 1, at 449.

[13] In the context of Canadian federalism, social assistance is a matter of provincial jurisdiction. However, the federal government has long played a critical role in social assistance policy through cost-sharing agreements with the provinces.

assistance policies are both critical sites for feminist engagement given the persistently high rates of poverty among women generally, and sole support mothers particularly. Moreover, social assistance policy has been an important terrain of contestation for feminists, both as a site for critique given its patriarchal character and moral regulation of women, and as a site of potential liberation given its potential to enable women to sustain households independently of men and to exercise choice between waged work and care.[14] As a residual, needs-tested programme' social assistance, accessible only after all employment related benefits have been exhausted, is also an integral component of any social protection floor, especially for women whose access to employment related social benefits is often more limited.

In both the poverty reduction planning and social assistance review processes feminists intervened in an attempt to ensure an understanding of the issues and the development of new policy directions attentive to the complex realities of women's lives and the gendered roots of poverty. These interventions sought to bring a gendered analysis to social assistance and to further women's substantive equality, attending not only to redistribution, but also to recognition, transformation and participation.[15] Problematically, in both the 2008 Poverty Reduction Strategy and the report staking out a vision for social assistance reform, the concerns and frameworks articulated by feminists were rendered as postscripts or afterthoughts. The 2008 Poverty Reduction Strategy concludes by noting that 'certain people' experience higher rates of poverty, among them women. Their acknowledged 'unique needs', requiring 'tailored solutions', rather than being understood as integral to the framing of the Strategy itself, are characterised as 'perspectives' that should inform the issue of poverty 'going forward'.[16] Significantly, when the Poverty Reduction Act Bill was introduced into the legislature on first reading, it omitted women as a group particularly impacted by poverty. The final report of the Social Assistance Review Committee concludes in a remarkably similar fashion; it acknowledges that a number of submissions had urged the 'use of specific "lenses" or frameworks to assess the impact of reforms on equity, including lenses focused on disability, gender, racialization, and health', and again, rather than engaging with these 'lenses', the Commissioners recommended to the Province that as part of its implementation

[14] The patriarchal character of the welfare state is evocatively captured in the notion of trading in a man for the man. See Kandaswamy, P, '"You Trade in *a* Man for *the* Man": Domestic Violence and the US Welfare State' (2010) 62 *American Quarterly* 253.

[15] See Fredman, in this collection; and Fredman, S, 'The Potential and Limits of an Equal Rights Paradigm in Addressing Poverty' in S Liebenberg and G Quinot (eds), *Law and Poverty: Perspectives from South Africa and Beyond* (Claremont, Juta & Company Ltd, 2012) for an elaboration of these components of substantive equality.

[16] Cabinet Committee on Poverty Reduction, 'Breaking the Cycle, Ontario's Poverty Reduction Strategy' (Ontario, Ministry of Children and Youth Services, 2008) 5, available at: www.children.gov.on.ca/htdocs/English/documents/breakingthecycle/Poverty_Report_EN.pdf.

plan, it should 'establish a framework (or frameworks) to assess the impact of changes on different groups'.[17]

This move to postscript, rather than integrate, a gendered analysis perpetuates the neo-liberal silencing of equality, and of the critical role of care and nurturing relationships. Individuals are assumed to inhabit a world in which structures of power are non-existent; where their membership in particular social groups—be it groups constituted by gender, race or disability—is irrelevant to, for example, their access to employment. Pervasive discrimination is obscured, and equality as a guiding norm and aspiration, never mentioned.[18] Central to the framing of the recommendations is a valorised, if not mythical, world of waged work, capable of adequately sustaining all, not the precarious employment that characterises a substantial segment of the Canadian labour market.

Part of what I seek to understand is why the ideas and positions advanced by feminists had so little traction and what we might learn from this as we go forward to engage in future political struggles over women's equality and women's right to security. Investments in human capital development form a central and unifying thread in both the Poverty Reduction Strategy and the blueprint offered for the future of social assistance policy. Both make clear that social returns—in the form of increased economic activity—are to be expected from these investments. While the Poverty Reduction Strategy is focused upon child poverty—with investments primarily in education but also in a child benefit—the social assistance reform recommendations are preoccupied with the movement of all adult beneficiaries from assistance and into waged work, through investments in individualised assessments, employment plans, training and skill development. At least as deployed within these processes in Ontario, the ideas and discourses of social investment are derived from an uncritical invocation of human capital theory. Persons experiencing low income are reduced to assets—commodified, dehumanised and stripped of context, histories and identities. Modest investments in skill development are assumed to increase the capacity of this 'asset' to yield future, collective returns and to guarantee a 'pathway' out of poverty. I do not mean to suggest that state support for education or skills training are, in themselves, wrongheaded. Rather, my concerns centre upon the preoccupation with a narrow band of activity—education and skill training—and the commodification of labour, both of which serve to obscure the many structural factors which together shape women's social

[17] Lankin, F and Sheikh, MA, Commissioners, Commission for the Review of Social Assistance in Ontario, 'Brighter Prospects: Transforming Social Assistance in Ontario' (A Report to the Minister of Community and Social Services, Ontario, Ministry of Community and Social Services, 2012), available at: www.mcss.gov.on.ca/documents/en/mcss/social/publications/social_assistance_review_final_report.pdf .

[18] See also Jenson, 'Lost in Translation', above n 1, at 466–67 on the disappearance of equality.

security: the devaluing of caring relationships; violence against women; labour market segregation; and discrimination, for example. This preoccupation with investments in human capital serves, in turn, to deepen neo-liberalism's evisceration of women's lives, concerns and aspirations for equality.

SOCIAL ASSISTANCE IN ONTARIO

Since 1997, social assistance in Ontario has been comprised of two programmes, 'Ontario Works' (OW) and the 'Ontario Disability Support Program' (ODSP). Both are residual, needs-tested programmes; OW is intended for the 'able-bodied', and ODSP, for those who meet a statutory test of 'disability'. For OW recipients, benefits are conditioned on participation in work or work readiness activities, and each adult beneficiary is required to enter into a 'participation agreement' with the state, outlining the activities in which she will participate. The penalty for a breach of this agreement is, in the first instance, a one-month suspension of benefits, with a three-month suspension for subsequent breaches.[19]

These—and other reforms, including a significant drop in benefit levels and a focus on fraud in the system—have been characterised by many as indicative of the unfolding of a neo-liberal social policy landscape. No longer entitled to benefits as a social right indicative of citizenship, and to protection from the vagaries of the market, a new conditional and contractual relationship was forged, requiring work-related activity as a precondition to benefit receipt. This 'workfarist' model, as Peck and Theodore observe, reflected something of a 'postwelfare consensus among transAtlantic policy elites'.[20] As they note, within this model it is welfare dependence, not poverty, which is understood to be the problem. The model is one that at its core draws upon and reinforces age-old stereotypes about welfare recipients as choosing idleness over industry, lacking a proper work ethic and in need of the discipline of the workhouse.

Significantly, the introduction of OW and ODSP marked an important step in the erasure of the gendered subject in Ontario social assistance policy. Prior to 1997, single parents were entitled to benefits until their youngest child reached the age of 18, or in some circumstances 21. With the introduction of OW, single mothers were re-grouped into the category of temporarily unemployed persons and subject to the work participation requirements, with an exemption until their youngest child reached school

[19] O Reg 134/98, s 33.

[20] Peck, J and Theodore, N, 'Recombinant Workfare, Across the Americas: Transnationalizing "Fast" Social Policy' (2010) 41 *Geoforum* 195, 196.

age (three or four). While benefits were never adequate, the precipitous reduction of benefit levels by 21.6 per cent when OW was introduced was intentionally designed to sharpen the spur of poverty and to incentivise recipients to seek employment. The combined impact of this reduction in rates and the new work participation obligations signalled a further devaluation of women's caring labour, a valorisation of waged work as the sole route to belonging and to social recognition, and a fundamental re-scripting of mothers as waged workers.

The reforms in Ontario also reflected significant elements of neo-conservatism. This is evidenced most clearly in the definition of 'spouse' introduced in 1997 (and modified somewhat subsequently), the active regulation of women's intimate lives and the enforcement of obligations to seek support.[21] Waged work and forced dependency upon deemed 'spouses' were dual strategies to move women off welfare rolls.

Since the introduction of these significant reforms in the late 1990s only relatively modest changes have been made to Ontario's social assistance regime and these, only after significant struggle:[22] rates have increased marginally to $599 for a single person as of 2012 (in real terms $225 less than what it was following the 21.6 per cent cut);[23] a lifetime ban on receipt of benefits if convicted of welfare fraud has been revoked; and a three-month 'grace period' before relationships are interrogated to determine if they are 'spousal' has replaced the presumption, introduced in 1997, that a spousal relationship arises upon co-residency. No doubt the most significant development has been the introduction of the Ontario Child Benefit, a benefit delivered outside the social assistance regime but which has had important implications for the financial well-being of families with children.

ONTARIO'S POVERTY REDUCTION STRATEGY

In the autumn of 2007 the Liberal government of Ontario announced that a new committee of Cabinet would be struck and tasked to develop 'poverty indicators and targets and a focused strategy for making clear-cut progress

[21] Mosher, J, 'Intimate Intrusions: Welfare Regulation and Women's Personal Lives' in SAM Gavigan and DE Chunn (eds), *The Legal Tender of Gender* (Hart Publishing, Onati Law & Society Series, 2010) 165.

[22] See *Falkiner et al v Director, Income Maintenance Branch* (2002), 59 OR (3d) 481 (challenging the definition of spouse); *Broomer v Ontario (AG)* (5 June 2002), Toronto 02-CV-229203CM3, Ontario Superior Court (challenging the lifetime ban, a case settled in advance of hearing); and *Chokomolin, Lance and Prince v Her Majesty the Queen in Right of Canada et al* (challenging the claw back of the national child benefit supplement from families in receipt of social assistance in Ontario, but as a result of the introduction of the Ontario Child Benefit did not proceed in the courts).

[23] Stapleton, J, 'Of the 1%, for the 1%, to the 1%?' (*Open Policy Ontario*, Ontario, 3 April 2012), available at: www.openpolicyontario.com/of-the-1-for-the-1-to-the-1.

on reducing child poverty'.[24] As such, it was clear from the outset that the focus would be on the reduction of child poverty.

Alongside this process, two feminist organisations based in Toronto, the Metropolitan Action Committee on Violence Against Women and Children (METRAC) and the Woman Abuse Council (WAC), assumed leadership of a project called 'Take Action', that brought together representatives from some 50 women's organisations across Ontario working with women experiencing violence. Poverty was identified as the single most pressing issue facing abused women and as such there was a sense of urgency to ensure that the poverty reduction framework reflected the gendered routes into and out of poverty, and in particular the integral role that violence plays in the impoverishment of women. The project's report, 'No Cherries Grow on our Trees', was submitted to the Poverty Reduction Cabinet Committee.[25] Drawing upon the influential work of Amartya Sen, the Report urged an understanding of poverty that went beyond low income to include voice, capabilities, access to opportunities and freedom from violence. It offered a gendered approach to poverty reduction grounded in an analysis of the intersecting axes of oppression that constitute poverty's roots, and attentive to the specific structures and systems that trap women in poverty. The report identified substantive equality and respect for human rights as overarching norms and called on the government to adopt specific targets and timelines for the reduction of women's poverty.

Ultimately, the government enacted new legislation, the Poverty Reduction Act, 2009[26] and a five-year plan, entitled 'Breaking the Cycle' (the Plan).[27] The Plan concentrates on the reduction of child poverty, setting a target for the reduction of child poverty by 25 per cent over five years (by 2013).[28] Although the process was ostensibly about poverty reduction, the Plan, as its title suggests, is much more singularly focused on breaking the intergenerational cycle of poverty.[29] Indeed, the Plan begins by trumpeting, 'We

[24] Onley, DC, 'Moving Forward, The Ontario Way' (Address given on the Opening of the First Session of the Thirty-Ninth Parliament of Ontario, 29 November 2007) 7.

[25] Take Action Project, 'No Cherries Grow on our Trees' (Social Research Paper for the Take Action Project, a Public Policy Initiative to Address Women's Poverty and Violence Against Women, October 2008), available at: http://www.metrac.org/wp-content/uploads/woocommerce_uploads/2014/07/take.action.report.dec08.pdf. I worked with METRAC and WAC as the research coordinator of the project, and with Nora Currie, the project coordinator.

[26] Poverty Reduction Act, SO 2009, c 10.

[27] Cabinet Committee on Poverty Reduction, above n 16.

[28] The federal government undertook in 1989 to end child poverty by 2000. A 2012 report card tracking progress in ending child poverty reveals that 979,000 or 14.5% of children in Canada lived in poverty as of 2010, compared with 912,000 or 13.7% in 1989. See Campaign 2000, 'Needed: A Federal Action Plan to Eradicate Child and Family Poverty in Canada' (2012 Report Card on Child and Family Poverty, Toronto, Family Service Toronto, 2012), available at: www.campaign2000.ca/reportCards/national/C2000ReportCardNov2012.pdf.

[29] See also Jenson, 'Lost in Translation', above n 1.

can break the cycle of poverty. That's the conviction that sits at the heart of Ontario's Poverty Reduction Strategy'. The first of the ten principles articulated in the plan makes clear that, 'Kids are our highest priority. By helping kids living in poverty get what they need to succeed, especially in school, the cycle of poverty can be broken'.[30]

The influence of social investment thinking and human capital theory in particular, is explicit. Children living in poverty are characterised as 'untapped potential', and 'investments' to develop this asset are promised to produce returns for all Ontarians in the form of a more prosperous economy. Principle 8, for example, states unambiguously that 'the research is clear—investing in the early years will give us the highest possible return on our investment'.[31] Education, and especially early childhood education, is identified as 'the best poverty reduction strategy' and the key to breaking the 'intergenerational cycle that makes poverty such an insidious problem'.[32] In a self-congratulatory manner, the government highlights its 'signature investments in education', referring to the expansion from part-day to full-day kindergarten and the reduction of class sizes in elementary education.[33]

This focus on children mirrors discourses and practices in other policy areas and among other social policy actors.[34] The Ontario Municipal Social Services Association, in a 2005 report for example, underscores the importance of greater investment in high quality, early learning and childcare.[35] It too relies on research ostensibly showing 'clear linkages between investments in quality childcare and future labour force success'.[36] Like the Poverty Reduction Plan, it also anticipates social returns on investments, favourably quoting Charles Coffey, Executive Vice-President of Government Affairs, for the Royal Bank of Canada Financial Group:

> [T]he bottom line is that the earlier we invest in a child's life, the greater the future dividend. As a business leader I clearly understand that improving shareholder value tomorrow has everything to do with investing in children today.[37]

[30] Cabinet Committee on Poverty Reduction, above n 16, at 1 and 5.

[31] *Ibid*, at 8.

[32] *Ibid*, at 3–4.

[33] *Ibid*, at 1.

[34] See McKeen, 'Diminishing the Concept', above n 6; and Dobrowolsky and Jenson, above n 3, for a fuller discussion of the emphasis within social investment on investing in children, and the resulting obfuscation of women's equality rights.

[35] Ontario Municipal Social Services Association (OMSSA), 'Demonstrating the Value of Social Investments: A Resource Document for OMSSA Members' (OMSSA, May 2005), available at: www.omssa.com/human-services/employment-income-security/employment-and-income-security-resources/poverty-reucation-strategies-across-ontario/campaign-47/campaign-47-member-toolkit/Demonstrating%20the%20Value%20of%20Social%20Investments%20-%20A%20Resource%20Document%20for%20OMSSA%20Members.pdf.

[36] *Ibid*, at 5.

[37] *Ibid*, at 6.

Indeed, these anticipated returns are quantified: investments in quality early learning and childcare programmes for children up to six years of age are said to yield returns at a minimum of $2 for every dollar invested; and up to $17 for every dollar invested in programmes for 'disadvantaged children'.[38]

The Plan identifies a 'moral imperative' for reducing poverty, an imperative that pulls most strongly in reference to children who 'should have the opportunity to succeed in life'.[39] But even here, and in relation to children, this moral imperative is narrowly construed in an equal opportunity framework, and devoid of attention to human dignity and human rights. Having noted this moral imperative, the Plan quickly shifts to an instrumental justification of proclaimed equal importance:

> As a society, we can't afford it. An educated, healthy and employable workforce is critical to the economic future of this province. Our economy is changing before our eyes and we need everyone to be ready to contribute to our future prosperity.[40]

The Plan is grounded in a monochromatic view of the roots of poverty and thus offers an equally simplistic solution: investments in children, especially in education. In this rendering, education severs poverty's sole root, its intergenerational transmission. Further, as the primary labourers of social reproduction, women are cast as poverty's vectors. The Plan is grounded in a view of children as homogenous (a mass of fungible individuals), ignoring the evidence that parents' income and social capital continues to matter significantly in the educational attainment of children,[41] and that the quality of education is varied (often based on class, race and gender).[42] The use of human capital theory to predict rates of return on social investments has been critiqued on a number of grounds, including its inattention to labour market demand[43] and to the reality that race and gender segregation within the labour market impacts the returns on similar investments. Indeed, Fortin and her co-authors caution against thinking that education necessarily reduces inequality, observing that under some conditions, it does just the opposite.[44] Lastly, a normative question ensues of whether we ought to construe education solely in terms of its potential to develop a commodity—human capital—for production.

[38] *Ibid*, at 6; and Cabinet Committee on Poverty Reduction, above n 16, at 5.

[39] Cabinet Committee on Poverty Reduction, above n 16, at 5.

[40] *Ibid*.

[41] Banting, above n 1, at 427.

[42] Bowles, S and Gintis, H, 'The Problem with Human Capital Theory—A Marxian Critique' (1975) 65 *The American Economic Review* 74, 79.

[43] Chattopadhyay, S, *Education and Economics: Disciplinary Evolution and Policy Discourse* (Oxford, Oxford University Press, 2012).

[44] Fortin, N et al, 'Canadian Inequality: Recent Developments and Policy Options' (2012) 38 *Canadian Public Policy* 121, 138–39.

The only recognition given at all to the principles and values identified by the 'Take Action' report[45] comes in the form of an acknowledgement of the intersections between violence and poverty and again, a self-congratulatory review of the government's pre-existing domestic violence action plan. That poverty mirrors and reinforces existing inequalities goes unexamined in the Plan, and the pervasive and destructive social practices of discrimination that contribute to poverty are rendered absolutely invisible. There is not a single mention of equality or human rights. The realities of twenty-first century labour markets are largely ignored, although the Plan notes in passing the over-representation of women in precarious work. The closest the Plan comes to an acknowledgement of the structural and systemic factors that contribute to poverty is in its recognition that the lack of adequate state enforcement of legislated minimum standards of employment (including of the minimum wage) contributes to poverty. As Evans observes, 'there's a rather striking evasion of having to deal with the real structural problems confronting Ontario's working families and communities'.[46]

The Plan concludes, in what reads much like a postscript, that for often complex reasons 'certain people are at higher risk of poverty', including 'women, racialized communities, newcomers, people with disabilities, and Aboriginal peoples'. But as noted in the Introduction, consideration of the acknowledged 'unique needs of these groups [that] require tailored solutions' is put over to another day, and poverty is to be viewed 'from these perspectives going forward'.[47]

In addition to the Plan, new legislation, the Poverty Reduction Act 2009 (the Act) was introduced.[48] The framing of the Act, while identifying an early focus on children, is broader than the Plan, with 'untapped potential' being identified as residing not only in children, but in all low-income Ontarians. The Act stresses the need to tap this potential 'by building and establishing supports for, and eliminating barriers to, full participation by all people in Ontario's economy and society'. In many respects, the legislation reflects the postscript to the Plan, acknowledging some groups are at higher risk of poverty and promising to involve such groups in the creation of future plans (again, put over to another day.) Section 3 of the statute specifically recognises that not all groups share the same level of risk of poverty. But as noted earlier, despite the deeply entrenched and higher rates of poverty for women than men, and that across all other social groups experiencing high rates of poverty—whether

[45] Take Action Project, above n 25.

[46] Evans, B, 'Importing Blair's Failure: Ontario's Poverty Reduction Strategy' (*Socialist Project*) 4, available at: www.socialistproject.ca/relay/relay22_evans.pdf.

[47] Cabinet Committee on Poverty Reduction, above n 16, at 5.

[48] Poverty Reduction Act, above n 26.

persons with disabilities, racialised groups, etc—women experience higher rates than men, in the first reading of the statute in the legislature, women were omitted as a group with a higher risk of poverty.[49] Women were added only after persistent advocacy by feminists. The groups now recognised by the legislation are immigrants, women, single mothers, people with disabilities, aboriginal peoples and racialised groups. These identified groups are to be consulted in the drafting of the five-year cyclical poverty reduction plans and targets.

Lastly, it is important to note that the Act, unlike the Strategy, does name both the problem of discrimination and the importance of human dignity. The Act notes that in eliminating barriers to full participation, particular attention needs to be paid to 'persons who face discrimination on the grounds of their race, ancestry, place of origin, colour, ethnic origin, citizenship, creed, sex, sexual orientation, age, marital status, family status or disability'.[50] Moreover, principle 5 provides, 'That all people in Ontario, including those living in poverty, deserve to be treated with respect and dignity'. Yet, as discussed below, at least with respect to the social assistance review—a review ostensibly grounded in the prior poverty reduction work—the anti-discrimination provision of the Act is totally ignored, and while dignity is mentioned, it is not a value which is engaged in any substantive way to guide the recommendations.[51]

THE SOCIAL ASSISTANCE REVIEW

A recurrent theme in the poverty reduction consultations was the failure of OW, and a critical component of the Poverty Reduction Plan was a commitment to a review of social assistance. The government-drafted terms of reference for the review reflect a continuing preoccupation with transitioning recipients off assistance and into waged work; indeed they read remarkably like the legislative statement of purpose for the existing Ontario Works programme, now expanding its reach to include persons with statutorily recognised disabilities.[52] Two Commissioners, Frances Lankin and Munir A Sheikh, were appointed to lead the review, and in October 2012 the final report, 'Brighter Prospects: Transforming Social Assistance in Ontario' (the Report) was released.[53]

[49] Women had been identified as a group experiencing higher rates of poverty in the Plan.

[50] Poverty Reduction Act, above n 26, at s 2(2)1.

[51] But see Mahon, R and Macdonald, L, 'Anti-poverty Politics in Toronto and Mexico City' (2010) 41 *Geoforum* 209.

[52] Lankin and Sheikh, above n 17, at 12.

[53] *Ibid*.

Feminists again engaged in the review process in an attempt to ensure attention to issues of gender inequality. Among these attempts was that of an ad hoc group of feminist academics and feminist service providers, who convened a day-long workshop to share ideas about the framing of the review.[54] One outcome of this gathering was a submission to the Commission, urging a 'gendered equity approach'—one attending to the intersections of gender with other axes of oppression, to existing dimensions of gender inequality, to the complex realities of women's lives and to the often different pathways into and out of poverty for men and women. The submission also posited substantive equality as the benchmark against which policy options ought to be evaluated. In reviewing the recommendations of the Commission below, I draw upon a number of the ideas put forward by this ad hoc group, as well as from the ideas generated through a community consultation project with low-income women called 'Bringing in Women's Voices'.[55]

Given the emphasis of the Poverty Reduction Plan, and the terms of reference of the Review itself, that the final Report is preoccupied with the movement of 'clients' from welfare and into waged work is entirely predictable. Employment is positioned as the 'starting point of the new system', one in which 'all social assistance recipients, including people with disabilities, should be supported to participate in the workforce to the maximum of their abilities and that income security should be guaranteed for those who cannot work'.[56] The first chapter of the Report, drafted to speak directly to individuals in receipt of benefits, reassures the 'client' that the programme is designed to

> help you [achieve your employment goals, with] services and supports ... matched to your individual needs ... Your Pathway to Employment Plan would provide you with a valuable employment planning tool and promote greater collaboration between you and your caseworker.[57]

Consistent with the approach to the Poverty Reduction Plan, the Commissioners embrace the view that moving more recipients into employment will not only 'ensur[e] human potential is not wasted' but 'improve

[54] I assisted in the organisation of the workshop and participated in both the crafting of the letter and two subsequent in-person meetings with the Commissioners. There were also a number of other feminist contributions.

[55] This was a joint project of the Income Security Advocacy Centre and Campaign 2000 in which more than 200 women participated. See Income Security Advocacy Centre (ISAC) and Ontario Campaign 2000, 'Social Assistance Review: Key Messages from the "Bringing Women's Voices" Project' (ISAC, 15 July 2011), available at: www.sareview.ca/isac-resources/key-messages-from-the-%E2%80%98bringing-in-women%E2%80%99s-voices%E2%80%99-project/.

[56] Lankin and Sheikh, above n 17, at 11.

[57] *Ibid*, at 19, 22, 26.

the quality of life for individuals and families in need and contribute to greater prosperity for all Ontarians'.[58]

The central place of employment in these proposals travels in lockstep with earlier neo-liberal reforms, so one might ask what, if anything, is new here beyond the extension of the expectation of employment to persons with disabilities? The Commissioners are cognisant of the dismal performance of the existing system in permanently moving welfare recipients from assistance and into non-poverty waged work, but rather than abandoning this policy direction, they seek to better operationalise it.[59] The source of the failure, they suggest, is rooted in the generally poor quality of training programmes (there is broad based agreement about this assessment of quality) and in the emphasis on moving recipients into the first available job.[60] They urge a shift in thinking, captured by a change in metaphors; the transition into employment should be understood not as a 'leap' but a 'journey'—a slower, more measured and deliberative approach.[61] Unlike the current 'participation agreement', the 'employment plan' of the future will provide a 'pathway' plotted through a careful assessment of each recipient, case management and pre-employment and post-employment supports tailored to individual needs, 'to ensure no one is left behind'.[62] The pathway promises not only a route to employment—itself the locus of 'increased independence, a sense of wellbeing, new networks, further opportunities, and the ability to plan for the future'—but 'the key route to escaping poverty'.[63]

Certainly, this vision—of individualised assessments of employability with resources and supports to develop one's human capital—is, at first blush, an appealing one. One might say that here we see evidence of a shift towards social investment in adult workers, and away from the purely punitive measures of neo-liberalism. However, such conclusions may be too hasty; given the central reliance placed upon human capital as an anti-poverty measure and as an engine of economic prosperity, it is critical to explore more fully the content and assumptions of human capital theory.

[58] *Ibid*, at 11.

[59] See Lightman, E, Mitchell, A and Herd, D, 'Cycling Off and On Welfare in Canada' (2010) 39 *Journal of Social Policy* 523; Mallon, AJ and Stevens, G, 'Making the 1996 Welfare Reform Work: The Promise of a Job' (2011) 15 *Journal of Poverty* 113; and Peck and Theodore, above n 20, at 196.

[60] See Pulkingham, J, Fuller, S and Kershaw, P, 'Lone Motherhood, Welfare Reform and Active Citizen Subjectivity' (2010) 30 *Critical Social Policy* 267; and Gingrich, L, 'Single Mothers, Work(fare), and Managed Precariousness' (2010) 21 *Journal of Progressive Human Service* 107.

[61] Lankin and Sheikh, above n 17, at 20 and 47.

[62] *Ibid*, at 45.

[63] *Ibid*, at letter of transmittal, 39 and 3.

Human capital theory, regarded as a staple of neo-classical economics, assumes 'peoples' learning capacities are comparable to other natural resources involved in the capitalist production process'.[64] The theory posits that when this 'resource is effectively utilised the results are profitable both for the enterprise and for society as a whole'.[65] Education and job training are regarded as central to the production of human capital, but other factors, including health and economic migration, are also relevant.[66] Both the Report and the Plan rely heavily upon claims regarding the 'returns' on investments in the development of human capital through job training and education. Yet these claims are contentious; some research finds training programmes (themselves heterogeneous) have at best only modest positive effects on future earnings, and that returns are greatest for those already at the high end of the wage distribution.[67] Other research comes to a similar conclusion, finding that training benefits the non-poor but not the poor.[68] Giving further pause is a study finding that job training actually worsened the economic position of non-whites, while post-secondary education made a difference in the poverty rates of women and minority groups (a level of education no longer supported by social assistance policies in Ontario).[69] Moreover, to be effective training programmes must be 'strongly tailored to local labour markets'.[70] Heckman and his colleagues come to the conclusion that overall 'job-training programs are an inefficient transfer mechanism and an inefficient investment policy for low-skilled adults'.[71] While there may not yet be sufficient research to come to a definitive conclusion, there is ample reason for at least measured scepticism about the claims currently being made in relation to investments in human capital.

A significant question also arises about the actual investments that are likely to materialise, for among the parameters dictated for the Review is that of cost-neutrality. The Commissioners do make other recommendations intended to free up funds for re-purposing, but without additional and significant cash infusions it seems unlikely that particularised assessments and substantial supports will materialise. Moreover, discourses of 'opportunity planning' in social assistance have existed in Ontario since the late

[64] Hong, PYP and Pandey, S, 'Human Capital as Structural Vulnerability of US Poverty' (2007) 26 *Equal Opportunities International* 18, 20.

[65] *Ibid*, at 20.

[66] *Ibid.*

[67] Heckman, JJ, 'Inequality in America: What Role for Human Capital Policies?' (2005) 23 *Focus* 1 (discussing issues addressed by James J Heckman, University of Chicago, in a seminar of the same title).

[68] Hong, PYP and Pandey, S, 'Differential Effects of Human Capital on the Poor and the Near Poor: Evidence of Social Exclusion' (2008) 12 *Journal of Poverty* 456, 473.

[69] Hong and Pandey, 'Human Capital', above n 64, at 32.

[70] Heckman, above n 67, at 8.

[71] *Ibid.*

1980s (when the metaphor invoked was that of welfare as a 'springboard') and yet have never led to widespread, meaningful, on-the-ground supports to access and sustain employment. Indeed, Canada's commitment to investing in human capital has been described as 'uncertain at best'.[72] Broader concerns regarding the decline in the quality of services as universal programmes give way to residual ones targeting the least well off (and frequently the most politically marginalised) are echoed in observations regarding the often poor quality of job training programmes for the most disadvantaged.[73]

A related critique of human capital theory is its obfuscation of macroeconomic conditions.[74] The Canadian labour market currently resembles something of an hourglass, with a significant decline in middle-income jobs and a growth of low income, precarious work and the highly skilled work required of the knowledge economy. There is an increasing divide between 'good jobs' and 'bad jobs' and a resulting growth in income inequality.[75] Much of the work at the bottom of the hourglass is increasingly precarious: it consists of various forms of temporary and part-time work, high levels of uncertainty, few if any benefits, low wages, little control over labour processes and not uncommonly, limited access to regulatory protections.[76] Using a combination of three or more characteristics—low wages, the absence of pensions, small firm and no union—as a measure of precariousness, fully one-third of workers in Ontario hold precarious jobs.[77] Modest investments in the training of social assistance recipients are not likely to move social assistance recipients out of the work offered at the lower end of the labour market, nor increase their wages, other than at best, marginally. Cynthia Williams aptly describes low wage work as the 'Achilles heel of our social security system for working-age adults', and as such, claims that full time employment is 'the best ticket out of poverty—rings hollow for many workers who are stuck in low-wage jobs'.[78] Moreover, as Hong and Pandey suggest, human capital development for the supply side may have little impact on poverty status when on the demand side opportunities ('good jobs' in particular) do not exist.[79] The Commissioners do briefly

[72] Banting, above n 1, at 425; see also McKeen, 'Diminishing the Concept', above n 6, at 881.

[73] Hong and Pandey, 'Human Capital', above n 64, at 33.

[74] Bowles and Gintis, above n 42, at 81.

[75] Zizys, T, *Working Better: Creating a High-Performing Labour Market in Ontario* (Toronto, Metcalf Foundation, 2011); and Fortin et al, above n 44, at 131.

[76] Noack, AM and Vosko, LF, 'Precarious Jobs in Ontario: Mapping Dimensions of Labour Market Insecurity by Workers' Social Location and Context' (2011), available at: www.lco-cdo.org/vulnerable-workers-commissioned-papers-vosko-noack.pdf; and Law Commission of Ontario (LCO), *Vulnerable Workers and Precarious Work* (Final Report, Toronto, LCO, December 2012).

[77] Noack and Vosko, above n 76, at 15.

[78] Williams, C, 'Asset-building Approaches', above n 5, at 56.

[79] Hong and Pandey, 'Human Capital', above n 64, at 36.

note the rise of temporary, part-time and low-wage work, and with it, growing income inequality.[80] To address this, they recommend that the province should build on its Jobs and Prosperity Council 'to develop a comprehensive human capital development strategy'. While not detailed in the Report, the inference implied is that a human capital strategy has the potential to reduce income inequality. Yet here too, the evidence is ambiguous; increasing skills may drive wages down at the upper end, and up at the lower end (with fewer workers competing here), but may also produce the opposite result.[81]

Critically absent from the human capital perspective is any acknowledgement that good and bad jobs are not equitably distributed; rather women, racialised women, recent immigrants, single parents (mostly women) and those with less than high school education are heavily concentrated among precarious workers.[82] The harsh reality is that much of the work low-income women are able to access is part time (women constitute 72 per cent of permanent part-time employees), without benefits, low-waged and without workplace policies designed to accommodate the needs of parents.[83] The lack of congruence between the character of work that women access and their child-caring needs is a significant source of women's job insecurity. While 9.3 per cent of women give as their reason not to work full time that they are caring for children, 0.8 per cent of men offer this reason.[84] Moreover, there is a significant gap between participation and employment rates, especially among lone mothers with young children (12 per cent for lone mothers with children under three in Ontario).[85] Unemployment and underemployment for women, as well as low-income status, often has more to do with the absence of childcare options, inflexible workplaces and discrimination, than with deficiencies in human capital.[86]

As noted in relation to education, human capital theory presupposes homogeneity of persons—an amorphous untapped potential—undifferentiated by structures of class, race or gender, with investments producing equivalent returns. As such, it ignores not only macroeconomic conditions, but also a host of systems and structures that play a fundamental role in women's poverty.[87] Waged work in the Report takes on an almost surreal quality where discrimination is non-existent, no one struggles to balance work and family, women do not experience violence pervasively, wages are

[80] Lankin and Sheikh, above n 17, at 107, and Fortin et al, above n 44, at 122–24.
[81] *Ibid*, at 138.
[82] Noack and Vosko, above n 76, at 26–27.
[83] *Ibid*, at 19.
[84] *Ibid*, at 10.
[85] Mitchell, A, Mosher, J and Jamal, R, 'How Lone Mothers Have Fared in Canada' (unpublished paper, 2011).
[86] Hong and Pandey, 'Human Capital', above n 64, at 22.
[87] See also Jenson, 'Lost in Translation', above n 1, at 466–67.

adequate, all have equal opportunities and labour markets are devoid of sex and race segregation.

A related and equally troublesome dimension of the positioning of waged work lies in the contrast drawn between work and receipt of social assistance. Being in receipt of welfare is to be 'left behind', in a space assumed to be unproductive, unfulfilling and devoid of value. But it is in precisely this space that significant numbers of women, particularly single mothers, are caring for their children. It further assumes that those in receipt of social assistance are 'doing nothing', a view typified by remarks from former Premier Mike Harris (1995–2002) that social assistance was paying 'people to sit at home and do nothing'.[88]

This devaluation of women's caring labour is reinforced by the Commissioners' discussion of 'fairness', a discussion fixated on a comparison between low-waged workers and persons in receipt of social assistance. The Commissioners assert that it is 'unfair' for those in receipt of social assistance (and presumed to be idle) to receive more than the waged worker (the principle of less eligibility continues). But 'adequacy' is another concern of the Commissioners, and so the reality of precarious, low-waged work creates a tension. Ultimately, in proposing a methodology to set social assistance rates, the minimum wage (itself determined without reference to adequacy) is selected as the benchmark. And while the Commissioners do conclude that current rates are inadequate, this methodology for setting future rates leaves benefit levels permanently below market incomes, irrespective of the inadequacy of the latter.

In stark contrast to the last major review of social assistance in Ontario in 1987, which devoted considerable attention to the social value of caring labour, in the recent review caring labour is not a subject of discussion. The admonition of the ad hoc group of feminists, urging attention to the variety of roles women play in their families, communities and economy and the value of women's caring labour—including its essential role in the well-being of society and the growth of the economy—obviously was not heard; in the world imagined by the Commission there is but one form of social contribution—waged work.[89]

Moreover, apart from a few oblique references to childcare as among a list of supports potentially needed to transition to employment (and to which women could be 'referred'),[90] and perhaps inferentially by the decision to leave untouched the current exemption of a parent with a pre-school aged child from mandated employment-related activities, workers appear in

[88] Legislative Assembly of Ontario, Oral Questions, Welfare Reform, 12 December 2000, available at: www.ontla.on.ca/web/house-proceedings/house_detail.do?locale=en&Parl=37&Sess=1&Date=2000-12-12#P302_59446.

[89] Letter from the ad hoc group to the Commissioners (6 May 2011).

[90] Lankin and Sheikh, above n 17, at 58.

the Report as unencumbered by caring obligations. There is, for example, no discussion of the complex realities of juggling, as sole support mothers do, the responsibilities of caregiver and wage-earner; a juggling act that is experienced as acutely stressful by many low-income women.[91] Even the work–life balance discourse—itself an individualising and responsibilising one—that has more recently shaped labour market policies is absent here.[92] The recommendations reflect a stark individualism, a world devoid of the caring relations that nurture and sustain each of us and indeed, contribute to our human capital.

The individualism is evident in other respects as well; the intense focus on assessments of each individual exudes a preoccupation with the reform of recipients. Human capital theory is at work here too in its obfuscation of the structural and its attention to the enhancement of the productivity of undifferentiated individuals. Recipients are rendered resources in the process of production to be assessed, groomed and prepared for a pathway to employment (productivity) which will, it is claimed, sustain them, connect them and fulfil them. As Lucy Williams so aptly describes, it is through the invocation of 'magical thinking' that the 'alienation and subordination experienced by low-wage workers, particularly women', is eliminated and waged work rendered a place of dignity, independence and self-actualisation.[93]

Finally it is imperative to note that the Commissioners envision a mixed carrot and stick approach—resources and supports for the development of one's human capital, but also sanctions for the failure to responsibly utilise these. Recipients are responsibilised to take up the 'opportunities' presented by these investments, to increase their asset value, their human capital. But who is in a position to take up these 'opportunities' (such as they are) and how is this impacted, for example, by caring obligations and the lack of access to childcare? As Green cautions, there is reason to worry that those who are not able to take up these 'opportunities' will be left further behind.[94]

The Report offers no analysis justifying the retention of sanctions notwithstanding the volumes of research, including a 2004 report by Deb Matthews, then Parliamentary Assistant to the Minister of Community

[91] See McMullin, JA, Davies, L and Cassidy, G, 'Welfare Reform in Ontario: Tough Times in Mothers' Lives' (2002) 28 *Canadian Public Policy* 297; Gazso, A, 'Balancing Expectations for Employability and Family Responsibilities While on Social Assistance: Low Income Mothers' Experiences in Three Canadian Provinces' (2007) 56 *Family Relations* 454; and Caragata, L and Cumming, SJ, 'Lone Mother Led Families: Exemplifying the Structuring of Social Inequality' (2011) 5 *Sociology Compass* 376.

[92] See McManus, above n 7.

[93] Williams, L, 'The Legal Construction of Poverty: Gender, "Work" and the "Social Contract"' (2011) 22 *Stellenbosch Law Review* 463, 465.

[94] Green, above n 9, at 399.

and Social Services (later chair of the Poverty Reduction Cabinet and now Minister of Health), that show recipients to be highly motivated, possessing a strong work ethic and anxious to seize opportunities for skill development and decent work.[95] Recipients of welfare are by no means immune to the message that the good neo-liberal citizen—someone who belongs and is accorded respect—sustains herself through paid employment. They are, in fact, very explicit targets of this message. As several authors have argued persuasively, the subjectivities of those in receipt of social assistance are 'acted upon to inculcate the notion of worker-citizen'[96] and low-income women 'schooled' to define themselves as low wage job-seekers.[97] This is not to suggest that this version of citizenship goes uncontested; many women attach value to their caring labour but they must, as McMullin et al describe, constantly negotiate the fundamental contradiction between the expectation that a good mother will stay home and raise her children and that of the good citizen who will sustain herself through paid employment.[98]

Yet by leaving sanctions intact the stereotype of the welfare recipient as a 'lazy loafer' who chooses to remain idle, parasitically living off the hard work of others, is reinforced. As less than ideal citizens, the termination of benefits for non-compliance from the programme of last resort—the pulling up of the floor of social protection—is deftly accomplished. As the 'Bringing in Women's Voices' project suggests, penalties themselves take on a gendered form, particularly when women are sanctioned for prioritising care obligations over compliance with the terms of their participation agreements; for example, when a woman misses a résumé writing workshop to care for a sick child or a skills workshop when a childcare arrangement has fallen through. Moreover, the shoring up of this stereotype serves to further entrench discriminatory practices; practices which are pervasive in the lives of low-income people, yet go unacknowledged in the Report.

As with the Poverty Reduction Plan, the concerns raised by feminists are largely postscripted.[99] They are not taken up by the Commissioners

[95] Matthews, D, *Review of Ontario Employment Assistance Programs in Ontario Works and Ontario Disability Support Program* (Ontario, Ministry of Community and Social Services, December, 2004); see also ISAC and Ontario Campaign 2000, above n 55.

[96] Pollack, S and Caragata, L, 'Contestation and Accommodation: Constructions of Lone Mothers' Subjectivity through Workfare Policy and Practice' (2010) 25 *Affilia: Journal of Women and Social Work* 264.

[97] Pulkingham et al, above n 60, at 279.

[98] Gingrich, above n 60, at 125; McMullin et al, above n 91, at 305; and Pulkingham et al, above n 60, at 284.

[99] A few of the recommendations do reflect some of the concerns raised by feminists: that the government no longer deducts child support dollar for dollar from benefits; and that women not be required to pursue child support.

in elucidating the nature of the challenges or in crafting new policy recommendations, but rather are merely acknowledged at the end of the Report, in what reads very much as an afterthought. The Commissioners note that some of the submissions they had received urged specific lenses, focused on 'disability, gender, racialization and health' and they offer a few examples.[100] But these lenses in no way steer their thinking on any of the major issues with which they grapple; rather they are postscripted into a recommendation that the 'Province establish a framework (or frameworks) to assess the impact of changes on different groups'.[101]

CONCLUSION

While in some jurisdictions the social investment paradigm has been accompanied by the reinsertion of the gendered subject,[102] this has not been the case for social assistance and poverty reduction initiatives in Ontario. Certainly in relation to these two critical sites of women's social security, the question of whether the social investment perspective offers an approach to gender relations that responds to women's equality claims and ambitions for full citizenship rights must be answered with a resounding 'no'. As the above review evidences, despite active interventions by feminists, neither the Poverty Reduction Strategy nor the social assistance review attend to the complex realities of women's lives and in denying the value of caring labour, they continue to undermine women's full citizenship rights. At least in Ontario, it is also clear that the 'child-centred and human capital foci of the social investment strategy' do not reinforce, but rather undermine, the agenda for gender equality and the realisation of women's right to social security. Rather, the discourses and practices of social investment in Ontario are fundamentally at odds with an engendered right to social security and corrosive of women's equality.

At one level, security and equality are undermined simply because human capital policy 'is being asked to carry too much weight ... and needs to be reinforced by attention to long-standing issues of poverty, inequality, and income redistribution'.[103] As Banting elaborates:

> [H]uman capital strategies hold out the promise of security in the future. Social investment requires long time horizons ... In the meantime, problems of low-skilled workers remain. In effect, the transition to a human-capital strategy requires

[100] Lankin and Sheikh, above n 17, at 117.
[101] *Ibid.*
[102] See, eg, Jenson, 'Writing Women Out', above n 11, for a discussion of developments within the European Union.
[103] Banting, above n 1, at 422.

> that most elusive of commitments, patient capital, on the part of normally impatient governments.[104]

And Canada has not evidenced that patience, moving to cut existing systems of support—among them social assistance, unemployment insurance, pensions, workers' compensation—before investments in human capital have 'come to fruition'. This poses as Banting maintains, 'a recipe for lower levels of economic security among low-skilled workers in this generation and perhaps several to come. Yet this is precisely the pattern Canada has followed'.[105]

More significantly, it is not just that human capital policy cannot do it all (even in the long run), but that human capital policy—its vocabulary, discourse and practice—is hostile to substantive equality and to an engendered right to social security. Human capital policy is inattentive to the social structures that shape inequality, its focus concentrated upon the individual. Indeed the theory is often invoked to blame low-income individuals for their failure to invest wisely in the development of their human capital, reinforcing individual, behavioural explanations of poverty.[106] Envisioned by the review of Social Assistance is an intense form of individual case management to correct flawed investors, reflecting as McKeen describes:

> [A] casework doctrine that assumes that social problems and the programmes of social cohesion can be addressed solely by treating the supposed deficiencies of the individuals ... structural understandings of social problems have been all but eliminated.[107]

The vocabulary of the market—capital, assets, investments, returns on investments—is profoundly dehumanising, reducing human beings to fungible commodities whose value is measured in terms of production. Within human capital theory persons are not entitled to an adequate level of social support in recognition of their human dignity or the indivisibility of fundamental human rights. Rather, 'investments' are justified on a purely utilitarian calculus—that of productivity and future returns. 'The idea of investing in human capital, either individually or as state policy, in order to produce readily aggregate units of human capital' is, as Krul maintains, 'offensive to all notions of human development and flourishing'.[108]

If, as I have argued, a human capital focus is antithetical to women's security and equality, there is an obvious need for alternative approaches. While the exploration of these alternatives is beyond the scope of this

[104] *Ibid*, at 426–27.
[105] *Ibid*, at 427.
[106] Hong and Pandey, 'Human Capital', above n 64, at 19.
[107] McKeen, 'Diminishing the Concept', above n 6, at 881.
[108] Krul, M, 'A Critique of "Human Capital" Theory' (11 October 2010), available at: www.mccaine.org/2010/10/11/a-critique-of-human-capital-theory/.

chapter, two areas of scholarship are particularly promising: feminist work on relational approaches to social rights, including a right to care; and Sen's capability theory in which claims upon the state derive not from our potential use value in production, but our ability to chose lives worth living.[109] Integral to both is the language of rights; a language that facilitates the transformation of 'universalistic utopian ideals of the good society into political realities'.[110]

[109] West, R, 'Rights, Capabilities, and the Good Society' (2000–01) 69 *Fordham Law Review* 1901; and Fudge, J, 'The New Discourse of Labor Rights: From Social to Fundamental Rights?' (2007) 29 *Comparative Labor Law & Policy Journal* 29.
[110] West, above n 109, at 1932.

10

What Would an Engendered Human Rights Approach to Social Security Mean for Sole Parents in Australia?

BELINDA SMITH

INTRODUCTION

IN THIS CHAPTER I use sole parents in Australia as a focus to examine what it would mean to take a gendered, human rights approach to interpreting the right to social security in international law. While this approach supports ongoing provision of social security in the form of cash transfers as a safety net for immediate alleviation of income poverty, the human rights approach points to complementary measures that are also needed. The right to social security should be understood as requiring the state to enable sole parents to undertake their caring roles while also protecting them against poverty in all its dimensions. Cash assistance has been the primary form of support and is essential. However, cash alone is not enough; a range of supports is needed for this disadvantaged group.

Sole parents are a useful focus for exploring an engendered human rights approach to social security. In Australia, as in many countries, responsibility for unpaid care and household work is primarily borne by women.[1] Sole parents, who are disproportionately women,[2] are an important subset of carers. Sole parents are by definition both the sole providers of childcare and the sole economic providers of the household. As a result, sole parent households are the family unit that most intensely experiences the competing demands

[1] Australian Human Rights Commission (AHRC), *Investing in Care: Recognising and Valuing Those Who Care, Volume 1: Research Report* (Sydney, AHRC, 2013).

[2] McLachlan, R, Gilfillan, G and Gordon, J, *Deep and Persistent Disadvantage in Australia* (Productivity Commission Staff Working Paper, Australian Government Productivity Commission, July 2013) 143.

of paid work and care responsibilities. They thus represent a litmus test for establishing whether the state ensures that citizens with caring responsibilities are protected against economic and social vulnerability.

An engendered human rights approach provides principles for evaluating and guiding a state's fulfilment of its obligation to provide social security. The human rights lens casts the state obligations wider than merely treating sole parents as 'citizen workers'. Human rights inhere in individuals because of their humanity, not because of their labour. A human rights approach therefore calls for support for sole parents to keep them from poverty but also enable them to engage in care and in society, including but not limited to the labour market. This approach is reflected in non-income notions of poverty such as social exclusion and deprivation that are gaining some traction in public debates and initiatives in Australia[3] and could be bolstered by a human rights framework. Attention to gender also means that the context of the unequal share of unpaid caring work performed by men and women must be factored into any sole parent policy.

I make the argument for a wider range of supports for sole parents in three parts. In the first part a brief outline is provided of Australia's general revenue based tax-transfer system of social security. Under this system sole parents have traditionally been supported through a cash transfer programme, now called the Parenting Payment (Single) (PPS), which is low but enables them to withdraw from employment and provide personal care for their children. This programme of income support helps to address the financial risks of poverty. However, a human rights framework and a growing body of research reveal that the cash transfer approach to supporting sole parents (a) does not ameliorate (and may even exacerbate) long-term poverty risks, and (b) does not address the non-income elements of poverty such as deprivation and social exclusion.

The high incidence of joblessness among sole parents is identified as a key factor explaining their poverty. The second part examines three reasons why sole parents have a low rate of employment and the role the state has played in creating, reinforcing and more recently trying to address this. The engendered human rights approach to social security guards against policies that actually entrench inequality, undermine agency and dignity for sole parents and ultimately fail to achieve the goal of enabling economic and social security in a way that values caregiving. Three reasons for this are considered. First, the provision of a cash transfer payment has reflected and

[3] See, eg, Saunders, P, Naidoo, Y and Griffiths, M, *Towards New Indicators of Disadvantage: Deprivation and Social Exclusion in Australia* (Sydney, Social Policy Research Centre, University of New South Wales, 2007); Australian Social Inclusion Board, *Social Inclusion in Australia: How Australia is Faring*, 2nd edn (Canberra, Department of the Prime Minister and Cabinet, 2012); McLachlan et al, above n 2.

reinforced a cultural understanding that sole parents are not expected to be employed. Further, by enabling sole parents to withdraw from employment, the state has perversely undermined their employability and thus limited their capacity to take up employment. Finally, there are problems with the availability of affordable and appropriate childcare.

The third part explores the family unfriendliness of work conditions as another barrier to sole parent workforce participation. Good jobs that provide decent pay, good conditions and security have traditionally been afforded to the 'ideal worker' who is unencumbered by caring responsibilities. Australia has recently seen a number of regulatory initiatives to change this to promote reconciliation of caregiving and employment demands. These include: a right to request flexible working arrangements, anti-discrimination provisions in the national labour law and a new gender affirmative action regime. Ultimately, however, it is 'decent work' that provides the best conditions for sole parents: this means work that is well paid, safe, secure and with predictable hours. The greatest challenge in supporting employment for sole parents is increasing casualisation of employment and prevalence of insecure jobs with unpredictable or insufficient hours.

SOLE PARENTS AND INCOME SUPPORT PAYMENTS

Well before Australia ratified international conventions with social security obligations it had developed an extensive system of social security, in the form of cash transfers or income support payments paid by the government.[4] The provision of this kind of social security to Australians is seen as a fundamental and legitimate part of what government does in providing a safety net and enabling social inclusion. While the language and notions of human rights have filtered into public debates and demands on government over the last half century, social security is not commonly characterised or understood as a human right in Australia.

Social Security Overview

Australia has historically separated work, welfare and health care. A comprehensive system of strong industry-wide arbitrated labour rights (discussed further in the third part below) has developed over time. This evolved separately but in conjunction with a general revenue funded income support system of social security payments for those who were unable

[4] Carney, T and Hanks, P, *Australian Social Security Law, Policy and Administration* (Melbourne, Oxford University Press, 1986).

(or not expected) to find employment. A national system of public health care is provided, which is independent of employment and income support, and supplemented by some private health insurance.

The general revenue funding of Australian social security is a fundamental feature of the system. It is entirely a public tax-transfer system of payments, not a contributory social insurance system. Category-based cash transfer payments are provided at flat rates and eligibility for any category of payment is based primarily on need. The categories represent policy decisions about recipients who are not able to support themselves through employment (for example, people with severe disabilities), those who are not expected to be in employment (for example, carers and the aged) and those who are seeking employment but have been unable to obtain it. Importantly, eligibility does not generally need to be 'earned' over time or through employment. Payments are individual, means-tested (on family income and wealth) and without time limits.

The cash payments are supplemented by other government supports, including: rental assistance (payments or concessions); various kinds of concession and benefit cards which entitle holders to discounts on some medical expenses, transport, utilities and other goods and services; extra payments or discounts for education and training; mobility allowances; and job search assistance.[5] In addition, for families with children, there are two specific benefits called Family Tax Benefit A (FTB A) and Family Tax Benefit B (FTB B) that are discussed below.[6]

The Australian tax-transfer system became significantly more redistributive over the past two decades, targeting low-income households and families. Over the 15 years from 1988 to 2003, spending on family allowances that target children increased from 0.5 per cent of GDP to 1.8 per cent of GDP.[7] When other payments to families are counted (including income support for sole parents), this spending was well over 2 per cent of GDP, which placed Australia second highest of the OECD countries in terms of cash benefits for families (although this was not the case with regard to spending on services).[8]

[5] Social Security Act 1991 (Cth).

[6] A New Tax System (Family Assistance) Act 1999 (Cth).

[7] Cass, B and Whiteford, P, Social Policy Research Centre, 'Social Inclusion and the Struggle against Child Poverty: Lessons from Australian Experience' (paper for Expert Group Meeting on Policies to Advance Social Integration, United Nations Department of Economic and Social Affairs, Division for Social Policy and Development, Social Perspective on Development Branch, Convened in Preparation for the 48th session of the Commission for Social Development, United Nations Headquarters, New York, 2–4 November 2009) 4, available at: www.un.org/esa/socdev/social/meetings/egm09/docs/bettinacass.pdf.

[8] *Ibid*.

One particular development since the 1990s in the Australian tax-transfer system is the extension of eligibility for many of the additional benefits and concessions to *all* low-income families, with a focus on families with children, not only those receiving social security payments.[9] In this way the system is generally redistributive and is used to address poverty, targeting those on the lowest incomes, either welfare or wage.[10] This is particularly true of family payments. FTB A is a payment available to families with children who have low to moderate income. If a parent is receiving an income support payment they will be eligible automatically for this additional family payment at the maximum level of $86 per week for one young child, with rates increasing for older and additional children.[11] The amount of FTB A reduces once a parent's income rises above a certain level, but the taper is gradual and thus payments do not cut out until the family income reaches $101,653 per annum,[12] which represents 175 per cent of average annual total earnings of employees[13] and excludes only the top 15 per cent of families with children.[14] Sole parents will also be eligible for up to $73 per week FTB B payment if they earn less than $150,000 per annum,[15] which is 259 per cent of average annual total earnings of employees.[16]

The redistributive nature of the Australian tax-transfer system and the particular focus on families with children can be seen by comparing average welfare and wage incomes across the OECD countries. Generally, a family with children in Australia receiving only government benefits (without employment income) will have an income that puts it above the poverty line of 50 per cent median household income, with an income of 60 per cent for sole parents and 62 per cent for couples.[17] Across the OECD countries this places Australia second in providing benefits as a proportion of median income. It means that welfare dependants with children in Australia require

[9] *Ibid*; and Adema, W and Whiteford, P, 'Matching Work and Family Commitments: Australian Outcomes in a Comparative Perspective' (2008) (80) *Family Matters* 9.

[10] Cass and Whiteford, above n 7.

[11] A New Tax System (Family Assistance) Act 1999 (Cth); for rates see Department of Human Services, 'Family Tax Benefits' (Australian Government Department of Human Services), available at: www.humanservices.gov.au/customer/services/centrelink/family-tax-benefit-part-a-part-b.

[12] This rate is for a parent of one child who is 0–12 years of age, with higher rates for additional children. Department of Human Services, 'Family Tax Benefit', above n 11.

[13] Average weekly total earnings from employment are $1115, and annualised $57,980. Australian Bureau of Statistics (ABS), '6302.0—Average Weekly Earnings, Australia, Nov 2013' (ABS, 2013), available at: www.abs.gov.au/ausstats/abs@.nsf/Products/6302.0~Nov+2013~Main+Features~Key+Figures?OpenDocument.

[14] Brennan, D, 'Babies, Budgets, and Birthrates: Work/Family Policy in Australia 1996–2006' (2007) 14(1) *Social Politics: International Studies in Gender, State, and Society* 31, 37.

[15] Department of Human Services, 'Family Tax Benefit', above n 11.

[16] Australian Bureau of Statistics, '6302.0', above, n 13.

[17] Cass and Whiteford, above n 7 (figures from Organisation for Economic Co-operation and Development (OECD 2007, for 2005).

no additional earnings to reach this poverty line,[18] a figure that contrasts with the United States, where lone parents need an additional 98 per cent of average wage, and an average of 44 per cent in the OECD countries.[19]

Even though this demonstrates that the payments to single parents are paid at a relatively high rate, there are long-term problems associated with it, as explored below.

Sole Parent Payments and Poverty

International policy approaches to child poverty and gendered poverty related to caring responsibilities can be divided into a work–welfare dichotomy.[20] The distinction is between approaches that primarily aim to ensure economic well-being and alleviate poverty for carers and children by providing financial support so parents can personally undertake the care work; and those that are directed more at enabling carers to earn income through paid employment.

In Australia, poverty alleviation for sole parents has been primarily achieved through a specific income support payment. Australia has a relatively long history of supporting sole parents through cash transfers; some type of social security payment for sole parents has been available since the 1940s.[21] Currently sole parents are eligible under the Australian social security system for a PPS, which is payable to parents who are 'single' or at least not in a recognised couple relationship. Currently the payment is fortnightly, and paid at the rate of approximately $350 per week[22] (or 31 per cent Average Weekly Total Earnings), supplemented by rental assistance and other benefits mentioned above. The PPS is income and assets tested, and to be eligible, the parent's youngest child must be under eight years of age.[23]

Despite the relatively high level of spending on family payments, the redistributive nature of the tax-transfer system, and the focus on addressing poverty especially for families with children, as noted above, child poverty in Australia remains above the OECD average.[24] The primary reason is that among families with children in Australia there is a very high level of

[18] *Ibid* (measured as 50% of the median income).

[19] *Ibid.*

[20] Adema and Whiteford, above n 9.

[21] Cass, B, 'Care Giving and Employment: Policy Recognition of Care and Pathways to Labour Force Return' (2006) 32(3) *Australian Bulletin of Labour* 240, 244.

[22] Department of Human Services, 'Parenting Payment' (Australian Government Department of Human Services), available at: www.humanservices.gov.au/customer/services/centrelink/parenting-payment.

[23] For a discussion of the changes to eligibility related to the child's age, see Goldblatt, in this collection.

[24] Cass and Whiteford, above n 7, at 5.

joblessness[25] and joblessness is strongly associated with high risks of child poverty.[26] In 2007 Australia had the 'fourth highest rate of children living in jobless families within the OECD' (falling behind the United Kingdom, New Zealand and Turkey).[27] While the proportion fell slightly after that time, in June 2010 of all families with children under 15 years of age, jobless families still constituted 13 per cent.[28] Furthermore, the 'vast majority of jobless families are headed by single mothers'.[29] The proportion of all families that are sole parent families has also steadily increased since the 1970s.[30] In summary, sole parent status and employment both play a role in determining poverty risks, with unemployed sole parents and their children facing particularly high risks.

Dimensions of Poverty

The focus in Australia on ensuring adequate income support under the social security payment system has meant that insufficient weight has been given to 'the broader context of social integration'.[31] An engendered human rights approach to social security warrants a broader, social inclusion understanding of poverty and disadvantage that has been slow to emerge in Australia.[32]

A social inclusion approach to poverty was adopted in various States, but did not see national adoption until 2008 when the Federal government established the Australian Social Inclusion Board. The Board was set up to 'advise Government on how to achieve better outcomes for the most disadvantaged in our community and report on our progress in building a socially inclusive community'.[33] Drawing on social policy research into dimensions of disadvantage beyond income poverty, to include notions of deprivation and social exclusion,[34] the Board articulated its aims as an agenda: reducing disadvantage, increasing social, civic and economic

25 *Ibid*, at 5, Table 2.

26 Australian Social Inclusion Board, *Addressing Barriers for Jobless Families* (Canberra, Department of the Prime Minister and Cabinet, 2011) 15.

27 *Ibid*.

28 *Ibid*, at 10.

29 *Ibid*. See also Baxter, J et al, 'Parental Joblessness, Financial Disadvantage and the Wellbeing of Parents and Children' (Occasional Paper No 48, Canberra, Department of Families, Housing, Community Services and Indigenous Affairs, 2012) 2.

30 Report of the Australian Government, *Families in Australia: 2008* (Canberra, Department of the Prime Minister and Cabinet, 2008) 7.

31 Cass and Whiteford, above n 7, at 2.

32 Australian Government, *Social Inclusion: Origins, Concepts and Key Themes* (Canberra, Department of the Prime Minister and Cabinet, 2008).

33 Australian Social Inclusion Board, *Social Inclusion in Australia*, above n 3, at 1.

34 Saunders et al, above n 3.

participation and promoting active involvement of the entire community.[35] Social inclusion was defined as people having the 'resources, opportunities and capabilities they need' to: learn by participating in education and training; work by participating in employment, in voluntary work and caring; engage by connecting with people and using their local community's resources; and have a voice so that they can influence decisions that affect them.[36] The Board was able to develop a set of indicators of social inclusion and use these to benchmark and subsequently monitor Australia's performance. It was, however, disbanded in September 2013 as one of the first acts of the current Federal government, which clearly suggests diminished support for the social inclusion approach.

Social measures of poverty reflect the fact that poverty is not merely a lack of resources. Like equality,[37] poverty needs to be understood as multidimensional to include an understanding of the extent to which people can participate and engage in economic, social and cultural life.[38]

SOLE PARENTS AND EMPLOYMENT

It is clear from the figures on poverty that the tax-transfer system operates to redistribute income across Australian society but it only partially addresses the risks of poverty. Since increasing the employment rate of sole parents would reduce the risk for these parents and their children of poverty in its various dimensions, the state's obligation to ensure an adequate standard of living requires more than the provision of income support or cash transfer payments; it also requires the state to ensure quality jobs are available and enable sole parents to obtain them. In this part I examine why sole parents have lower workforce participation rates than other parents and the role the state has played in creating, reinforcing and more recently, trying to address this.

Not Expected to Work

One of the most fundamental ways in which the Australian State has influenced the employment level of sole parents is by providing a social security cash payment at a level that has enabled withdrawal from the workforce. This policy decision reflected and reinforced a view that it 'was not culturally

35 Australian Social Inclusion Board, *Social Inclusion in Australia*, above n 3, at 12.
36 *Ibid*.
37 See Fredman, in this collection.
38 Australian Government, *Social Inclusion*, above n 32.

or politically expected that sole mothers would be employed'.[39] Care work was seen as a legitimate reason why the parent was not sufficiently engaged in employment to be financially independent.

The sole parent payment was originally designed, in effect, to compensate for the missing breadwinner. Starting with a pension for widows and 'deserted' wives (de jure or de facto) in the 1940s, and later extended to other sole parents, the state stepped in as the income provider. Developed in a time of war, the mothering provided by widowed or deserted wives was seen as a kind of national service[40] to be supported through social security payments.

Although the wartime rationales diminished in significance, the characterisation of sole mothers as in need of special support and protection actually grew. There was a strong cultural view that mothers in the traditional model of nuclear family should be able to 'choose' to stay at home to personally provide their children with care.[41] Correspondingly, financial payments were developed to ensure that sole parents could also provide such personal care. There was no work test applied to be eligible for the payment, which clearly indicates that employment was not expected for the citizen mother.

It is clear that gender, not merely family status, influences sole parent workforce participation because sole fathers are much more likely to be employed than sole mothers, and certainly more likely to be employed full-time.[42] This might reflect the gender pay gap,[43] which means rewards for work are gendered, but arguably it also reflects the greater legitimacy of mothers than fathers being outside the workforce.

Employment Withdrawal and Employability

Providing a cash payment that enables sole parents to withdraw from the workforce might ease the work–care conflict for sole parents in the short term, but it can undermine long-term economic and social security. Withdrawal from employment for a substantial period of time for care

[39] Cass, above n 21.

[40] Shaver, S, 'Women and the Australian Social Security System: From Difference Towards Equality' (SPRC Discussion Paper No 41, Sydney, Social Policy Research Centre, University of New South Wales, 1993) 7.

[41] Brennan, above n 14.

[42] Australian Bureau of Statistics, '4102.0—Australian Social Trends 2007: One-parent Families' (Canberra, ABS, 2007) 3.

[43] The gap is approximately 16%. Australian Social Inclusion Board, *A Compendium of Social Inclusion Indicators: How's Australia Faring?* (Canberra, Commonwealth of Australia, May 2009) 22.

work reduces employability,[44] making it more difficult for sole parents to get jobs. This is not new: a major study in the 1990s of sole parents in the period after their child reached the cut-off age for benefit eligibility concluded that:

> The most significant factors affecting pathways either to employment or income support were employment and employment-related experience in the preceding five years; having had contact with a Jobs, Education and Training [JET] Advisor; and having participated in one or more training programs.[45]

More specifically, in the study, 'women who were unemployed 12 months after the cessation of their eligibility' for the sole parent pension identified as key barriers to their employment 'the length of time spent outside the labour force' and 'lack of work experience'.[46] Since this study there has been further research that establishes a negative impact on women of long periods of withdrawal or absence from the workforce.[47]

The state must balance ensuring short-term poverty alleviation through income support with avoiding entrenching long-term disadvantage by providing autonomy to maintain a household without expectations of returning to work. While policies need to recognise and support the essential caregiving reproductive work of sole parents, the risks of ongoing poverty clearly suggest that policies also need to encourage and enable carers to re-enter the workforce. As Adema and Whiteford conclude, 'when adequate benefits are provided without a clear signal to clients that they are expected to work and/or they are without adequate employment supports (including childcare), sole parent employment rates are low and poverty risks high'.[48] International comparative research suggests that sole parents do best economically when they are not treated distinctly from other parents, but this requires adequate employment supports, such as education and training, childcare and possibly a longer period of paid parental leave.[49]

There have been some significant policy developments that reflect a move towards increasing the employment expectations on sole parents. First there has been a gradual reduction in the eligibility period for PPS: a parent was eligible until their youngest child turned 24 years of age, and this was

[44] McLachlan et al, above n 2, at 129–30.

[45] Cass, above n 21, at 251, citing Shaver, S, King, A, McHugh, M and Payne, T, *At the End of Eligibility: Female Sole Parents Whose Youngest Child Turns 16* (Social Policy Research Centre Reports and Proceedings, No 117, Sydney, the University of New South Wales, December 1994).

[46] Cass, above n 21, at 251.

[47] See, eg, Evertsson, M and Duvander, AZ, 'Parental Leave—Possibility or Trap? Does Family Leave Length Effect Swedish Women's Labour Market Opportunities?' (2011) 27 *European Sociological Review* 435.

[48] Adema and Whiteford, above n 9, at 14.

[49] *Ibid*.

reduced to 16 in 1987 and then down to eight in 2006. Second, in 2006, an 'activity test' was also introduced requiring recipients whose youngest child had turned six to undertake some work or look for work of at least 15 hours per week or undertake approved study.[50]

These changes might subtly shift the cultural expectation of employment for sole mothers, but they do little to facilitate or support transition to employment and are arguably designed to reduce government costs without necessarily promoting sole parent employment. There have been more active labour market programmes for sole parents in the past, including an entirely voluntary programme called the Jobs, Employment and Training (JET) programme that phased in from 1989.[51] The programme was personalised and integrated, providing individual advice and counselling by trained JET advisers, access to childcare, education, training and employment programmes, including subsidies for study or training. The initiative was relatively well resourced and comprehensive, and represented a key element in the Federal government's National Agenda for Women, which was a broad strategy aimed at improving the status, economic independence and security of women in Australia.[52] Importantly, this programme was entirely voluntary and had no punitive elements. Interest in the programme was high, with about 20 per cent of all sole parent pensioners in 1991 participating. In the early years of its operation, labour force participation of sole parents increased from 48 per cent in 1988 to 55 per cent in 1991.[53] Some commentators, however, argued that even this programme was still disabling for sole parents because it was shaped and limited by gendered stereotyping that prescribed motherhood as the most important job for women and assisted sole parents only to find precarious work that fit with this role.[54]

Childcare

While a lack of appropriate childcare influences maternal employment generally, accessible and appropriate childcare is particularly critical for

[50] Australian Bureau of Statistics, '4102.0', above n 42, at 5; see also Goldblatt, in this collection for a discussion of more recent changes.

[51] Walters, C, 'The JET Program' in P Whiteford (ed), *Sole Parents and Public Policy* (Social Policy Research Centre Reports and Proceedings, No 89, Sydney, University of New South Wales, February 1991).

[52] *Ibid*, at 53.

[53] Australian Government, *Women in Australia: Australia's Second Progress Report on Implementing the United Nations Convention on the Elimination of All Forms of Discrimination Against Women* (Barton, ACT, Office of the Status of Women, Department of the Prime Minister and Cabinet, 1992) 119.

[54] Gardiner, J, 'Putting Sole Mothers in their Place: The Normalising Discourse of Social Policy' (1999) 34(1) *Australian Journal of Social Issues* 43.

sole parents who, by definition, do not have access to care by a partner. Access to alternative care for a sole parent's child (or children) is necessary for workforce participation. Adema and Whiteford note that 'countries with the best outcomes for sole parents' combine 'activity requirements for all unemployed persons' with 'good quality childcare supports'.[55]

In Australia, childcare has been the focus of numerous Federal and State government initiatives designed to meet demand from mothers increasingly taking up employment and also to promote this trend. These initiatives have tackled many different aspects of childcare—increasing the number of places, making them more affordable for parents, increasing quality and developing national standards for ratios of carers to children and carer qualifications.[56]

To address affordability, the government has significantly increased its expenditure on childcare over the last decade.[57] Spending has increased on two subsidies paid to parents, for childcare provided by registered providers. The first is a non-means-tested Childcare Rebate, the second, a means-tested Childcare Benefit, whereby up to 80 per cent of fees could be paid by government.[58] The effectiveness of these subsidies has been undermined by a very high proportion of places being provided by for-profit centres.[59] The subsidy is paid as a proportion of fees, up to a ceiling, but there is no cap on the fees a centre can charge, so there can be a significant gap between the subsidy and the out-of-pocket expenses.

One of the few remnants of the JET scheme noted above is a special payment available to sole parents for childcare expenses. For sole parent recipients of social security payments like PPS, the JET Childcare Fee Assistance is available to help cover the gap between what the childcare provider charges and assistance provided by the Childcare Benefit and the Childcare Rebate.[60]

There has been a significant increase in the proportion of children who use formal childcare in Australia,[61] but there are still considerable

[55] Adema and Whiteford, above n 9, at 14.

[56] Boyd, W, 'Maternal Employment and Childcare in Australia: Achievements and Barriers to Satisfying Employment' (2012) 38 *Australian Bulletin of Labour* 199.

[57] Brennan, above n 14, at 47.

[58] Introduced in 2004, the Rebate provides 50% of the cost of childcare, up to $7500 per child per year and is not means-tested. A New Tax System (Family Assistance) Act 1999 (Cth).

[59] In 2001, 67 per cent of the most used type of formal childcare for pre-school children—long day care centres—were owned by private-for-profit bodies. Australian Institute of Health and Welfare (AIHW), *Australia's Welfare 2003* (AIHW Cat No AUS 41, Canberra, AIHW, 2003) at 235 (Table 6.11). By 2006, a single company—ABC Learning—was providing a quarter of all centre-based childcare services. Brennan, above n 14, at 47. After ABC Learning collapsed, 650 centres were transferred to not-for-profit management. Boyd, above n 56, at 207.

[60] A New Tax System (Family Assistance) Act 1999 (Cth).

[61] Brennan, above n 14, at 47.

shortfalls in appropriate care, either because of affordability, geography or a mismatch in hours of the childcare provision and work.[62]

MAKING WORKPLACES MORE FAMILY FRIENDLY?

While it is clear that joblessness increases the risk of poverty, a number of studies have concluded that to enable sole parents to transition off income support and gain protection against poverty the goal cannot be employment per se.[63] As Cass and Whiteford identify, 'public policy development must also be focussed on providing decent, secure jobs that are not short-term and precarious, but provide job security as well as family and carer friendly flexible practices and family leave arrangements'.[64] Laws and policies that reflect and reinforce the ideal worker as one who is 'unencumbered' by caring responsibilities will marginalise sole parents with caring responsibilities, who therefore do not fit this norm. Employment policies need to recognise and support the essential caregiving responsibilities of sole parents, and other carers. If jobs are not 'family-friendly'—failing to support and enable reconciliation of employment and caregiving—sole parents will not be able to take them, or in taking them may undermine their family's emotional and social well-being.

Before turning to initiatives to make working conditions more family-friendly, it is worth providing some context about the Australian labour market and labour law. First, the Australian economy is in reasonable shape, having weathered the global financial crisis relatively unscathed. The national unemployment rate recently rose to 5.9 per cent, but this is the highest it has been since 2003.[65] Importantly, child poverty did not increase following the global financial crisis.[66]

Second, Australian labour laws are generally strong and comprehensive. The Federal Minimum Wage in Australia is currently $16.37 per hour or $622.20 per week and is updated each year. This minimum wage is relatively high. As a proportion of the median wage it was the highest of all OECD nations during the 1980s and 1990s, although since then it has fallen; in 2011 it ranked seventh with the minimum wage representing

[62] *Ibid*, at 49.

[63] Cass and Whiteford, above n 7; Baxter et al, above n 29, at vii.

[64] Cass and Whiteford, above n 7, at 10.

[65] Australian Bureau of Statistics (ABS), 'ABS 6202.0—Labour Force, Australia, Jan 2014' (ABS, 2013), available at: www.abs.gov.au/ausstats/abs%40.nsf/mf/6202.0.

[66] Redmond, G and Whiteford, P, 'Middle Class Welfare—Are We Hitting the Target?' (*The Conversation*, 16 May 2013), available at: theconversation.com/middle-class-welfare-are-we-hitting-the-target-14257.

54 per cent of the median wage.[67] Working conditions and labour rights historically have been regulated by industrial tribunals setting industry-wide awards, initiated and negotiated by unions through a system of conciliation and arbitration. While there has been little focus specifically on gender or other status differentiations,[68] the collective and industry-wide development of award minimum conditions generally was beneficial for those who were in employment. Eventually they even narrowed the gender pay gap, although this has since increased with a move over the past 20 to 30 years away from industry awards towards conditions being set through enterprise bargaining.[69]

Although increasingly employees' conditions are set by enterprise bargaining, an important exception is the introduction in 2009 of a legislated set of National Employment Standards (NES) in the Fair Work Act.[70] The NES provide for: a minimum federal wage (noted above); maximum hours of work; minimum hours per shift; four weeks' annual paid leave; 10 days' paid personal or carer's leave; and rights to notice for termination, overtime pay and penalty rates for unsocial hours and allowances. Industry-wide awards and enterprise agreements generally provide for higher conditions than the NES.

While women's employment has increased steadily and substantially, there has also been a related growth in part-time jobs and casual employment. Despite a long period of opposition to part-time work by unions, Australia now has a particularly high rate of part-time workers (30 per cent of employees).[71] Women are substantially more likely to work part-time, especially mothers: 45 per cent of employed women work part-time, compared with only 15 per cent of male employees.[72] Part-time workers would not count as unemployed, but might still be underemployed because they are not working as many hours as they would like.[73]

Casual work, a regulated, well-accepted employment status within the Australian system of workplace regulation, has also increased. Casual employees are employees in the formal economy who may work intermittently for their employer but have an expectation of continuing work. Casual

[67] Cowgill, M, 'How Does Australia's Minimum Wage Compare?' (*We Are All Dead; a Discussion of Australian Political and Economic Issues and Ideas*, 13 February 2013), available at: mattcowgill.wordpress.com/2013/02/13/australian-minimum-wages/.

[68] Smith, B, 'What Kind of Equality Can We Expect from the Fair Work Act?' (2011) 35(2) *Melbourne University Law Review* 545.

[69] Pocock, B and Masterman-Smith, H, 'Work Choices and Women Workers' (2005) 56 *Journal of Australian Political Economy* 126.

[70] Fair Work Act 2009 (Cth).

[71] Australian Bureau of Statistics (ABS), '6359.0—Forms of Employment' (Canberra, ABS, November 2012).

[72] Australian Social Inclusion Board, *A Compendium of Social Inclusion Indicators*, above n 43, at 21.

[73] *Ibid*.

employees receive a loading of approximately 25 per cent of ordinary earnings on top of their base rate of pay but do not have guaranteed hours, paid leave and tenure security. The casual loading is meant to compensate for the lack of important employment conditions such as regular work hours, personal or carers' leave and annual leave. Women are more likely than men to work casually: almost a quarter of female employees are now engaged on a 'casual' basis.[74]

The growth in part-time jobs, and especially women's uptake of these jobs, has enabled women to participate in employment without the 'stay at home' expectations of mothering being directly challenged. Working part-time is seen as a way for women to participate economically while also meeting their caring responsibilities. Importantly, as a result, employers generally have not had to accommodate workers with caring responsibilities—rather women bear the risks themselves by accepting part-time and casual work. While women are no longer restricted to the private sphere, there is still a pervasive norm about their responsibility for this sphere. Thus, work and family debates and workplace policies and initiatives are often framed as needing to reduce the conflict between the demands of work and family care *for women* and accommodating *women* so that they are better able to combine these dual responsibilities. Part-time work has helped minimise work–family conflict, but it has largely left intact the expectation that women will be the ones to bear the responsibility of managing any such conflict. The traditional family model has become a 'modified breadwinner' model in which women have taken up short hours of paid work and continue to perform most of the caring and household work while the hours of work for men, regardless of parental status, have grown.[75]

Probably the greatest weakness of the Australian labour law system of protection for workers is the existence, wide use and general acceptance of 'casual' employment.[76] For the price of a small premium in pay, employers are able to avoid a great swathe of employee protections. While this mechanism enables employers to offer small parcels of work as the work arises, work which might not otherwise be offered, it thereby also enables those employers to avoid bearing many of the standard risks of employment. Casual employees bear the risk of uncertainty, not knowing the number or schedule of work hours in any particular week or whether they will get any

[74] Australian Bureau of Statistics (ABS), '1370.0—Measures of Australia's Progress, 2010: Future Directions for Measuring Australia's Progress' (Canberra, ABS, September 2010).

[75] Leahy, M, 'Women and Work in Australia' (Australian Policy Online, 28 November 2011), available at: apo.org.au/sites/default/files/Women_and_work_in_Australia_APO_guide_Mary_Leahy_0.pdf.

[76] Owens, R, 'Decent Work for the Contingent Workforce in the New Economy' (2002) 15(3) *Australian Journal of Labour Law* 209.

work at all. With short stints of work rather than full days, casual workers are less able to recoup the fixed costs of transport to work, training courses, clothing or other equipment. Without any entitlement to paid leave, casual employees also bear all the risks of insuring against the need to take leave for reasons of sickness, caring responsibilities, recreation and recovery.

The entrenchment of 'casual' as a normal and acceptable form of employment for businesses poses a specific problem for women and particularly those with caring responsibilities. Casual employment is characterised as ideal and even desirable for such workers because it is 'flexible', unlike full-time employment, and may allow workers to combine employment with family responsibilities. It is questionable whether workers benefit from this flexibility. The fact that women take up casual employment is often seen as evidence of a preference for casual work rather than a preference for hours that can accommodate caring responsibilities or an acceptance that casual work is the only kind of work available.

Having considered the context of the Australian labour market, three legal initiatives to accommodate workers' caring responsibilities will now be examined: the right to request flexible working arrangements; new anti-discrimination provisions in the national labour law; and amendments to the gender affirmative action regulatory framework.

Right to Request Flexible Working Arrangements

The national labour law, the Fair Work Act (FW Act) enacted in 2009, introduced a right to request flexible working arrangements and this was seen as promising but limited. The 'right' had some symbolic importance: it was seen to reconnect the apparently separate spheres of work and family by requiring the employer to consider requests for flexible working arrangements to accommodate a worker's caring responsibilities. However, the provision really only has symbolic effect because, unlike other labour law rights and unlike other equivalent laws in Europe, it is unenforceable, as a number of commentators have explored.[77] Employers are required to respond to an employee's request within 21 days and failure to do so can amount to a breach of the Act. Employers are not to refuse a request other than on 'reasonable business grounds' but the Act provides no capacity for review of the reasons for refusing any such request.

The right to request flexible work arrangements is limited in two other important ways. The first is that only some categories of employee have

[77] See, eg, Himmelweit, S, 'The Right to Request Flexible Working: A "Very British" Approach to Gender (In)Equality?' (2007) 33 *Australian Bulletin of Labour* 246; and Charlesworth, S and Campbell, I, 'Right to Request Regulation: Two New Australian Models' (2008) 21(2) *Australia Journal of Labour Law* 116.

a right to request flexible work, although the number of categories has recently been expanded. Originally, the right was only available in respect of employees responsible for the primary care of pre-school children, or children with a disability up to the age of 18. Amendments passed in June 2013 have extended the right to employees who are carers and others.[78]

The second limitation, an eligibility period of 12 months' ongoing employment, was not changed by the 2013 amendment. This requirement operates to exclude many workers who have interrupted tenure or casual, irregular employment. Importantly it also reinforces the idea that such accommodation provisions are not really core rights that adhere to employment, but benefits that need to be earned over time and, even then, only granted when the request is reasonable according to the employer.

Protections Against Family Responsibilities Discrimination

Other provisions of the FW Act that have the potential to challenge the carer-hostile working conditions are new protections against discrimination on the ground of carer's or family responsibilities. Federal and State anti-discrimination laws already contain some protections against discrimination on the basis of sex, pregnancy and family or carer's responsibilities, but the regulatory framework for these laws is very individualistic and has little power to bring about systemic changes in employment conditions.[79] The new FW Act protections have been inserted in two different but related ways: as a right against discrimination and as a prohibition on discriminatory terms being contained in awards and enterprise agreements.

First, building on earlier unlawful termination provisions, the FW Act provides 'General Protections' for employees against 'adverse action' by employers because of status grounds, including 'family or carer's responsibility', and the usual ones of sex, race and disability.[80] The provision applies to employees and potential employees, and 'adverse action' is defined widely to include refusing to employ, dismissing, discriminating with respect to terms and conditions of employment and altering the position of an employee to the employee's prejudice.[81] The term 'family or carer's responsibility' is not defined, so the protection is not limited to parents or even to family relationships. These protections are bolstered

[78] Fair Work Amendment Act 2013 (Cth) sch, 1 cl 17(1A). The other groups also included are: employees with a disability; employees who are 55 years or older; and employees who are experiencing family violence or who are caring for or supporting a family or household member who is experiencing family violence.

[79] Smith, B, 'Not the Baby and the Bathwater: Regulatory Reform for Equality Laws to Address Work–Family Conflict' (2006) 28(4) *Sydney Law Review* 689.

[80] Fair Work Act 2009 (Cth) s 351.

[81] *Ibid*, at s 342.

further by: a favourable evidentiary mechanism that amounts to a shifting burden of proof that is absent from Australian anti-discrimination legislation; enforcement supports, such as a public prosecutor (the Fair Work Ombudsman); and a range of penalties that can be ordered for breaches.[82]

Second, the Act provides that awards and enterprise agreements must not include terms that discriminate because of 'sex, … marital status, family or carer's responsibilities, [or] pregnancy'.[83] A term that is found to be discriminatory is of no effect.[84]

While seemingly very broad, these protections have some limitations.[85] One particularly critical question is whether the protections extend to indirect discrimination (otherwise known as adverse impact) or only cover direct discrimination (adverse treatment). The provisions have already been used to combat direct discrimination in situations where a pregnant woman or person with caring responsibilities has been treated differently because a prejudicial assumption has been made about their suitability to perform work. The Fair Work Ombudsman has been quite active in providing educational materials specifically about pregnancy discrimination, pursuing claims, denouncing breaches and publicising settlements to increase compliance. Many of the barriers faced by sole parents, however, are more likely to constitute indirect discrimination where all workers are treated the same but the impact of an apparently neutral condition disproportionately affects workers with caring responsibilities. These apparently neutral conditions could be provisions in awards or agreements, or a matter of practice such as rotating rosters, unpredictable schedules and requirements to work overtime at short notice.

Whether the protections extend to indirect discrimination is a question because the FW Act does not define discrimination. Under anti-discrimination law in Australia discrimination is defined in some detail to include both direct and indirect discrimination. Under the definition of indirect discrimination, a condition that disparately impacts on a protected group, such as women or workers with caring responsibilities, is not unlawful unless it is unreasonable.[86] There is no indication in the FW Act that a test of reasonableness should be adopted if the provision were interpreted to include indirect discrimination, but there is no other model at hand in Australia.

Assuming the discrimination provisions were interpreted this way, the challenge would be to prove that a condition was not reasonable. Many practices which exclude and marginalise workers with caring responsibilities

[82] Smith, B, 'Fair and Equal in the World of Work: Two Significant Federal Developments in Discrimination Law' (2010) 23(3) *Australian Journal of Labour Law* 199.

[83] Fair Work Act 2009 (Cth) ss 136(2)(a), 186.

[84] *Ibid*, at ss 137, 194, 195.

[85] Smith, 'Fair and Equal', above n 82.

[86] See, eg, Sex Discrimination Act 1984 (Cth) s 7B.

are so well entrenched they represent the status quo, which looks natural and neutral.[87] Those seeking to challenge the status quo can appear to be seeking special treatment rather than equality.

The key condition that fundamentally disadvantages workers with caring responsibilities is 'casual' employment status which denies them paid leave, regular hours of work and security of tenure. It is apparently neutral and applied to everyone, but impacts disproportionately on women and workers with caring responsibilities. There seems little scope, however, for this to be challenged because the status of casual has been so normalised it is almost unassailable. In the most high profile case in which casual employment was challenged in this way as indirectly discriminatory under sex discrimination legislation, the courts rejected the claim and appeared reluctant to even examine the question of whether casual employment was reasonable.[88] Instead of addressing this central question in the case, Australia's highest court sidestepped the issue and dismissed the case on narrow, technical grounds.

The approach taken in a recent High Court case[89] further stokes concerns that the judiciary may stifle rather than promote the transformative potential of the general protections in the FW Act. The way in which the Court interpreted the general protections was extremely narrow, and suggests that in practice these protections would be useful only to limit direct discrimination. Protections against direct discrimination are important for addressing different treatment that arises from stereotyping, prejudice and assumptions, so even a narrow interpretation of the new protections could be helpful. But for sole parents to participate equally in work ultimately they need to be able to challenge the conditions of work that marginalise and disadvantage workers with family responsibilities. If the adverse action provisions are interpreted only to guarantee that sole parents are treated the same as ideal, unencumbered workers the laws will not enable the underlying conditions to be challenged.

Gender Affirmative Action Legislation

A third legislative initiative that has some scope for challenging carer-hostile working conditions is the new Workplace Gender Equality Act 2012 (WGE Act), which replaces the Equal Opportunity for Women in the Workplace Act 1999. Like the old Act, the WGE Act imposes duties on large private

87 Minow, M, *Making all the Difference: Inclusion, Exclusion and American Law* (Ithaca, Cornell University Press, 1990) 70.

88 *New South Wales v Amery* [2006] HCA 14.

89 *The Board of Bendigo Regional Institute of Technical and Further Education v Barclay & Anor* [2012] HCA 32.

sector employers designed to promote gender equality in employment. The old Act imposed entirely procedural obligations on employers—to audit, consult and develop a gender equality plan and report to the agency.

The reporting obligations in the new Act are different in a few key ways. The Act requires employers to audit their workforce and consult and report on their findings, but the reporting requirements are more specific and transparent. Under the WGE Act, employers must report on specific 'gender equality indicators',[90] which reflects a slight shift from reporting on processes to reporting on outcomes. These include the gender composition of the workplace and governing bodies, and the gender pay gap. Of particular interest here is that the Act also includes the indicator of availability and uptake of flexible working arrangements. The reporting is more transparent because, unlike the old provisions, there is no capacity for the agency to grant 'waivers', so every relevant employer must report every year. Under new provisions, in addition to consulting with staff in developing the report, the employer is required to notify its employees and members or shareholders of the report and advise them on how they can access it and comment on it directly to the agency.[91] These notice and access provisions took effect in 2013.

There are three other new provisions that might make the legislation more effective than its predecessor. First, there are stronger powers given to the agency to identify non-complying employers, publicise their non-compliance and exclude them from government procurement and subsidies.[92] Further, the minister is to establish 'minimum standards', including quantitative outcomes or evidence of actions to improve quantitative outcomes, against which non-compliance is to be measured.[93] These are in addition to 'industry benchmarks' that the Workplace Gender Equality Agency can develop, based on actual, submitted figures, to enable employers to evaluate their own performance against peers.[94]

This regulatory framework offers some promise that employers will pay more attention to the gender composition of their workforce and possible barriers to equality because reporting will be more public and data will be comparable. However, because this is soft regulation without accompanying punitive measures, change will depend on stakeholders having the will and capacity to use the data to press for change in existing norms. Reporting on specific indicators may expose employers to more scrutiny, but ultimately, change might depend on the extent to which a 'market'

[90] 'Gender equality indicators' defined in s 3, and the duties are imposed under ss 13 and 13A, Workplace Gender Equality Act 2012 (Cth).

[91] Workplace Gender Equality Act 2012 (Cth), ss 13, 13A and 13B.

[92] *Ibid*, at ss 18, 19A–19D.

[93] Workplace Gender Equality Act 2012 (Cth), s 19.

[94] *Ibid*, at s 10(1)(aa).

for gender equal employment develops. It is possible that only employers competing for higher-end, professional employees—those with greater market power—will offer equal opportunities, not necessarily affording such opportunities to the most disadvantaged.

These three employment law initiatives have some potential to change the norm of a strict separation between spheres of work and family. They each have substantial limitations and any one of them on their own would likely have little effect. Collectively, however, they could represent an increasing challenge to the norm of the ideal worker being unencumbered by caring responsibilities, a norm that particularly hurts sole parents.

CONCLUSION

Australia has adopted a welfare focused approach to sole parents, providing them with up to eight years of parenting payments. While this may validate and support the care work they do and allow short-term poverty alleviation, it has not been enough to ensure economic and social security. In fact, by enabling and encouraging women to not participate in employment for long periods of time, the income support system has undermined rather than supported long-term economic and social security. Increasingly, it has become clear that sole parents need to gain or retain attachment to the workforce. An engendered human rights approach further illuminates the limits of a cash transfer programme, showing how a safety net of cash payments must be complemented by an expectation of and support for employment, the provision of affordable and appropriate childcare and workplace regulations that address precariousness and ensure decent work. The state needs to provide supports to ensure workforce attachment and not to entrench long-term disadvantage by enabling sole parents to maintain a household without the expectation they will return to work.

There has been a move towards a work-orientated approach to supporting sole parents. Changes and specific initiatives across a range of supports—the social security cash transfer system, social services and labour law—have been directed at encouraging or enabling sole parents to participate in employment. Reduction in the eligibility period for sole parents is the most obvious signal that sole parents are expected to undertake paid work once childcare demands ease. Substantial increases in the availability of formal childcare have facilitated maternal employment, but there are still significant gaps in availability and problems of affordability.

For sole parents, the pattern of changes in women's employment over time has a particular significance. The growth in part-time positions has enabled mothers, including sole mothers, to take up employment while also balancing the caring responsibilities they have retained. The increasing casualisation of work, however, undermines the poverty protection potential of employment. This is particularly problematic for sole parents. If employment is precarious, offering few guarantees of hours, decent wages, or conditions, women who are secondary earners in a household may be underemployed, undervalued and frustrated. But for sole parents who are the only source of income for a household, precarious employment might increase stress, financial pressures and the challenges of running a household. Unless casualisation is addressed as a fundamental weakness of the labour law regulatory framework, the anti-poverty potential of employment for sole parents will remain limited.

Part IV

Crisis and Austerity: Shaping Women's Rights to Social Security

11

Gendering the Right to Social Security in the Era of Crisis Governance: The Need for Transformative Strategies

DIANNE OTTO*

INTRODUCTION

IN THE CONTEMPORARY era of international crisis governance,[1] it is commonplace to see concerns about the 'security' of women harnessed to militaristic agendas. Lack of security, in this paradigm, is associated with terror and violence, especially sexual violence.[2] This flurry of alarm stands in stark contrast to the silence about the quotidian lack of *social* security that many—perhaps even most—women experience, even though it is an underlying cause of sexual violence. Women's social insecurity has been compounded by the gendered effects of free market globalisation, including cutbacks in publicly provided social benefits and protection schemes, the privatisation of responsibility and, with the 2008 global economic crisis, further cuts to social security protections justified by the mantra of austerity.[3] This seemingly inexorable shift, from social security as entitlement to social security as individual responsibility, employs well-worn techniques of

* Thanks to my ever attentive research assistant, Candice Parr, for her invaluable assistance.

[1] Otto, D, 'Remapping Crisis through a Feminist Lens' in S Kouvo and Z Pearson (eds), *Feminist Perspectives on Contemporary International Law: Between Resistance and Compliance?* (Oxford, Hart Publishing, 2011); and Klein, N, *The Shock Doctrine: The Rise of Disaster Capitalism* (Melbourne, Penguin/Allen Lane, 2007).

[2] AFP, 'G8 and Angelina Jolie Pledge Action on Rape as Weapon of War' *The Australian* (Sydney, 12 April 2013), reporting that the G8 Foreign Ministers meeting in London, in April 2013, agreed to commit US$35.5 million to tackle war-time rape and sexual assault.

[3] Ortiz, I, Chai, J and Cummins, M, 'Austerity Measures Threaten Children and Poor Households: Recent Evidence in Public Expenditures from 128 Developing Countries' (Social and Economic Working Paper, New York, UNICEF, September 2011).

crisis governance by shifting the blame, and its burden, onto those already disadvantaged and marginalised, and reneging on human rights obligations in the name of emergency, which then becomes the norm.[4]

Efforts to resist these moves have been slow to gather momentum, although in the background, many human rights and development NGOs have been working steadily towards building an alternative consensus, powerful enough to contest these trends.[5] At the institutional level, the United Nations (UN) Committee on Economic, Social and Cultural Rights (CESCR) has been amassing evidence that reduced social protections do not provide a solution to economic crisis and may indeed make the situation worse,[6] while the International Labour Organization (ILO) has laid the foundations for a global campaign to promote social protection floors and comprehensive social security systems for everyone.[7] As women increasingly shoulder the responsibility for dealing with the everyday effects of poverty, in the face of declining social assistance, including basic services and food subsidies,[8] these counter moves, in the shadows of crisis governance, are imperative. Yet, destabilising the certainties of the present, including public austerity and individual responsibility, remains a daunting task.

One attempt to draw international attention to the need to address women's quotidian survival struggles using human rights was the Montréal Principles on Women's Economic, Social and Cultural Rights (Montréal Principles), collaboratively authored during the zenith years of the global rise of crisis governance.[9] The impetus was to contribute to the CESCR's anticipated General Comment (authoritative interpretation),[10]

[4] Grabham, E and Smith, J, 'From Social Security to Individual Responsibility (Part Two): Writing Off Poor Women's Work in the Welfare Reform Act 2009' (2010) 32 *Journal of Social Welfare and Family Law* 81. See generally, Agamben, G, *State of Exception* (Chicago, University of Chicago Press, 2005).

[5] McCord, A and Vandemoortele, M, 'The Global Financial Crisis: Poverty and Social Protection—Evidence from 10 Country Case Studies' (Briefing Paper, United Kingdom, Overseas Development Institute, August 2009); and Green, D, King, R and Milller-Dawkins, M, *The Global Economic Crisis and Developing Countries* (United Kingdom, Oxfam Research Report, 28 May 2010).

[6] Pillay, AG, Letter on behalf of the Committee on Economic Social and Cultural Rights to all States Parties to the ICESCR on the Protection of Rights in the Context of Economic and Financial Crisis (16 May 2012); and Pillay, AG, Chairperson of CESCR, 'Statement to the General Assembly' (67th Session, 23 October 2012).

[7] International Labour Organization (ILO), *The Strategy of the International Labour Organization—Social Security for All: Building Social Protection Floors and Comprehensive Social Security Systems* (Geneva, ILO, 2012).

[8] Chant, S, 'The "Feminisation of Poverty" and the "Feminisation" of Anti-Poverty Programmes: Room for Revision?' (2008) 44 *Journal of Development Studies* 165, 178.

[9] 'Montréal Principles on Women's Economic, Social and Cultural Rights' (2004) 26 *Human Rights Quarterly* 760.

[10] Otto, D, '"Gender Comment": Why Does the UN Committee on Economic, Social and Cultural Rights Need a General Comment on Women?' (2002) 14 *Canadian Journal of Women and the Law* 1.

which would mainstream gender in the monitoring and implementation of the International Covenant on Economic, Social and Cultural Rights (ICESCR).[11] Eventually, in 2005, the CESCR adopted General Comment 16 on the equal right of men and women to enjoy all economic, social and cultural rights,[12] and later, in 2008, General Comment 19 shed further light on gender mainstreaming the right to social security.[13] Pre-dating these developments, the Human Rights Committee (HRC), which monitors implementation of the International Covenant on Civil and Political Rights (ICCPR),[14] had several opportunities to consider issues of gender equality in relation to social security entitlements through its individual complaints mechanism. Reviewing all these developments from the point of view of women's right to social security, three issues emerge that demand urgent attention. The first is whether the comparative standard of equality—even if it is substantive equality—can really do all the work we need it to do to ensure women's full and effective enjoyment of the right. Related to the first, the second issue is how to conceptualise the substantive content of the right in light of the incredible diversity of women's (and men's) participation in paid and unpaid work over the span of their lives. The third is the importance of addressing the dire situation of those most disadvantaged by the current arrangements, in a way that can challenge the prevailing discourse of public austerity and private responsibility.

For present purposes, I understand the provision of 'social security' broadly, following the ILO and CESCR, as covering the whole range of measures that are designed to secure protection from inadequacy of work-related income, lack of access to health care, insufficient family support and general poverty and social exclusion, which can take many forms including social transfers, benefits, social protection, social assistance and social protection floors.[15] I begin, in the first part of the chapter, with the story of recent efforts to frame women's right to social security in international human rights law, starting with the Montréal Principles, moving then to the CESCR's General Comments and recent Concluding Observations

[11] International Covenant on Economic, Social and Cultural Rights (ICESCR) (adopted 16 December 1966, entered into force 3 January 1976) 993 UNTS 3.

[12] UN Committee on Economic, Social and Cultural Rights (CESCR), *General Comment No 16: The Equal Right of Men and Women to the Enjoyment of all Economic, Social and Cultural Rights (art 3)*, 11 August 2005, UN Doc E/C.12/2005/4.

[13] UN Committee on Economic, Social and Cultural Rights (CESCR), *General Comment No 19: The Right to Social Security (art 9)*, 4 February 2008, UN Doc E/C.12/GC/19.

[14] International Covenant on Civil and Political Rights (ICCPR) (adopted 16 December 1966, entered into force 23 March 1976) 999 UNTS 171.

[15] International Labour Organisation (ILO), *Social Security for Social Justice and a Fair Globalization: Recurrent Discussion on Social Protection (Social Security) under the ILO Declaration on Social Justice for a Fair Globalization, 2011* (Report VI, International Labour Conference, 100th Session, Geneva, ILO, 2011) 9–10; and CESCR, *General Comment No 19*, above n 13, at paras 2–5.

and finally to the HRC's jurisprudence on this issue. My conclusion is that this groundwork is inadequate for the task of addressing the many complex challenges, both old and new, that impede realisation of women's right to social security today; that we are in urgent need of a fundamental reformulation—a transformation—of the right to social security. In the second part of the chapter I suggest two strategies towards transformation. The first is to develop a more gender inclusive account of the content of the right to social security which would obviate some of the need for comparisons with men, and be more inclusive of both women and men. The second is to urge that priority be given to identifying the 'minimum core obligation' of the right to social security, assumed by states parties to the ICESCR.[16] Further, I argue that the redistributive ICESCR obligation, to seek or provide international assistance and cooperation,[17] needs more robust interpretation and promotion, in order to tackle the entrenched inequities of the quotidian which are so regularly dismissed by invoking, what Maria Grahn-Farley calls, the 'politics of inevitability'.[18] Strengthening commitment to redistributive obligations requires working against the grain of crisis governance, which treats everyday structural inequalities as inevitable and fosters highly gendered, quick-fix, technocratic, market-friendly and often militarised responses to those global problems of inequality and exclusion that are temporarily elevated to the level of crisis,[19] before they fall again into the fog of inevitability.

EXAMINING THE GROUNDWORK

In this section I chart the human rights developments that have contributed to our understanding of women's right to social security. My argument is that elucidation of the legal obligation to progressively implement the right to social security, on the basis of equality between women and men, has stalled. The assumption that women are always dependent on male breadwinners has been hard to shake and, where it has been shaken, as in the jurisprudence of the HRC, an approach of formal equality has been adopted, which fails to attend to the cumulative structural disadvantages

[16] UN Committee on Economic, Social and Cultural Rights (CESCR), *General Comment No 3: The Nature of States Parties' Obligations (art 2, para 1 of the Covenant)*, 14 December 1990, UN Doc E/1991/23, para 10.

[17] ICESCR, above n 11, at art 2(1).

[18] Grahn-Farley, M, 'The Politics of Inevitability: An Examination of Janet Halley's Critique of the Criminalisation of Rape as Torture' in S Kouvo and Z Pearson (eds), *Feminist Perspectives on Contemporary International Law: Between Resistance and Compliance?* (Oxford, Hart Publishing, 2011) 120–21.

[19] Charlesworth, H, 'International Law: A Discipline of Crisis' (2002) 65 *Modern Law Review* 377.

that accrue to most women. The inadequacies of conceptions of equality, both formal and substantive, which rely on comparisons with a masculine standard, are all too apparent. I argue that these developments point to the need for a transformative re-visioning of the right to social security, in order to shake off enduring gender stereotypes, value all forms of paid and unpaid work and overcome the limitations of the comparative standard of equality.

The Montréal Principles: Substantive Equality

One attempt to unsettle the assumption of women's economic dependency came from a group of feminist human rights advocates, including myself, who set out to draft a model General Comment on women's equal enjoyment of the rights enumerated in the ICESCR, to provide guidance for the CESCR. Two international collaborations were organised, in Cape Town in 2000 and in Montréal in 2002. Following the lead of earlier efforts by human rights experts to assist the CESCR in its work,[20] the Montréal Principles, as the draft came to be called, sought to provide normative guidance on the interpretation and implementation of the ICESCR. The Montréal Principles[21] promote a substantive equality approach to realising women's economic, social and cultural rights and emphasise the immediacy of many of the relevant ICESCR obligations.

Adopting the approach of the Convention on the Elimination of all forms of Discrimination against Women (CEDAW),[22] the Montréal Principles propose that the ICESCR be interpreted to require the realisation of women's substantive or de facto equality, as well as their formal equality,[23] and emphasise that attention must be paid to eliminating the structurally embedded impediments to women's equal enjoyment of economic, social and cultural rights, such as the traditional assignment of domestic and caring responsibilities to women and the historical devaluation of their work, both paid and unpaid.[24] The need to recognise women's full legal personhood and autonomy is highlighted,[25] including their 'economic autonomy',[26] and the negative impacts on women of neo-liberal economic policies,

[20] Limburg Principles on the Implementation of the International Covenant on Economic, Social and Cultural Rights, UN Doc E/CN.4/1987/17, annex (8 January 1987); Maastricht Guidelines on Violations of Economic, Social and Cultural Rights (Maastricht, 22–26 January 1997); and Maastricht Principles on Extraterritorial Obligations of States in the area of Economic, Social and Cultural Rights (Maastricht, 28 September 2011).

[21] 'Montréal Principles', above n 9.

[22] Convention on the Elimination of All Forms of Discrimination against Women (CEDAW) (adopted 18 December 1979, entered into force 3 September 1981) 1249 UNTS 13.

[23] 'Montréal Principles', above n 9, at para 9.

[24] *Ibid*, Introduction, at 762.

[25] *Ibid*, at para 11.

[26] *Ibid*.

such as 'privatization, economic austerity and structural adjustment' are emphasised.[27] A number of CEDAW obligations are thus imported into the ICESCR, including the definition of discrimination against women, which identifies men as the relevant comparator and robustly proscribes both direct and indirect discrimination.[28] Also following CEDAW, the adoption of temporary special measures, or positive discrimination, is promoted as a means to address the structural dimensions of women's disadvantage and thus hasten the realisation of de facto equality.[29]

The Montréal Principles justify their asymmetrical focus on women's inequality on the basis that '[s]ex or gender inequality is a problem experienced primarily by women' and that 'implicit' in understanding social norms that are 'considered appropriate for women and men' is that 'male and female norms have been constructed so as to privilege men and disadvantage women'.[30] In recognising that sex discrimination 'primarily' affects women and conceding that the social construction of gender affects both men and women, the Montréal Principles leave room for acknowledging that men may also experience discrimination on the basis of their sex/gender. Yet they consistently assume a gender hierarchy that always works to the advantage of men and the detriment of women. While today I still agree that women are primarily disadvantaged by sex/gender discrimination, my concern has shifted to the need to understand that gendered power functions in complex ways, and not always as duality, sometimes disadvantaging men and nearly always legitimating discrimination against those who transgress the prevailing gender codes, whether they identify as a woman, a man or another gender, such as intersex, transgender or third sex.[31]

In addition to adopting CEDAW's asymmetrical substantive equality approach, a second feature of the Montréal Principles is the way they draw on the considerable work undertaken by the CESCR to clarify the 'progressive' implementation obligations that states parties assume on ratification of the ICESCR, under Article 2(1),[32] which have often been dismissed as toothless. They emphasise that the obligation to eliminate discrimination and ensure women's equal enjoyment of ICESCR rights is both immediate and justiciable,[33] and this point is underlined by stressing that the 'maximum

[27] *Ibid*, Introduction, at 763.
[28] *Ibid*, at para 7.
[29] *Ibid*, at para 16.
[30] *Ibid*, Introduction, at 760–61.
[31] Otto, D, 'International Human Rights Law: Towards Rethinking Sex/Gender Dualism' in M Davies and VE Munro (eds), *The Ashgate Research Companion to Feminist Legal Theory* (Farnham, Ashgate Publishing Limited, 2013) 197.
[32] ICESCR, above n 11, at art 2(1).
[33] 'Montréal Principles', above n 9, at paras 13, 14. See also, UN Committee on Economic, Social and Cultural Rights (CESCR), *General Comment No 9: The Domestic Application of the Covenant*, 3 December 1998, UN Doc E/C.12/1998/24, para 10.

available resources' must be distributed in such a way as to provide for women's substantively equal exercise and enjoyment of ICESCR rights.[34] The immediacy of the obligation to make provision for basic needs in the context of scarcity, as well as in situations of conflict and post-conflict (which the CESCR has described as the 'minimum core obligation'), is stressed with respect to 'health care, access to potable water, sanitation services, housing, education, energy, and social protection'.[35] Repeatedly emphasised is the overall and primary responsibility of states parties to ensure the enjoyment of ICESCR rights, including their obligations to regulate non-state actors consistently with the ICESCR.[36]

While the Montréal Principles do not provide specific guidance as to how substantive equality applies, in practice, to women's social security rights,[37] the taxonomy developed would require that states parties ensure that women are able to enjoy the panoply of social security rights (article 9 ICESCR) so as to benefit, in real terms, on a basis of equality with men, in addition to providing 'special protection' before, during and after childbirth, including paid leave for working mothers (article 10(2) ICESCR). That is, with the exception of assistance related to pregnancy and early motherhood, men's experience is instantiated as the normative standard. Such a comparison can provide a very powerful means for women to claim rights, especially as it assumes that women, like men, enjoy economic autonomy. However, the comparative standard also means that if men are not in a situation that is comparable to women's situation, there are no associated rights that women can claim by means of equality. The way that social security entitlements have traditionally been conceived provides a clear example of the limitations of comparative equality. The model, based on (some) men's experience of formal workforce participation and the idea that they earn a family wage, still underpins contemporary conceptions of social security.

To some extent, the limitations of such comparisons are ameliorated by assessing equality between women and men substantively, which can legitimate different treatment in order to achieve de facto equality. In its most robust form, substantive equality necessitates equality of outcome

[34] 'Montréal Principles', above n 9, at para 18.

[35] *Ibid*, at para 21.

[36] *Ibid*, at paras 22 and 23. However, there is a curious absence of reference to the obligation to regulate individuals in the private sphere of the home, such as fathers and husbands, who may obstruct women's enjoyment of economic, social and cultural rights by, eg, preventing their freedom of movement or trapping them in cycles of domestic violence.

[37] *Ibid*, at para 1(d) makes reference to women's right to 'Social security, social protection, social insurance and social services, including special assistance before, during and after childbirth'.

or results.[38] So, for example, if women's unequal pay and interrupted workforce participation due to family responsibilities reduces their ability to contribute to a social insurance scheme as compared with men, the state would be required to take measures to ensure equality in outcome, by supplementing women's contributions or requiring equal distribution despite unequal contributions.[39] However few, if any, states embrace such a strong definition of substantive equality. It is more commonly interpreted in a softer way as requiring that conditions for equality of opportunity are established by, for example, introducing more flexible workplace practices that enable women to assume family responsibilities without affecting their workforce participation. Adopting positive measures, including affirmative action, to overcome systemic and entrenched discrimination also assists in making the comparison between women and men, demanded by substantive equality, more nuanced and proactive. However, affirmative action is often poorly understood and very vulnerable to challenge, so its effects can even be counterproductive.[40]

Yet the comparative rubric of gender equality is utterly unhelpful when women's experience differs from men's, as it does so often and so dramatically in this highly gendered world. When comparison fails, the practice has been to adopt 'special' exceptional measures that too often take the form of protection, rather than rights, as with the ICESCR's provision for 'special protection' for pregnant women and young mothers. Special provisions for women reinvigorate earlier legal representations of women as less than fully human, as dependent and vulnerable (like children) and therefore in need of protection by husbands, fathers and the state.[41] Such paternalism is patently inconsistent with the human rights principles of equality and universality.

Yet the substantive equality model promoted by the Montréal Principles does not come to grips with these problems. In the context of the right to social security, the assumption of a male breadwinner is not challenged, care work and other family and community responsibilities are simply not visible and the protectiveness of the special maternity measures is not questioned. The threats to women's social security presented by the rise of precarious work, and by poorly remunerated work in the informal sector,

[38] Moeckli, D, 'Equality and Non-Discrimination' in D Moeckli, S Shah and S Sivakumaran (eds), *International Human Rights Law* (Oxford, Oxford University Press, 2010) 192.

[39] This approach is proposed in CESCR, *General Comment No 19*, above n 13, at para 32.

[40] See, eg, *Maloney v The Queen* [2013] HCA 28, 19 June 2013, which interpreted 'special measures' under the International Convention on the Elimination of Race Discrimination, art 1(4), restrictively so that prior consultation with affected [Aboriginal] communities was not required.

[41] See also Otto, D, 'The Exile of Inclusion: Reflections on Gender Issues in International Law over the Last Decade' (2009) 10 *Melbourne Journal of International Law* 11.

are also not mentioned and there is no reference to the specific forms of discrimination faced by single mothers and women household heads. The Montréal Principles fail to anticipate the momentum of the movement towards individual responsibility and austerity, which perhaps accounts for their failure to discuss the redistributive obligations associated with international cooperation and assistance and their importance for women.

The Committee on Economic, Social and Cultural Rights: Gender Mainstreaming

Like the Montréal Principles, the CESCR's General Comment 16 takes a substantive equality approach and emphasises implementation obligations. However, in a significant departure from the Montréal Principles, General Comment 16 adopts a 'symmetrical' or 'gender inclusive' understanding of sex/gender discrimination, which enables gender relations, and gendered violations of economic, social and cultural rights experienced by men, as well as women, to be acknowledged. Implementing article 9, for example, is interpreted as requiring

> inter alia, equalizing the compulsory retirement age for both men and women; ensuring that women receive the equal benefit of public and private pension schemes; and guaranteeing adequate maternity leave for women, paternity leave for men, and parental leave for both women and men.[42]

The requirement that parental leave be made available to both men and women is a good illustration of the General Comment's gender inclusivity and the way it can challenge long-standing gender stereotypes. Instead of gender being used as a synonym for women, as in the Montréal Principles, it is defined as referring to 'cultural expectations and assumptions about the behaviour, attitudes, personality traits, and physical and intellectual capacities of men and women, based solely on their identity as men or women'.[43] In the same vein (direct) discrimination is described as occurring when differential treatment relies on distinctions 'based exclusively on sex and characteristics of men or of women, which cannot be justified objectively'.[44] Other illustrations of the CESCR's symmetrical approach include the identification of both boys and girls as needing protection from practices that promote child marriage (article 10(1))[45] and the concern that both women and men are able to reconcile work and family responsibilities

[42] CESCR, *General Comment No 16*, above n 12, at para 26.
[43] *Ibid*, at para 14.
[44] *Ibid*, at para 12.
[45] *Ibid*, at para 27.

(article 7(a)).[46] Acknowledging men's family responsibilities and the vulnerability of boys to child marriage works to de-feminise these issues, which has the important effect of disrupting gender stereotypes, militating against protective responses to women and opening possibilities for transformative change in gender relations. Unfortunately, however, no reference is made anywhere in the General Comment to gender identities that do not fit the male/female binary, such as transgender and intersex people.[47]

Yet the inclusion of men as possible victims of sex discrimination in General Comment 16 does not whitewash the reality that sex/gender discrimination and inequality largely operate to women's disadvantage, which should provide some reassurance to those concerned that symmetrical treatment will result in the re-marginalisation of women's experiences of discrimination and inequality.[48] That women bear a disproportionate burden of gender disadvantage is consistently acknowledged with respect to specific rights violations—for example, women are described as 'primarily' the victims (domestic violence),[49] as 'particularly' affected (historical disadvantage),[50] as 'generally' placed at a disadvantage (cultural assumptions and expectations)[51] and as requiring 'particular attention' as marginalised workers (the right to form and join trade unions).[52] Thus, the silence about human rights abuses suffered by men because of their gender is broken, without denying the general reality of women's systemic inequality. This outcome is achieved by making calibrated assessments of women's and men's gender inequality, in the context of each specific right, rather than assuming women's subordination/men's dominance as always the rule.

While the CESCR's recognition that men may be disadvantaged by sex/gender discrimination has the important effect of militating against the acceptability of protective stereotypes of women in human rights law, protective assumptions remain at the heart of the key ILO Conventions relating to social security. For example, Convention 102 on Social Security (Minimum Standards) adopted by the ILO in 1952,[53] which is still regarded

[46] *Ibid*, at para 24.

[47] See Yogyakarta Principles on the Application of International Human Rights Law in relation to Sexual Orientation and Gender Identity, drafted by an International Panel of Experts (Yogyakarta, Indonesia, 6–9 November 2006).

[48] Persram, N, 'Politicizing the *Féminine*, Globalizing the Feminist' (1994) 19 *Alternatives* 275; and Esperanza Hernández-Truyol, B, 'Unsex CEDAW? No! Super-Sex It!' (2011) 20 *Columbia Journal of Gender and Law* 195.

[49] CESCR, *General Comment No 16*, above n 12, at para 27.

[50] *Ibid*, at para 8.

[51] *Ibid*, at para 14.

[52] *Ibid*, at para 25.

[53] ILO Convention C102: Social Security (Minimum Standards) Convention (Convention Concerning Minimum Standards of Social Security) (adopted 28 June 1952, entered into force 27 April 1955).

as providing the foundation for international social security law,[54] makes specific reference to women only as 'wives'. Although women workers are presumably included in the categories of prescribed workers which are taken into account when establishing classes of protected persons, 'the constant references to the male industrial worker for various technical reasons provided for by the Convention, such as the level of benefits, clearly "leaves the women at home"', as Lucie Lamarche has observed.[55] The symmetrical approach of General Comment 16 challenges this normative framework, pointing to the need for a complete re-imagining of social security as it has traditionally been conceived. Gender inclusivity also draws attention to the social and relational nature of gendered assumptions, highlighting the point that changing gendered stereotypes of men, as well as women, is essential to the project of achieving full equality between women and men. To focus only on women, as in the Montréal Principles (and CEDAW), is to address only half the problem.[56]

The CESCR builds on its gender inclusive interpretation of the right to social security in General Comment 19 by promoting substantive equality in its strongest sense of equality in outcome. The General Comment calls for the elimination of factors that prevent women from making equal contributions to social security schemes that link benefits with contributions by ensuring that such schemes take account of factors, such as intermittent workforce participation because of family responsibilities, in the design of benefit formulas.[57] Further, in the case of non-contributory social security schemes, states should take account of the fact that women are more likely to live in poverty than men and are also more likely to have responsibility for the care of children.[58] Going against the grain of the contemporary logic of austerity measures, the General Comment urges that 'social security should be treated as a social good, and not primarily as a mere instrument of economic or financial policy'.[59]

Yet the CESCR seems unwilling or unable to incorporate the progressive vision of its General Comments into the guidance it provides to states

[54] C102 was confirmed by the ILO Governing Body in 2002 as an instrument corresponding to contemporary needs and circumstances. The nine categories of social security C102 identifies were also affirmed by states and trade union and employer representatives at the ILO Maritime Labour Convention (adopted 23 February 2006, entered into force 20 August 2013) reg 4.5, standard A4.5. The CESCR also endorses the approach of C102 in CESCR, *General Comment No 19*, above n 13, at para 12.

[55] Lamarche, L, 'The Right to Social Security in the International Covenant on Economic, Social and Cultural Rights' in A Chapman and S Russell (eds), *Core Obligations: Building a Framework for Economic, Social and Cultural Rights* (Antwerp, Intersentia, 2002) 92.

[56] Rosenblum, D, 'Unsex CEDAW, or What's Wrong with Women's Rights' (2011) 20 *Columbia Journal of Gender and Law* 1.

[57] CESCR, *General Comment No 19*, above n 13, at para 32.

[58] *Ibid.*

[59] *Ibid*, at para 10.

parties on the implementation of article 9. A survey of the Concluding Observations adopted by the CESCR in 2012, after considering the periodic reports of 10 states, shows that its guidance is agonisingly general. In response to the austerity measures adopted by Spain, New Zealand and Iceland in the context of economic and financial crisis, the CESCR did not hold back from expressing concern, but its recommendations fall short of remedying their dire consequences and seem to capitulate to the use of social security as a tool of economic management. In the case of Spain, for example, the CESCR expresses concern about the drastic cuts to family benefit payments, the reduction of pensions below subsistence levels, especially for women in receipt of widows' pensions and queries the gender stereotypes that maintain inequality between women's and men's wages and their right to work, resulting in violations of the ICESCR, including article 9.[60] Yet its recommendations that Spain ensure all austerity measures are 'temporary and proportionate',[61] that they comply with the 'minimum core content' of ICESCR rights (without further elucidation as to what this is) and that the core is protected 'under any circumstances, especially for disadvantaged and marginalised individuals and groups'[62] seem feeble in the face of such widespread suffering, and do nothing to challenge the use of austerity as acceptable fiscal policy. In relation to New Zealand, concern is expressed about the 'retrogressive nature and possible discriminatory effects' of welfare reforms, followed by similarly tepid recommendations that punishing work-test requirements and income management practices be reviewed.[63] The CESCR's recommendations to Iceland are somewhat more robust, recommending social transfers to mitigate inequalities and the identification of a social protection floor,[64] but it still refrains from questioning the wisdom of austerity measures in the first place.

By contrast, the situation in the other seven states parties reviewed is not seen as a crisis, despite the fact that they all have seriously inadequate social security systems and everyday poverty is pervasive. As a result, the guidance provided by the CESCR is even more general than what was given to the crisis-marked developed states. In the total absence of a social security system in Ethiopia, it is recommended that steps be taken to establish one in line with General Comment 19,[65] and in response to the narrow coverage

[60] UN Committee on Economic, Social and Cultural Rights (CESCR), *Concluding Observations of CESCR: Spain*, 6 June 2012, UN Doc E/C.12/ESP/CO/5, paras 17, 20, 13.

[61] *Ibid*, at para 17.

[62] *Ibid*, at para 8.

[63] UN Committee on Economic, Social and Cultural Rights (CESCR), *Concluding Observations of CESCR: New Zealand*, 31 May 2012, UN Doc E/C.12/NZL/CO/3, para 17.

[64] UN Committee on Economic, Social and Cultural Rights (CESCR), *Concluding Observations of CESCR: Iceland*, 11 December 2012, UN Doc E/C.12/ISL/CO/4, para 6.

[65] UN Committee on Economic, Social and Cultural Rights (CESCR), *Concluding Observations of CESCR: Ethiopia*, 31 May 2012, UN Doc E/C.12/ETH/CO/1-3, para 13.

of Peru's social security system, it is recommended that steps be taken to include all workers in the private sector and persons with disabilities.[66] Bulgaria is requested to establish an effective system of indexation to ensure social assistance enables a decent standard of living; Ecuador is asked to develop a plan for providing universal coverage;[67] Mauritania is urged to extend coverage to the vulnerable majority of the population, including to unemployed and elderly people;[68] and Tanzania is advised to take steps to extend its low coverage towards establishing a universal system.[69] Gender-specific social security issues are raised in just three cases and then only in relation to women: Slovakia with respect to reduced coverage of reproductive and health services, including the removal of contraceptives from coverage, under the new law on social security, adopted in September 2011;[70] Ecuador with respect to disproportionately low rates of coverage of indigenous and Afro-Ecuadorian women;[71] and Mauritania with respect to the over-representation of women among the poor.[72]

Even this cursory examination of the CESCR's monitoring work indicates that it is in danger of capitulating to the politics of inevitability when it comes to the structural disadvantage of large swathes of the population in developing countries. There is obviously an urgent need for more effective tools to guide implementation of article 9 generally, as well as in relation to addressing the gendered effects of most, if not all, existing arrangements, despite the immediacy of the obligation of non-discrimination and even without the intensifying ideologies of austerity. In theory, there is a great deal to be gained by engaging creatively with substantive conceptions of equality and gender inclusive understandings of sex/gender discrimination. Yet translating this into country-specific recommendations seems stubbornly elusive. Minimum core obligations are rarely mentioned, despite the fundamental importance of social assistance in enabling a decent living for those who are most disadvantaged. And the point made in the CESCR Statement to the General Assembly in 2012—that taking retrogressive steps in relation to economic, social and cultural rights 'does not … constitute an escape route out of crisis'[73]—is nowhere to be found.

[66] UN Committee on Economic, Social and Cultural Rights (CESCR), *Concluding Observations of CESCR: Peru*, 30 May 2012, UN Doc E/C.12/PER/CO/2-4, para 13.

[67] UN Committee on Economic, Social and Cultural Rights (CESCR), *Concluding Observations of CESCR: Ecuador*, 13 December 2012, UN Doc E/C.12/ECU/CO/4, para 20.

[68] UN Committee on Economic, Social and Cultural Rights (CESCR), *Concluding Observations of CESCR: Mauritania*, 10 December 2012, UN Doc E/C.12/MRT/1, para 17.

[69] UN Committee on Economic, Social and Cultural Rights (CESCR), *Concluding Observations of CESCR: Tanzania*, 13 December 2012, UN Doc E/C.12/TZA/CO/1-3, para 12.

[70] UN Committee on Economic, Social and Cultural Rights (CESCR), *Concluding Observations of CESCR: Slovakia*, 8 June 2012, UN Doc E/C.12/SVK/CO/2, para 24.

[71] CESCR, *Concluding Observations of CESCR: Ecuador*, above n 67, at para 20.

[72] CESCR, *Concluding Observations of CESCR: Mauritania*, above n 68, at para 22.

[73] Pillay, 'Statement to the General Assembly', above n 6.

The Human Rights Committee: Formal Equality

In contrast, the HRC's approach to complaints about sex/gender discrimination in social security benefits schemes has been one of formal, rather than substantive equality. While this approach has the advantage of rejecting arrangements based on the assumption of women's economic dependency, in determining eligibility and level of benefit for example, the problem of the cumulative effects of women's past disadvantage, like lower pay and interrupted workforce participation, is completely ignored. The result is what might be called 'symmetry with a vengeance'.[74] The cases thus provide further illustration of the inadequacies of the comparative standard of equality when it comes to addressing the gendered dimensions of social insecurity, and also point to the need for gender inclusive frameworks of analysis.

In the course of monitoring implementation of the ICCPR, the HRC has considered a number of individual complaints alleging discrimination with regard to social security payments, in violation of equal protection of the law (article 26 ICCPR). Six of these cases challenged the legislative presumption of a male breadwinner/female dependent arrangement between (heterosexual) married couples, which resulted in different (allegedly discriminatory) social security entitlements for married men and married women. The requirement in Dutch law that an unemployed married woman had to prove that she was a 'breadwinner' in order to be eligible for unemployment benefits, a requirement that did not apply to unemployed married men, was challenged by women in three cases.[75] The three other cases were brought by men, two of whom challenged survivor benefits schemes which awarded lower benefits to widowed men than to widowed women,[76] while the third challenged a scheme that resulted in smaller civil service pensions for married men than for married women.[77] In all six cases, the HRC interpreted equal treatment narrowly, focusing on whether the laws were formally neutral in their

[74] With thanks to CA MacKinnon who uses the term 'equality with a vengeance' to dismiss the kind of equality that results from applying male standards to women. See MacKinnon, CA, *Feminism Unmodified: Discourses on Life and Law* (Cambridge, Harvard University Press, 1987) 72.

[75] *SWM Brooks v The Netherlands*, Communication No 172/84, 9 April 1987, UN Doc CCPR/C/29/D/172/1984; *Zwaan-de Vries v The Netherlands*, Communication No 182/84, 9 April 1987, UN Doc CCPR/C/29/D/182/1984. See also, *Araujo-Jongen v The Netherlands*, Communication No 418/90, 22 October 1993, UN Doc CCPR/C/44/D/418/1990, para 7.4 where the Human Rights Committee found that subsequent legislative changes had rectified the discrimination in the author's claim.

[76] *Pauger v Austria*, Communication No 415/1990, 26 March 1992, UN Doc CCPR/C/44/D/415/1990; *Pepels v The Netherlands*, Communication No 484/1991, 15 July 1994, UN Doc CCPR/C/47/D/484/1991.

[77] *Vos v The Netherlands*, Communication No 786/1997, 26 July 1999, UN Doc CCPR/C/66/D/786/1997.

application to women and men, which led to the finding that all the gender differences in social security entitlement complained of constituted prohibited discrimination, and thus violated article 26. The European Court of Justice has taken a similarly formal approach to gender equality in this field.[78]

If the HRC had gone on to consider whether gender neutrality of the laws might have, or maintain, discriminatory effects, the outcome may well have been different. While removing the assumption of married women's economic dependency from social security schemes can have empowering effects for women, it must be removed in such a way that does not leave women even more exposed to inadequate social protection coverage because of their unpaid work and/or intermittent and low-paid employment histories.[79] Further, the process of awarding widows and widowers the same pension entitlements has generally resulted in a levelling down of provision,[80] while equalising the retirement age of men and women has increased women's age of retirement. These developments threaten to deepen the poverty of women who lose entitlements—in the name of equality. There is a clear need for frameworks that combine substantive conceptions of equality with gender symmetry, which would assess equality in a more contextualised manner, yet without relying on protective stereotypes.

While formal interpretations of equality, and levelling down, can severely limit the potential to achieve equal outcomes for women, the more pressing problem with the paradigm of equality is its instantiation of men's experience as the norm. Comparative notions of equality do not enable a rethinking of the existing gendered social arrangements, as illustrated by the interpretive guidance offered by General Comment 16 discussed earlier,[81] which, despite the progressiveness of its gender inclusivity, still seeks merely to promote the inclusion of women and men in the existing social protection arrangements by equalising the retirement age, advocating for women's inclusion in existing pension schemes and extending parental leave to men (although the last move does have the potential to be transformative).

As recognised by the Expert Working Group on the promotion of women's economic and social rights in its 1998 report, prepared to assist the work of the Commission on the Status of Women,[82] the full realisation

[78] Luckhaus, L, 'Equal Treatment, Social Protection and Income Security for Women' (2000) 139(3) *International Labour Review* 149, 154–55.

[79] *Ibid*, at 155–56.

[80] *Ibid*, at 161.

[81] See CESCR, *General Comment No 16*, above n 42, and accompanying text.

[82] Expert Group Meeting, UN Division for the Advancement of Women, *Promoting Women's Enjoyment of their Economic, Social and Cultural Rights*, UN Doc EGM/WESR/1997/Report (Abo/Turku, Finland, Report, 1–4 December 1997). See also, Otto, D, 'Defending Women's Economic and Social Rights: Some Thoughts on Indivisibility and a New Standard of Equality' in I Merali and V Oosterveld (eds), *Giving Meaning to Economic, Social and Cultural Rights* (Philadelphia, University of Pennsylvania Press, 2001).

of women's human rights requires a number of strategies. Among those suggested were the creative gender-sensitive (re)interpretation of existing human rights norms, the possible recognition of new human rights that take account of women's life patterns and experiences where they differ from men's and mainstreaming a gender perspective in all legislation, policies and programmes.[83] In relation to gender mainstreaming, the report observed that it will, in many cases, require 'a fundamental restructuring—a transformation—of institutions and systems such as the labour market, social security systems and the operation of property markets'.[84] These strategies all push beyond the limits of comparative equality and, in combination, promote much more radical change than either the Montréal Principles or the gender mainstreaming work of the CESCR.

BUILDING ON THE GROUNDWORK: TOWARDS TRANSFORMATION

Following the transformative encouragement of the Expert Working Group, I will now pursue its strategy of creative gender-sensitive (re)interpretation of the right to social security, which is closely linked with the other two strategies of recognising 'new' human rights and gender mainstreaming. My aim in re-imagining the substantive content of the right is to ensure that it establishes a universal standard that is inclusive of both women's and men's experience. Such reinterpretation would reduce reliance on the comparative principles of equality and non-discrimination, and challenge protective stereotypes of women and paternalistic stereotypes of men. This approach is described by Beth Goldblatt and Lucie Lamarche as 'gendering the social security right'.[85] In addition, I will urge a second strategy of transformation—to strengthen the focus of implementation on addressing the situation of those who are most disadvantaged by clarifying the content of the minimum core of the right to social security and finding ways to actualise the redistributive obligations in the ICESCR that require states parties to seek and provide international assistance and cooperation.

Gendering the Social Security Right: Creative Reinterpretation

As I have argued, there are many problems with relying solely or primarily on the principles of sex/gender equality and non-discrimination, as the means to ensure that human rights violations suffered largely by women

[83] Expert Group Meeting, above n 82, at paras 33, 44 and 45.
[84] *Ibid*, at para 33.
[85] Goldblatt and Lamarche, in this collection.

are included in the universal register. At the heart of a gender inclusive reinterpretation of the right to social security is the challenge to conceptualise the right in light of the huge diversity of women's and men's participation in paid and unpaid work, and the interconnectedness of social security rights with the enjoyment of other human rights.

One method of gender-sensitive reinterpretation of existing human rights is illustrated by the HRC in its gender mainstreaming General Comment 28, where it re-imagines the universal subject of the ICCPR as a woman.[86] Applying this method to the right to life (article 6 ICCPR),[87] a number of new violations are identified, including failure to address conditions under which women have no options but to resort to life-threatening backyard abortions to prevent unwanted pregnancy, inadequate measures to protect women from childbirth related deaths and failure to eliminate social practices that violate women's right to life, such as female infanticide and dowry killings.[88] Although the HRC takes an asymmetrical approach, focusing only on women's gender disadvantage and not men's, its reinterpretation of ICCPR rights is groundbreaking. Importantly, especially for present purposes, the HRC acknowledges the interdependence of the right to life and economic and social rights by recognising that situations of poverty and deprivation, which pose a threat to women's lives, may also violate article 6.[89] Thus, a state's failure to ensure that everyone enjoys at least the minimum core content of the right to social security may violate ICCPR, as well as ICESCR, obligations.

Following the approach of the HRC, what happens to our understanding of the right to social security if the universal subject is re-imagined as a woman? A number of novel violations of article 9 become immediately visible if we look, from this point of view, for arbitrary and unreasonable restrictions on social security coverage, social risks and contingencies that are not currently recognised and groups that are not covered because of discriminatory assumptions. For example, arbitrary and unreasonable restrictions on the coverage of social security would include entitlements calculated solely on formal workforce participation, the exclusion of workers in the informal economy from eligibility and the omission of unremunerated work from the calculation of entitlements, including domestic, reproductive and caring work in the family or community. Additional social risks and contingencies, which are central concepts in social security formulation, also become visible including income that falls below a minimum liveable

86 UN Human Rights Committee (HRC), *General Comment No 28: Equality of Rights Between Men and Women (art 3)*, 29 March 2000, UN Doc CCPR/C/21/Rev.1/Add.10.

87 ICCPR, above n 14, at art 6.

88 *Ibid*, at para 10.

89 *Ibid*.

level, income insecurity due to precarious work, interrupted work due to domestic violence and the inability to secure paid employment because of caring responsibilities. Also evident are female dominated groups who are currently ineligible because of discriminatory beliefs and practices, including agricultural workers, home-workers, domestic workers, sex workers, migrant workers, subsistence workers and unpaid workers providing care or contributing to family enterprises. In sum, imagining a woman as the subject of social security rights, rather than the male industrial worker, makes it very clear that the traditional design of social security systems needs thorough reconstruction.

A new definition of work may be the best starting point for transforming the right to social security—a definition which encompasses unremunerated reproductive, domestic and caring labour, as well as all forms of remunerated employment in the informal, casualised and formal sectors.[90] Equally valuing feminised work in the domestic sphere and family enterprises would help to change the breadwinner model and unequal gender relations in the context of the family. Acknowledging the precarity of many forms of remunerated work, much of which is undertaken by women, would necessitate admitting that work-related income may be inadequate for survival in the absence of any of the social risks or contingencies currently recognised as grounding claims for social protection. A transformed right to social security would need to ensure support to workers whose income falls below the minimum wage or poverty line, as well as to those engaged in unpaid work. Such a transformation involves rejecting the false promises of free market ideologues about individual entrepreneurialism and trickle-down wealth, and instead reasserting the importance of public responsibility for human well-being. In this new vision, states would be expected to take the lead in restructuring their labour markets so as to promote inclusion, socially useful and environmentally sustainable work, adequate remuneration and family-friendly workplace practices, supplemented and supported by universal social security coverage.

An alternative starting point for transforming the right to social security would be to reconceptualise social security as a social good, rather than as primarily related to work. The first step would be to guarantee universal coverage that ensures that everyone enjoys, at the very least, the minimum core. From this foundation, efforts to reduce the burden on the state could be promoted; including contributory or insurance based work-related schemes, and privately run, self-help, informal sector arrangements. This alternative reverses the neo-liberal crisis thinking that promotes individual responsibility as the foundation and reduces state responsibility to a minimal

[90] For a related discussion of principles for a substantively equal, gendered social security right, see Goldblatt, in this collection.

residual function. In keeping with the 1944 Declaration of Philadelphia on the ILO, social security measures are understood as 'provid[ing] a basic income to all in need of such protection and comprehensive medical care'.[91]

Transforming the right to social security is imperative if we are ever to universally realise the basic conditions for human flourishing and equality, whether it is achieved by adopting a gender inclusive definition of work or by reconceiving social security as a universal social entitlement. Transformation is necessary to dislodge the standard of the industrial male worker and, instead, recognise the huge diversity of women's and men's participation in paid and unpaid work, which eliminates reliance on harmful gender stereotypes and obviates much of the need for gendered comparisons. Transformation is also necessary to challenge the naturalised account of dualistic and hierarchical gender relations and, instead, treat gender identities and roles as socially produced and shifting forms of human expression and desire.

Focusing on the Most Disadvantaged: Reviving Social Responsibility

Among its efforts to give substance to ICESCR rights in the context of the progressive nature of many ICESCR obligations, the CESCR has embraced the concept of a minimum core obligation which requires states parties 'to ensure the satisfaction of, at the very least, minimum essential levels of each right'.[92] Although neither the Montréal Principles nor General Comment 16 use the terminology of minimum core, the former emphasises the obligation to provide for women's 'basic needs',[93] and the latter emphasises the importance of rigorous monitoring of the enjoyment of ICESCR rights by disadvantaged or marginalised people.[94] In adopting the concept of a minimum core, the CESCR hoped to achieve three things: establish a common legal standard that would mitigate the relativism of the obligation of progressive realisation; advance a baseline that would apply across diverse economic systems and differences in availability of resources; and provide the basis for promoting 'manageable' redistributive obligations, as Katharine Young has argued.[95] I will look first at the idea of a common

[91] International Labour Organization (ILO) *ILO Declaration Concerning the Aims and Purposes of the International Labour Organization (Declaration of Philadelphia)*, 10 May 1994, s III(f), available at: www.ilo.org/dyn/normlex/en/f?p=1000:62:0::NO:62:P62_LIST_ENTRIE_ID:2453907:NO#declaration.

[92] CESCR, *General Comment No 3*, above n 16, at para 10.

[93] 'Montréal Principles', above n 9, at para 21.

[94] CESCR, *General Comment No 16*, above n 12, at para 21.

[95] Young, KG, 'The Minimum Core of Economic and Social Rights: A Concept in Search of Content' (2008) 33 *Yale Journal of International Law* 113, 121–22.

legal standard in the form of a baseline, before turning to the question of redistributive obligations.

In relation to the right to social security, General Comment 19 identifies several components of the minimum core obligation, including ensuring access is non-discriminatory, protecting against retrogression, adopting a national strategy and action plan, targeting those who are most disadvantaged and establishing monitoring mechanisms.[96] The substantive baseline proposed is

> [universal] access to a social security scheme that provides a minimum essential level of benefits to all individuals and families that will enable them to acquire at least essential health care, basic shelter and housing, water and sanitation, foodstuffs, and the most basic forms of education.[97]

The General Comment goes on to make it clear that states parties are expected to make every effort to use all resources at their disposal 'to satisfy, as a matter of priority, these minimum obligations'.[98] While there has been a great deal of discussion about the desirability of a minimum core approach, with some fearing that the minimum will become the standard,[99] and others concerned that it is impossible to apply in practice,[100] it nevertheless has an important role to play when the vast majority of people have no access at all to social security. The CESCR clearly needs to treat this immediate obligation far more seriously in its Concluding Observations.

General Comment 19 also calls on states parties and others, 'in a position to assist', to 'provide international assistance and cooperation' to enable developing countries to fulfil these core obligations.[101] This call indicates that the 'redistributive character' of the right to social security, acknowledged earlier in General Comment 19,[102] is not confined to redistribution within a state, but refers also to global redistribution in the form of wealthy states assisting poor ones. The obligations that arise in relation to international cooperation and assistance are not to be confused with a state's extraterritorial human rights obligations which apply when its actions (or omissions) have deleterious effects on the enjoyment of human rights in the

[96] CESCR, *General Comment No 19*, above n 13, at para 59(b)–(f).

[97] *Ibid*, at para 59(a).

[98] *Ibid*, at para 60.

[99] Salomon, ME, 'Why Should it Matter That Others Have More? Poverty, Inequality, and the Potential of International Human Rights Law' (2011) 37 *Review of International Studies* 2137, 2140.

[100] *Government of South Africa v Grootboom* (Constitutional Court of South Africa, Case CCT 11/00, 4 October 2000) paras 32–33 (Jacoob J for the Court).

[101] CESCR, *General Comment No 19*, above n 13, at para 61.

[102] *Ibid*, at para 3.

territory or jurisdiction of another state.[103] The obligation of international cooperation and/or assistance, referred to four times in the ICESCR,[104] relies on international solidarity and shared commitment to changing the inequitable international order as a necessary condition for the global realisation of human rights. As the CESCR explains in General Comment 3, these obligations are in accord with 'well-established principles of international law' that require international cooperation for development, and thus are binding on all states parties 'in a position to assist others in this regard'.[105] These obligations also apply to developing states which have the corresponding responsibility to 'make every effort' to seek and obtain international assistance to ensure the realisation of economic, social and cultural rights[106] and, as Magdalena Sepúlveda Carmona has argued, all states whether providing or receiving international assistance, have associated obligations of non-discrimination, participation and transparency.[107]

The wording used by the CESCR makes it clear that it considers these obligations to be legally binding; yet their scope remains unclear, particularly with respect to the obligation to fulfil. While the CESCR has regularly questioned developed states about the level of their international development assistance, often recommending that it should be increased to the level of 0.7 per cent of Gross Domestic Product as recommended by the UN, it has not treated this aspect of assistance as a legally binding obligation.[108] The CESCR has been more comfortable with requiring states parties to refrain from activities such as economic sanctions, that would have a negative impact on economic, social and cultural rights in other countries[109] and asking them to provide technical assistance, as in assisting to devise a national action plan for progressively implementing compulsory and free primary

[103] Maastricht Principles, above n 20; Skogly, S, *Beyond National Borders: States' Human Rights Obligations in International Cooperation* (Antwerp, Intersentia, 2006); and Coomans, F, 'The Extraterritorial Scope of the International Covenant on Economic, Social and Cultural Rights in the Work of the United Nations Committee on Economic, Social and Cultural Rights' (2011) 11 *Human Rights Law Review* 1.

[104] ICESCR, above n 11, at arts 2(1), 11(1), 11(2) and 23.

[105] CESCR, *General Comment No 3*, above n 16, at para 14.

[106] UN Committee on Economic, Social and Cultural Rights (CESCR), *General Comment No 2: International Technical Assistance Measures (art 22 of the Covenant)*, 2 February 1990, UN Doc E/1990/23, para 10.

[107] Carmona, MS, 'The Obligations of "International Assistance And Cooperation" Under The International Covenant on Economic, Social and Cultural Rights: a Possible Entry Point to a Human Rights Based Approach to Millennium Development Goal 8' (2009) 13 *The International Journal of Human Rights* 86, 96–97.

[108] See, eg, UN Committee on Economic, Social and Cultural Rights (CESCR), *Concluding Observations of CESCR: Germany*, 2002, UN Doc E/2002/22, para 675; UN Committee on Economic, Social and Cultural Rights (CESCR), *Concluding Observations of CESCR: Australia*, 12 June 2009, UN Doc E/C.12/AUS/CO/4, para 12.

[109] UN Committee on Economic, Social and Cultural Rights (CESCR), *General Comment No 8: The Relationship between Economic Sanctions and Respect for Economic, Social and Cultural Rights*, 12 December 1997, UN Doc E/C.12/1997/8.

education.[110] Clearly, providing international cooperation and assistance towards realising the minimum core of the right to social security has some important technical components, such as designing a non-discriminatory system and formulating a national action plan. However, in the case of many developing countries, accumulating the resources to provide everyone with access to a social security system that provides essential health care, basic shelter and housing, water and sanitation, foodstuffs and the most basic forms of education would require substantial monetary assistance. Yet, as noted, the CESCR has not treated this kind of assistance as obligatory, and the individual responsibility focus of neo-liberal economics has fostered diminishing confidence in international aid. To make matters even worse, many developed countries have reduced their meagre development aid budgets in the current climate of economic crisis and austerity.

Adopted in 2008, General Comment 19 acknowledges that the situation is dire, estimating that, globally, about 80 per cent of people lack access to formal social security and that 20 per cent of these people live in 'extreme poverty'.[111] In its earlier statement on poverty, the CESCR admits that there are structural impediments to developing states addressing poverty that 'lie beyond their control', including 'the absence of an equitable multilateral trade, investment and financial system'.[112] This admission suggests that the problem needs to be understood as an issue of unequal distribution of global resources, as Margot Salomon has proposed, rather than an issue of scarcity.[113] Yet there is a disturbing disconnect between admitting the calamitous general situation described, and the specific recommendations of the CESCR in its Concluding Observations. In response to the ten periodic reports that it considered in 2012, which were discussed earlier, the CESCR makes reference to the minimum core only once, in the general context of Iceland's domestic austerity measures adopted in reaction to the recent economic crisis.[114] The importance of establishing a common legal standard, in the form of a non-derogable baseline of minimal social security entitlements, has been lost in translation of general obligations into country-specific recommendations. The idea of promoting 'manageable' redistributive obligations appears to have completely lost traction, as there is no reference

[110] UN Committee on Economic, Social and Cultural Rights (CESCR), *General Comment No 11: Plans of Action for Primary Education (art 14 of the Covenant)*, 10 May 1999, UN Doc E/C.12/1999/4, para 11.

[111] CESCR, *General Comment No 19*, above n 13, at para 7.

[112] UN Committee on Economic, Social and Cultural Rights (CESCR), *Substantive Issues Arising in the Implementation of the International Covenant on Economic, Social and Cultural Rights: Poverty and the International Covenant on Economic, Social and Cultural Rights—Statement Adopted by the Committee on Economic, Social and Cultural Rights on 4 May 2001*, 10 May 2001, UN Doc E/C.12/2001/10.

[113] Salomon, above n 99, at 2145.

[114] CESCR, *Concluding Observations of CESCR: Iceland*, above n 64, at para 6.

at all to the obligations to seek international cooperation and assistance in any of these Concluding Observations, and only two expressions of concern about reducing levels of official development assistance, aimed at Spain and New Zealand.[115]

Not least because of the overwhelming number of people who do not have access to formal provision of social security, the right to social security in the ICESCR needs to be interpreted as a robust international redistributive measure, and efforts to promote international cooperation and assistance should not be confined to realising the minimum core or allowed to stop once a social protection floor has been achieved—despite the landmark achievement this would be. Instead, we need to rethink the standard account of international human rights law as a means to protect human dignity from the excesses of sovereign power and, as Patrick Macklem suggests, shift to a distributive understanding of this body of law, as a means to mitigate some of the inequitable consequences of the operation of the international legal order.[116] He argues, convincingly, that redistributive obligations arise because international law has contributed, and continues to contribute, to the vast disparities between the resources available in developed and developing countries. He cites, as examples, the legal regulation of the processes of decolonisation, which ensured that many natural resources remained in control of the former imperial powers,[117] and contemporary international institutions, like the World Trade Organization, which enable economically powerful states to benefit disproportionately from trade liberalisation and global economic growth.[118] Salomon argues along similar lines that developed states have obligations of cooperation and assistance because they are often deeply implicated in the inability of people in developing countries to exercise their socio-economic rights.[119] For her, the challenge for human rights law is to confront the scandalously unequal global allocation of resources by accommodating a 'doctrine of fair global distribution'.[120] Only then, she argues, will human rights advocates move beyond seeking fulfilment of minimum essential living standards for almost half the world's population who live in poverty, to demanding equality for all. A transformative understanding of international human rights law would reposition the redistributive obligations to seek and provide

[115] CESCR, *Concluding Observations of CESCR: Spain*, above n 60, at para 10; CESCR, *Concluding Observations of CESCR: New Zealand*, above n 63, at para 29.

[116] Macklem, P, 'What is International Human Rights Law? Three Applications of a Distributive Account' (2007) 52 *McGill Law Journal* 575.

[117] *Ibid*, at 602. See also, Anghie, A, *Imperialism, Sovereignty and the Making of International Law* (Cambridge, Cambridge University Press, 2004).

[118] Macklem, above n 116, at 599. See also Pogge, T, *World Poverty and Human Rights*, 2nd edn (Cambridge, Polity Press, 2008).

[119] Salomon, above n 99, at 2142.

[120] *Ibid*, at 2152.

international cooperation and assistance from the margins to the heart of the whole regime.

CONCLUSION

The groundwork laid by the Montréal Principles and the CESCR's General Comments needs urgently to be built upon, if we are to address the many complex and seemingly intractable problems that attend realisation of women's right to social security today. To this end I have proposed two transformative strategies. The first is to develop a more gender inclusive formulation of the content of the right to social security, which could be achieved either by radically revising the definition of 'work' so that it is inclusive of all forms of paid and unpaid labour, or by severing the link with work and treating social security as a universal entitlement. Both approaches would avoid many of the current problems that come with reliance on comparative conceptions of equality to realise social security rights for women. The second strategy is to urge that the immediate minimum core obligations of the right to social security be clarified and that the redistributive obligations associated with international cooperation and assistance be seriously engaged as a means to promote a more equitable global distribution of resources. This strategy works against the received wisdom of crisis governance, which treats the structural inequalities of the quotidian as the norm that must simply be endured, rather than recognising that the institutions and practices of international law and politics are deeply implicated in the politics of inevitability. Those same institutions have the potential to transform the inequities of the present, although this requires courage to expose the false claims of neo-liberal economic policies and attentiveness to the alternatives proposed by grass roots social movements seeking to eliminate poverty in all its dimensions. International human rights law, particularly efforts to universally realise the right to social security, has a role to play in bringing about this transformation by giving shape to transformative obligations and helping to forge an international movement strong enough to debunk the certainties of crisis governance and pursue, in its place, the fair distribution of global resources and adequate social security for everyone.

12

A Gendered Right to Social Security and Decent Work? The Debate in the Context of Irish Austerity

MARY P MURPHY AND CAMILLE LOFTUS

INTRODUCTION

THIS CHAPTER DISCUSSES key concerns in relation to women's rights to social security. We first introduce some of the central theoretical concepts, including human rights and feminist principles, and then apply these to a national case study. We use this Irish case study to generalise some of the major challenges and tensions in enabling women's access to social security. We conclude by drawing attention to core themes including issues of ideology, governance and those concerning the relationship between work and social security.

The chapter is divided into three sections. The first section introduces some broad theoretical tools including feminist principles and human rights frameworks, and considers key tensions in gendering access to social security and human rights. We also consider the global and regional contexts of social security regimes and issues concerning convergence between the global north and south. Section two applies these theories and principles to an Irish case study of gender and social security. It critically applies gendered human rights frameworks to examine the recent Irish experience of austerity and then considers, in more depth, reforms to lone parents' social security rights. It assesses these reforms against human rights and feminist principles. Section three draws some broad conclusions concerning governance, ideology and convergence and comments on the usefulness of human rights approaches as mitigating tools to develop women's access to social security and decent paid employment.

THEORETICAL FRAMEWORK

To develop a broad theoretical framework we first introduce and promote the value of feminist principles and explore how accessibility to social protection can be enhanced through an appropriate gendered design of social security. We then critically engage with the human rights frameworks outlined by Goldblatt and Lamarche,[1] drawing particular attention to the core debate about the degree to which social security rights are, or should be, delinked from labour market conditionality. We focus on somewhat under-theorised issues concerning activation and sanctions as well as parallel debates about decent work and employment regulation. We then engage with Otto, who rightly insists on the importance of the international political and economic context, and we address the issue of convergence between the global north and south.[2]

Feminist Principles

This section first explores feminist principles and approaches to ensuring a gender-sensitive approach to care, individualised rights to social security and maximal economic independence through provision of social security, quality services and access to decent work. A feminist framework seeks to recognise, but also break down, past path dependencies. Women's specific needs and interests must be ensured if social and economic rights are to be fully and equally realised, but it is crucial to avoid locking women (and men) into historically gendered patterns.

Social security is central to recognition of women's care work, but such recognition needs to avoid perpetuating traditional gender divisions. This necessitates recognising informal economic sectors and, particularly, migrant women's work. It also means giving due attention to cumulative gendered experiences across the lifecycle and recognising how these can perpetuate pension inequality. Gendering the lifecycle helps recognise, as Luckhaus[3] does, that over-focusing on the fight for gender equality in the workplace largely hid the centrality of women's unpaid caring work as the source of women's poverty and exclusion.[4] However, it also draws attention to the difficulties in accommodating both work and care. Income support means different things at different stages of the lifecycle.

[1] Goldblatt and Lamarche, in this collection.
[2] Otto, in this collection.
[3] Luckhaus, L, 'Equal Treatment, Social Protection and Income Security for Women' (2000) 139(2) *International Labour Review* 149.
[4] Goldblatt and Lamarche, in this collection.

The ILO concept of the Social Protection Floor means basic social security guarantees that ensure universal access to essential health care and income security at a nationally defined minimum level for four basic social security supports (essential health care services; income security for children; social transfers in cash or in kind for active age groups that cannot earn sufficient income; income security for older persons; and people with disabilities).[5] We argue it is difficult to design for the active working age category. This is particularly so where the adults are in the early stages of family formation, but also when care needs of older children and dependant adults mean paid employment has to be balanced against reciprocal care obligations.

While drawing essentially on Western gendered experiences of care and work, the framework below is useful in visioning alternative ways to share and balance reproductive care and productive work, to understand how they interrelate and to analyse how to break patterns of path dependencies.

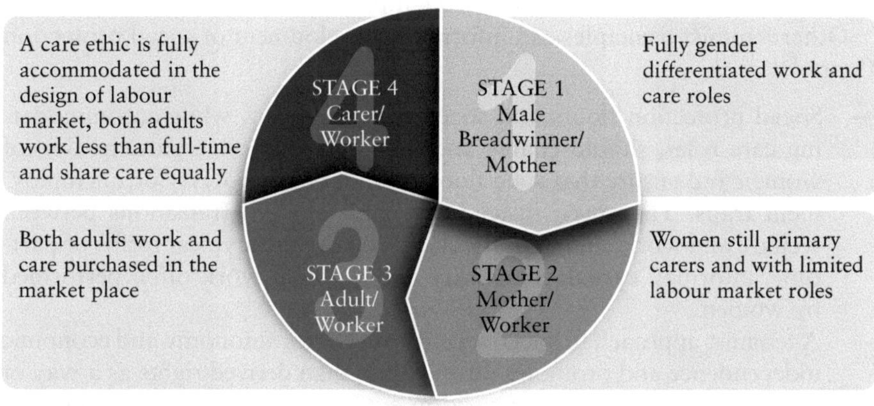

Figure 1: Typologies of Gendered Work/Care Combinations[6]

[5] ILO Recommendation R202: Social Floors Protection Recommendation (Recommendation Concerning National Floors of Social Protection) (101st Conference Session, Geneva, 14 July 2012).

[6] Murphy, MP, 'Careless to Careful Activation: Making Activation Work for Women' (Dublin, National Women's Council of Ireland and SIPTU, 2012).

At stage one, typologies like 'male breadwinner' or 'modernised male breadwinner' reflect deeply differentiated gender roles where women perform 'wifely labour'.[7] In stage two, 'mother/worker' models reinforce gender differentiation while acknowledging the dual roles women undertake as mothers or carers, and increasingly as workers. In stage three, 'adult worker' models see both adults in paid employment and purchasing commodified care,[8] which is similar to what Fraser terms the 'universal breadwinner' model.[9] Stage four, the 'carer/worker' model, is a feminist approach informed by a care ethic and the concept of affective equality, and greater sharing between men and women of both care and paid employment.[10] This approach is similar to Fraser's 1994 seminal idea of a *universal caregiver*, as well as the European concept of the *individual carer-earner* regime[11] which includes well developed gender equality friendly policies.[12] The focus on accommodating work and care for mothers and fathers implies a residual need for care which may be provided by the market or the state. It requires state policy to enable sharing of care with intervention at the level of the family and the market to promote family friendly policies for men and women, as well as the promotion of male care roles through paid parental leave.

Other feminist principles can inform the development of social protection floors:[13]

- Social protection floors and social security policy, while accommodating care roles, should enable and maximise economic participation of women and ensure that such floors do not create poverty or unemployment traps. They need instead to enable smooth transitions between welfare and work, and in particular recognise the atypical forms of part-time, informal, casual, temporary and seasonal work often performed by women.
- A feminist approach to social security advocates autonomy and economic independence and promotes direct rather than derived rights as a way of ensuring women are not trapped in exploitative domestic relationships.

[7] Shaver, S and Bradshaw, J, 'The Recognition of Wifely Labour by Welfare States' (1995) 29(1) *Social Policy and Administration* 10.

[8] Lewis, J and Guillari, S, 'The Adult Worker Model Family, Gender Equality and Care: The Search for New Policy Principles and the Possibilities and Problems of a Capabilities Approach' (1995) 34(1) *Economy and Society* 76.

[9] Fraser, N, 'After the Family Wage: Gender Equity and the Welfare State' (1994) 22(4) *Political Theory* 591.

[10] Hobson, B, 'Squaring the Circle? The Individualised Worker, the Gender Participatory and the Gender Equity Models in Sweden' (2003) 3(1) *Social Policy and Society* 75.

[11] Sainsbury, D (ed), *Gender and Welfare State Regimes* (Oxford, Oxford University Press, 1999).

[12] Sörensen, K and Bergqvist, C, *Gender and the Social Democratic Welfare Regime: A Comparison of Gender-Equality Friendly Policies in Sweden and Norway* (Stockholm, National Institute for Working Life, 2002).

[13] We acknowledge here Fraser's normative principles of anti-poverty, exploitation, marginalisation and andocentralism and pro-equality of income, leisure and respect; Fraser, above n 9.

There are various practical ways to promote women's economic autonomy. Paying child income directly to mothers maximises intra-household distribution as does addressing historical pension justice and enabling economic participation to open women's future access to pensions. Even within derived rights, administering incomes individually to all adults in the household enables a degree of financial autonomy—a basic principle of rights and dignity. There is also the question of whether to have family or individualised units of assessment.

Designing a Feminist Social Security System for Working Age Women: Some Tensions

The above principles enable policymakers to design a feminist social security system, paying particular attention to implementation and removing hidden gender obstacles to social protection floors and employment.[14] Core tensions in the design of feminist working age social security schemes are now briefly sketched.

Conditionality

Attaching behavioural conditions to social security payments creates core tensions for a rights-based feminist approach.[15] While the International Labour Organization (ILO) has always stressed the centrality of freely chosen work to dignity and human rights, it also advocates an active rather than passive use of guaranteed income to promote economic participation. The trade-off between conditionality and social security rights is complex, and recent evaluations of conditionalities in Latin America suggest they reinforce traditional gender roles.[16] Economic participation should be encouraged through incentives, not compelled through sanctions.

Paid Employment

Feminist design avoids an over-focus on productive paid work (formal or informal) while accommodating care (paid or unpaid, formal or informal). The quality of work available is crucial as is the question of how, or whether, social security interacts with earned income. Addressing these questions requires careful design entailing further questions such as: what counts as work (formal, informal, self-employment, micro-enterprise); how

[14] Lynch, K and Lyons, M, 'The Gendered Order of Caring' in U Barry (ed), *Where Are We Now? New Feminist Perspectives on Women in Contemporary Ireland* (Dublin, New Island, 1995).

[15] Fredman, in this collection.

[16] Bastagli, F, 'Conditional Cash Transfers as a Tool of Social Policy' (2011) 46(21) *Economic and Political Weekly* 61.

earnings are assessed against social security entitlements; and how work is regulated to ensure decent working conditions.

Care Ethic

There are crucial trade-offs between universal—but tailored—care services, and cash transfers to support the purchase of care in the market. A feminist framework favours a universal care infrastructure for children and care-dependant adults over cash transfers, which tend to reinforce existing gendered care patterns. Flexible work arrangements can also accommodate a care ethic and safeguard against over-commodification of care.[17] Nordic social policy has pioneered social security that generates more neutral care relations, but even there, gender neutral care remains a very long-term project.[18] The relationship between paid work and unpaid care is crucial, as is the quality of the work available. Recent UK and US research stresses the intractable conflict in the Western world in combining informal unpaid care with low paid, low quality, employment, where dignity and child well-being is often eroded for very little economic return.[19]

Adequacy

Dignity and autonomy require an adequate income and there is some trade-off between adequacy (vertical extension—increasing the amount) and coverage (horizontal extension—increasing the proportion of people included in an income guarantee). Anti-poverty and equality principles need to be balanced but the priority has to be on alleviating poverty, vulnerability and social exclusion.[20] While a range of technical instruments is available to determine adequacy benchmarks and indexation, the question of 'how much' is ultimately a political choice and is related to wider fiscal choices.[21]

Policy Monitoring

The choice of tools to review or monitor policy, and mechanisms to involve stakeholders, are crucial. Women's under-representation in capital and formal labour organisations leads to tensions in mechanisms that give

[17] Orloff, AS, 'Gender and the Social Rights of Citizenship: The Comparative Analysis of Gender Relations and Welfare States' (1993) 58 *American Sociological Review* 303.

[18] Bergmann, BR, 'A Swedish-Style Welfare State or Basic Income: Which Should Have Priority?' (2004) 32 *Politics and Society* 107.

[19] Christopher, K, 'Welfare as We [Don't] Know It: A Review and Feminist Critique of Welfare Reform Research in the United States' (2004) 10(2) *Feminist Economics* 143.

[20] International Labour Office, *Report IV (2B): Social Protection Floors for Social Justice and a Fair Globalisation* (International Labour Conference, 101st Session, Geneva, International Labour Organization, 2012) 8.

[21] *Ibid*, at 10.

traditional corporate stakeholders (trade unions and employers) a more privileged role in determining the balance between horizontal and vertical extension. So do the basic rules: the concepts, definitions and methodology used in the production of social security data and indicators are highly gender sensitive, as are processes that enable exchange of information, experiences and expertise.

Revenue

Distributive justice requires contributive justice. Methods to ensure financial, fiscal and economic sustainability of national social protection floors need to take the contributory capacities of different population groups into account.[22] Gendering this discourse may be useful in generating consensus about strategies to develop a sense of solidarity and interdependence and a 'politics of the common good'.[23] Taxpayers need to be convinced that in the longer term such investment generates social and economic cohesion that ultimately benefits all and that a human rights framework can provide good governance to ensure reasonable and proportional policy.

Human Rights Frameworks

Goldblatt and Lamarche's[24] introductory chapter outlines three different approaches to undertaking the task of engendering the right to social security, with the first centred on an equality guarantee and ensuring that the right to social security is realised in a gender equal way.[25] The second ensures that every part of the International Covenant on Economic, Social and Cultural Rights (ICESCR) takes account of gendered considerations and results in rights with a deeply gendered content.[26] The third involves mainstreaming gender using a set of guidelines to test compliance of social protection programmes with human rights obligations informed by a gender perspective.[27] We now critically engage with these frameworks and consider the constructive intersection between human rights and feminist approaches to securing access to social security for women. There are particular challenges in designing social security systems that adequately address the

[22] *Ibid*, at 12.

[23] Vail, J, 'Decommodification and Egalitarian Political Economy' (2010) 38 *Politics and Society* 310, 326.

[24] Goldblatt and Lamarche, in this collection.

[25] As approached by Fredman, in this collection.

[26] As approached by Otto, in this collection.

[27] The approach followed by M Sepúlveda Carmona, Independent Expert on the Question of Human Rights and Extreme Poverty, *The Importance of Social Protection Measures in Achieving Millennium Development Goals (MDGs)*, 9 August 2010, UN DOC A/65/259, 16–18.

reality of care in women's lives, while also striving to enable economic participation at decent wages. We draw particular attention to a core debate about the degree to which social security rights are, or should be, delinked from labour market participation, and somewhat under-theorised issues concerning activation, conditionality, decent work standards and employment regulation.

While the principle of indivisibility of rights is well established, in practice the relationship between the right to work and the right to social security is complex. Social security rights are often productivist and narrowly defined as, for example, in the focus on workers' mobility and entitlements in EU social policy,[28] or even in the Convention on the Elimination of All Forms of Discrimination against Women (CEDAW), article 11.[29] The role of social security can vary from enabling income security in the absence of employment-based security or income supports, to providing in-work income supports in full-time employment. The challenge is not to choose between women's role in economic development and women's social security rights; the challenge, for both developed and developing worlds, is the relationship between complementary goals.

Thus, in moving from a labour to a human rights perspective on social security rights needs we must ensure that a human right to social security is itself indivisible from a human right to work and development. So while work-based entitlement evades 80 per cent of the global population and the 70 per cent of workers located in precarious and unregulated employment regimes, the question is how to extend social security rights while also enabling access to decent work, and in particular, realising both. Chapters in this collection dealing with how human rights instruments engage with paid employment and unpaid work[30] point to the limitations of the Committee on Economic, Social and Cultural Rights (CESCR) General Comment 19[31] and the 2012 ILO initiative—Recommendation 202 for National Social Protection Floors[32]—in fully integrating women's caregiving responsibilities into social security rights and the failure to address the negative impact of women's peripheral connection to work as a fundamental obstacle to substantive gender equality.

As Razavi asks, how far can we go in promoting the link between welfare and work when work is both precarious and peripheral in so many women's lives?[33] In trying to determine where the balance should be struck

[28] Ó Cinnéide, S, 'Ireland as the European Welfare State' (1993) 21(2) *Policy and Politics* 97.
[29] Fredman, in this collection.
[30] Lamarche, in this collection; and Otto, in this collection.
[31] UN Committee on Economic, Social and Cultural Rights (CESCR), *General Comment No 19: The Right to Social Security (art 9)*, 4 February 2008, UN Doc E/C.12/GC/19.
[32] ILO Recommendation R202, above n 6. See also Lamarche, in this collection.
[33] Lamarche, in this collection, at 11.

between 'work linked' and 'work delinked' models, the frameworks and guidelines introduced in the introductory chapter are of practical assistance in testing compliance of social protection programmes with human rights obligations informed by a gender perspective.

The Global Dimension

Before proceeding to discuss a national setting (Ireland), we need to problematise the task of applying global principles to divergent national systems in a highly unequal world. Otto stresses the international political and economic context, and regional dimensions to social security policy.[34] We need to understand how, for example, the global economic crisis translates into a national context and how this happens through institutions, programmes and ideologies.

Nicaise identifies three competing ideologies through which social security policy evolves; each actively influences policy and has strong implications for gendering work and care.[35] Following Rosanvallon,[36] a *social democratic* approach champions the right, but also the obligation, to participate in employment. Social solidarity assumes, and requires, high levels of participation and full employment. Following the Friedmans,[37] the *neo-liberal* approach assumes that rational humans will take up paid employment if it pays to do so. A focus on incentivising low-paid work ignores the care ethic that informs choices between paid employment and unpaid care. Following Murray,[38] the *conservative* approach focuses on the moral imperative to work and avoid intergenerational joblessness and a dependency culture; it stresses behavioural obligations and sanctions and ignores and devalues unpaid care work. The Irish case study in the next section examines how ideologies inform the national gendered development of social security policy. These ideologies are also evident at regional governance level, for example, the European Commission Social Investment Package (discussed below) can be understood as an amalgam of such ideologies.

Taking a global dimension points to the importance of accounting for international governance and how globally dominant ideologies frame thinking about social security. They are the context within which the ILO

[34] Otto, in this collection.

[35] Nicaise, I, 'Social Protection: Between Rights and Duties, Between Dependency and Social Investment' (paper to Alliances Against Poverty, Lisbon, 23–24 May 2013).

[36] Rosanvallon, P, *The New Social Question: Rethinking the Welfare State* (Princeton, Princeton University Press, 2000).

[37] Friedman, M and Friedman, R, *Free to Choose: A Personal Statement* (New York, Harcourt Press, 1980).

[38] Murray, C, *Losing Ground: American Social Policy, 1950–1980* (New York, Basic Books, 1984).

attempts to promote a social protection floor and decent work. Indeed Reynaud[39] describes how the ILO initiative was in part triggered by the need to counter ideas of poverty alleviation and consumption-smoothing promoted by the World Bank to the exclusion of other objectives such as redistribution, inclusion, and equality.[40]

At regional governance level, the social investment approach was adopted by the European Union (EU) Commission Communication[41] on the Social Investment Package (SIP)[42] in February 2013 and is perceived as a new EU social model. SIP aims at better coordinating and boosting EU funds to deliver inclusive growth. Its consideration of social investment cannot be divorced from the context of austerity and the current framework for European economic governance (Economic and Monetary Union (EMU)). The context of austerity means that social investment is justified for generating savings that can be used to deliver fiscal consolidation rather than improving social outcomes. Ex ante conditions can attach requirements for structural reforms; this has clear implications for shifts in power and consequences for subsidiarity and democracy that are inconsistent with the key feminist and human rights principle of participation. Employment is a central focus with 'work for those who can' given greater priority than 'social protection for those who cannot'. This has serious gender implications especially given there is little reference to decent work. SIP proposals for micro-behavioural conditionality, making cash transfers conditional on Early Childhood Care and Education (ECCE) registration, and to oblige claimants, including mothers, to participate in precarious labour markets also have implications for human rights.

Regional governance is translated into national governance through a variety of methods. In the Irish case study we see the recent role of the Troika (European Commission, International Monetary Fund and European Central Bank) in the domestic governance of vulnerable European states. The Irish Troika bail out programme includes policy conditionalities that limit the future development of Irish social security and directly limit the capacity of Irish social security to promote gender equality or

[39] Reynaud, E, *The Extension of Social Security Coverage: The Approach of the International Labour Office* (ESS Paper No 3, Geneva, International Labour Organization, 2002) 1.

[40] *Ibid*, at 4–5.

[41] European Commission (EC), 'Communication from the Commission to the European Parliament, the Council, the European Economic and Social Committee and the Committee on the Regions: Towards Social Investment for Growth and Cohesion—Including Implementing the European Social Fund 2014–2020' (COM (2013) 83 final, Brussels, EC, 2013).

[42] SIP is series of eight papers; a Commission Communication on Social Investment; a Commission Recommendation Investing in Children: Breaking the Cycle of Disadvantage; six staff working documents providing background on active inclusion, long-term care, homelessness, health, demographic trends change and social investment.

promote 'compassionate neo-liberalism'. While the Troika regime ended in November 2013, new EU treaty governance mechanisms are now in place alongside softer EU coordination methods.

Human rights frameworks are global, yet we cannot ignore the stark differences between individual countries, nor can we assume any social security convergence between the global north and south. Compare, for example, the same instrument applied to Ireland, a small open economy in the European Union, with a well developed economy and welfare state, and South Africa, a large state and member of the BRICS group of fast growing emerging economies, but with a relatively underdeveloped welfare state without comprehensive coverage.[43] While the economic and social differences are stark in these two nations, the broad gendered differences in patterns of work, care and time use are similar.[44] Likewise, while key debates are different, the basic underlying themes of conditionality, adequacy and comprehensiveness are evident in both national discourses. It is also interesting to observe that the challenge and debate in South Africa is on the need to develop rights, minimum wages and working age social security,[45] while in Ireland the focus is on a diminution of working age welfare and dismantling of the minimum wage and employment regulation infrastructure.[46] While we observe a slow convergence across developed countries,[47] it is less clear as to whether global convergence might occur by the global north levelling down and the global south levelling up.

IRISH CASE STUDY OF GENDER AND SOCIAL SECURITY

This section applies some of the principles and considerations discussed above to an Irish case study of gender and social security over the Great Recession. We begin by outlining the historical development of, and recent changes to, women's social security rights. We then apply a gendered human rights framework to the recent Irish experience of austerity and

[43] Knijn, T and Patel, L, 'Introduction: Social Policy Change in a Transition Society—the Case of South Africa' (2012) 46(6) *Social Policy and Administration* 597.

[44] McGinnity, F et al, *Time Use in Ireland 2005: Survey Report* (Dublin, The Economic and Social Research Institute and the NDP Gender Equality Unit, Department of Justice, Equality and Law Reform, 2007); and Floro, M and Komatsu, H, 'Gender and Work in South Africa: What Use Can Time-Use Data Reveal?' (2011) 17(4) *Feminist Economics* 33.

[45] Surrender, R et al, 'Social Assistance and Dependency in South Africa: An Analysis of Attitudes to Paid Work and Social Grants' (2011) 39(2) *Journal of Social Policy* 203.

[46] Murphy, MP and Loftus, C, 'A Precarious Ireland: Dual Labour Markets, Dual Social Protection' (paper to International Working Group on Labour Market Segregation Conference, Trinity College, Dublin, 11–13 September 2013).

[47] EZ Brodkin and G Marston (eds), *Work and the Welfare State: Street-Level Organizations and Workfare Politics* (Washington, DC, Georgetown University Press, 2013).

find it rich in illuminating gender impact of cuts to social security rights. We complement this with the CESCR principles in paragraph 42 of General Comment No 19 on the Right to Social Security[48] for monitoring retrogression, and find these lacking in Irish experiences of austerity. To further unpack the degree to which social security can, or should be, delinked from paid employment, we then look, from the perspective of feminist principles, at recent changes to lone parents' social security entitlements.

Women's Access to Social Security in Ireland

Gender segregation has always been a feature of the Irish social security system. Yeates argues that gender is an organising category in Irish social security, with gendered notions of 'deserving' and 'undeserving' grounded in men's status as breadwinners, and women's marital and family status.[49] Despite the elimination of direct discrimination in the 1970s, there remains a gendered legacy of indirect discrimination against women in the Irish social security system. The 1990s saw significant change in gender expectations concerning care and employment and, in particular, a shift in the perception of mothers as carers to mothers as workers. This was reflected in reforms to earnings assessments for both adult dependants (1996) and lone parents (1994 and 1997) to encourage participation in employment. Such movement from social security as social protection to social security as an agent of economic participation is consistent with the experience of other European and liberal welfare states, albeit Ireland is a late starter in this regard.

Assessing Ireland's Austerity Programme from a Gendered Human Rights Perspective

We now overview the main changes to social security entitlements[50] implemented in successive austerity budgets since the onset of the 'Great Recession'. Specific changes to lone parents' payments are discussed in greater detail in the subsequent section.

Reductions in entitlements for people of working age have been a recurring theme. All working age social welfare payments have been reduced by at least 8 per cent, while young unemployed people have experienced

[48] CESCR, above n 31, at para 42.

[49] Yeates, N, 'Gender and Development of the Irish Social Welfare System' in A Byrne and M Leonard (eds), *Women and Irish Society* (Belfast, Beyond the Pale, 2003).

[50] The overview is not comprehensive, focusing on the main changes implemented.

more drastic cuts (50 per cent plus for those under 21 years of age). In relation to unemployment, the duration of jobseeker social insurance payments has been cut by 40 per cent, while contribution rates and the level of prior earnings required to qualify for full payment have both doubled. Structural reforms have made it more difficult for part-time and atypical workers to qualify for unemployment payments, and have reduced the income support available. These are highly gendered reforms: more onerous eligibility criteria make it harder for women—over-represented in low paid, atypical and part-time work—to qualify, and reduces their social protection.

Some controversial cuts, related to disability and caring social security entitlements, are under review and have not yet been implemented.[51] However, entitlement to Carer's Allowance (CA) was made more restrictive for non-residential carers, and both CA and home help payments are now included in social security means-tests; the Respite Care Grant was also cut. Nearly two-thirds of all carers[52] and 80 per cent of CA recipients are women, making these changes highly gendered.

Supports for low income private tenants have also seen significant reductions. Tenants' weekly rent contribution has increased from €13 to €30 per week, and maximum allowable rents have been reduced on three occasions. Access to support was restricted while the capital budget for social housing construction was severely curtailed. These reforms have contributed to 'ghettoisation' of the most vulnerable tenants seeking lower rents; there is also evidence of increased homelessness.[53]

Ireland's austerity regime has also seen severe cuts in child income supports. Entitlement to universal Child Benefit (CB) was withdrawn for children aged 18, and successive CB cuts accumulate to a 22 per cent reduction for smaller families and a third for larger families. Universal Early Childcare Supplement[54] was abolished, but partially replaced with a universal (school) year of free, half-time pre-school—ECCE. Up until 2010, families relying on social welfare had been protected from cuts in universal supports with increases in means-tested payments, but from 2011, no protective measures were put in place; in fact, means-tested supports were also cut.

[51] Raising the age a person can apply for Disability Allowance (DA) from 16 to 18 years, and extending the reduced rates for younger unemployed people to DA claimants.

[52] Central Statistics Office (CSO), 'Quarterly National Household Survey: Special Module on Caring, Quarter 3 2009' (Dublin, CSO, 29 July 2010).

[53] TSA Consultancy, 'Out of Reach: The Impact of Changes in Rent Supplement' (Dublin, Focus Ireland, 2012).

[54] For children under 6.

Older people's incomes had been largely insulated from the austerity regime, but the 2012 budget reduced the pension paid to those with fewer social insurance contributions—restricting access for women, who are more likely to have interrupted careers—and increased the contributions needed to claim a survivor's pension—86 per cent of survivors assistance claimants are women.

This section now applies Fredman's equality framework, set out in her chapter in this book,[55] to test whether the Irish austerity cuts violate gender equality. Fredman's approach to equality incorporates four dimensions: redistribution to break the cycle of disadvantage; recognition to promote respect for dignity and worth; transformation to accommodate difference and achieve structural change; and participative mechanisms to facilitate full participation. A similar equality framework developed by Irish academics, Baker et al,[56] understands inequality across four interrelated dimensions: economic equality; socio-cultural equality; political equality; and affective equality.

Fredman's rights-based approach articulates the principles underpinning the right to equality. These are used to test specific Irish cuts (see Table 1 below). We find the Irish government fails on all four dimensions of Fredman's framework. While the indicator of participation is partially met in that the state engages in pre-budget consultations, these are largely symbolic.[57] There is no positive indicator of breaking the cycle of disadvantage through redistribution, little evidence of engagement with recognition, dignity and worth and limited focus on accommodation of difference or attempts to achieve structural transformative change. We conclude that there has been a substantive failure by the Irish government to meet the equality rights of citizens and given the disproportionate focus on cuts to carers, lone parents, widows and children, that women have been particularly failed in this respect.

Assessing Ireland's Austerity Programme: CESCR Retrogression Scrutiny

We further examine rights approaches in recessions by focusing on the CESCR principles for monitoring retrogression: reasonable justification; examination of alternatives; genuine participation; non-discrimination; sustained

[55] Fredman, in this collection.

[56] Baker, J et al, *Equality: From Theory to Action* (Basingstoke, Palgrave Macmillan, 2004).

[57] Holland, L, 'Mauled by the Celtic Tiger: Human Rights in Ireland's Economic Meltdown' (Rights in Crisis Briefing Paper, Madrid, Center for Economic and Social Rights, February 2012).

Table 1: Assessing the Impact of Austerity Budgets on Social Security in Ireland—Equality Approach (Fredman)[58]

Key changes	Redistribution: break the cycle of disadvantage	Recognition: promote respect for dignity and worth	Transformation: accommodate difference and achieve structural change	Participative: facilitate full participation
Unemployment payments	Make already precarious work harder to sustain; greater impact on women	Minus	No recognition of needs of precarious workers	Symbolic pre-budget consultation
Rate cuts for people of working age	Less redistributive, reduces capacity; gender neutral	Minus	No	Symbolic pre-budget consultation
Rate cuts for young unemployed	Less redistributive, reduces capacity; greater impact on men	Minus	No	Symbolic pre-budget consultation
Lone parent payments	Less redistributive, reduces capacity; greater impact on women	Minus	No	Supporting lone parents (DSFA 2006)[59] SWAP consultation
Disincentivise Active Labour Market Programmes (ALMP's)	Less redistributive, reduces capacity; greater impact on women	Minus	No	ALMP forum

(Continued)

58 Fredman, in this collection.
59 Department of Social and Family Affairs, 'Supporting Lone Parents' (Dublin: DSFA, 2006).

Table 1: (*Continued*)

Key changes	Redistribution: break the cycle of disadvantage	Recognition: promote respect for dignity and worth	Transformation: accommodate difference and achieve structural change	Participative: facilitate full participation
Disability payments	Less redistributive, reduces capacity; greater impact on men	Minus	No	Symbolic pre-budget consultation Advisory Group on Tax and Social Welfare
Carers' payments	Less redistributive, reduces capacity; greater impact on women	Minus	No	Symbolic pre-budget consultation
Rent supplement	Less redistributive, reduces capacity; gender neutral	Minus	No	Symbolic pre-budget consultation
Supports for children	Where poor families not protected, less redistributive, reduces capacity; greater impact on women	Minus	No	Symbolic pre-budget consultation Advisory Group on Tax and Social Welfare
State pensions	Less redistributive, reduces capacity; greater impact on women	Minus	No	Symbolic pre-budget consultation

impact; realisation of rights; and independent review.[60] The discrimination indicator enables examination of the gender impact of cuts and retrogressive measures. In line with the Centre for Economic and Social Rights,[61] we concur that the most vulnerable populations—such as women, children, Travellers, migrants, older persons and the disabled—are suffering the human rights impacts of the crisis disproportionately. The brief assessment in Table 2 shows that austerity measures implemented by the Irish State fail the test of proving that 'they have been introduced after the most careful consideration of all alternatives and that they are duly justified by reference to the totality of the rights provided for in the Covenant'.[62] In most cases, reasonable justification for the measures cannot be identified, nor has there been serious consideration of alternatives, even when they have been identified in government sponsored reports. There are substantive concerns about the discriminatory nature of many austerity reforms.

We concur with the Centre for Economic and Social Rights' conclusion:

> The substantive human rights principles of progressive realization, use of maximum available resources and non-retrogression, along with the procedural principles of transparency, accountability and participation have meanwhile been largely ignored in Ireland's recovery measures, ... government is not taking all necessary steps to comply with its international obligations to respect, protect and fulfill economic and social rights. In particular, fiscal policies (both budget and tax-related) do not appear to be in line with the obligation to devote the maximum of available resources to fulfill economic and social rights progressively, and to guard against retrogression and ensure the rights of the most vulnerable, even in times of scarcity. [63]

Hogan[64] argues that the non-retrogression test implies a strong presumption that retrogressive measures taken 'are not permissible' and that the burden of proof rests with states to show that such measures are warranted. However, he recognises that these are weak obligations on the Irish State and have had little impact over this recession. He argues that such rights might be made meaningful through a 'commitment by States coming before the CESCR to introduce human rights assessments'. These 'could put teeth' into what is meant by 'deliberate, concrete and targeted' steps towards realisation of economic and social rights.

[60] CESCR, above n 31, at para 42.

[61] Holland, above n 57.

[62] *Ibid.*

[63] Holland, above n 57, at 4.

[64] Hogan, D, 'Human Rights and Austerity in Ireland: Response to CESR Paper' (Seminar Presentation on Austerity and Human Rights in Europe: The Impact of European Austerity Policies on the Realisation of Economic, Social and Cultural Rights, European Group of National Human Rights Institutions, Berlin/ Brussels, 12–13 June 2013).

Table 2: Assessing the Impact of Austerity Budgets on Social Security in Ireland—CESCR Non-Retrogression Approach

Key changes	Reasonable justification	Alternatives examined	Genuine participation	Discriminatory Equality grounds	Sustained Impact realisation rights	Independent review
Unemployment payments	No	No	No	Yes	Yes	No
Rate cuts for people of working age	No	No	No	No	Yes	No
Rate cuts for young unemployed	No/some	No	No	Yes: age	Yes	No
Lone parent payments	No/some	No	Yes	Yes: women, family status	Yes	No
Disincentivise ALMPs	No/some	No	No	Yes: women, family status	Yes	No
Disability payments	No/some	Yes	No	Yes: men, disability	Yes	Independent?
Carers' supports	No	No	No	Yes: women	Yes	No
Rent supplement	No	No	No	No	Yes	No
Supports for children	No	Yes	No	Yes: women, children	Yes	No
State pensions	No	No	No	Yes: women	No	No

Assessing Changes to Lone Parents' Entitlements Using Feminist Principles

Reforms to lone parent payments provide a useful test case to examine the impact of austerity on women's social security rights, and to consider the policy direction being pursued in relation to the double burden of care and paid work. The reforms reflect the ambiguities and tensions involved in this debate in Ireland.

Historically, lone parents with a child up to 18 (or 21 in full-time education) were eligible for the means-tested One Parent Family Payment (OFP). In 2006, the state proposed compulsory labour market participation for lone parents and adult dependants[65] when their youngest child reached seven years of age. In 2010, the State proposed a single social assistance payment for people of working age (SWAP) which proposed applying labour market conditionality, on the same basis as for unemployment payments, to a range of groups previously exempted from labour market activity requirements including lone parents, adult dependants, people with disabilities and carers.

Various measures since the crisis have reduced eligibility to the OFP. A special earned income disregard for lone parents (which recognised high childcare costs), will be cut by 60 per cent by 2016 so it is in line with means-testing of earned income for jobseekers. In other cuts, a phased withdrawal of OFP when earnings reach a threshold was abolished, and eligibility for additional half-rate payments was withdrawn. Entitlement to OFP for Community Employment participants—an active labour market programme with high rates of lone parent participation—was also abolished. The reforms meant a reduction in the overall return from paid employment (even before childcare costs—which remain very high in Ireland—are factored in); in particular, the cuts disincentive part-time work.

Many women, if forced to choose between low paid full-time work and full-time care, will choose the latter. The stated aim of these reforms was to reduce long-term dependence on social security, but they will make it harder for lone parents to engage in economic activity, particularly in the absence of substantive measures to reduce childcare costs. By 2014, the OFP was to be available only to lone parents whose youngest child was seven or under. Following protest by lone parents groups in May 2013 about the failure to enable part-time and flexible employment options, the Government announced new transitional arrangements[66] for the lone

[65] Adult dependants are the partners or spouses of claimants: 98% of the 120,000 Irish adult dependants are women.

[66] Department of Social Protection (D/SP), 'Briefing for the Lone Parent Representative Groups on the Transition of One-Parent Family Payment Recipients as a Result of the Reforms to the Scheme' (Dublin DSP, May 2013).

parents with children between 7 and 14 years who were due to lose OFP entitlement by 2015. Almost half of lone parents with a child between seven and 14 will now transfer to a transitional unemployment payment with some conditionality exemptions, namely allowing them to seek more flexible part-time work but with reduced income disregards.[67] They will not be counted on the official count of unemployment and may have restricted access to labour market supports. These reforms, while originally proposed for adult dependants, only apply to lone parents.

While it is too early to assess the impact of these reforms, it is ironic that policy change ostensibly motivated by the goal of increasing economic participation will possibly worsen outcomes for employed lone parents. The somewhat softer transitional arrangements in part recognise the inadequacy of the states' proposals to expand affordable childcare. The reforms are unlikely to achieve a reorientation towards full-time work (due to the high cost of childcare), and whatever their optimal work–life balance combination, lone parents will have less social protection. Without a more comprehensive and effective solution to the high cost of childcare, social security reform is unlikely to secure increased labour market participation by lone parents, and may indeed reduce it. Little wonder then that the state feels the need to use conditionality and sanctions to force its policy direction.

Shifting Discourses and Ideologies

The original 2006 policy proposals to enhance low-income mothers' participation in paid employment were ultimately implemented in the period between 2010 and 2014 and in the context of austerity and without complementary investment in childcare. The key goal over this period was reducing the fiscal deficit, rather than enabling women's economic autonomy or tackling poverty. Policy that was already inadequate to properly support mothers—and in particular lone parents—to reconcile care and paid work has been undermined, implying much greater reliance on conditionality if the goal of increased labour market participation by mothers is to be achieved. The outcome is far removed from feminist and human rights principles.

Rather, such reforms reflect a deep ambivalence on the part of the state towards easing the double burden of care and work faced by women. It is possible to identify in discourse an amalgam of the three ideologies identified earlier: social democratic, neo-liberal and conservative. The dominant ideology is not 'compassionate liberalism', but an ideology that sees poverty

[67] To qualify for an unemployment payment, a claimant must have no work on at least four days in seven; this will not apply in the transitional arrangement.

of women and children as an acceptable risk and an economically viable choice for the state.

The debate about these proposals also highlights significant societal and policy ambiguity surrounding the issue of mothering, welfare and paid work in Ireland.[68] On the one hand, proposals to support women's economic participation were welcomed. Paid employment offers the potential to overcome the lack of financial power that is fundamental to any discussion of women's poverty or gender equality. Economic power is also fundamental to women's civic and political participation. On the other hand, women remain reluctant to undervalue the important role of caregiving relative to paid employment, or to divorce policy to increase economic participation from the debate about accommodating care, unpaid work and work–life balance.

CONCLUSIONS

First, our chapter demonstrates, both theoretically and practically, the usefulness of human rights and feminist approaches in developing thinking about the design of systems to enable women's access to social security. It also demonstrates the theoretical and practical usefulness of aligning human rights and feminist frameworks, and draws attention to the need to further problematise the difficulty of designing accessible systems that reward economic participation while also valuing care.

Second, we drew attention to key issues concerning convergence and the experience of developing women's access to social security in the global north and south (and the challenges this presents to deriving generalised conclusions). While a process of levelling-down and levelling-up may lead to a convergence, the underlying nature of the debate concerning women's access to social security remains qualitatively different in both regions. Ideology works at a global level, but key issues and language can only really be understood in the context of developed and developing states or regions. Hence, governance at international and regional level is key. We noted the global governance and regional processes promoting human rights and minimum standards frameworks for social security. However, we drew attention to contradictory regional and global governance processes that have disregarded the rule of law and forced an undermining of rights on national sovereigns and people. It is ironic that the same regional governance mechanism of the European Commission simultaneously promotes and denigrates human rights. This ambiguity is reflected in ideological shifts at EU level in the 2013 Social Investment Package.

[68] Daly, M, 'What Adult Worker Model? A Critical Look at Recent Social Policy Reform from a Gender and Family Perspective' (2011) 18(1) *Social Politics* 1.

Third, our case study and the application of feminist principles to understand reforms in Ireland demonstrates the complexity and ambiguity of the relationship between work and social security and the importance of quality services, particularly in relation to care, and in enabling access to decent work. In this Irish case we see a shift from a language of unemployment to joblessness, suggesting an ideological shift from social democratic to conservative values. Ultimately, our review shows that Irish austerity reforms have been disproportionately negative for women. It also evidences retrogression of human rights and lack of any meaningful consultation or participation.

Seguino argues that job creation and women's economic participation are central to responding to the crisis, and that social protection plays a vital investment and multiplier role in boosting economic growth and enhancing social cohesion.[69] Social security design is crucial to enabling this. The Irish State has missed the opportunity to reform towards these goals and has instead made it harder for women to access employment. In this context, from a feminist perspective, we question the use of conditionality and sanctions and argue against linking income support and activation, conditionality and temporary supports. We point instead towards a focus on rights and quality standards—both in terms of supports provided, and in relation to the regulatory framework that can increase the availability of decent work. Strong legal safeguards concerning rights to social security are required to protect universality and fundamental rights. An active rights approach means delivering social security in a local integrated way that maximally enables and empowers people's agency and productive capacity but also recognises and accommodates the reality of care in people's lives.

Finally, we observe through our case study, and indeed through our own experience, that human rights frameworks, while limited in terms of their enforcement capacity, still supply a language that contests power and strengthens arguments concerning distribution of resources. Our chapter confirms that policy is rarely driven by one ideology, but rather is an interplay of competing forces. Rights enable a voice of protest and a way to articulate demand; a global framework allows a common language to develop solidarity across and within countries, regionally and globally.

We end on an optimistic note. In February 2014 an Irish Constitutional Convention voted to afford greater constitutional protection to economic, social and cultural rights. They recommended the Irish government to enhance the level of protection for such rights, making them amenable to supervision by the Irish courts and that certain rights (including health,

[69] Seguino, S, 'The Global Economic Crisis, Its Gender and Ethnic Implications, and Policy Responses' (2010) 18(2) *Gender and Development* 179.

housing and social security) should be expressly stated in the Constitution.[70] Government is obliged to respond to this recommendation within four months. A stronger framework for such rights would make non-retrogression principles more meaningful in Irish policy and practice. This recommendation reflects a growing awareness amongst Irish citizens of the role human rights can play in balancing power and addressing inequalities in both the developed and developing world. Clearly women and other vulnerable groups will benefit from a stronger specification of precise economic and social rights obligations on states parties to core UN Conventions and how these should frame governance responses in economic crisis.

[70] The Convention on the Constitution, 'Press Release—The Convention on the Constitution has Voted to Afford Greater Constitutional Protection to Economic, Social and Cultural (ESC) Rights' (*The Convention on the Constitution*, 23 February 2014), available at: www.constitution.ie/NewsDetails.aspx?nid=a531341a-a19c-e311-a7ce-005056a32ee4.

13

Testing Women's Right to Social Security in Australia: A Poor Score

BETH GOLDBLATT

INTRODUCTION

THE RIGHT TO social security, when interpreted from a gender perspective, requires an appreciation of the impact of the sexual division of labour on the situation of women in relation to work of different kinds: unpaid subsistence work; work in the formal and informal sectors; and unpaid reproductive work in maintaining households and in providing care.[1] The right to social security has historically been linked to formal and, hence, male-biased conceptions of work that disadvantage women. In addition to rethinking the way work is conceived within the right to social security, the right should also be understood as a citizenship entitlement, delinked from work, which is available to address poverty and social exclusion. Such a right will respond, along with other rights, to the needs of the millions of women who face disproportionate poverty, lack of access to paid work or underemployment and numerous additional barriers to dignified inclusion in society.

A gendered right to social security is intimately tied to the right to equality given the principle of the interdependence of rights and the importance of substantive gender equality in realising women's rights. Sandra Fredman's multidimensional approach to equality, pursuing the four overlapping aims of recognition, redistribution, transformation and participation,[2] is the equality standard used here against which to measure compliance with the

[1] These ideas are discussed and developed in Goldblatt, B, 'Gender poverty and the development of the right to social security' (2014) *International Journal of Law in Context*, forthcoming.

[2] Fredman, in this collection. See also, Fredman, S, *Discrimination Law*, 2nd edn (Oxford, Oxford University Press, 2011).

social security right. Fredman explains the four aims entailed in substantive equality as follows:

> First, it aims to break the cycle of disadvantage associated with status or out-groups. This reflects the redistributive dimension of equality. Secondly, it aims to promote respect for dignity and worth, thereby redressing stigma, stereotyping, humiliation, and violence because of membership of an identity group. This reflects a recognition dimension. Thirdly, it should not exact conformity as a price of equality. Instead, it should accommodate difference and aim to achieve structural change. This captures the transformative dimension. Finally, substantive equality should facilitate full participation in society, both socially and politically. This is the participative dimension.[3]

This approach offers a comprehensive formulation of substantive equality that is well suited to inform the equality right, from a gender perspective, in its relationship to the social security right.

The above ideas about work and equality are central to developing a set of principles for a substantively equal, gendered right to social security. These principles include: first, that women's household reproductive labour and care work (of children, the sick, elderly and disabled) is recognised and supported and that care is understood as a responsibility of the whole society; second, that women's other unpaid work such as occurs in subsistence production and family industries is recognised and supported for the purpose of social security; third, that women's work in the informal sector in the many forms this takes requires accompanying social security rights; fourth, that women's work within formal employment is valued and attracts sufficient and equal social security; fifth, that social security is provided to all men and women who need it, regardless of their relationship to work; sixth, that the design of social security systems promotes gender equality; and seventh, that women have full and equal access to social security.[4]

These principles should apply beyond national boundaries to address the circumstances of migrant workers and within states, at all levels of governance, to address internal labour migration; and they should inform international cooperation and assistance. They should also take account of the diversity of women's experience across age, race, disability, sexuality, caste, ethnicity and so on, in recognising intersectional disadvantage. The principles can be used to engender existing interpretations of the right to social security, most recently articulated in detailed form in the United Nations (UN) Committee for Economic, Social and Cultural Rights (CESCR) General Comment No 19 on the Right to Social Security.[5]

[3] Fredman, *Discrimination Law*, above n 2, at 25.

[4] Goldblatt, above n 1.

[5] UN Committee on Economic, Social and Cultural Rights (CESCR), *General Comment No 19: The Right to Social Security (art 9)*, 4 February 2008, UN Doc E/C.12/GC/19.

In this chapter, the above conceptual approach, including the principles for a substantively equal, gendered right to social security, is used to analyse the realisation of this right for women in Australia. The Australian social security system is found somewhat wanting when examined through this lens. The chapter briefly outlines the history and nature of the Australian social security system. It then discusses the position of women in Australia, including the gender considerations that informed welfare developments and some of the critiques of the social security system from a gender perspective. It considers Australia's human rights framework and the capacity for the realisation of the right to social security in the Australian context. It then selects for examination two recent issues that highlight the relationship between gender, social security and human rights: the cuts to Parenting Payments (a social assistance measure) that primarily affect poor, single mothers; and, the introduction of income management (controls placed on social assistance spending) and its impact on indigenous women. Analysis of these issues using a gender rights framework points to human rights violations by Australia in relation to access to and adequacy of social security and of equality and non-discrimination in the provision of the right.[6]

AUSTRALIA'S SOCIAL SECURITY SYSTEM

Australia, with a population of 23 million, is an advanced industrial country with a strong economy and a wealthy population.[7] Despite this, poverty affects a sizeable portion of the population and is skewed against women.[8]

Australian social security takes the form of social assistance rather than social insurance as found in many European countries. The payments are funded through the tax system and paid at a flat rate on the basis of means-testing of targeted groups.[9] The major grants are the aged pension, disability pension, parenting payments and unemployment payments (known as Newstart). Approximately 4.9 million people (about 20 per cent of the

[6] Access, adequacy and non-discrimination are elements of the right to social security as set out in CESCR, *General Comment No 19*, above n 5.

[7] Whiteford, P, 'Poverty in a Time of Prosperity' (2012) 21(2) *Human Rights Defender* 7, 7, citing a 2011 Credit Suisse Global Wealth Report estimating that Australia has the 'highest median household wealth in the world'.

[8] Between 12.8% and 20.9% of Australians live below the poverty line depending on the measure used. Women are somewhat more likely to be poor than men while single parent families (usually women) are significantly over-represented amongst the poor. Australian Council of Social Service (ACOSS), 'Poverty in Australia' ('Poverty and Inequality in Australia' Reports, Strawberry Hills, ACOSS, 2012).

[9] Mendes, P, *Australia's Welfare Wars Revisited: The Players, the Politics and the Ideologies* (Sydney, UNSW Press, 2008) 15.

population) receive income support.[10] Esping-Andersen, famous for his welfare state typology, has placed Australia's welfare system within the 'liberal' or residual welfare state regime-type. He sees this regime as restrictive of social rights with stratification of the poor on welfare from others within the market.[11] This characterisation has been challenged by writers who argue that the Australian welfare system is supported by high wage rates through wage fixing and home ownership.[12] They argue that despite lower levels of social spending and lower taxes relative to other OECD countries, Australia is very effective in reaching the poorest people,[13] including through its system of universal health insurance. The caveat to this is that in recent years, unemployment payments have fallen significantly in relation to wages and other pensions. This group of welfare recipients is falling deeper into poverty as are larger numbers of lone parents who are being moved onto Newstart.[14]

The conservative Howard government (1996–2007) adopted the ideology and policies of the US workfare approach in linking unemployment (and other) benefits to job seeking and work-for-the-dole and the introduction of a more punitive system including monitoring and harsh penalties for fraud and violation of welfare rules.[15] Conservative welfare reform shifted public perceptions away from notions of welfare as a social right of citizenship to a more conditional idea based on mutual obligation.[16] There was also a shift from sovereignty of the welfare consumer to state supervision and the removal of choice—'a denial of the equality of selfhood as the price of welfare assistance'.[17] Under the Labor government (2007–13) many of these neo-liberal policy features and the accompanying ideology remained with low unemployment and parenting payments seen by government as incentives to find work. The new Liberal government (elected in 2013) is

[10] As at June 2010: Australian Bureau of Statistics (ABS), '1301.0—Year Book Australia 2012' (ABS, 2012), available at: www.abs.gov.au/ausstats/abs@.nsf/Lookup/by%20Subject/1301.0~2012~Main%20Features~Income%20and%20community%20support~194.

[11] Esping-Andersen, G, *The Three Worlds of Welfare Capitalism* (London, Polity Press, 1990) 167–68.

[12] Saunders, P and Deeming, C, 'The Impact of the Crisis on Australian Social Security Policy in Historical Perspective' (2011) 45(4) *Social Policy & Administration* 371, 376.

[13] Whiteford, P, 'How Fair is Australia's Welfare State?' *Inside Story*(Sydney, 2011), available at: inside.org.au/how-fair-is-australia%E2%80%99s-welfare-state/.

[14] Whiteford 'Poverty in a Time of Prosperity', above n 7, at 8.

[15] Mendes, *Australia's Welfare Wars Revisited*, above n 9, at 33–34; Chenoweth, L, 'Redefining Welfare: Australian Social Policy and Practice' (2008) 2(1) *Asian Social Work and Policy Review* 53. See also Carney, T, 'Neoliberal Welfare Reform and "Rights" Compliance' (2006) 12(1) *Australian Journal of Human Rights* 223.

[16] Shaver, S 'Australian Welfare Reform: From Citizenship to Supervision' (2002) 36(4) *Social Policy & Administration* 331. Also see Carney, T, *Social Security Law and Policy* (Leichhardt, The Federation Press, 2006).

[17] Shaver, above n 16, at 342.

unlikely to alter this approach, other than to further limit certain welfare payments both in terms of eligibility and amount.

Gender in the Australian Social Security System

Australia's welfare system began with a focus on wage fixing and the protection of the family through the male wage earner, alongside income support for those in need such as the aged. The assumption was that if men were paid adequately they could provide for their families.[18] In 1907, the *Harvester* judgment set a minimum wage as the amount required for a male worker, his wife and three children to live in 'frugal comfort'.[19] The model of a male breadwinner with a wife at home has been eroded over the past century to the point where about two-thirds of couple families involve two working parents. However, women are likely to work part-time and earn half the income of men,[20] while performing the major care functions. This 'modified-breadwinner model reinforces gender inequality, casting women as the primary carers and men as the primary earners'.[21] Two-thirds of women participate in the labour market (compared with more than three-quarters of men) but almost half are in part-time work (as opposed to 16.5 per cent of men).[22] These workers face income and job insecurity as well as limited access to benefits usually attached to work.[23] Women face job segregation and a persistent gender pay gap of 17.1 per cent.[24] As a result of lower pay over the life course and work interruptions, on retirement, men have 1.7 times the amount of superannuation (retirement savings) as women.[25] Women perform a significant majority of unpaid

[18] Chenoweth, above n 15, at 54.

[19] Referred to in Leahy, M, 'Women and Work in Australia' (Australian Policy Online Topic Guide, 28 November 2011) 2, available at: apo.org.au/sites/default/files/Women_and_work_in_Australia_APO_guide_Mary_Leahy_0.pdf.

[20] *Ibid.*

[21] *Ibid*; Charlesworth, S, 'Law's Response to the Reconciliation of Work and Care: the Australian Case' in G James and N Busby (eds), *Families, Care-Giving and Paid Work: Challenging Labour Law in the 21st Century* (Cheltenham, Edward Elgar, 2011) 86.

[22] Australian Human Rights Commission (AHRC), *Investing in Care: Recognising and Valuing Those Who Care* (Volume 1: Research Report, Sydney, AHRC, 2013) 5. See also Baird, M, Charlesworth, S, Cooper, R and Heron, A, 'Women, Work and the Global Economic Downturn' (Department of Social Services, Australian Government, 2011), available at: www.fahcsia.gov.au/our-responsibilities/women/publications-articles/general/women-work-and-the-global-economic-downturn?HTML#fn_13; and Smith, in this collection.

[23] Charlesworth, above n 21, at 89.

[24] Workplace Gender Equality Agency, 'Gender Pay Gap Statistics' (Australian Government, 2014), available at: www.wgea.gov.au/sites/default/files/2014-03-04-Gender_Pay_Gap_fact-sheet_website.pdf.

[25] Easteal, P (ed), *Women and the Law in Australia* (Chatswood, LexisNexis Butterworths, 2010) 6.

reproductive and care work in Australia.[26] The employment rate of mothers with young children is lower than in many OECD countries.[27] It is in this context that women make up a higher portion of the poor than men in Australia[28] and are in greater need of income support. Single mothers are a particularly vulnerable group.

Australian social security policy has been implicated in creating and reinforcing gender inequalities in work and care in the particular form they take in this country.[29] During the 1940s, a range of transfers were provided to address the needs of children and spouses.[30] Some of the social security transfers were overtly gendered, such as widow's pensions and different pension ages for men and women. From the 1970s onwards, feminists, in alliance with the trade union movement and various Labor governments, removed most of the manifest inequality from the Australian social security system. Various child support and childcare policies were introduced to bring women into the labour force and support families. However, the Howard years (1996–2007) resulted in some inconsistent policies that both encouraged women to earn wages and play a caring role in the home.[31] Howard refused to introduce paid maternity leave but instead introduced the 'Baby Bonus'—a one-off payment to new mothers whether in or outside the workforce. The ideology behind this measure was to encourage women to have children and to stay at home to care for them. Brennan suggests that Howard's deep conservatism included a 'commitment to full-time mothering'.[32] Two further policies were introduced during the Howard years: family tax benefits that effectively encouraged women to become primary carers rather than joint earners and carers[33] and which reinforced women's dependent status; and, a policy requiring poor parents receiving parenting payments to seek or engage in certain hours of paid work in order to retain benefits.[34] Brennan notes the class divide in Howard's policies—the 'choice' to remain out of work for mothers in income-earning families as opposed to the compulsion to work for families (usually single mothers)

[26] *Ibid*, at 3–4.

[27] Baxter, J, Australian Institute of Family Studies, 'Timing of Mothers' Return to Work After Childbearing: Variations by Job Characteristics and Leave Use' (Research Paper No 42, Canberra, Commonwealth of Australia, July 2008) 1.

[28] ACOSS, 'Poverty in Australia', above n 8, at 14–15.

[29] Cass, B, 'Citizenship, Work, and Welfare: The Dilemma for Australian Women' (1994) 1(1) *Social Politics* 106.

[30] Hodgson, H and Boden, R, 'Not-so-Distant Cousins: Family Benefits in the United Kingdom and Australia' (2008) 61(3) *International Social Security Review* 29, 30.

[31] Brennan, D, 'Babies, Budgets, and Birthrates: Work/Family Policy in Australia 1996–2006' (2007) 14(1) *Social Politics: International Studies in Gender, State, and Society* 31.

[32] *Ibid*, at 37.

[33] *Ibid*, at 38–39.

[34] *Ibid*. See also Cortis, N and Meagher, G, 'Women, Work and Welfare in the Activation State: An Agenda for Australian Research' (2009) 35(4) *Australian Bulletin of Labour* 629.

relying on social assistance.[35] Childcare benefits to pay for approved childcare, like family tax benefits, have been criticised for failing to provide strong incentives to encourage women into full-time work.[36]

There were some efforts by the Labor government (2007–13) to introduce reforms aimed at assisting working women (such as Paid Parental Leave)[37] but problematic features of the social security system such as low unemployment and parenting payments as well as conditionalities attached to social assistance for single parents and indigenous women were retained or started under this government.[38]

Recent proposals to improve women's retirement savings by recognising the impact of care on their working lives have been advanced by the Australian Human Rights Commission within a broader set of recommendations to better structure the role of care in the society, but it remains to be seen whether these will be adopted.[39] The chances of improved social security policies for women under the new Liberal government (since 2013) are slim. The Government has already indicated that it wishes to look for budget savings through an 'overhaul' of the welfare system—such changes are likely to further harm already disadvantaged women.

Australia's Human Rights Framework and the Right to Social Security

Australia is a party to the International Covenant on Civil and Political Rights (ICCPR)[40] and the International Covenant on Economic, Social and Cultural Rights (ICESCR)[41] as well as many of the major human rights conventions including the Convention on the Elimination of All Forms of Discrimination against Women (CEDAW).[42] Australia has also ratified seven of the eight fundamental ILO Conventions and a reasonable number of governance and technical conventions. It has not however, ratified ILO Convention No 102 on Social Security (Minimum Standards)[43] or any of

[35] Brennan, above n 31, at 38–39.

[36] Carney, T, 'Women and Social Security/Transfer Payments Law' in P Easteal (ed), *Women and the Law in Australia* (Chatswood, LexisNexis Butterworths, 2010) 430.

[37] This was introduced in January 2011 whereby government provides 18 weeks' pay at the minimum wage.

[38] Discussed in further detail below.

[39] AHRC, *Investing in Care*, above n 22.

[40] International Covenant on Civil and Political Rights (ICCPR) (adopted 16 December 1966, entered into force 23 March 1976) 999 UNTS 171.

[41] International Covenant on Economic, Social and Cultural Rights (ICESCR) (adopted 16 December 1966, entered into force 3 January 1976) 993 UNTS 3.

[42] Convention on the Elimination of All Forms of Discrimination against Women (CEDAW) (adopted 18 December 1979, entered into force 3 September 1981) 1249 UNTS 13, art 5(b).

[43] ILO Convention C102: Social Security (Minimum Standards) Convention (Convention Concerning Minimum Standards of Social Security) (adopted 28 June 1952, entered into force 27 April 1955).

the related conventions dealing with social risks or contingencies such as unemployment, sickness, old age, maternity and so on. While it attempts to fulfil its international human rights obligations through certain domestic mechanisms including anti-discrimination legislation,[44] human rights commissions and more recently, parliamentary oversight mechanisms, it does not have general human rights legislation (at the federal level) or a bill of rights. Australia has been widely criticised for this gap and encouraged to improve its human rights protections.[45] Human rights, as found in government discourse and public consciousness, is generally understood to include civil and political rights rather than social and economic rights. There is a very limited understanding across Australian society of social security as a human right,[46] let alone the gender dimensions of this right.

Treaty bodies, in particular the CESCR, and various UN special rapporteurs have commented on and made recommendations regarding Australia's social security system. In 2009, the CESCR recommended measures to address the gender wage gap and the level of unemployment affecting indigenous people, asylum-seekers, migrants and people with disabilities.[47] These recommendations related to the Committee's concern that Australia's social security benefits were not adequate as an 'effective income support system'.[48] The Committee also expressed concern at the rate of poverty in Australia, especially amongst disadvantaged and marginalised groups.[49] The CEDAW Committee, in its 2010 report on Australia, called on Australia to improve the newly introduced Paid Parental Leave Scheme and the system of childcare.[50]

Additional strong criticism of Australia has come from the UN Special Rapporteur on the situation of human rights and fundamental freedoms of indigenous people, James Anaya. In his 2010 report, Anaya found that in particular, aspects of the Northern Territory Emergency Response (NTER or 'the Intervention') violated Australia's human rights obligations and

[44] Social security legislation is broadly exempted from anti-discrimination legislation. See Carney, 'Neoliberal Welfare Reform', above n 15, at 231.

[45] See the Conclusions and Recommendations of the Universal Periodic Review of Australia: Human Rights Council, *Report of the Working Group on the Universal Periodic Review (Australia)*, 24 March 2011, UN Doc A/HRC/17/10, para 86.22; and Australia's Response (Attorney General's Department, Australian Government, 8 June 2011), available at: www.ag.gov.au/RightsAndProtections/HumanRights/UniversalPeriodicReview/Documents/AustraliasformalresponsetotheUPRrecommendations.pdf.

[46] Carney, 'Neoliberal Welfare Reform', above n 15, at 238.

[47] UN Committee on Economic, Social and Cultural Rights (CESCR), *Concluding Observations of CESCR: Australia*, 22 May 2009, UN Doc E/C.12/AUS/CO/4, paras 17–18.

[48] *Ibid*.

[49] *Ibid*, at para 24.

[50] UN Committee on the Elimination of Discrimination against Women (CEDAW), *Concluding Observations of CEDAW: Australia*, 30 July 2010, UN Doc CEDAW/C/AUS/CO/7, para 39.

were racially discriminatory.[51] This included the introduction of income management of social security payments.[52] In 2012, the UN Special Rapporteur on extreme poverty and human rights and the Working Group on the issue of discrimination against women in law and in practice wrote to the Australian government to ask them to respond to allegations that the cuts to Parenting Payments were a violation of human rights.[53] The issues of income management and cuts to Parenting Payments as (gendered) violations of human rights are now discussed in more detail.

Parenting Payments Cuts

Removal of Benefits

As discussed above, historically Australia supported wives/widows and single mothers on the basis that they were needy recipients without male breadwinners to rely on. In 1973, the Commonwealth Supporting Mother's Benefit was introduced as an entitlement without conditions attached. From 2002, compulsory interviews were introduced as well as a minimal activity requirement for parents of older children. A major shift occurred in 2006 when parents with school age children were brought under the job-search requirements applied to the unemployed.[54] Single parents are now defined by their employment status rather than their caring status as they are moved onto Newstart when their children start school.[55]

Newstart is paid at a lower rate and with 'tighter income and activity tests and a more punitive compliance regime'.[56] This policy change was seen as a 'significant' shift 'in the structure of the Australian welfare state' from a 'male-breadwinner' to an 'adult worker family model'.[57] For new claimants after 1 July 2006 job-search requirements and the Newstart rate apply for single parents with children over the age of six. The rules mean that parents must be in paid work for a minimum of 15 hours a week or jobseeking for 15 to 25 hours per week. Jobseekers may also be required to

[51] Anaya, J, Special Rapporteur on the Situation of Human Rights and Fundamental Freedoms of Indigenous People, *Situation of Indigenous People in Australia*, 4 March 2010, UN Doc A/HRC/15/37/Add.4, Appendix B, para 37.

[52] *Ibid*. See below for a more detailed discussion of income management.

[53] This is discussed in greater detail below.

[54] Grahame, T and Marston, G, 'Welfare-to-Work Policies and the Experience of Employed Single Mothers on Income Support in Australia: Where are the Benefits?' (2012) 65(1) *Australian Social Work* 73, 74.

[55] Cortis and Meagher, above n 34, at 632.

[56] *Ibid*.

[57] *Ibid*, at 631.

participate in activities aimed at improving their chances of work.[58] Those who had already made claims before this date would receive Parenting Payments for children born prior to 1 July 2011 and still under the age of 16[59] and would be expected to meet participation requirements once their youngest child turns seven.[60] This latter group is known as 'grandfathered' or 'saved' beneficiaries. In 2012, the Labor government took a decision to remove the benefits previously provided to the 'grandfathered' group of parents with effect from 1 January 2013 and to move them onto Newstart, at a lower rate of pay.[61] Not all people would be eligible for Newstart as the income threshold is lower.[62] The government described this as a measure to introduce consistency between groups of parents in receipt of Parenting Payments and a measure to encourage parents of school age children to 're-engage with the workforce and provide strong working role models for their children'.[63]

This change was clearly also a cost-saving measure to reduce spending by $728 million over four years.[64] Welfare advocates said the cuts affected more than 100,000 sole parents with income reductions of more than $100 per week.[65] They noted that 95 per cent of Parenting Payment (single) recipients were female in August 2011 (304,589 women).[66] An analysis of government data showed that despite government rhetoric about getting parents back to work, 60 per cent of the affected group were already

[58] There were some minor changes made in 2009 to include study and volunteering. Grahame and Marston, above n 54, at 74.

[59] This age was changed to 12 or 13 for applicable groups in May 2012.

[60] O'Halloran, M (ed), *The Independent Social Security Handbook*, 7th edn (Sydney, Welfare Rights Centre, 2012) 300.

[61] Eligibility for all Parenting Payments (including the grandfathered group) would cease when the youngest child turns 6 (partnered) or 8 (single). Participation requirements for grandfathered parents would kick in when the youngest child turned 6 instead of the previous 7. Explanatory Memorandum, Social Security Legislation Amendment (Fair Incentives to Work) Bill 2012 (Cth) 9.

[62] It was estimated that almost a third (30%) of Parenting Payment recipients would not be eligible for Newstart and with a lower income free area they would thus face earlier reductions in payments than they had previously experienced. Parliamentary Joint Committee on Human Rights, *Examination of Legislation in Accordance with Human Rights (Parliamentary Scrutiny Act) 2011: Social Security Legislation Amendment (Fair Inventives to Work) Act 2012: Final Report* (Canberra, Commonwealth of Australia, 2013) 5.

[63] *Ibid.*

[64] Karvelas, P, 'Single-Mother Cuts to Hit Hardest in PM's Seat' *The Australian* (Sydney, 22 September 2012).

[65] Around 63,000 people were affected by the change on the commencement date of the legislation, 1 January 2013. Eventually, the changes will affect 147,000 grandfathered recipients. Parliamentary Joint Committee on Human Rights, *Examination of Legislation: Final Report*, above n 62, at 4.

[66] Based on government figures, Australian Council of Social Service (ACOSS), 'Inquiry by the Parliamentary Joint Committee on Human Rights into the Social Security Legislation Amendment (Fair Incentives to Work) Bill 2012 (Supplementary Submissions)' (Strawberry Hills, ACOSS, 2012) 9.

in work.[67] Testimony from single mothers showed that they would have to give up studying, move states and cancel their children's participation in certain activities following the cuts. Many talked about the hardships relating to inadequate family support, the need to escape violence, children with special needs and the lack of childcare and its impact on their job situations and how reduced income would compound these difficulties.[68] The implications of moving single mothers, an already vulnerable and disadvantaged group,[69] onto Newstart, criticised by the government's own tax review as inadequate, appeared harsh, unfair and even counterproductive.[70] It was seen as a breach of a promise made by the government to support this cohort of parents who had counted on the higher income for a longer period of time.

Human Rights Responses to the Removal of Benefits

The cut to single mothers' benefits, even by a Labor government, was not entirely surprising in the context of international austerity measures following the global financial crisis that began in 2008. Australia was looking for ways to bring the budget out of deficit and grandfathered sole parents might have seemed one possible revenue source. What was significant, however, was the new role for human rights in efforts to oppose the measure. Welfare and human rights advocates attempted to challenge the Bill introducing the changes by calling for an inquiry into the proposed legislation by the Parliamentary Joint Committee on Human Rights. The Committee is a new body set up under the Human Rights (Parliamentary Scrutiny) Act 2011.[71] The Act was introduced following a national human rights consultation in 2008 that called for human rights legislation along the lines of the English model. This was rejected, but a more limited scrutiny function was given to Parliament requiring new Bills to be accompanied by statements of compatibility with international human rights.[72] The Act also created the Parliamentary Committee to examine and inquire into Bills in terms of Australia's international human rights obligations.

[67] O'Halloran, M, 'Working Single Parents Kicked' *The Australian* (Sydney, 6 March 2013).

[68] Verbatim testimony provided by the National Council for Single Mothers and their Children. ACOSS, 'Supplementary Submissions', above n 66, at 11–12.

[69] Saunders, P and Wong, M, *Promoting Inclusion and Combating Deprivation: Recent Changes in Social Disadvantage in Australia* (Social Policy Research Centre (SPRC) Report Series, Sydney, SPRC, University of New South Wales, December 2012) 54.

[70] Cox, E, 'What the Government Wants to Ignore About Sole Parents and Jobseeking' (*The Conversation*, 17 January 2013), available at: theconversation.edu.au/what-the-government-wants-to-ignore-about-sole-parents-and-jobseeking-11582.

[71] Human Rights (Parliamentary Scrutiny) Act 2011 (Cth).

[72] See Williams, G and Burton, L, 'Australia's Exclusive Parliamentary Model of Rights Protection' (2013) 34(1) *Statute Law Review* 58.

The Parenting Payment cuts were the subject of the first inquiry by the new Committee and thus an important test of Australia's somewhat minimalist new human rights framework. The Australian Council of Social Service (ACOSS), together with 14 other individuals representing welfare and human rights organisations[73] across Australia, requested an inquiry by the Parliamentary Committee on 15 June 2012 into the Bill which contained the cuts.[74] The letter of request described the proposed removal of Parenting Payments to the grandfathered recipients as a human rights violation.[75] It said that the Bill violated rights under ICESCR and CEDAW as it impinged on the social security rights of sole parents, most of whom are women. It also argued that the measure violated the principle of non-retrogression by removing an existing benefit and went against the obligation of progressive realisation of rights. The letter said that the minister's statement of compatibility which accompanied the Bill was manifestly inadequate and called for a public inquiry by the Committee.

The Committee agreed to hold an inquiry and invited oral evidence by the government and the letters' authors on 21 June 2012.[76] It also allowed further written submissions after the hearing. It produced an interim report in September 2012 recommending that the Bill be deferred until the outcome of a Senate Committee into the adequacy of Newstart,[77] since it said that if Newstart could not provide an adequate standard of living for beneficiaries then the proposed Bill would 'risk being incompatible with the obligation in article 9 of ICESCR to ensure minimum essential levels of

[73] The author was a signatory of the letter in her capacity as Visiting Fellow, Australian Human Rights Centre, Faculty of Law, University of New South Wales. She also provided oral evidence at the inquiry and contributed to the supplementary written submissions provided to the Committee following the inquiry.

[74] The Social Security Legislation Amendment (Fair Incentives to Work) Bill 2012.

[75] Letter from the Australian Council of Social Service (ACOSS) to Harry Jenkins MP, Committee Chair, Parliamentary Joint Committee on Human Rights, 'Request for Inquiry by the Parliamentary Joint Committee on Human Rights into the Social Security Legislation Amendment (Fair Incentives to Work) Bill 2012' (15 June 2012), available at www.aph.gov.au/Parliamentary_Business/Committees/Joint/Human_Rights/Committee_Activity/socialsecurity/correspondence/~/media/Committees/Senate/committee/humanrights_ctte/activity/social_security/correspondence/letter_inquiry_joint_committee_human_rights.ashx.

[76] Parliamentary Joint Committee on Human Rights, Parliament of Australia, *Examination of Legislation in Accordance with the Human Rights (Parliamentary Scrutiny) Act 2011 Interim Report: Social Security Legislation Amendment (Fair Incentives to Work) Bill 2012: Fourth Report* (Canberra, Commonwealth of Australia, September 2012) 6.

[77] An inquiry by the Senate Education, Employment and Workplace Relations References Committee which was due to report by 29 November 2012. For the Committee's report see The Senate Education, Employment and Workplace Relations References Committee, *The Adequacy of the Allowance Payment System for Jobseekers and Others, the Appropriateness of the Allowance Payment System as a Support into Work and the Impact of the Changing Nature of the Labour Market* (November 2012).

social security'.[78] Despite this recommendation, the Bill was passed by both Houses of Parliament on 9 October 2012. The Senate inquiry into Newstart did in fact find that the payment was not providing for an acceptable standard of living for anyone but the short-term unemployed, with different parties proposing different solutions to this.[79] The Parliamentary Human Rights Committee produced a final report in March 2013.

The Parliamentary Human Rights Committee's reports demonstrated a real engagement with the meaning of the right to social security and the right to non-discrimination. The Committee also carefully considered issues of justification in relation to limitations of rights under the ICESCR as well as issues of non-retrogression. It developed a framework for analysis looking at the legitimate objective of the measure, the rational connection between the measure and the objective and whether the measure is proportionate to the objective.[80] Its final report raised concerns that the cuts to Parenting Payments would create additional financial stress for single parent families without improving their employment prospects.[81] It also questioned the unwillingness of government to establish an official poverty measure.[82] It found that the government had failed to adequately incorporate its human rights obligations in developing the new laws. In particular, it found that the government had failed to consult properly or consider alternatives measures; failed to explore the likely impact of the measures on the human rights of affected people; and had not put in place impact assessment mechanisms for the future.[83] On this last point, the Committee proposed a review after 12 months to consider the impact of the legislation and whether reasonable adjustments would be needed. Overall, it found that the government had not demonstrated that the right to social security of affected individuals was being met. It was thus unable to conclude that the 'measures are compatible with human rights'.[84] The Committee's report is a welcome first consideration by the Australian Parliament of social security measures in terms of Australia's international human rights obligations.

At an earlier point, the ACOSS network that had initiated the inquiry, fearing that Parliament would ignore the Committee's recommendations and pass the Bill, wrote to the United Nations Special Rapporteur on Extreme Poverty and Human Rights on 5 October 2012. The letter called

[78] Parliamentary Joint Committee on Human Rights, *Examination of Legislation: Interim Report*, above n 76, at 19.

[79] See Senate Education, Employment and Workplace Relations References Committee, above n 77.

[80] Parliamentary Joint Committee on Human Rights, *Examination of Legislation: Final Report*, above n 62, at 14–15.

[81] *Ibid*, at 28.

[82] *Ibid*.

[83] *Ibid*, at 29.

[84] *Ibid*, at 30.

on the Special Rapporteur to send an 'urgent appeal' to the government to delay the Bill pending the Senate Newstart inquiry.[85] The UN Special Rapporteur together with the Chair-Rapporteur of the Working Group on the issue of discrimination against women in law and in practice wrote to the Australian government on 19 October 2012.[86] In this letter they said they did not want to prejudge the issue but wished to draw the government's attention to the applicable human rights norms and standards. These included, inter alia, article 9 of ICESCR and CESCR General Comment No 19 dealing with the right to social security and its adequacy. They also raised issues of non-discrimination and the rights of children and women. The authors set out the ICESCR and CESCR requirements regarding limitations of rights and non-retrogression. Finally, they asked for the Australian government's cooperation and observations on a set of questions that they said would inform their report to the UN Human Rights Council. The questions concerned the alternative measures considered; an assessment of the impact of the Act on the groups affected; what consultations had occurred; what measures were put in place to avoid indirect discrimination of women and children; monitoring and redress mechanisms; and why the Act was not seen as violating human rights.

The questions are significant in that they emphasise consultation with affected groups, principles of non-discrimination and impact assessment in testing the reasonableness of the law and its compliance with the right to social security. The Special Rapporteur's letter appears to have had some impact on the approach taken by the Parliamentary Human Rights Committee in its Final Report, particularly with reference to the issues of consultation, impact assessment and monitoring. To date the government has not responded to the Special Rapporteur's letter. The legislation took effect on 1 January 2013.

Discussion

Despite Australia's stated commitment to international human rights, the above narrative of events surrounding Parenting Payment cuts highlights a failure to properly engage with calls for it to respect its obligations. Nevertheless, the efforts to bring human rights arguments into the debate

[85] Letter from Australian Council of Social Service, (ACOSS) 'Urgent appeal to the United Nations Special Rapporteur on Extreme Poverty and Human Rights on the proposed introduction of the Social Security Legislation Amendment (Fair Incentives to Work) Bill 2012 in Australia' (5 October 2012), on file with the author.

[86] Letter from Maria Magdalena Sepúlveda Carmona, Special Rapporteur on Extreme Poverty and Human Rights and Kamala Chandrakirana, Chair of the Working Group on the Issue of Discrimination Against Women in Law and Practice (19 October 2012), Reference: UA Poverty AUS 2/2012, available at: spdb.ohchr.org/hrdb/22nd/public_-_UA_Australie_19.10.12_(2.2012).pdf.

around welfare reform were important in the Australian context as they offered welfare rights advocates an additional set of strategic tools and a discourse for framing the Parenting Payment issue.

The legislation which is now in place has had a harsh impact on thousands of families. It violates the right to social security of affected sole parents in terms of adequacy as it provides too little for an adequate standard of living and a dignified life. It is also unreasonably retrogressive in removing existing benefits from a group that had expected to continue receiving these. The cuts are also indirectly discriminatory against women which is the group overwhelmingly affected. By expecting these mothers to seek work, retrain or work and look after children without the necessary supports to do so, and on very limited incomes, effectively marginalises this group even further. This measure fails to provide recognition of single mothers' care responsibilities in assuming that single mothers are equally well placed with dual parent families and childless individuals to find their way out of unemployment or to manage work and childcare. Ironically, almost two-thirds of the parents affected by the new law were already working and it was these parents who lost the most from the cuts.[87] Removing some of their social assistance simply made life more difficult for this group.

The government's response shows a lack of understanding of the challenges of caring, alone, for school age children who need care in school holidays, when they are ill and before and after school hours, while also balancing these demands against employer expectations that are not always sensitive to these realities.[88] The caring work that these women are providing is also not valued as socially necessary and beneficial labour. The removal of Parenting Payments tested against the conceptual approach, including the principles for a substantively equal, gendered right to social security, set out at the start of this chapter, illustrates infringements of the right in the following respects.

First, the failure to consider the context in which the cuts would operate reflects a lack of acknowledgment of the gendered realities faced by this group of parents. Their access to the labour market is shaped by their unremunerated childcare work and the impact that sole responsibility for children has on their life circumstances. Failure to take account of this context leads to violations of their rights to social security. In terms of the principles set out at the start of the chapter, removal of Parenting Payments shows disregard for principle one relating to the recognition of care work; principle five relating to social security as an entitlement regardless of the

[87] O'Halloran, 'Working Single Parents Kicked', above n 67.

[88] Cox, E and Priest, T, 'Welfare to Work: At What Cost to Parenting?' (2008), available at: pandora.nla.gov.au/pan/95161/20090223-1020/www.women.nsw.gov.au/PDF/Welfare_to_Work_At_what_cost_to_parenting.pdf.

person's relationship to work; principle six relating to the design of social security to promote gender equality; and principle seven regarding full and equal access to social security.

Second, a substantive equality approach using the dimensions of recognition, redistribution, participation and transformation points to gendered rights violations. On the level of recognition there was a failure to acknowledge single parents' care responsibilities and the challenges they face as well as the contributions they make while burdening them with conditions and stigma. With regard to redistribution, parents were further impoverished rather than being provided with greater resources to place them on a more equal footing with others in society. In relation to participation, there was a failure to involve single parents in formulating approaches to address their specific circumstances while imposing new conditions on them contrary to past promises. Further, with respect to transformation there was a failure to develop policies that consider ways of changing the conditions that lead to a significant group of vulnerable single mothers being unable to compete in the labour market, care for themselves and their children and contribute fully to society. Transformative responses that assist single mothers are likely to be linked to broader social policies that address gendered divisions of labour and inadequate provision of care.[89]

The principles for a substantively equal, gendered social security right have been overlooked in the limiting of women's access to adequate social security. Rather than progressively realising the rights of this disadvantaged group, their existing provision has been diminished. Tested in this way, the Australian government has failed to meet its human rights obligations for this group of single parents.

Income Management

The chapter now considers another legislative development, the introduction of income management, in testing Australia's compliance with the right to social security, viewed through a gender lens.

Background

In June 2007, the conservative Howard government introduced the Northern Territory Emergency Response (NTER, also known as 'the Intervention') in response to shocking reports of child abuse and violence

[89] Cortis and Meagher, above n 34, at 643, point to comparative research by Lambert that links higher labour market participation and income by working mothers to supportive policies such as childcare and paid leave. Australia does not do well in this regard in comparison with other rich democracies.

against women in Aboriginal communities in the Northern Territory.[90] The most significant report, prepared by the Northern Territory Board of Inquiry into the Protection of Aboriginal Children from Sexual Abuse entitled 'Little Children are Sacred', called for a wide range of measures and services along with extensive consultation with the communities affected.[91] The government used the rhetoric of crisis to speedily introduce a raft of measures without any consultation with local people. Measures included bans on alcohol, pornography, reforms to the justice system and employment projects, compulsory acquisition of Aboriginal land and significantly, the introduction of compulsory income management.[92] The idea behind income management was 'the belief that undesirable behaviour can be modified by the regulation of personal income'.[93] Quarantined income was to be used for goods needed for the care of children. Women were also to be protected from 'humbugging' whereby they are forced, sometimes violently, to share their income support payments with relatives. The Racial Discrimination Act was suspended so that the measures could be applied only to indigenous residents of listed communities.[94] This aspect led to severe criticism by domestic human rights groups and international human rights bodies.[95] When Labour came to power late in 2007 it continued supporting the NTER, only reinstating the Racial Discrimination Act in 2010 when it extended the measures to non-indigenous members of the Northern Territory.[96] In June 2012, the government enacted the 'Stronger Futures' legislation which extended income management for a trial period

[90] Australia is made up of states and territories with the federal government having certain additional powers in relation to territories. The Northern Territory, while sparsely populated, has a disproportionately large indigenous population compared with other states and territories.

[91] Northern Territory Board of Inquiry into the Protection of Aboriginal Children from Sexual Abuse, *Ampe Akelyernemane Meke Mekarle: 'Little Children are Sacred'* (Northern Territory Government, 2007), available at: www.inquirysaac.nt.gov.au/pdf/bipacsa_final_report.pdf. Discussed in Watson, N, 'The Northern Territory Emergency Response—Has it Really Improved the Lives of Aboriginal Women and Children?' (2011) 35 *Australian Feminist Law Journal* 147, 148–49.

[92] Mendes, P, 'Compulsory Income Management: A Critical Examination of the Emergence of Conditional Welfare in Australia' (2012) *Australian Social Work* 1, 4; Watson, above n 91, at 149–50 and 161–63.

[93] Watson, above n 91, at 150.

[94] In terms of s 132(1) and (2) of the Northern Territory Emergency Response Act 2007 (Cth) and ss 4(1), (2) and (4) and 6(2) and (3) of the Social Security and Other Legislation Amendment (Welfare Payment Reform) Act 2007 (Cth).

[95] Such as the Australian Human Rights Commission and the UN Special Rapporteur on the Situation of Human Rights and Fundamental Freedoms of Indigenous People, James Anaya.

[96] Social Security and Other Legislation Amendment (Welfare Reform and Reinstatement of Racial Discrimination Act) Act 2010 (Cth). The Act allowed 'special measures' to continue to be taken to address issues such as alcohol related harm.

of five years to five areas outside the Northern Territory.[97] It also extended the School Enrolment and Attendance through Welfare Reform Measure (SEAM), designed to suspend or cancel income support where a person fails to ensure school enrolment and attendance, to further sites in the Northern Territory.[98]

Income management applies to certain categories of people such as 'long-term welfare recipients' or 'disengaged youth' and can also be required for people identified as vulnerable. In addition to compulsory income management there is provision for voluntary income management. A portion of income support is withheld and placed in a managed account which can be accessed only for use on certain items of expenditure with a 'basics card' that can only be used at approved stores.[99]

Responses to the NTER

General Criticisms

The NTER and Stronger Futures have been met with angry criticism from many quarters. A general complaint has been the lack of consultation. This was patently problematic in the top-down way in which the Howard government introduced the legislation, but even subsequent consultation efforts by the Labour government were the subject of scathing condemnation. The National Congress of Australia's First Peoples said the consultations were flawed and did not involve sufficient opportunity for indigenous people to come up with their own solutions to the problems based on requirements of international human rights.[100] The Intervention has also been divisive within the indigenous community both within and beyond the Northern Territory.[101] Despite the government's claim that the Stronger Futures

[97] Stronger Futures in the Northern Territory Act 2012 (Cth). The additional areas contain high numbers of culturally and linguistically diverse communities of recent migrants and refugees. Australian Human Rights Commission (AHRC), 'Stronger Futures in the Northern Territory Bill 2011 and Two Related Bills: Australian Human Rights Commission—Submission to the Senate Community Affairs Legislation Committee' (Sydney, AHRC, 6 February 2012) 29.

[98] Social Security Legislation Amendment Act 2012 (Cth).

[99] O'Halloran, *The Independent Social Security Handbook*, above n 60, at 108.

[100] National Congress of Australia's First Peoples (NCAFP), 'Statement to the Parliamentary Joint Committee on Human Rights on the Parliamentary Scrutiny of Human Rights as applied to the Stronger Futures in the Northern Territory Bills (2011)' (Redfern, NCAFP, June 2012) 6. See also Partridge, E, Maddison, S and Nicholson, A, 'Human Rights Imperatives and the Failings of the Stronger Futures Consultation Process' (2013) 18(2) *Australian Journal of Human Rights* 21.

[101] See Watson, above n 91, for a discussion of some of the differences between Aboriginal women around the Intervention. Also see Mendes, 'Compulsory Income Management', above n 92, at 8–9 on some of the reasons for the different perspectives.

legislation promotes rather than violates human rights,[102] the measures arguably constitute indirect race discrimination since they apply primarily to indigenous people. Government's claim that they are 'special measures' to advance the interests of a disadvantaged group has not been well justified or demonstrated. On the contrary, they appear to violate social security beneficiaries' autonomy and choice, create stigma and reinforce existing inequalities and stereotypes experienced by Indigenous Australians.

Another concern, particularly relating to the income management provisions, is that the Intervention has been used to mask a significant policy change from welfare entitlement to control, using the NTER as a 'pilot' for further roll out to the broader non-indigenous population and particularly to those marginalised individuals and groups who are regarded as dysfunctional.[103] In a similar vein, Mendes suggests that compulsory income management reflects a shift from structural to individualistic explanations of social disadvantage and is a continuation of the increasing conditions being imposed on social security recipients.[104] There is also a strong argument about the failure of the government to support its assertion that the measures are beneficial with adequate evidence.[105] In addition, the situation facing children and others that were meant to be assisted by the Intervention has only worsened.[106]

Gender Related Criticisms

What has not always been evident in the wide-ranging public debate on the Intervention is the gendered impact of the measures. In pure numerical terms, the income management provisions affect women disproportionately since three-fifths (61 per cent) of income managed people in October 2011 were women.[107] It is generally women who do the shopping for families. A study of women's experience of income management showed a majority were feeling demeaned by having to use the basics card and most did not

[102] Letter from Jenny Macklin MP to the Honourable Harry Jenkins MP, 'Assessment of Policy Objectives with Human Rights—Stronger Futures in the Northern Territory Bill 2012; Stronger Futures in the Northern Territory (Consequential and Transitional Provisions) Bill 2011' (letter and attached submission to the Parliamentary Joint Committee on Human Rights, 27 June 2012),, available at: www.aph.gov.au/Parliamentary_Business/Committees/Joint/Human_Rights/Committee_Activity/strongerfutures/background/~/media/Committees/Senate/committee/humanrights_ctte/activity/stronger_futures/correspondence/mfcsia_chair_280612.ashx.

[103] Cox, E, 'Evidence-Free Policy Making? The Case of Income Management' (2011) (12) *Journal of Indigenous Policy* 1.

[104] Mendes, 'Compulsory Income Management', above n 92.

[105] Cox, 'Evidence-Free Policy Making?', above n 103.

[106] Cox, 'Evidence-Free Policy Making?', above n 103, at 85, says this is evidenced by government's own statistics.

[107] Bray, JR et al, 'Evaluating New Income Management in the Northern Territory: First Evaluation Report' (Sydney, Social Policy Research Centre, July 2012) 57–58.

feel any safer since its introduction.[108] Many interviewees found the basics card confusing and limiting of their choices such as to shop at smaller non-approved stores or to buy medicine from a pharmacy that was closer but did not take the card. Interviewees expressed feelings of shame at being identified as basics card holders and for the assumption that they could not manage their finances responsibly on their own.

Family violence (often directed at women) is one of the triggers for the categorisation of a person requiring income management. The Australian Law Reform Commission has examined the link between family violence and income management and has found that compulsory income management can be dangerous and inappropriate in the context of family violence.[109] It recommends that it should not be used in such cases. Ironically, the prevention of family violence is one of the stated objectives for the introduction of income management. The Commission suggests that people experiencing family violence are often denied agency and control over themselves and their households so government measures that further remove control are likely to be harmful and deepen their sense of disempowerment.[110]

Watson argues for the need to locate an understanding of the Intervention within the historical context of control over Aboriginal women coupled with their invisibility as holders of rights.[111] Protectionist legislation was used to control Aboriginal women's sexuality, relationships and families. As wards of protectors, Aboriginal women had to surrender their wages which were administered on their behalf, a practice which continued late into the twentieth century. Similarly, welfare payments were controlled or recipients were subject to surveillance until their trustworthiness was established.

Discussion

The women's rights dimensions of income management have also been missing from human rights objections to the measures. Yet the measures, in impacting harshly on indigenous women, constitute indirect discrimination on the basis of race and gender. This results in both multiple and intersectional forms of discrimination for the group of women involved. Because of their race and their gender, women in the income-managed communities are facing daily indignities and a loss of autonomy. Their vulnerability as a marginalised group in Australia is being intensified—indigenous women in the Northern Territory have very low visibility in the wider society and

[108] Equality Rights Alliance, 'Women's Experience of Income Management in the Northern Territory' (Canberra, Equality Rights Alliance, 2011).

[109] Australian Law Reform Commission (ALRC), *Family Violence and Commonwealth Laws—Improving Legal Frameworks: Final Report* (ALRC Report 117, Sydney, ALRC, November 2011) 247–83.

[110] *Ibid*, at 260.

[111] Watson, above n 91, at 156–58.

are seen as 'other' or different from the 'rest of Australia'. This location allows for legislated indignities to go largely unnoticed and unchallenged. Violations of the right to social security have been identified in human rights objections to the Intervention as involving issues of discrimination based on race, but these have not considered the specific gender dimensions of the right to social security in relation to women who are the subjects of the laws.

Women's care responsibilities and unpaid work in household reproduction contribute to their disproportionate representation as welfare recipients. Indigenous women face discrimination in their access to the right to social security, which serves to deepen their already considerable disadvantage. Using the conceptual approach and principles set out at the start of this chapter, the violations of women's right to social security become apparent in the context of income management in the Northern Territory and the further sites where it is being introduced. The NTER measures fail in relation to the first principle on the recognition and support for care work; the fifth principle concerning the provision of social security to all who need it regardless of their relationship to work; the sixth principle relating to the design of social security systems that promote equality; and the seventh principle of full and equal access by women to social security.

Bringing a substantive equality lens into an examination of the right to social security focuses attention on issues of recognition, redistribution, participation and transformation. Women who are subject to the income management provisions face 'misrecognition'[112] in the way in which they are targeted, demeaned and stigmatised by the laws.[113] From a distributive point of view they are prevented from making choices about expenditure, sometimes leading to financial disadvantage.[114] With regard to participation, they have been inadequately consulted and have not been able to shape measures to address the difficulties they face—instead, they feel imposed upon and confused by the changes.[115] Rather than seeking transformative means of empowering indigenous communities to find ways of tackling violence against women and children, income management has reinforced an historical pattern of colonial paternalism and control, particularly over women.

Worryingly, these measures are being extended to other vulnerable communities containing recent migrants and refugees, where women face additional forms of discrimination on the basis of sex, race, ethnicity, religion, language and culture alongside their migrant status. The introduction of

112 To use Nancy Fraser's term: Fraser, N, *Scales of Justice* (Cambridge, Polity Press, 2008) 16.
113 Equality Rights Alliance, above n 108, at 29–32.
114 For examples see *ibid*, at 21–25.
115 *Ibid*, at 17 and 39.

compulsory income management goes further down the path of conditionality and control within the Australian social security system. This shift from social security as a right to something that requires ongoing proof of a person's deservingness is a dangerous trend. Greater conditionality is accompanied by increased monitoring and punitive controls that undermine the right to social security.[116] Income management imposes hardships on women recipients of social security who are carrying care burdens of the society and who should be entitled to welfare support, without limitations, despite their lack of paid work. This support should be fully accessible without harsh, discriminatory and inappropriate conditions attached to it, within a social security system that is designed to improve the position of women rather than stigmatise and burden them. Tested against the principles for a substantively equal, gendered right to social security, the income management measures fail in that they hamper women's access to the right and, rather than promoting gender equality, the design of the measures reinforces women's disproportionate household responsibilities while imposing new and additional hardships.

CONCLUSION

The Australian social security system, while sufficient in parts, is not adequately meeting the needs of a significant section of the poor. This failing has important gender dimensions as women comprise the majority of the poor and of those providing care in society and an overwhelming majority of single parents. Social security, once seen as an entitlement, is increasingly dependent on the fulfilment of conditions, many of which are difficult for women with care responsibilities. Single mothers are being moved onto social assistance that does not provide for an adequate standard of living, particularly in a country with such wealth. The Northern Territory measures added a race dimension to social security provision that has impacted harshly on indigenous women and is being rolled out to other vulnerable groups. Both issues relate in part to the structuring role of care in the gendered division of labour and its adverse impact on women across the life course in Australia. They also highlight the failure of government to address this structural inequality. On the contrary, the current policies reinforce the marginalisation of the most disadvantaged groups of women and leave existing divisions intact.

Tested against the conceptual approach and the principles for a substantively equal, gendered social security right discussed at the start of this chapter, Australia scores poorly in relation to the two issues discussed here.

116 Walsh, T, 'Breaching the Right to Social Security' (2003) (12) *Griffith Law Review* 43.

Parenting Payment cuts are pushing a large group of single women and their children into poverty in the guise of efforts to encourage their further employment. This is somewhat cynical given that many of the mothers are already in work, will struggle to balance further work and care without adequate social provision of affordable child care and will face difficulties in finding appropriate work in the current employment context. Poor single mothers are facing violations of their rights to social security since the current measures are inadequate, substantively unequal and fail to address principles of the inclusion of care and unpaid work. Similarly, indigenous women and other marginalised women have encountered violations of their rights to social security with the introduction of income management. Their full and equal access to social security has been circumscribed as a result of their race, their physical location as well as their gender location, which is in turn related to their caring responsibilities in society. The principles advanced in this chapter relating to recognition of care and unpaid work, and access to and design of social security, are not being followed. The stigma and stereotyping that accompanies these measures results in indirect, intersectional race and gender discrimination in violation of their equality and social security rights.

The lack of comprehensive human rights laws within the domestic context means that options to challenge these deficiencies using human rights are restricted. International bodies are being resorted to but these clearly have limited persuasive power in the Australian setting. Nevertheless, there appears to be a new, albeit small, space for engagement around human rights with the establishment of the Parliamentary Joint Committee on Human Rights. The recent advocacy around both the Parenting Payment Cuts and the Northern Territory laws has introduced some human rights discourse on social security into public debate. The gender dimensions of this debate have, however, been more limited. The use of a gender analysis within a human rights approach enables an understanding of the specific violations of the right to social security that affect certain groups of disadvantaged women in Australia. This understanding can be used to address such violations and deficiencies in the social security system to ensure that these groups of women are substantively included and that the system advances rather than impedes the realisation of gender equality in society. This deeper understanding of the right to social security from a gender perspective is needed to inform improvements to social security in Australia.

14

Mainstreaming Gender in Spanish Labour and Pension Reforms and in European Social Policies

NÚRIA PUMAR BELTRÁN

MODELS OF SOCIAL SECURITY AND THEIR IMPACT ON GENDER

THE INTERNATIONAL LABOUR Organization's (ILO) Social Protection Floor Initiative,[1] one of the objectives identified in the global programme for a Decent Work Agenda, calls on states to extend their social security systems in line with ILO Conventions and Recommendations. Recommendation No 202 of the Social Protection Floors[2] specifically declares that states should establish social security guarantees by law, ensuring that individuals have access to essential health care and basic income security, to which end social security systems should include universal benefit schemes.

In Europe,[3] where states typically have advanced social security systems, social protection reforms are being implemented in a context of economic crisis and budgetary restraint. Those governments that have had to be bailed out or which are suffering serious problems of financial stability—as

[1] International Labour Organization (ILO), *Social Security for All: Building Social Protection Floors and Comprehensive Social Security Systems* (Geneva, ILO, 2012).

[2] ILO Recommendation R202: Social Floors Protection Recommendation (Recommendation Concerning National Floors of Social Protection) (101st Conference Session, Geneva, 14 July 2012).

[3] Mechanisms for extending social security systems are necessarily different in developing countries where most of the population does not have access to social security and where the economic and institutional fabric is weaker. See Filali Meknassi, R, 'Extending Social Security in the Developing Countries: Between Universal Entitlement and the Selectiveness of International Standards' (2006) 27(2) *Comparative Labor Law & Policy Journal* 207.

is the case of Spain—have had to introduce austerity measures,[4] under the supervision of the European Union. These measures affect above all the most vulnerable groups of society who have seen themselves deprived of the basic income security that can guarantee their most fundamental needs.[5] Moreover, some of these austerity measures infringe the social rights recognised in the International Covenant on Economic, Social and Cultural Rights (CESCR)[6] and in the European Social Charter,[7] as their respective treaty committees have observed.

The UN's gender mainstreaming approach[8] in turn serves as a key instrument to analyse the distinct impact that social security reforms have on men and women. Specifically, austerity measures that impact on the adequacy of social security benefits, preventing individuals from attaining minimum standards of living, have a greater negative effect on women who 'are disproportionately represented among the poor'.[9]

This chapter analyses the Spanish legal reforms that have been introduced in response to the economic crisis in the areas of labour relations and pensions and examines their impact on gender equality. The adoption of a gender mainstreaming approach to the austerity measures implemented by governments in their attempt to overcome the crisis and, more specifically, to the measures that affect the reconciliation of work and family life, social protection and support for employability[10] should enable us to

[4] These include, among others: measures that reduce social expenditure (eg, cash benefits and public services), cuts in public sector employment and raised taxes and contributions. Leventi, C et al, 'Research Note 8/2010—Modelling the Distributional Effects of Austerity Measures: The Challenges of a Comparative Perspective' (European Commission, 5 December 2010).

[5] The percentage of the Spanish population that is at risk of poverty or social exclusion has increased nearly five points between 2007 and 2012 (23.3%–28.2%). Eurostat (European Commission), available at: epp.eurostat.ec.europa.eu/portal/page/portal/eurostat/home/.

[6] UN Committee on Economic, Social and Cultural Rights (CESCR), *Consideration of Reports Submitted by States Parties under Articles 16 and 17 of the Covenant: Concluding Observations of the Committee on Economic, Social and Cultural Rights: Spain*, 6 June 2012, UN Doc E/C.12/ESP/CO/5.

[7] European Committee of Social Rights, Conclusions XX-2 (2013), Spain (Articles 3, 11, 12, 13 and 14 of the 1961 European Social Charter Council of Europe, January 2014), available at: www.coe.int/t/dghl/monitoring/socialcharter/conclusions/State/SpainXX2_en.pdf.

[8] Understood as the promotion of 'gender sensitive actions in all policy areas and at all levels of decision-making'. Economic and Social Council, *Report of the Economic and Social Council*, 18 September 1997, UN Doc A/52/3, Ch IV 'Gender Mainstreaming'.

[9] Report of the Advisory Group chaired by Michelle Bachelet, Convened by the International Labour Organization (ILO) with the Collaboration of the World Health Organization, *Social Protection Floor: for a Fair and Inclusive Globalization* (Geneva, ILO, 2011) 58. For more on the impact of the current economic crisis on women, see International Labour Organization (ILO), *Report VI: Gender Equality at the Heart of Decent Work* (Geneva, ILO, 2009).

[10] Rodríguez, LM, 'Unemployment and Difficulties for Reconciliation. Key Gender Issues in the Economic Crisis in Spain' (2013) 2(4) *About Gender Rivista Internazionali di Studi di Genere*, available at: www.aboutgender.unige.it/ojs/index.php/generis/article/view/86.

determine the gap in gender equality,[11] and the human development and empowerment capabilities[12] that both sexes will be able to call upon once we have emerged from the crisis. Consideration will also be given to the extent to which these measures adhere to the 'flexicurity' model and pension sustainability, as proposed by the European Union. Finally, the chapter considers the extent to which the strongly labour-market oriented policies on reconciliation and pensions being promoted in Europe may conflict with the gendered human rights approach of international social standards—most specifically the right to social security.

Numerous studies[13] analysing gender issues in public policies of social protection show—with varying degrees of intensity depending on the specific welfare model being applied and the social and cultural reality of each country—a lack of neutrality in terms of the ways they impact on men and women respectively. This lack of neutrality towards the genders is particularly evident in the way that social protection policies regard the social roles that men and women assume in relation to the family and the workplace. In this way, most European social security systems respect formal equality on the grounds of sex, yet at the same time ignore the social and economic subordination of women and the traditional division of social roles, which leads to discrimination against women.[14] This situation has given rise to numerous reflections and proposals on the need to mainstream gender in social security policies, so that they might respond to the various necessities, experiences and life models of women.[15]

[11] This is the strategy that the authorities should adopt in all regulatory frameworks affecting the family and gender inequality. In the words of López, Chacartegui and Canton: 'What is needed is a gender mainstreaming strategy that integrates in a holistic regulatory framework all policies related to families and gender inequality'. López, J, Chacartegui, C and Cantón, CJ, 'Social Rights in Changing Labor Markets: Caring for Caregivers in the European Union' in KVW Stone and H Arthurs (eds), *Rethinking Workplace Regulation: Beyond the Standard Contract of Employment* (New York, Russell Sage Foundation, 2013) 345.

[12] On the theory of human development linked to capabilities and women's empowerment, see Nussbaum, MC, *Women and Human Development: The Capabilities Approach* (Cambridge, Cambridge University Press, 2000); and Sen, A, 'Human Rights and Capabilities' (2005) 6(2) *Journal of Human Development* 151.

[13] Feminist literature on social protection is broad and includes studies primarily within sociology, political science and economics. Without seeking to be exhaustive, see, eg, Lewis, J, 'Gender and the Development of Welfare Regimes' (1992) 2(3) *Journal of European Social Policy* 159; Daly, M, 'Paid Work, Unpaid Work and Welfare: Towards a Framework for Studying Welfare State Variation' in TP Boje and A Leira (eds), *Gender, Welfare State and the Market: Towards a New Division of Labour* (London, Routledge, 2000); Leira, A, 'Combining Work and Family: Nordic Policy Reforms in the 1990s' in TP Boje and A Leira (eds), *Gender, Welfare State and the Market: Towards a New Division of Labour* (London, Routledge, 2000); and Sainsbury, D, 'Gender and Social-Democratic Welfare States' in D Sainsbury (ed), *Gender and Welfare State Regimes* (Oxford, Oxford University Press, 1999).

[14] See Luckhaus, L, 'Equal Treatment, Social Protection and Income Security for Women' (2000) 139(2) *International Labour Review* 149.

[15] This approach is taken by Goldblatt and Lamarche, in this collection.

Feminist studies of the welfare state, in general, concur with the idea that models of social protection[16] are much fairer from a gender perspective when social rights are linked to the individual as a citizen irrespective of their participation in the labour market and the role they fulfil in the family. The international recognition of the right to social security requires that it be considered a personal and inalienable right, and that the link between social security systems and notions of citizenship and universality be defended.[17]

Yet, by contrast, we see that European Union guidelines on pensions and social security recommend that Member States seek to strengthen their contributory pension schemes so as to guarantee future financial stability.[18] As the European Commission recognises, pension benefits 'will increasingly depend upon the workers' entire career'.[19] In short, an individual's work history, and the contributions they make over their lifetime, is being given increasing importance in determining their level of protection and their benefit entitlements.

In general, social security systems based on contributory schemes perpetuate the differences between men and women in the labour market, since social protection is a fairly faithful reflection of their respective situations. Thus, work-related benefits are better suited to the traditional male professional career path, as they require a long history of uninterrupted, full-time employment. In fact, this model of social protection marginalises women,

[16] In the European Union the term 'social protection' is given different meanings depending on the context in which it is being employed—be it statistical (see the definition of the European System of Integrated Social Protection Statistics), political or normative. The Founding Treaties (art 151 of the Treaty on the Functioning of the European Union, art 34 of the Charter of Fundamental Rights of the European Union) adopt a strict definition of 'social protection' that coincides with the notion of 'social security' understood both as 'social insurance' and 'social assistance'. Art 34 of the Charter distinguishes between the right to social security and the right to social assistance. Although the list is not closed, the right to social security is formed by a series of classic risks ('in cases such as maternity, illness, industrial accidents, dependency or old age, and in the case of loss of employment') that are covered by both work-related and non-contributory benefits and social services. Social assistance has a more universal character referring to the 'right to social and housing assistance so as to ensure a decent existence for all those who lack sufficient resources'. See Moussis, N, *Access to European Union: Law, Economics and Policies,* 20th edn (UK, Intersentia Ltd, 2013) 247.

[17] Universal Declaration of Human Rights (UDHR) (adopted 10 December 1948) 217 A (III), arts 22, 25; International Covenant on Economic, Social and Cultural Rights (ICESCR) (adopted 16 December 1966, entered into force 3 January 1976) 993 UNTS 3, arts 9, 10, 11; and UN Committee on Economic, Social and Cultural Rights (CESCR), *General Comment No 19: The Right to Social Security (art 9)*, 4 February 2008, UN Doc E/C.12/GC/19.

[18] European Commission (EC), 'Green Paper: Towards Adequate, Sustainable and Safe European Pension Systems' (COM(2010) 365 final, Brussels, EC, 7 July 2010); European Commission (EC), 'White Paper: An Agenda for Adequate, Safe and Sustainable Pensions' (COM(2012) 55 final, Brussels, EC, 16 February 2012).

[19] European Commission, *Progress on Equality between Women and Men in 2011: A Europe 2020 Initiative* (Luxembourg, European Union, 2012).

and leaves many that do not perform paid work, or who work in the informal economy,[20] unprotected.

In Spain, current successive reforms to the pension system are following this same approach. In the analysis of legislative policy that follows, the key features of the labour and pension reforms implemented in Spain during the current period of economic crisis will be examined. Particular focus will be given to their impact on the socio-occupational situation of women.

Beginning with the situation of working women in Spain, what we notice immediately is the sustained increase in their participation in the labour market since first entering en masse in the 1980s. Statistics confirm a steady rise, even in times of recession, in the number of active women in the Spanish labour market, as well as an increase in their levels of qualification. Today, in fact, they are better educated than men; prompting predictions of improved job prospects for women in the future.[21]

This positive trend should not, however, disguise the position of inequality suffered by women in the labour market, nor the fact that women in Spain continue to have a considerably lower activity rate than that of men (53.31 per cent versus 65.9 per cent in 2013)[22] in keeping with the EU mean.[23] Although the socio-occupational position of women is not homogeneous, dependent to a considerable degree on their level of education, certain qualitative aspects of their respective working conditions can be identified. These factors highlight the distance separating men and women, and include: the concentration of women in productive sectors characterised by highly precarious labour conditions; the wage gap with men; and women's greater incidence of temporary employment and unemployment.

Yet, for the first time since 2010, this difference has been tempered somewhat due to the massive destruction of jobs in more traditionally male sectors, such as construction and industry, as a result of the economic crisis. Additionally, women experience greater disruptions in their work histories

[20] Informal economy has been defined by the International Labour Conference as 'all economic activities by workers and economic units that are—in law or in practice—not covered or insufficiently covered by formal arrangements'. International Labour Organization (ILO), *Resolution Concerning Decent Work and the Informal Economy* (90th Session, ILO, 2002) para 3.

[21] Economic and Social Council (ESC), *Tercer Informe Sobre la Situación de la Mujeres en la Realidad Sociolaboral Española* (Informe No 1/2011, ESC, 2012).

[22] *Instituto Nacional de Estadística* (Spanish Statistical Office), available at: www.ine.es.

[23] The percentage of inactive women in the European labour market (who are neither employed nor seeking work) is 14 points higher than the corresponding figure for European men, and more than half of these women of childbearing age remain outside the labour market because of their family duties. European Institute for Gender Equality (EIGE), *Review of the Implementation of the Beijing Platform for Action in the Area F: Women and the Economy—Reconciliation of Work and Family Life as a Condition of Equal Participation in the Labour Market* (Luxembourg, EIGE, 2011).

and are much more likely to undertake part-time employment, which can be explained by the continuing unequal distribution of family responsibilities.

The differing socio-occupational situations of men and women are reflected in the level of protection provided for them by social security, being markedly lower for women than for men.[24] Despite the fact that in the Spanish social security system the number of male pensioners is practically the same as that of women, the gender inequality becomes evident if we consider the type of pension and the degree of protection provided.[25] In the case of retirement pensions, which provide the highest degree of protection in the system, the majority of beneficiaries are male (in December 2011, 65 per cent of pensioners were men). Conversely, in the case of those receiving widows' pensions and what was the compulsory old-age and disability insurance, which provides the lowest degree of protection in the system, more than 95 per cent of beneficiaries are women. Moreover, in the case of retirement pensions, in 2011 female pensioners received on average 61.41 per cent of what their male counterparts received.[26]

Despite its apparent neutrality, the social security system as it currently operates has unequal consequences for women and men. The question posed here is whether any of these differences can be identified in legal terms as being discriminatory. Both European legislation and the case law of the European Court of Justice on equality and non-discrimination on the grounds of sex offer frames of reference for addressing this question. As will be shown, the problem does indeed assume a legal nature due to the notion of 'indirect discrimination', which has been recognised on various occasions by the Court of Justice of the European Union (CJEU)[27] and the Spanish Constitutional Court in cases involving the social protection of part-time workers.

The subject matter dealt with in this chapter is 'especially delicate'[28] and has yet to be tackled fully. This is recognised in the cited judgments of the CJEU, which state that the achievement of equal rights between men

[24] Pérez del Río, MT, 'Mujer y Protección Social en España' (1998) 1 *Revista de Derecho Social* 39.

[25] Employment and Social Security Ministry, Statistics, Budgets and Studies, available at: www.seg-social.es/Internet_6/Estadistica/index.htm.

[26] Figures provided by the Employment and Social Security Ministry, 'Annual Statistics Report 2011', available at: www.empleo.gob.es/estadisticas/ANUARIO2011/welcome.htm.

[27] See Case C-96/80 *Jenkins v Kingsgate (Clothing Productions) Ltd* [1981] ECR 911; Case C-286/85 *Norah McDermott and Ann Cotter v Minister for Social Welfare and Attorney-General* [1987] ECR 1453; Case C-171/88 *Rinner-Kühn v FWW Spezial-Gebäudereiningung* [1989] ECR 2743; Case C-102/88 *Ruzius-Wilbrink v Bedrijfsvereniging voor Overheidsdiensten* [1989] ECR 4311; and Case C-395/08 *Bruno Pettini and others* [2010] ECR I-5119.

[28] Fernández López, MF, 'Igualdad y Sistemas de Seguridad Social: Efectos de la Incorporación de las Mujeres al Trabajo' (2007) 1 *Revista del Ministerio de Trabajo y Asuntos Sociales* 116.

and women could lead to a financial imbalance in the pension system. Furthermore, for indirect discrimination to exist, the discriminatory treatment, as opposed to the apparent neutrality of the rule, must be demonstrated by examining practical aspects of its implementation, or de facto situations.[29]

The problems of indirect discrimination in the field of social security seem to highlight two particular situations in which women appear to be under-protected. First, there is a predominance of female workers in groups working in the most precarious economic sectors and receiving less social protection than others. This is particularly evident in the social security system provided for domestic workers and for care providers for dependants, and highlights the need to review the system of social protection of these groups. Second, the eligibility requirements for receiving contributory benefits tend to be prejudicial to women in precarious jobs, particularly those in part-time employment. This is another area in need of review.

However, an adjustment of legal protection cannot alone resolve the structural problem caused by the lack of income that above all affects women, and which lies within the narrow channels of formal equality 'that imperfectly levels a specific playing field between certain groups of male and female workers'.[30] For this reason, rectifying the de facto inequalities that exist between men and women requires that states extend their nets of social protection to cover the various ways in which women participate in unpaid jobs, as well as to include the most socially disadvantaged groups.[31]

CONSTRUCTING GENDER EQUALITY AND SOCIAL SECURITY IN THE EUROPEAN UNION

The European Union and the Member States, 'having in mind fundamental social rights such as those set out' in the European Social Charter … and in the Community Charter of the Fundamental Social Rights of Workers', should have as their goals the promotion of employment, improved living and working conditions and proper social protection (article 151 of the Treaty on the Functioning of the European Union, TFEU).[32]

[29] Brocas, A, Cailloux, AM and Oget, V, *Women and Social Security. Progress Towards Equality of Treatment* (Geneva, International Labour Organization, 1990) 49: 'One of the greatest difficulties … is to distinguish between situations which really do constitute indirect discrimination, that is, which have their origins in social security provisions as such, and those which reflect pre-existing inequalities—unequal remuneration, for instance'.

[30] Goldblatt and Lamarche, in this collection.

[31] See Otto, in this collection; and Fredman, in this collection.

[32] Consolidated Version of the Treaty on the Functioning of the European Union (TFEU) [2008] OJ C115/47.

The Charter of the Fundamental Rights of the European Union[33] recognises the right to social security benefits and social services 'in accordance with the rules laid down by Union law and national laws and practices'. The Charter does not, however, employ the traditional language of the international treaties that recognise fundamental rights as individual rights. It only recognises an entitlement to the social advantages of those 'residing and moving legally within the European Union'. The rights recognised in the Charter are addressed to the institutions of the European Union and to the Member States only when they are implementing Union law and, under no circumstances, do they suppose a change in the scope of their established powers (article 51 EU Charter of Fundamental Rights). The Charter guarantees a minimum level of protection with respect to the human rights recognised in international treaties to which all the Member States are party, while nothing in the Charter can be interpreted as restricting or adversely affecting these international standards (article 53 EU Charter of Fundamental Rights). Article 53 explicitly refers to the European Convention for the Protection of Human Rights and indirectly to the European Social Charter,[34] with the implication that the European legislator must respect the basic social rights recognised in them.[35]

Social security is an area that falls under the exclusive competence of the Member States, so that the European Union can only intervene under the principle of subsidiarity.[36] Based on this premise, the Social Security Directives see the field as falling under the shared competence of the European Union and the Member States, which need to agree to regulate such matters by applying the rule of unanimity.[37] The European Union has promoted governance through an open method of coordination, not only in the field of employment, but also in those related to policies of social inclusion and social protection, principally health care and pensions. This

[33] Charter of Fundamental Rights of the European Union [2000] OJ C364/01.

[34] Schlachter, M, 'The European Social Charter: Could it Contribute to a More Social Europe?' in N Contouris and M Freedland (eds), *Resocialising Europe in a Time of Crisis* (Cambridge, Cambridge University Press, 2013). The author also notes the importance that the case law of the European Court of Human Rights, which takes the European Social Charter as a necessary reference for the effective implementation of the rights recognised in the European Convention for the Protection of Human Rights, based on the theory of the 'indivisibility of human rights', would have for the enforcement of social rights in the framework of the European Union.

[35] However, although the Commission has recommended that Member States ratify the ILO Conventions in order to raise the level of social protection, some have yet to ratify a number of basic ILO standards. Casale, G, 'International Labour Standards and EU Labour Law' in N Contouris and M Freedland (eds), *Resocialising Europe in a Time of Crisis* (Cambridge, Cambridge University Press, 2013) 82.

[36] Consolidated Version of the Treaty on European Union (TEU) [2010] OJ C83/01, art 5(3).

[37] Consolidated Version of the Treaty on the Functioning of the European Union, above n 32, art 153.

means that the Member States are subject to the guidelines and common objectives established by the European institutions.

At the beginning of the 1990s in its application of the Community Charter of the Fundamental Social Rights of Workers, the European Commission recommended[38] that the Member States agree to common criteria concerning social protection so as to guarantee a minimum floor of protection, while respecting the diversity of national systems. This convergence has not received the backing of the Member States and European regulations provide for the coordination of national social security systems within the framework of the free movement of persons. There is only one European social security right regarding questions of gender equality that is applied to completely national situations.[39]

As for gender equality, this constitutes a fundamental value and right in the European Union in accordance with the provisions to that effect in the founding treaties[40] and in the European Charter of Fundamental Rights.[41] However, the value of gender equality has undergone an intense and expansive development in European law and policy since the signing of the founding Treaty of Rome in 1957, which recognised the right to equal pay for men and women. In 1999, the Amsterdam Treaty amended the founding treaties and committed the European Union to the promotion of gender equality and gender mainstreaming in all its activities and policies, and in turn legitimised the positive actions of Member States in the field of employment.

The Gender Equality Directives have established a common basis for national regulations concerning the principal notions of anti-discrimination laws in matters of employment and working conditions,[42] the self-employed,[43] social security[44] and the access to and supply of goods and services.[45] This framework has been completed by Directives on the protection

[38] European Council, *Recommendation on Common Criteria Concerning Sufficient Resources and Social Assistance in Social Protection Systems,* 24 June 1992, Recommendation 92/441/EEC, OJ L245.

[39] Moussis, above n 16, at 248.

[40] Consolidated Version of the Treaty on European Union, above n 36, arts 2 and 3; and Consolidated Version of the Treaty on the Functioning of the European Union, above n 32, arts 8, 10, 19 and 157.

[41] Charter of Fundamental Rights, above n 33, art 23.

[42] Directive 2006/54/EC on the Implementation of the Principle of Equal Opportunities and Equal Treatment of Men and Women in Matters of Employment and Occupation (Recast) [2006] OJ L204/23.

[43] Directive 2010/41/EU on the Application of the Principle of Equal Treatment Between Men and Women Engaged in an Activity in a Self-Employed Capacity and Repealing Council Directive 86/613/EEC [2010] OJ L180/1.

[44] Directive 79/7/EEC on the Progressive Implementation of the Principle of Equal Treatment for Men and Women in Matters of Social Security [1979] OJ L006.

[45] Directive 2004/113/EC Implementing the Principle of Equal Treatment Between Men and Women in the Access to and Supply of Goods and Services [2004] OJ L373/37.

of pregnant workers and workers who have recently given birth or are breastfeeding[46] and those on parental leave.[47] Likewise, the Directives on atypical employment (part-time work, fixed-term contracts and temporary agency work) have been given a gendered application by the CJEU, particularly with regard to part-time work.

Directive 79/7/EEC[48] on the equal treatment for men and women in statutory social security schemes establishes the norm for regulating the prohibition of sex discrimination in matters of social security in the EU, and will be discussed here in some length. Also of great importance are the two Gender Equality Directives referring to privately run schemes: Directive 86/378/EC (recast as Directive 2006/54/EC)[49] on occupational social security schemes, and Directive 2004/113/EC[50] on equality in the access to and supply of goods and services. The first of these directives recognises the right to equality in complementary protection of a collective and professional nature; in other words, it essentially refers to occupational pension schemes. Its application has led to the development of a consolidated and persuasive case law. The CJEU has included occupational pension schemes within the notion of wage and has subjected them to rules of non-wage discrimination on the grounds of sex.[51] Directive 2004/113/EC also concerns social protection, as it prohibits the use of sex as an actuarial factor for the purposes of insurance and related financial services when it leads to differences in individuals' premiums and benefits.[52] The same rule however allows Member States to derogate from the principle of equal treatment with regard to insurance contracts under certain circumstances.[53] Although the CJEU in an important ruling declared this Directive invalid, as it is not subject to a time limit.[54] This ruling should be read in relation to the CJEU doctrine, according to which the parties cannot claim that, on average, women enjoy a longer life expectancy to justify differences in treatment that may be prejudicial to them, 'since that is a factor directly based on sex

[46] Directive 92/85/EEC on the Introduction of Measures to Encourage Improvements in the Safety and Health at Work of Pregnant Workers and Workers Who Have Recently Given Birth or are Breastfeeding [1992] OJ L348.

[47] Directive 2010/18/EU Implementing the Revised Framework Agreement on Parental Leave Concluded by BUSINESSEUROPE, UEAPME, CEEP and ETUC and Repealing Directive 96/34/EC [2010] OJ L68/13.

[48] Directive 79/7/EEC, above n 44.

[49] Directive 2006/54/EC, above n 42.

[50] Directive 2004/113/EC, above n 45.

[51] See, eg, Case C-170/84 *Bilka v Weber von Hartz* [1986] ECR 1607; Case C-262/88 *Barber v Guardian Royal Exchange Assurance Group* [1990] ECR I-01889.

[52] Directive 2004/113/EC, above n 45, art 5(1).

[53] *Ibid*, at art 5(2).

[54] See Case C-236/09 *Association Belge des Consommateurs Test-Achats and Others* [2011] ECR I-773.

which, in the light of the case law of the Court of Justice, cannot, by its nature, be taken into account'.[55]

Directive 79/7/EEC was adopted in order to address the social security rules that were directly or indirectly prejudicial to women, principally because of their marital or family status. However, the application of this Directive has been extremely limited, due first and foremost to its restrictive material and personal scope. The Directive applies to the working population and the risks that it addresses are of a professional, occupational nature.[56] Thus, Directive 79/7/EEC does not include welfare benefits, except for the 'social assistance' provided when supplementing or replacing these professional risks.[57] As such, the Directive excludes from its scope women who have never worked or who had to interrupt their careers because of family responsibilities.[58] Similarly, it does not contemplate unpaid work; protecting 'a male model of life'[59] and, in turn, only taking into account the professional-contributory model of protection.

To this consideration of Directive 79/7/EEC should be added the fact that it fails to consider death and survivors' benefits and family benefits, despite the fact that these benefits are precisely those for which distinctions on the grounds of the sex of the beneficiary are most frequently made. Additionally, the Directive provides for significant exceptions to the application of the principle of equality in certain matters, such as the determination of pensionable age, the granting of benefits to persons raising children and the granting of benefits 'by virtue of the derived entitlements of a wife'.[60] It can be seen that the Directive qualifies benefits typically accorded to women as exceptions to the principle of equality, rather than as positive actions. On the basis of this reading it can be concluded that this Directive have been interpreted restrictively by the CJEU.

The case law of the CJEU concerning indirect discrimination in matters of social security has typically focused on two main situations: when social security rules penalise women within the prevailing male breadwinner model and when they treat part-time workers unequally. However, the CJEU has shown great caution and sought to avoid any possible economic consequences that might derive from its decisions, being governed by the fear of interfering in the social policies of national legislatures.

[55] Case C-317/93 *Nolte v Landesversicherungsanstalt Hannover* [1995] ECR I-4625; Case 123/10 *Brachner* [2011] ECR I-10003.

[56] Directive 79/7/EEC, above n 44, art 3(1)(a).

[57] See, eg, Case C-243/90 *Smithson* [1992] ECR I-00467; Case C-228/94 *Atkins v Wrekin District Council* [1996] ECR I-03633.

[58] See Case C-48/88 *Achterberg-te Riele ea v Sociale Verzekeringsbank* [1989] ECR 01963; and Case C-77/95 *Züchner v Handelskrankenkasse Bremen* [1996] ECR I-05689.

[59] Cousins, M, 'Equal Treatment and Social Security' (1994) 19(2) *European Law Review* 142.

[60] Directive 79/7/EEC, above n 44, art 7(1).

In this sense, the CJEU has not considered regulations that conditioned access to or increased the amount of benefits on the grounds of marital status or the income earned by the applicant's spouse as being discriminatory,[61] despite recognising that such measures are more prejudicial to women than they are to men. It also considered the Dutch regulation requiring a minimum income in order to be entitled to a benefit for incapacity for work (in the *Posthuma-van Damme* case[62] which revised the doctrine of the *Roks* case)[63] as being compatible with Community law.

In the specific instance of the social protection of part-time workers, the CJEU has recognised situations of discrimination in certain cases.[64] However, the Court did not recognise indirect discrimination in the German social security rules that excluded employment of a minor or short-term nature from having any benefit entitlement,[65] despite the fact that the doctrine governing part-time work could be readily applied to this type of employment. In these cases, the Court ruled as reasonable the arguments put forth by the German government in defence of its employment policy and its need to achieve budgetary equilibrium.

In two recent decisions concerning indirect discrimination and social security, the CJEU has examined the equality test more strictly. In the *Elbal Moreno* case[66] the Court ruled that Spanish legislation requiring part-time workers to pay contributions for a longer period than full-time workers in order to access retirement pensions was incompatible with the principle of gender equality. The Court gave a similar ruling in the *Brachner* case[67] which considered an Austrian law excluding pensioners from entitlement to the compensatory supplement if their income, including that of the spouse forming part of their household, exceeded the standard rate; a situation that mostly affected women.

Although the legal instruments discussed above have resulted in significant advances in the recognition of rights, they are obviously insufficient to overcome the structural inequalities faced by European men and women. A clear example of this is found in the so-called atypical Work Directives whose 'effectiveness in bringing workers in non-standard employment

[61] See Case C-30/85 *Teuling v Bedrijfsvereniging voor de Chemische Industrie* [1987] ECR 02497; Case C-229/89 *Commission v Belgium* [1991] ECR I-02205; and Case C-226/91 *Molenbroek v Sociale Verzekeringsbank* [1992] ECR I-05943.

[62] Case C-280/94 *Posthuma-van Damme* [1006] ECR 179.

[63] Case C-343/92 *Roks and Others* [1994] ECR I-00571.

[64] See Case C-102/88 *Ruzius-Wilbrink* [1989] ECR 4311.

[65] Case C-317/93 *Nolte v Landesversicherungsanstalt Hannover* [1995] ECR I-4625; and Case C-444/93 *Megner and Scheffel v Innungskrankenkasse Vorderpfalz* [1995] ECR I-04741.

[66] Case C-385/11 *Ebal Moreno* [2012], 22 November 2012.

[67] Case 123/10 *Brachner* [2011] ECR I-10003.

within the scope of employment protection legislation or social protection systems is questionable'.[68]

In this dialogue between legislation and case law for the construction of the right to gender equality in matters related to social security, indirect discrimination emerges somewhat timidly as a legal instrument for eliminating inequities and levelling up to the benefits of the most advantaged.[69] However, it is true that the European Court of Justice, in its decisions concerning the rules of social protection that have a more negative impact on women, has not strictly adhered to the criteria of proportionality.[70] According to the Court, these rules can be considered reasonable and justifiable on the grounds of guaranteeing financial stability and of achieving social policy goals.

Nevertheless, this would not rule out the possibility that drastic reductions in social security benefits, which caused them to fall below the poverty threshold, could be considered discriminatory to women given their greater impact on their living conditions. A reference in European international law, although not linked to gender issues, is that of the non-binding case law of the European Committee of Social Rights delivered via its collective complaint procedure.[71]

At the political level, the European Union has undertaken an institutional commitment to advance equality through the use of various policies and strategies, ranging from the promotion of equal opportunities and the principle of gender mainstreaming, to ensuring the implementation of positive action 'for the underrepresented sex' in matters of employment.[72] The European commitment to policies of equality has been most clearly influenced by the concepts and approaches developed in the UN World Summits on Women held in Nairobi (1985) and Beijing (1995). This is especially so with regard to the

[68] Ashiagbor, D, 'Promoting Precariousness? The Response of EU Employment Policies to Precarious Work' in J Fudge and R Owens (eds), *Precarious Work, Women, and the New Economy* (Oxford, Hart Publishing, 2006).

[69] Suk, J, 'Work–Family Balance and Gender Equality: Pension Reform and Antidiscrimination Law' in KVW Stone and H Arthurs (eds), *Rethinking Workplace Regulation: Beyond the Standard Contract of Employment* (New York, Russell Sage Foundation, 2013) 328.

[70] On the principle of proportionality and the justiciability of social rights in reference to constitutional litigation, see Contiades, X and Fotiadou, A, 'Social Rights in the Age of Proportionality: Global Economic Crisis and Constitutional Litigation' (2012) 10(3) *International Journal of Constitutional Law* 660.

[71] Some of the decisions of the European Committee of Social Rights have ruled certain drastic austerity measures to be contrary to the European Social Charter. This was the case in the Greek government's pension reforms which were considered not to have respected the essence of the rights guaranteed by the European Social Charter. European Committee of Social Rights, *General Federation of Employees of the National Electric Power Corporation (GENOP-DEI)/Confederation of Greek Civil Servants' Trade Unions (ADEDY) v Greece*, Decision No 66/2011 and 65/2011.

[72] Directive 2006/54/EC, above n 42, art 3; and Consolidated Version of the Treaty on the Functioning of the European Union, above n 32, art 157.

need to achieve the greater social empowerment of women and to promote gender-sensitive actions in all policy areas and at all levels of decision making.[73] Indeed, as provided by articles 9 and 10,[74] equality between men and women should be upheld in all areas and activities of European public policy and at all levels of decision making, whether involving European, state or sub-state actors.

Since the beginning of the 1980s, the European Union has introduced successive strategic action plans aimed at achieving equality of opportunities. These have focused on goals including: gender mainstreaming in all the Union's policies, and placing the strategy at the heart of employment policies that integrate women in the workplace. Within the open method of coordination as applied to employment, scholars such as Rubery[75] see such integration from a gender perspective, thus offering an opportunity to implement policies of change in Europe. However, the European Union has recognised in its own evaluation of EU Employment Strategy that 'gender mainstreaming continues to be weak and non-systematic, lacking gender impact assessment of existing systems and new policy proposals' and that national level policy makers have yet to 'internalise the full implications of a mainstreaming approach'.[76]

POLICIES OF CO-RESPONSIBILITY IN SPAIN IN TIMES OF ECONOMIC CRISIS

The issue of gender inequality remains the main obstacle to women's economic empowerment, encompassing the unequal distribution of provision of care responsibilities. Recent statistics continue to show that the activity rates of European women with young children are significantly lower than those of men in similar circumstances.[77]

As many authors have pointed out, reconciliation between family life and work as a tool for achieving greater equality has been relegated to a position of secondary importance in European policies, where the main goal remains the creation of jobs for women.[78] European authorities insist on

[73] Economic and Social Council, above n 8.

[74] Consolidated Version of the Treaty on the Functioning of the European Union, above n 32, arts 9 and 10.

[75] Rubery, J, 'Gender Mainstreaming and Gender Equality in the EU: The Impact of the EU Employment Strategy' (2002) 33(5) *Industrial Relations Journal* 500.

[76] Ashiagbor, above n 68, at 96, citing European Commission (EC), 'Draft Joint Employment Report 2003/2004' (COM(2004) 24 final/2, Brussels, EC, 2004).

[77] European Institute for Gender Equality (EIGE), *The European Institute for Gender Equality Annual Report 2011* (Belgium, EIGE, 2012).

[78] Stratigaki, M, 'The Cooptation of Gender Concepts in EU Policies: The Case of "Reconciliation of Work and Family"' (2004) 11(1) *Social Politics* 30; and Lewis, J, *Work–Family Balance, Gender and Policy* (Cheltenham, Edward Elgar, 2009).

the need for women with family responsibilities to re-join the labour market. In keeping with this strategy, the Lisbon target of increasing the female participation rate should serve as an incentive for increased birth rates and for addressing the challenges of demographic ageing.

In the throes of the economic crisis in 2011, the European Council in Luxembourg opted to back reconciliation as the means of assisting European women to have children and to face the ageing challenge. It is worth noting that governments have abandoned the numerical targets of enrolment previously fixed at the Barcelona European Council in 2002, and now place greater emphasis on promoting family-friendly policies in the workplace without specifying their content. This current unilateral approach is very much aligned with the philosophy of corporate social responsibility and overlooks somewhat European commitments to greater investment in the outsourcing of care.

The recognition of the right to reconcile work and family life in the European Charter of Fundamental Rights under the heading of Family and Professional Life[79] is formulated in a very incomplete and restrictive way because it refers to basic guarantees that had previously been incorporated within several directives.[80] Directive 2010/18/EU on parental leave,[81] which replaces Directive 93/34/EC, recognises a series of workers' rights and guarantees linked to the enjoyment of parental leave, which should be upheld by the various national systems. Although the impact of the Directive on national laws has been discreet, it clearly has a symbolic value as it definitively ties reconciliation to questions of gender discrimination and promotes the co-responsible use of the right to leave among men.[82] Here, the Directive provides for the reservation of part of the parental leave to be taken up by fathers. However, the Directive recommends, but does not require Member States to cover the leave with social security benefits so as not to generate new obligations for states.[83] Recently, in the *Roca Alvárez* case,[84] the CJEU changed its doctrine concerning previous statements from that previously set forth in the *Hofmann* case.[85] The Court ruled that national legislation preventing a man from enjoying parental leave should be considered discriminatory on grounds of sex. One of the arguments forwarded by the Court was that such exclusions are likely to perpetuate the traditional roles allocated to men and women.

[79] Charter of Fundamental Rights, above n 33, art 33(2).

[80] Caracciolo Di Torella, E and Masselot, A, *Reconciling Work and Family Life in EU Law and Policy* (London, Palgrave Macmillan, 2010).

[81] Directive 2010/18/EU, above n 47.

[82] Ballester Pastor, I, 'La Era de la Corresponsabilidad: Los Nuevos Retos de la Política Antidiscriminatoria' (2012) 25 *Revista de Relaciones Laborales* 53.

[83] Case C-537/07 *Gómez-Limón Sánchez-Camacho* [2009] ECR I-06525.

[84] Case C-104/09 *Roca Alvárez* [2010] ECR I-08661.

[85] Case 184/83 *Ulrich Hofmann v Barmer Ersatzkasse* [1984] ECR 03N047.

The impact of the economic crisis in Spain has been well documented, showing that since 2008 it has advanced inexorably. This has left Spain with massive unemployment figures, as successive financial crises have undermined the value of the Spanish economy, threatening it with bankruptcy. Since 2008, successive governments, headed first by the Socialist Party and today by the Partido Popular have, with the approval of the European Union and other international economic organisations such as the Organisation for Economic Co-operation and Development (OECD) and International Monetary Fund (IMF), significantly reduced public spending with the aim of balancing the country's finances. The first cuts saw pay reductions for civil servants and the freezing of pensions. Parallel to this, both governments introduced liberalising reforms of the economy and labour relations, which, in the latter instance, led to a labour reform aimed primarily at lowering labour costs. The Spanish response to the economic crisis through a draconian budget has coincided with gender equality policies being virtually wiped off the political agenda.

The same fate has been shared by equality policies that seek to make men and women co-responsible in terms of unpaid time. The cuts implemented by Spain's central government and regions (the Autonomous Communities) have severely affected reconciliation policies. This is evidenced in the cuts to long-term care insurance for dependants, increases in kindergarten and nursery fees, suspension of the *Educa3* programme for schooling children under the age of three and the postponement of the extension of paternity leave.

These cutbacks in reconciliation policies represent a major setback in attempts to achieve gender equality. The statistics show that it is in countries that can provide more and better care infrastructure that women have achieved an economic independence comparable to that of men, and where the fight against the global phenomenon of the feminisation of poverty has been most successfully waged.[86] Moreover, state support in terms of care services reduces infant poverty and equalises opportunities from childhood onwards.[87]

The political commitment to strengthening the network of nurseries and care services for dependants serves to achieve two major goals in European employment policies. First, it strengthens the stability and presence in the labour market of women with family responsibilities, and second, it promotes the creation of new jobs, especially in the education and socio-health sectors.

[86] EIGE, *Review of the Implementation*, above n 23.

[87] Esping-Andersen, G, *The Incomplete Revolution: Adapting Welfare States to Women's New Roles* (Cambridge, Polity Press, 2009) 141.

It has yet to be seen whether current policies are extraordinary measures responding to exceptional circumstances, or whether they represent a paradigm shift. Moreover, Spain's pension and labour reforms of 2011–12 are markedly transversal in nature and not so visible from a gender perspective. Regardless, they will have a clearly negative impact on women. The 2012 labour reform, much applauded by the European institutions, has profoundly changed the rules and principles governing Spanish labour relations.

This reform has led to a strengthening of employers' powers when seeking to introduce changes in working conditions, and represents a marked increase in flexibility of labour relations, benefiting above all the employer. Indeed, certain specific legal provisions, such as those affecting part-time workers, infringe both constitutional and European law.[88]

Basically, the reform has reduced employers' costs of laying-off workers and has increased the flexibility of working conditions to the exclusive benefit of the interests of the company. This new regulation means that employers can unilaterally make substantial modifications to working conditions in areas such as working hours and wages. In doing so, they are not required to consult with the workers' representatives unless the measure affects a considerable number of employees. At the same time, companies can negotiate opt-out agreements, thus disassociating themselves from working conditions previously established under collective agreements. Other provisions that increase this so-called 'internal flexibility' include granting companies the right to establish the 'irregular distribution' of working hours without having to negotiate with workers, and allowing part-time workers to work overtime that is simply included in their 'additional' hours. The reform also lowers the costs of dismissal, eliminates the need for official administrative authorisation in the case of collective redundancies and increases the flexibility for the justification of layoffs for economic reasons; redundancies that can also be applied to civil servants.

In aspects directly related to reconciliation, the reform reduces the right of workers requesting a reduction in their working hours for reasons of childcare to make flexible work arrangements. Therefore, despite the sacrifice such workers have to make in terms of their wages, their chances of reconciling their work schedule with their family responsibilities are severely limited.

In short, the increased flexibility in labour relations gained at the expense of employees makes it especially difficult for those women with young children or dependants to enter and remain in paid work. Most of the

[88] López López, J, 'Elementos de Definición del Modelo de Relaciones Laborales por las Normas de OIT y Comunitarias: la Desestabilización por la Reforma Laboral (2012)' (2012) 57 *Revista de Derecho Social* 37.

new legislation adheres to the European flexicurity model, which is not specifically designed to create an 'inclusive labour market'. On the contrary, the reforms seem set to drive women with family responsibilities out of the labour market.

To the above, the issue of Spanish work schedules should be added. The irrational nature of work hours in Spain hinders enormously the reconciliation of work and personal life in almost all facets of day-to-day living, and causes serious health problems due to the inability of people, especially women workers, to control the time dedicated to their personal lives.

Many studies point to the urgent need to take legislative initiatives across the board that might rectify these dysfunctions.[89] A key question in this regard concerns the working day. Spain is one of the EU countries with the longest working hours. The work culture—reflected in the prolongation of the working day and in the irregularity and unpredictability of work schedules—forces women out of the labour market or into part-time work or casual jobs. When accompanied by the insufficient supply of care services, this explains why in the countries of southern Europe, such as Spain and Italy, the number of people working in domestic service is significantly higher than in central and northern Europe.[90] This also explains why grandparents are typically called upon to help in looking after their grandchildren in Spain. It should not be forgotten that the unequal division of family responsibilities leads not only to a gender wage gap but also to a gender gap in working hours, so that it is generally women who request flexible work arrangements.

It can thus be seen that the 2012 labour reform has served to further widen the gender gap in working hours. For this reason, it is becoming increasingly necessary to rethink the organisation of work so as to improve the competitiveness and productivity of enterprises, while ensuring workers have greater autonomy in relation to their working day. Labour laws need to promote a change in the organisation of the workplace based on a more rational use of time, which in turn might foster creativity and make use of the untapped talent of women, as opposed to the current work culture which fosters long working hours and unpredictable schedules.[91]

[89] Fagan, C, Hegewisch, A and Pillinger, J, *Out of Time: Why Britain Needs a New Approach to Working-Time Flexibility* (Manchester, Trade Union Congress, 2006); and Chacartegui, C, 'Tiempo de Trabajo, Racionalidad Horaria y Género: un Anàlisis en el Contexto Europeo' (2006) 2 *Revista de Relaciones Laborales* 1201.

[90] Those who work in this sector in all these countries present a common profile: they are mostly immigrant women, many of whom work in the informal economy. International Labour Organization (ILO), *Domestic Workers Across the World: Global and Regional Statistics and the Extent of Legal Protection* (Geneva, ILO, 2013).

[91] Fagan, Hegewisch and Pillinger, above n 89.

ADVANCES IN SOCIAL PROTECTION POLICIES AND THEIR IMPACT ON WOMEN: LIGHTS AND SHADOWS OF SPANISH PENSION REFORMS

The Spanish social security system has made some progress towards achieving gender equality, inasmuch as the legislator has eliminated any 'direct' discrimination. Thus, the system encompasses the individual nature of the right to social security, so that marital status is of no relevance when determining entitlement to most of the benefits, with the logical exception of widowhood, where the law currently provides protection not only to spouses, but also to cohabiting partners, regardless of their sexual orientation.

The Spanish health care system is a universal, public model that covers almost the entire population including those without a source of income. Previous legislation recognised the right of foreigners without legal residence to receive health care, provided they were enrolled on the municipal register. But since 2012 the government has excluded illegal aliens from the right to health care, except in cases of emergency, which is a clear step backwards in the process towards a universal model.[92]

In the Spanish social security system, contributory protection continues to have much more economic weight than that of social assistance. The development of social assistance has been belated and insufficient in terms of fulfilling the constitutional mandate of guaranteeing adequate assistance and benefits for all citizens.[93] Social assistance benefits are far from universal, as they are unable to cover the scarcity of resources and coincide with other contingencies required for an individual to be entitled to support, such as old age, disability, or family benefits. In the case of unemployment benefit, support is conditional on the prior exhaustion of the contributory benefits. By way of a second safety net, the Autonomous Communities provide social assistance in cases of poverty and social exclusion, although their budget allocations, regulations and degrees of coverage vary greatly from one region to the next.[94]

The women facing the greatest risk of social exclusion in Spain are those who are heads of single-parent households and elderly women who live alone, of which there are many in Spain. It should not be forgotten that this group, which comprises a large part of the phenomenon of the feminisation of poverty in Spain, has suffered the direct discrimination of Francoist legislation embodied in the numerous labour regulations and ordinances that directly discouraged or prohibited the employment of women once

[92] RD-Ley 16/2012, de 20 de abril del 2012, Official State Gazette, April 2012.
[93] Spanish Constitution, art 41 CE.
[94] Alarcón Caracuel, MR, *La Seguridad Social en España* (Pamplona, Aranzadi, 1999).

married or on becoming mothers.[95] Poverty among elderly women is manifest, above all in their lack of direct entitlement to pensions because they participated little, or not at all, in the labour market. Likewise, many elderly women are not entitled to social assistance either, because what is taken into consideration is the husband's income and so those who are widows do not receive very much in terms of benefits.

Moreover, the fact that a significant number of women find themselves excluded from the system of protection provided by Spain's social security is no exception to a global phenomenon that sees a greater concentration of women, especially immigrants, in informal sectors of the economy, working primarily as domestic employees or as caregivers. Such informality is also frequent in family businesses where the contribution of women remains invisible in the eyes of public authorities.

The new pension scheme has been introduced with the urgency dictated by the economic crisis, and has largely avoided entering into a broader political and social debate, being justified almost exclusively on the grounds of forecasts of demographic ageing.[96]

This restrictive reform can be added to those undertaken previously in other European countries, including Sweden, Germany, Italy and France, which have followed the recommendations of the European Union. It is worth remembering that the European Union, even in times of economic prosperity, has stressed the need for Member States to cut spending on pensions in order to cope with the progressive ageing of the European population and to ration public spending. This is reflected in the Green Paper on the need for sustainable pensions,[97] which calls for the prolongation of working life, discourages early retirement and calls for pensions that reflect the contributory efforts of people throughout their working lives. The goal is to prevent an increase in public spending on pensions, and to raise the activity rate, especially among older people approaching retirement age. This is the same line as in the revision of the Pact of Toledo in 2011,[98] which recommends strengthening the contributory nature of the system and bringing the effective or real age of retirement nearer to that of the statutory age. However, the parliamentary paper also foresees measures to strengthen solidarity for disadvantaged groups who are not specifically provided for under the reform.

[95] See Ortiz Heras, M, 'Mujer y Dictadura Franquista' (2006) 28 *Aposta: Revista de Ciencias Sociales* 1.

[96] Demographic forecasts in which many long-term variables are not so predictable. See in this sense the European Economic and Social Council Opinion on the 'Green Book on Pensions', January 2011, which raises concerns as to the demographic 'determinism' wielded by European authorities. European Commission, 'Green Paper', above n 18.

[97] European Commission, 'Green Paper', above n 18.

[98] Congreso de los Diputados, 'Boletín Oficial de las Cortes Generales' (No 513, 31 January 2011).

The pension reforms have been carried out by adopting two sets of regulations. The first, Law 27/1 August 2011, on updating, adapting and modernising the social security system,[99] significantly restricts entitlement to pensions and changes the way in which pensions are calculated, especially retirement pensions. This law was the result of a negotiated agreement between trade unions and employers' associations, while the second, Royal Decree Act 5/15 March 2013, to promote the continuity of the working lives of older workers and active ageing, was passed as an emergency measure by the government of the Partido Popular in response to comments made periodically by the Commission and the European Council encouraging Spain to reduce its deficit.[100]

In the lines that follow, the main innovations of the pension reforms (2011–13) will be analysed from a gender perspective, focusing on that of 2011 given its greater size.

During the reform negotiations, the Government, leading unions and employers' associations, made mutual concessions until they reached what some authors have called a 'defensive agreement'[101] from the unions' perspective. The Government, as it had proposed from the outset, raised the retirement age to 67 while maintaining the previous retirement age of 65 for workers who had paid their full quota of pension contributions. The door was not dramatically shut on early retirement as had originally been intended; rather, a new voluntary system was incorporated, although this possibility is reserved for those who have contributed over a period of many years and is counterbalanced by a reduction in the pension paid linked to their date of retirement.

The effect of the pension reform, which did not spark the types of social protests roused by other reforms, can be attributed to the dates scheduled for its implementation. This served to neutralise its negative impact on those close to the retirement age, as the new rules only apply to those retiring after January 2013, while the new provisions are to be gradually phased in over a period of up to 15 years.

The main provisions of Law 27/2011 can be summarised as follows: a normal retirement age of 67 will be applied to those who have not made social security contributions for 38 years and six months; the contribution period applied for calculating the retirement pension will be gradually

[99] Ministerio de la Presidencia, 'Official State Gazette (BOE)' (No 184, 2 August 2001).

[100] Council of the European Union (CEU), 'Recommendation with a View to Bringing an End to the Situation of an Excessive Government Deficit in Spain' (ECOFIN 669 UEM 252, Brussels, CEU, 9 July 2012); and European Commission (EC), 'Assessment of Action Taken by Spain in Response to the Council Recommendation of 10 July 2012' (COM(2012) 683 final, Brussels, EC, 14 November 2012).

[101] Baylos Grau, A, 'Reforma del Sistema de Pensiones en España' (*Insight*, 2011), available at: www.insightweb.it/web/content/reforma-del-sistema-de-pensiones-en-espa%C3%B1.

extended from 15 to 25 years; new less advantageous rules will be adopted for 'filling' the gaps in workers' contributions; and the percentages applicable to the regulatory base for determining the pension will be modified so that 37 years will now be required instead of 35 for the pension to reach 100 per cent.

Moreover, Law 27/2011 places a limit on the amount of supplementary benefits available before completing the minimum pension, which cannot exceed the amount of non-contributory pensions. These supplementary benefits improve contributory pensions (retirement, permanent disability, widows, orphans and relatives) until the minimum pension, as established in the annual budget, is reached. This serves as a tool of solidarity, correcting the strict contributory nature of the pension scheme and benefiting pensioners who have not made enough contributions to obtain the minimum legal amount. This supplementary benefit is incompatible for pensioners who obtain incomes for work or capital gains above a certain amount (fixed at €7063.07 in 2013).[102]

The gender impact of this measure is obvious, considering that most beneficiaries of these supplementary benefits are women. In 2009, 62 per cent of beneficiaries of supplementary benefits for minimum incomes were women, while the number of women collecting pensions from social security was almost half of all pensioners (48 per cent). This measure will also have an impact on the special social security scheme for domestic workers, which presently supplements pensions to reach the minimum level.

The new rules for calculating the retirement and permanent disability pensions significantly reduce the amount of benefits available. According to OECD estimates,[103] when the reform is complete, the replacement rate of the salaries of Spain's pensioners who have contributed regularly and worked full time will fall by 7.3 per cent, from 81.2 per cent to 73.9 per cent. In contrast, for those with long periods of interruption in their working lives, the rate could be 3 per cent higher (10.7 per cent). Thus, the greatest penalisations will be for those with the most irregular working lives.

Despite the clearly restrictive nature of these measures, pension reform has made three improvements to social protection that should have a particularly positive impact on women.

First, a legal formula has been introduced that seeks to compensate those with family responsibilities for the greater contributory effort required by the reform. Thus, periods before the birth or adoption of children, in which

[102] 'RD 1794/2010, de 30 de diciembre del 2011, on Revaluing the Pensions in the Social Security System and Other Social Benefits for 2011', BOE, 31 December 2011.

[103] Organisation for Economic Co-operation and Development (OECD), 'Spain: Country note: Pensions at a Glance 2011', available at: www.oecd.org/pensions/public-pensions/47367529.pdf.

there have been interruptions in contributions, are considered as having been paid. 'Fictitious' contributions, which can be claimed by either of the parents and which in 2019 will reach 270 days per child, cannot be used to complete the minimum contribution period and will only be recognised if there are gaps in contributions in periods identified as falling close to the date of birth or adoption of a child.

Arguably, the inclusion of this formula ought to be welcomed and can be added to others that similarly recognise periods in which there have been interruptions in contributions for reasons of childbirth or childcare, for example, the three years of leave of absence granted for caring for young children.[104] The essential difference though, with respect to the existing compensatory formulae, is that under this new provision the contributions cannot be used to fulfil the minimum period of contribution to be entitled to benefits. This is despite the fact that the reform has expanded the period required for partial retirement and new cases of early retirement to more than 30 years.

Without entering into the debate regarding the possible disincentives of this recognition for mothers who do not work, it seems that the compensation formula adopted by the Spanish legislator will be of limited operational use given the major constraints placed on its application.[105] Clearly the legislator could have provided more generous options, whereby the contributions of working mothers would be recognised regardless of whether they have interrupted their careers or not.

The second positive measure involves the integration of a special scheme for domestic workers within the general scheme. This special scheme for domestic workers has been distinguished since its foundation by the provision of less protection than is provided by all other social security schemes. The policy changes include improvements in protection in the case of sickness, requiring employers to pay the workers' contributions during the first few days of sick leave. The changes also include protection in cases of work-related accidents. However, domestic workers have no protection against unemployment, and less advantageous rules are applied to them than those applied to other workers in the case of gaps in their contributions. In turn, these improvements are accompanied by two important changes in the management and financing of this new special scheme. First, as a counterweight, the contribution base rate is gradually increased until a comparable rate is reached with that of the contributions made in the general system. Second, responsibility for paying the contributions is shifted

[104] Art 180, Royal Legislative Decree No 1/1994 of 20 June, approving the Codified Text of the General Law on Social Security.

[105] Ballester Pastor, A, 'Reformas en Materia de Protección Social e Impacto de Género: un Estudio Crítico' (2011) 112 *Temas Laborales* 51.

to the families who employ domestic workers regardless of the number of hours these workers are hired for and whether or not they work for other employers. Under the former system, domestic workers were responsible for paying their own contributions if they worked less than 80 hours per month and they did so for more than one employer.

This regulatory change has sought to promote equal social protection for domestic workers, bringing their conditions more closely in line with all other workers in paid employment. Although as was predicted, the increased tax burden resulting from the reform in such a precarious sector has led to a 'flight from the system'.[106] In fact, the new law has had the opposite effect to that sought by the legislator, since rather than exposing previously unreported employment there has been a noticeable decline in social security membership. This is why, barely one year after its entry into operation, the Government has modified the 2011 reform and re-established the obligation on workers working a marginal number of hours to pay their own contributions. This exposes the need for a full study of the impact of the reform on this sector of workers who receive the lowest benefits in the whole system (in December 2009 the mean benefit paid was just €464.86) and who suffer the precarious state of an informal sector characterised by great instability and irregularity.

The other expected improvement, announced in 2011 but still pending implementation, concerns the raising of the widow's pension to 60 per cent for those aged 65 or over and receiving a pension and with little income. The aim of this reform is to mitigate situations of poverty in old age. Despite the shortcomings and the limited scope of these improvements, they should be seen in a positive light. Although it must be recognised that they can do little to counter the gender impact derived from the reform as a whole.

Finally, Royal Decree Act 5/2013 amends certain aspects of the 2011 reform. Specifically, in response to observations from the EU, the measure increases restrictions on taking early retirement as provided for under Law 27/2011 in order to contain spending on pensions, while at the same time making it more difficult to take partial retirement. This possibility of taking early or partial retirement is reserved for those who have been contributing over long periods.

The above rules strengthen the links between the social security system and the labour market. In this brief overview of the key aspects of this reform it has been shown that the new pension regulations will impact most negatively on those with unstable careers and those who conduct their activity in precarious working conditions.

[106] *Ibid.*

Developments in the legal system regulating pensions accentuate even further the inequalities in the labour market, as it rewards those who have made their social security contributions over long periods and raises the bar for eligibility for those who have had more unstable, irregular careers. The people most affected, therefore, are those who belong to groups facing the greatest problems of labour market integration: young people, immigrants and women, especially those with fewer professional qualifications and greater family obligations.[107]

The set of rules for determining the age of retirement, and for calculating benefits and limiting supplementary benefits to reach a minimum pension, are set to have more negative repercussions on women in regard to their pensions. It remains to be seen whether this lowering of the level of protection will hinder predicted future trends towards convergence, if not equality, in the protection of the pensions of men and women.

One exception to this trend is the legal reform of the social protection of part-time workers that has been imposed by the aforementioned judgments of the EU Court of Justice[108] and Spain's Constitutional Court.[109] In essence, the new legal system[110] requires workers to fulfil minimum contribution periods that differ from those included in the general system in accordance with the length of time that they have been insured and working on a part-time basis. This measure seeks to put an end to the penalisation suffered by such workers when applying for social security benefits.

However, the chapter on restrictive reforms in the pension system does not yet appear to be complete. The present Government has recently commissioned an expert panel to present a proposal for pension reform. According to press reports, these experts are considering, among other measures, the possibility of introducing the sustainability factor in the calculation of retirement pensions and the adoption of new different mechanisms for updating pensions.

CONCLUSION

The austerity measures being implemented by Spain as a result of the economic crisis are seriously compromising the minimum core content of the state's social rights and the rights of equality as recognised under the

[107] For further details on this tendency, see Aparicio Tovar, J, 'La Evolución Regresiva de la Seguridad Social en el Periodo 1996–2002: Hacia el Seguro y el Asistencialismo' (2002) 19 *Revista de Derecho Social* 19.

[108] Case C-385/11 *Ebal Moreno*, above n 66.

[109] *Cuestión de inconstitucionalidad 5862-2003. Planteada por la Sala de lo Social del Tribunal Superior de Justicia de Galicia en relación con la disposición adicional séptima del texto refundido de la Ley General de la Seguridad Social, aprobado por el Real Decreto Legislativo 1/1994, de 20 de junio.* Constitutional Court of Spain, 61/2013, 3 March 2013.

[110] RD-Ley 11/2013, de 2 de agosto del 2013, BOE de 3 de agosto del 2013.

International Covenant on Economic, Social and Cultural Rights.[111] The adoption of a gender mainstreaming approach in the analysis of the austerity measures adopted by the Spanish authorities concerning reconciliation, social protection and employability allows us to conclude that when emerging from the crisis, women will be in a much worse position than men in their attempt to achieve economic independence.

These reforms have various points in common with the approaches adopted in other European countries, based as they are on the models of labour relations and pensions promoted by the European institutions. In its 2020 strategy, the EU has once again established the goal of increasing the labour participation of women by promoting policies of reconciliation. In parallel, the 2010 to 2015 strategy of gender equality seeks to ensure that women achieve a degree of economic independence comparable to that of men. However, these objectives are unlikely to receive the necessary institutional support at a time when European budgetary policies require Member States to reduce public spending considerably. Likewise, what can be gathered from the various proposals for pension reform made by the European authorities is a conception of social security that is dependent on the labour market and which diverges markedly from providing a universal system and from a human rights perspective.[112] Both the strengthening of the work-related criteria that prevent the access of non-standard workers to social security benefits and the cuts affecting the adequacy of welfare benefits have a strong impact on gender. In some cases, the drastic reduction in the amount of benefits (as has occurred in Spain and Greece) fails to respect the 'sufficiency' criterion, with payments falling below the poverty threshold. These austerity measures undoubtedly have a greater impact on women,[113] and despite this gender-mainstreaming criteria have not been taken into consideration in their adoption.

Whether in a period of boom or recession in the economy, the European Union remains unwavering in its support of these lines of reform. This suggests that many of the measures taken by the Spanish government with the approval of the European Union are in fact long-term reforms that represent a paradigm shift, rather than extraordinary responses to combat a situation of budget deficit and economic crisis. In Spain, the suspension of investment in care services, and the development of a model for labour relations that is competitive in terms of wage costs and highly flexible in

[111] CESCR, *Consideration of Reports*, above n 6.

[112] For a more in-depth discussion, see Goldblatt and Lamarche, in this collection.

[113] See gender implications of the current finantial crisis in Walby, S, 'Gender and the Financial Crisis' (paper for UNESCO Project on 'Gender and the Financial Crisis', 9 April 2009), available at: www.lancs.ac.uk/fass/doc_library/sociology/Gender_and_financial_crisis_Sylvia_Walby.pdf. See also UNAIDS, *Impact of the Global Economic Crisis on Women, Girls and Gender Equality* (discussion paper, Geneva, UNAIDS, August 2012).

terms of working conditions, seems set to lead to a reduction in the work options available to women with familial responsibilities who seek to earn their own income.

The Government needs to give its backing to the provision of quality public care services so that childcare is not an issue that each family has to manage in accordance with the time it has available and the economic resources it can count upon.

Index

Printed by Libri Plureos GmbH in Hamburg,
Germany

9 781509 912957